Books of the People
Revisiting Classic Works of Jewish Thought

MAGGID

Yeshiva University
THE ZAHAVA AND MOSHAEL STRAUS
CENTER FOR TORAH AND WESTERN THOUGHT

BOOKS OF
THE PEOPLE

EDITOR

Dr. Stuart W. Halpern

Straus Center for Torah and Western Thought
Maggid Books

Books of the People
Revisiting Classic Works of Jewish Thought

First Edition, 2017

Maggid Books
An imprint of Koren Publishers Jerusalem Ltd.

POB 8531, New Milford, CT 06776-8531, USA
& POB 4044, Jerusalem 9104001, Israel
www.maggidbooks.com

ISBN 978-1-59264-470-4, *hardcover*

A CIP catalogue record for this title is
available from the British Library

Printed and bound in the United States

*Dedicated to members of the Grunberger and Pollack families
of Slovakia who perished, or survived but lost family, in the Holocaust*

Grunberger

Henrich (Chaim) Grunberger
Zali (Sarah) Friedman Grunberger
Erno Grunberger
Olga Grunberger
Emil Bernstein
Vera, Judith and Tibor Bernstein
Helen Grunberger
Munsie Grunberger
Rozsi Grunberger
Misi Klein
*Yoshka Grunberger ***
*Rozsi Grunberger ***
Miklos and Sandor Grunberger
*Dezso Grunberger ***
Ibolika and Edith Grunberger
*Jeno Grunberger Kormendi ***
*Benjamin (Bela) Grunberger ***
*Moti (Matilda) Grunberger ***

*Survived

Pollack

Moric Pollack
Gisella (Gittel) Pollack
Yosef Pollack
Draizel and Henya Pollack
*Alexander Pollack ***
*Riftshu Srulovic Pollack ***
Leah Pollack
Lily Pollack
*Ibi (Viola) Pollack ***
*Susan Pollack ***
*Moric Berman ***
Hersh-Baruch Pollack
*Irene Pollack ***
*Eugene Herskovitz ***
Olga Pollack
Miriam Pollack

תנצב"ה
May their memories be a blessing to all future generations

Contents

Editor's Preface

"Exactly what kind of eternity *does* a library provide? How likely is it for a manuscript to become a book on a library shelf? How hard is it to stay there?" In her 2014 book, *The Shelf: Adventures in Extreme Reading*, author Phyllis Rose explored these and other questions as refracted through her experience reading a randomly selected group of books in the New York Society Library.

In the Jewish tradition we believe that our books are what define us as a people – our library of texts, beginning with the Tanakh, followed by the Mishna and Talmud, is what make us who we are. These ancient but timeless works have inspired an ever-growing number of subsequent works of Jewish provenance, despite the warning of Ecclesiastes 12:12 that "of making books there is no end." These writings are the keys to our eternity, both as religiously committed individuals and as a nation. To this day, a family's library of Jewish books is a source of pride in countless homes and volumes are passed down from generation to generation.

In thinking about which works of Jewish thought can and should be an essential part of every Jewish library, I conceived of the volume you hold in your hand. Each chapter in this book features a scholar of Jewish studies revisiting a particularly foundational and salient work of *maḥshevet Yisrael* (Jewish thought), from medieval to modern, and discussing its themes, its historical context, the circumstances and background of its author (the "person of the book"), and, most importantly, its contemporary relevance. My hope is that this volume inspires you, the reader, to make each of the works featured in these chapters a permanent part of your personal library, if they aren't already, and if they are, to dust them off the shelf and revisit them with a new perspective. The chapters in this volume can also serve as useful guides for those looking into more extensive learning projects covering each of the books systematically.

While the list of books discussed in this work is not exhaustive, nor does it represent a formal canon in any way, it reflects the changing priorities and religious sensibilities of readers and students, whether in the academy or among the general population. Whereas a discussion of Jewish thought only a generation ago might have focused almost exclusively on the *Rishonim* (medieval rabbinic scholars) who wrote volumes focused on Jewish philosophy, today there is a much greater emphasis on mysticism and Hasidism and a developing awareness that Jewish theology might be embedded in biblical commentary or other texts. If this collection sparks debate as to what should have been included but was not, *harei zeh meshubaḥ* (this would be praiseworthy).

The authors in this volume faced a fundamental methodological challenge; namely, explaining how contemporary readers might find meaning and relevance in texts written in intellectual and religious climates so different from our own and utilizing categories of thinking that seem, on the surface, foreign to contemporary readers. Yet, as religious Jews wedded to our ancient traditions, we cannot let this challenge paralyze us. The very project of an intellectually and spiritually vibrant Judaism has no choice but to face this task head-on – and indeed, so many religious people have found inspiration in these works, despite the contexts of their original composition. I fervently hope that this volume contextualizes while contemporizing, losing neither the vitality of the original works nor the concerns of today's readers.

Special thanks are due to the Director of the Straus Center, Rabbi Dr. Meir Y. Soloveichik, for his support of this project, as well as to our dedicated benefactors, Zahava and Moshael Straus, and to Yeshiva

University President Richard M. Joel. I would like to also express my gratitude to the Maggid team, particularly Rabbi Reuven Ziegler, for his always appreciated guidance, as well as to Dr. Yoel Finkelman for his insightful review of the manuscript and Nechama Unterman, Shalom Dinerstein, Tomi Mager, and Rabbi Daniel Tabak for their diligence and warmth in preparing the book for publication. The care the Maggid team took in ensuring the beauty of this work is, as always, appreciated. Having the honor of Rabbi Lord Sacks writing a foreword for this book is a priceless privilege, given that he himself has composed his own library of timeless Jewish classics. Lastly, I would like to dedicate this book to my maternal grandfather, Martin Wagner, for, among many other things, instilling in me a love of Jewish books of all kinds.

Dr. Stuart W. Halpern
Winter 5777

Foreword

Rabbi Lord Jonathan Sacks

The Koran calls Jews people of the book, but they were so long before. Already at Sinai, the Torah tells us, Moses wrote the laws in a book and read them to the people as they made a covenant with God. Deuteronomy tells us about a king that "he should write a copy of this Torah for himself as a book" and that "it should be with him and he should read it all the days of his life" (Deut. 17:18–19). Blessing Moses' successor Joshua, God charged him: "This book of the Torah should not leave your mouth and you shall think about it day and night, so you may be careful to do all that is written in it. Then all will go well with you" (Josh. 1:8). Other religions had holy places, holy times, and holy people. Judaism was the first faith to focus on holy words, on a book and its power to transform the lives of those who learn and live its teachings.

Judaism is the supreme example of a faith, a civilization, predicated on books and bookishness, education and the life of the mind. Aristotle's pupil Theophrastus searched for a way to describe this to his fellow Greeks: he called the Jews a nation of philosophers. So fundamental is this bookishness to Jewish identity that something of it persists even among lapsed or secular Jews. Heinrich Heine famously called the Torah the "portable homeland of the Jew." George Steiner wrote a fine article entitled "Our homeland, the text," describing dedication to literacy as "the open secret of the Jewish genius and its survival."

The text, he said, is "home" and each commentary "a return." The novelist Amos Oz called the book he wrote with his daughter about their own secular Jewish identity *Jews and Words*.

What created this remarkable affinity between Jews and books, Jews and study, Jews and words? We hear it in the several commands of Moses urging parents to educate their children, speaking of the Torah and its laws "when you sit in your house, when you walk by the way, when you lie down, and when you rise up" (Deut. 6:7). We hear it again in the penultimate command of the Torah instructing the people, men, women, and children, to gather together as a nation every seven years to hear the Torah read in public. We encounter it in the great assembly convened by Ezra and Nehemiah, rededicating the people after the Babylonian exile by means of a collective Torah reading. We hear it yet again when Rabban Yoḥanan b. Zakkai, just before the destruction of Jerusalem, wins a concession from Vespasian: "Give me Yavneh and its sages" (Gittin 56b). The result was the salvaging of the academy, the beit midrash, as the carrier of Jewish education and identity. Paul Johnson memorably called rabbinic Judaism "an ancient and highly efficient social machine for the production of intellectuals."

This is a history that turns time and again on learning and literacy, and there is nothing quite like it in the annals of any other nation. I have argued that one of the shaping factors in the religious history of Israel was that it coincided with the birth of the alphabet – the word "alphabet" itself comes from *aleph-bet*, later adopted by the Greeks as *alpha-beta*. This created the possibility, for the first time in history, of a society of universal literacy. The move from orality to literacy was itself a monumental shift in the direction of the abstract thought essential to the monotheistic mind.

At the heart of this history is the Book of Books itself, the Torah. For a thousand years, from the days of Moses to Malachi, Jews wrote commentaries to the Torah in the form of Nevi'im and Ketuvim, the prophetic books and the holy writings. For another thousand years, from late Second Temple times to the era of the *Geonim*, they wrote commentaries to the commentaries in the form of the vast literature of the Oral Law, Midrash, Mishna, and Gemara. For the next thousand years, they wrote commentaries to the commentaries to the commentaries in the form of biblical interpretation, and the clarification and codification of Jewish law. Jewish thought has been a series of ever-wider circles at whose center is the Book, the Torah, that forms the text and texture of Jewish life.

What lies behind this extraordinary set of phenomena is the basic premise of Judaism that our relationship with God is defined by a covenant, a document, a written text, detailing the pledge our ancestors took at Mount Sinai and the history that surrounded it. Everything we know as a people about the divine acts of Creation, Liberation, and Redemption, everything sacred about the structure of the society and the shape of the moral life, is contained in the words of the Torah. The Book became our constitution of liberty as a nation under the sovereignty of God, and its words were "our life and the length of our days."

In the modern world, for complex reasons, while Jews made signal contributions to scholarship in almost every field, in economics, sociology, anthropology, psychology, physics, chemistry, and medicine, the connection between Jews and Judaism, and between books and the Book, was broken. Early in the twentieth century, Thorstein Veblen, in an article entitled "On the Intellectual Pre-eminence of Jews in Modern Europe," argued that it was specifically the alienated quality of the Jewish intellectual that was the source of his creativity: "He becomes a disturber of the intellectual peace, but only at the cost of becoming an intellectual wayfaring man, a wanderer in the intellectual no-man's-land, seeking another place to rest, farther along the road, somewhere over the horizon."

After the Holocaust, Jewish intellectuals struggled with the question of whether it was possible to write books any more, whether words could ever be adequate to describe that black hole in human history, and whether language had been broken beyond repair. Theodor Adorno said it was barbaric to write poetry after Auschwitz. Jacques Derrida, one of the architects of deconstructionism, wrote that "a text is not a text unless it hides from the first comer, from the first glance, the law of its composition and the rules of its game." The image of a ghostly, surreal book haunts the work of the Egyptian-French-Jewish intellectual Edmond Jabès. "The fragment," he wrote, "the exploded book, is our only access to the infinite." We exist, he said, in the infinite space "where all we write is erased, even as you write it." Each of these figures testifies in some way to a loss of faith in literature, and in the power of civilization to civilize. One of the first acts of the Nazis against the Jews – following in the footsteps of Christians in the Middle Ages – was to burn Jewish books, and, as Heine had warned, when people begin by burning books, they end by burning people.

Even so, most Jews kept their faith in books and writing as a form of redemption of a world gone mad. In December 1941, the 81-year-old historian Simon Dubnow was shot and killed. It is said that his last words were, "*Yidn, shreibt un farschreib,*" "Jews, write and record." It is what many of them did, writing their last memories on scraps of paper they then buried in the grounds of the ghettos and concentration camps. The poet and Holocaust survivor Paul Celan said that "only one thing remained reachable, close and secure amid all losses: language. Yes, language. In spite of everything, it remained secure against loss. But it had to go through its own lack of answers, through terrifying silence, through the thousand darknesses of murderous speech."

To a remarkable degree, then, Jewish sense and sensibility, whether in ages of faith or crisis of faith, is bound to a book. That is what makes this work so valuable and illuminating. It is about a series of very special books, from Saadia Gaon's *Emunot VeDeot* to Rav Joseph B. Soloveitchik's *Halakhic Man,* in which outstanding Jewish thinkers from the tenth to the twentieth centuries wrestled with the relationship between Judaism and the wider culture of their day. To what extent were they compatible? Where and why did they conflict? Could Judaism be translated into the concepts and categories of the world outside, and if not, why not?

Jews tend not to philosophize. Philosophy is a Greek mode of thought more than a Jewish one. Greeks thought of truth in terms of system; Jews thought of it in terms of story. The Greeks sought the truth that is timeless; Jews pursued the truths that unfold through the course of time. The Greeks perfected the logical imagination, Jews the dialogical and chronological imagination – truths that emerge from conversation and from the ticking clock of history. The great Greek thinkers put their faith in reason; Jews had access to revelation also, and thus to truths that cannot be arrived at by reason alone.

Western civilization was to a large degree formed by the tension between these two ancient ways of thinking, mediated at times by Christianity, and at others by the great philosophers of Islam. But the Jewish contribution was an important one, and it should remain so to us as we seek to meditate on our faith and understand its role in the conversation of humankind.

The works that emerged from this encounter are the "great books" of Jewish thought, and a familiarity with them is essential to Jewish literacy. For while the codes of Jewish law and the commentaries on the Torah are about the details – and God is in the details – the works of Jewish philosophy and mysticism are ways of standing back and, in Matthew Arnold's phrase, seeing life steadily and seeing it whole. Saadia, Judah Halevi, Maimonides, Albo, Maharal, the Alter Rebbe of Chabad and Rav Nachman of Bratslav, Hirsch, the Netziv, Rav Kook, Rav Soloveitchik, and Rav Hutner, these are the great-souled Jewish thinkers who scaled the mountain of thought and described the view from the heights. To be sure, you cannot live on a mountaintop, but no one, at least some time in his or her life, should miss the climb.

So congratulations to Stuart Halpern for editing yet another outstanding collection of essays on Jewish thought by today's modern masters, and to all the contributors themselves. This is a wonderfully enlightening work, testifying to the ongoing vitality of Yeshiva University as a center of contemporary Jewish thought at the highest level. This is where the work begun by Saadia ten centuries ago continues today: the dialogue between Judaism and the world, captured in books about the Book that enlarge our intellectual horizons and lift our engagement with God, our people, and the world.

Emunot VeDeot: The Contemporary Relevance of Rav Saadia Gaon's Thought

Rabbi Yitzchak Blau

INTRODUCTION

Contemporary Jews, including even the philosophically inclined, rarely study Rav Saadia Gaon's *Emunot VeDeot* (*The Book of Beliefs and Opinions*). Much has changed since the medieval era, and we may find categories of his thought outdated. Moderns do not think of the world's matter as made up of the four elements of earth, wind, water, and fire, nor do we accept the geocentric view of the universe. In truth, the gap between modern and medieval thinkers is deeper than a shift in scientific conceptions about the cosmos. In our current intellectual horizon, we no longer affirm our ability to definitively demonstrate absolute truth through a set of logical arguments. Even given the above, some medieval analysis remains quite relevant. Medieval thought in areas such as ethical philosophy, theories of punishment, reasons for the commandments, biblical interpretation, and the balance between reason and revelation still have as much resonance today as they did then. Surprisingly, I will even argue that Rav Saadia Gaon provides significant insight into combating contemporary radical skepticism and has much to say about epistemological theory. While someone might think that theories of knowledge have changed so much that a sage from the tenth century could not possibly enhance the contemporary discussion, this essay attempts to show that this is not the case.

Sometimes, medieval categories utilized by a philosopher are not truly crucial to the position he takes. Rav Saadia argues that humanity is the pinnacle and purpose of Creation. One of his arguments supporting this position begins with the idea that the main item always lies at the center. The edible part of a nut is in its middle and the heart is located at the center of the human body. Since the earth is situated at the center of the universe, the purpose of Creation must live on earth. Humanity represents the greatest creature on earth; ergo, we are the pinnacle of Creation.[1] Given the Copernican revolution and the move to a heliocentric model, we moderns could say that Rav Saadia's entire argument collapses. On the other hand, Rav Saadia also cites verses such as Genesis 1:26 ("And God said: 'Let us make man in our image, after our likeness; and let them have dominion over the fish of the sea, and over the fowl of the air, and over the cattle, and over all the earth, and over every creeping thing that creeps upon the earth'"), Isaiah 45:12 ("I, even I, have made the earth, and created man upon it; I, even My hands, have stretched out the heavens, and all their host have I commanded"), and Psalm 8 (particularly, vv. 5–6: "What is man, that You are mindful of him? And the son of man, that You think of him? Yet You have made him but little lower than the angels, and hast crowned him with glory and honor") to buttress his claim, and it seems that his position does not truly depend on this one specific argument. Thus, the Copernican shift does not mean abandoning the position.

Emphasis on the centrality and significance of humanity raises an intriguing parallel with a twentieth-century author. Some argue that our current knowledge of the immensity of the cosmos disproves any notion of humanity as the purpose of Creation. Rav Saadia writes that we should not deny mankind's importance merely because the human body is small and weak: "Even though his body is small, his soul is wider than the heavens and earth since his knowledge encompasses

---

1. *Emunot VeDeot* (henceforth, *EV*) 4: Introduction.

all of them."[2] In analogous fashion, G. K. Chesterton cautioned against trying to "rebuke spirit by size."[3]

Maimonides' towering and overshadowing presence may also play a role in students of Jewish thought not encountering Rav Saadia. Those inclined toward exploring the classics of medieval Jewish philosophy are more likely to begin with *The Guide of the Perplexed*. The great influence of Maimonides' *Guide* is evident even for those utterly uninterested in philosophy. Anyone who reads Nahmanides' commentary on the Torah or Rav Tzadok HaKohen's hasidic works encounters ideas from the *Guide*. The same cannot be said of *Emunot VeDeot* or other parallel works. Without denying the *Guide's* greatness, there is no reason to assume that Maimonides had a monopoly on medieval philosophic insight. Rather, there is plenty of worthwhile material in Rav Saadia, and contrasting his positions with those of Maimonides proves instructive. Of course, much "rationalist" commonality exists between these two titans of Jewish thought as well. Rav Saadia agrees with Maimonides that magic does not exist and affirms that the Egyptian magicians trading "miracles" with Moses utilized sleight of hand.[4] He also preceded Maimonides in affirming God's incorporeality and dedicates part of the second treatise to explaining anthropomorphic terms in Tanakh. Furthermore, he preceded Maimonides in outlining a list of fundamental Jewish beliefs.[5] Yet the differences between them offer greater illumination than the similarities.

Rav Saadia's aforementioned position on humanity's centrality in the created order serves as a good example of a contrast with that of Maimonides. In the *Guide* (as opposed to a contrasting passage in the introduction to Maimonides' *Commentary on the Mishna*), Maimonides rejects the view that humanity is the purpose of the created order and that all the mineral, vegetable, and animal worlds as well as the planets

---

2. *EV* 4:2.

3. G. K. Chesterton, *The Everlasting Man* (San Francisco, 1993), 23.

4. *EV* 3:5.

5. Haggai Ben-Shammai, *A Leader's Project: Studies in the Philosophical and Exegetical Works of Saadia Gaon* [Hebrew] (Jerusalem, 2015). Ben-Shammai's work discusses many aspects of Rav Saadia's thought. The discussion on principles of belief appears in chapter 5.

and the stars were created to serve humanity.[6] Rav Abraham Isaac Kook pointed out how balancing the two serves an important religious purpose as each position can inspire greater religious sensitivity. Rav Saadia's position, says Rav Kook, challenges humankind to realize the goal of the universe whereas Maimonides' reminds humanity not to adopt an arrogant position toward the rest of the created order.[7]

Another instructive contrast relates to optimism or pessimism about our current world of human experience. Maimonides outlines three causes of human suffering: forces of nature, other humans, and the evils that each individual's folly brings upon himself. Those who realize that the third category is the most common cause of our troubles and begin to function with greater wisdom can conclude that the goods of this world outweigh the evils.[8] In contrast, Rav Saadia argues that this world cannot be where God rewards the righteous since all joys and pleasures of this world come suffused with sadness and suffering. As we shall see, this fits with Rav Saadia's great emphasis on the next world.[9]

BIOGRAPHY

Rav Saadia was born in Egypt in 882 but we know little else about his early family life and education. He lived in Syria and *Eretz Yisrael* before ultimately settling in Babylon, serving as the head of the academy in Sura. Rav Saadia was involved in various debates and polemics with external and internal opponents. In terms of the former, he wrote criticisms of both the Karaites and of the radical Hiwi al-Balkhi. In terms of the latter, Rav Saadia backed the Babylonian exilarch in his debate with Aharon ben Meir of *Eretz Yisrael* regarding control of the Jewish calendar. He also had a falling out with the exilarch, David ben Zakkai, which led to Rav Saadia losing his position as head of the academy before the two

---

6. *Guide* III:13.
7. *Maamarei HaRe'iya* 110–111.
8. *Guide* III:12.
9. For more on this contrast, see Shalom Carmy, "Tell Them I've Had a Good Enough Life," *Jewish Perspectives on the Experience of Suffering*, ed. Shalom Carmy (Northvale, 1999), 107–111. Carmy suggests that it is not the mere rewards of future existence that alter the evaluation but the perspective of eternity that does so.

men ultimately reconciled and Rav Saadia was restored to his place. He passed away in 942.

A prolific and versatile author, Rav Saadia contributed to an impressive range of Jewish subjects. He wrote halakhic monographs, a poem enumerating the mitzvot (later immortalized by Rabbi Yerucham Fischel Perla's epic commentary), a commentary on sections of the Bible, a translation of Tanakh (known as the *Tafsīr*), poetry and liturgical works, volumes on language and grammar, a siddur, a commentary on *Sefer Yetzira*, and of course the philosophical classic that is the subject of this essay. Just as Maimonides worked within the framework of Aristotelian thought in crafting the *Guide*, so too Rav Saadia utilized the categories of the predominant philosophy of his time, that of the Mutazilite Kalām.[10]

This essay addresses central themes in Rav Saadia's philosophy with a particular focus on ideas impactful on contemporary religious life. (Thus, I shall not discuss Rav Saadia's critique of twelve theories of Creation[11] or his reasons for rejecting ten erroneous conceptions of the soul.[12] Suffice it to say, regarding these matters, that he affirms Creation ex nihilo and that he conceives of the soul as a corporeal substance, albeit of a lighter nature than regular physical matter, independent of the body. When the body dies, the soul lives on ultimately to be reunited with the body at the End of Days.) Rather than purely theoretical interest, this essay aims for existential relevance for today. Though topical headings break up the essay, some of the issues discussed straddle two categories so the reader should not expect a fully neat division between topics.

REASON AND REVELATION

In response to the critique that our sages discouraged philosophical study, Rav Saadia responded that our sages' concern was only that Jewish thinkers might begin their philosophical inquiries without the

---

10. For a discussion of Rav Saadia's relationship with Kalām philosophy, see Sarah Strousma, *Saadia Gaon: A Jewish Thinker in a Mediterranean Society* [Hebrew] (Tel Aviv, 2002).

11. *EV* 1:3.

12. Ibid., 6:1.

data of revelation. Their caution against speculation regarding "what is below and what is above, what was before and what is to come" (Mishna Ḥagiga 2:1) does not apply to those starting with true information gleaned from the prophets.[13] But why engage in philosophical speculation altogether? Rav Saadia argues that there is value to fortifying our prior belief through reasoned argument. It is like the ability to work out a math problem instead of looking up the answer in the back of the book.[14] Furthermore, such study enables us to respond to various critics. While his initial discussion mentions only these two justifications, a later passage adds another possible reason that we shall now explicate.

Analysis of resurrection leads Rav Saadia to address the nature of biblical interpretation. He states that we should interpret the biblical text literally unless it contradicts one of the following: empirical knowledge, logic, another verse, or our tradition.[15] In those four instances, we must interpret metaphorically. For example, we know that Eve was not literally the "mother of all living things" (Gen. 3:20) and that God cannot actually be a consuming fire (Deut. 4:24). Malachi was not instructing his listeners to test God (Mal. 3:10) since the Bible cautions against doing so (Deut. 6:16). Finally, despite the verse's mention of forty lashes as being the punishment that a court should administer to sinners (Deut. 25:3), tradition tells us that this means thirty-nine. Absent these four conditions, however, we must interpret the Torah literally lest religious life turn into an arbitrary free-for-all, in which every legal and narrative section could be creatively reread so that not kindling a fire on Shabbat could refer to not going to war, not eating *ḥametz* on Passover could mean avoiding sexual immorality, and the Jewish people entering the ocean when leaving Egypt could mean that they moved among an army.[16] Along these lines, Rav Saadia determines that we should interpret verses about resurrection literally since none of the four conditions apply. Logic dictates that the same God who brought the world into being ex nihilo could also resurrect the dead.

---

13. Ibid., Introduction: 6.
14. Dr. David Shatz suggested this analogy.
15. *EV* 7:1.
16. Ibid., 7:2.

Note that here reason plays a constructive role in interpreting revelation. It is one factor instructing us whether to interpret verses literally or metaphorically. This provides a model for the contemporary man of faith. Even if we ultimately ground belief in faith, experience, intuition, and tradition, this does not mean that we completely neutralize reason; on the contrary, reason and logic greatly influence how we interpret and apply the tradition.

Having addressed why, according to Rav Saadia, we utilize reason to supplement revelation, we turn to why we need revelation in addition to reason. Admittedly, this question carried much more weight in the medieval world when there was greater confidence in reason's ability to work out the cosmic truths about ethics and religion. Rav Saadia indeed assumes that reason would suffice, and his initial discussion provides two reasons for revelation.[17] First, philosophical reasoning takes time, while revelation allows a person to arrive at the truth without the years of doubt while waiting for conclusions. Moreover, not everyone has the intellectual and personal wherewithal to successfully conclude intellectual investigation. Revelation therefore proves crucial for this less capable group. In a later section, Rav Saadia provides additional reasons for requiring revelation, and we shall discuss them within the next topic heading.

RATIONAL AND REVELATORY COMMANDMENTS

Rav Saadia divides the mitzvot between commandments the intellect obligates even without the word of God and those we know about and are obligated to fulfill only because of the divine word.[18] The former comprises three different categories. Reason demands that we pay homage and give thanks to someone who has done great things for us. It further demands that a sage not allow others to curse him. Finally, logic dictates that the created beings should not be allowed to harm each other. The first category creates the obligation to know God and worship Him, the second prohibits blasphemy, and the third outlaws stealing from or cheating fellow humans. In addition, God prescribed

---

17. Ibid., Introduction: 6.
18. Ibid., 3:1.

other mitzvot not obligated by the intellect so that we may perform them and receive greater reward. At first, it seems that these mitzvot have no intrinsic purpose, but Rav Saadia proceeds to state that they must have some slight justification even if not as great as the justifications of the rational commandments. Revelatory mitzvot include Shabbat and the festivals, Jewish dietary laws, and some sexual restrictions such as incest. Regarding Shabbat and the festivals, Rav Saadia notes how these institutions promote rest and community building while providing the opportunity to study and pray with greater depth and devotion.[19] At the same time, he clearly categorizes Shabbat in the category of commandments based on revelation.

The contrast with Maimonides is quite striking. Maimonides denies the existence of revelatory mitzvot entirely, insisting that all commandments have a significant telos (ultimate aim). For Maimonides, divine wisdom demands that God's commands not be vain or frivolous but rather rooted in logic, wisdom, and purpose.[20] Maimonides accepts a division between commandments whose purpose is self-evident and those whose purpose is more mysterious, but this division reflects the limitations of human reasoning and not the nature of the commandments themselves. The red heifer has as much logic and purpose as honoring parents even though humanity understands one easily and struggles to comprehend the goal of the other. Indeed, the *Guide* attempts to offer a rationale for every Torah commandment.

Now, Rav Saadia could claim that it is rational for God to give commandments to humans in order to provide them with heavenly reward even if the specific acts have no inherent purpose. Ironically, this argument resembles Maimonides' approach to the details of a commandment, which he concedes need not have a specific rationale. In the context of details, Maimonides agrees that in some instances rationality requires an arbitrary choice. Apparently, though, Maimonides distinguishes between the two scenarios. Once reason demands a certain general command, it also requires specific details, even if arbitrary, so that the act of the commandment has a concrete identity or so as

---

19. Ibid., 3:2.
20. *Guide* III:26.

to enable a strong sense of communal performance. However, this is not akin to God issuing a commandment with no rational basis on the general level either.

We should avoid identifying Rav Saadia's categories of rational and revelatory commandments with one common usage of *ḥukkim* and *mishpatim*. The category of *ḥukkim* can refer to commandments with some kind of paradoxical or irrational quality. Those who associate *ḥukkim* with the paradoxical emphasize the question of why would the red heifer purify the ritually impure and yet make some priests active in the purification impure. How can we send a goat to Azazel on Yom Kippur when such a practice seems to violate halakhic prohibitions against offerings outside the Temple and may even resemble idolatrous ritual? Nothing paradoxical or irrational can be attributed to the institution of Shabbat, one of the most understandable commandments in our tradition. We would not classify it among the *ḥukkim*. However, the intellect does not compel Sabbath observance so it is categorized as revelatory.

Rav Saadia returns to the purpose of revelation and explains its benefit regarding each of these categories of commandments.[21] By definition, we would not know the revelatory commandments without God's word so they depend upon revelation. Even the rational commandments require divine help in their application and definition. Reason demands that we thank God in prayer, but we depend on prophets to clarify the timing of prayer, the text of prayer, and the location of prayer. As Rabbi Kafih notes in his commentary, this example requires further thought since we usually assume that these prayer details are rabbinic in nature and were thus not taught via revelation. Reason prohibits adultery but does not detail how a marital union is formed. Logic forbids theft but does not say how property is acquired. Furthermore, logic recognizes the wrongness of various actions without being able to determine the appropriate punishment for each transgression. Revelation fills in this missing information.

With regard to the means of forming a marriage and acquiring property, we can question whether any given method is truly superior to another. Perhaps we need some definitive rule, but many options

---

21. *EV* 3:3.

could work equally well. Determining appropriate punishments, on the other hand, seems to clearly depend on a discerning wisdom. A version of this argument appearing in Rav Joseph Albo's writings offers further examples where divine direction clearly does more than just provide an arbitrary standard. Aristotle famously favored the golden mean for each character trait. For example, we should be brave, not cowardly or foolhardy. Regarding physical pleasures, we strive for temperance while avoiding hedonism or asceticism. However, this concept is more easily affirmed than practiced. How do we determine where the middle point is and how do we cultivate the appropriate character traits? Rav Albo writes that the halakhic system provides the recipe when it restricts certain foods permanently while prohibiting others in particular situations.[22] Again, revelation aids in working out the details of goals we recognize through reason.

ETHICAL THEORY

Several passages in *Emunot VeDeot* strike a pragmatic and consequentialist note. In other words, the wrongness of actions depends on the negative results they produce rather than on any inherent wrongness. Theft is wrong because if people are allowed to steal, no one will have motivation to work and produce goods and society will not have enough resources to survive. Adultery is negative because offspring will not successfully identify their parents and this will destroy all the precious aspects of stable family life.[23] A Kantian or deontological approach would see theft and adultery as wrong irrespective of which results they produce. We shall see shortly that Rav Saadia incorporates Kantian elements as well but the utilitarian emphasis is quite strong. Furthermore, Rav Saadia sees human motivation as very much influenced by rewards and punishments. One of his arguments in favor of life after death is the biblical example of martyrs. People would not be willing to die for a cause unless they knew that compensation awaited them in another world.[24] This claim ignores the possibility of a martyr being so committed to his ideals that

---

22. *Sefer HaIkkarim* 1:8.
23. *EV* 3:2.
24. Ibid., 9:2.

he would prefer doing the right thing to prolonging life irrespective of hopes for compensation in a future existence.

On the other hand, Rav Saadia does incorporate deontological or intuitive elements of ethics as well. Recall his first category within the rational commandments. The need to repay or at least acknowledge debts of gratitude is not explained by consequentialist considerations but rather is regarded as an inherent truth. He also declares that there is no point in arguing with someone who denies the goodness of truth and the evils of falsehood.[25] Here too, he relates to this principle as a self-evident truth rather than as a point of utilitarian consideration.

Eliezer Goldman makes an insightful point in his analysis of Rav Saadia's ethics. While modern ethical philosophers attempt to find one principle that undergirds all our ethical obligations, common sense theories adopt a variety of ethical sources.[26] For example, most of us have both deontological and consequentialist ethical intuitions. We feel that there is an inherent wrongness to particular actions and yet also we feel that results sometimes must be a factor in ethical decision making. Perhaps we should view the different strands of ethical theory in *Emunot VeDeot* as a strong point rather than as an inconsistency or a weakness.

A third element of Rav Saadia's ethics emerges from his concluding treatise. Reminiscent of Aristotle's *Nicomachean Ethics*, this section calls for balancing between thirteen different pursuits of humanity. Each one has its place but exclusive focus on any one of them is dangerous. According to Rav Saadia, this reflects the essential theme of Ecclesiastes. Ecclesiastes does not reject joy, wisdom, or money but only converting one such item into the solitary goal. Even the pursuit of wisdom and the desire to serve God in seclusion require balancing factors. Someone who only studies may not procure the physical necessities for survival. Relying on others to provide will generate enmity and resentment.[27] A person who secludes himself in order to exclusively worship God

---

25. Ibid., 3:8.
26. Eliezer Goldman, "Rav Saadia Gaon's Ethical Theory" [Hebrew], *Daat* 2/3 (1978–1979): 7–28. The point is on page 23. The rest of the paragraph reflects my viewpoint and not necessarily that of Goldman.
27. *EV* 10:14.

may also suffer from physical deprivation and such a life precludes religious fulfillment in the realms of business, agriculture, and the fullness of a varied life.[28]

Goldman points out that Rav Saadia's analysis implicitly rejects the idea of a sharp division of labor in Jewish society.[29] One might suggest that only the elite should study while the masses take care of society's physical needs. Some passages in Maimonides seem comfortable with such an arrangement. In his introduction to his *Commentary on the Mishna*, Maimonides states that the purpose of the multitudes not proficient in wisdom is to provide material needs and companionship for the select wise individuals. Another view could posit that different sectors of society perform divergent tasks but all contribute to the whole. The roles of priests and Levites provide an example of such a model. In opposition to those possibilities, Rav Saadia assumes that both sages seeking wisdom and those drawn to the single-minded pursuit of cleaving to God must personally involve themselves in the world of economic and domestic responsibilities.

For each one of the thirteen pursuits, Rav Saadia explains its limitations and its value. His focus on the next world emerges clearly. Rather than viewing rest as a way of recharging batteries for the challenges of this world, he explains its value as a reminder and taste of the ultimate tranquility in the next world.[30] So too, God implanted the desire for honor within us so that we would yearn for honor in the World to Come.[31] The very topical divisions of *Emunot VeDeot* reflect the same focus. Note how little discussion of eschatology and the future existence appear in *The Guide of the Perplexed*. Rav Saadia dedicates three of the ten treatises in the entire work to the Messiah, resurrection, and the World to Come. This choice reflects his view of reward and punishment as crucial motivating factors. In fact, he justifies the eternality of reward and punishment as a way of providing the most powerful incentive to

---

28. Ibid., 10:15.
29. Goldman, "Rav Saadia Gaon's Ethical Theory," 20.
30. *EV* 10:16.
31. Ibid., 10:12.

live a godly life.[32] Beyond his interest in motivating religious observance, Rav Saadia's concern for divine justice also encourages this focus.

PROVIDENCE

We affirm the justice of God yet we do not experience this world as rewarding the righteous and punishing the wicked. Rav Saadia's theodicy emphasizes the compensatory power of the rewards of the next world. Why do the righteous suffer? Sometimes, they receive punishments in this world for their small number of transgressions; they are then free to exclusively collect reward in the World to Come. Other times, God afflicts the righteous as a test in order to increase their reward in the World to Come.[33] Rav Saadia draws an interesting distinction between the two categories. Regarding the first, God can inform the sufferer via prophecy so that he will take the punishment to heart and in turn repent. In contrast, God cannot inform the second type of sufferer since the heroism consists of loyally bearing the difficulty without concrete knowledge of a resulting reward. In alliance with a major strand of thought in our tradition, Rav Saadia does not think that all suffering can be attributed to sin. Indeed, Ḥazal already introduced the concept of "afflictions of love." In elucidating this concept, other thinkers mention the character growth that suffering can engender; for example, Rabbenu Nissim, a fourteenth-century Spanish rabbi, writes of becoming less attached to physicality.[34] Rav Saadia does not mention any personal development but simply writes of faithfully enduring the pain. Rav Saadia raises the obvious question of why God needs to afflict in order to reward and answers by referring back to his doctrine that earned rewards are superior to freely dispensed gifts.

The death of children particularly concerned Rav Saadia and he affirms that they will receive compensation in the next world. He even mentions the children of the flood generation and of the Midianites as examples of this phenomenon.[35] Apparently, a war waged against an

---

32. Ibid., 9:7.
33. Ibid., 5:3.
34. *Derashot HaRan, Derasha* 10.
35. *EV* 9:2.

enemy nation does not obliterate the moral question regarding children and even though God commands their death, He must compensate those children. Note also that Rav Saadia implicitly rejects Maimonides' notion that only someone who knows basic metaphysical truths can find a place in the World to Come[36] and that only gentiles who affirm mono-theism merit salvation in the hereafter.[37] We imagine that the Midianite children would not perform well on the theological exam. The children question resurfaces in the context of Rav Saadia's rejection of reincarna-tion. He does not so much provide an argument against this doctrine; instead, he neutralizes all the claims in favor of it. None of the verses cited in favor of reincarnation truly refer to it. The claim that this idea explains the suffering of children is neutralized by Rav Saadia's argu-ment that compensation of the World to Come already addresses the conundrum.[38] Perhaps Rav Saadia does not need a specific critique of reincarnation since mention of this doctrine does not appear in Tanakh or Ḥazal. Once he has negated all the arguments in favor, the default position remains that this is not a part of our tradition.

The importance of divine justice and the idea that the World to Come realizes this value help explain Rav Saadia's great interest in the future existence. As noted, the righteous and wicked do not always receive their just deserts in this world. Rav Saadia does say that God sometimes administers just deserts in this world so that people will see an example of the divine justice they can anticipate in the World to Come.[39]

PROPHECY

According to Rav Saadia, we authenticate a prophet when God performs a miracle on his behalf.[40] To prevent any attribution of divinity to the prophet, prophets have all the limitations of humanity including mor-tality, dependence on food and drink, and the occasional struggle with illness and poverty. They cannot perform miracles on demand nor do

---

36. *Mishneh Torah, Laws of Repentance* 3:7.
37. Ibid., *Laws of Kings* 8:11, according to one textual variant.
38. *EV* 6:8.
39. Ibid., 5:1.
40. Ibid., 3:4.

they always have access to hidden information. These limitations clarify that miracles and prophetic message stem ultimately from God and not from the independent powers of the prophet. Beyond the miraculous, the content of the prophecy also helps an audience evaluate a prophetic claimant. If he directs us to do something against reason or tradition, such as calling for theft or adultery, then we know that he is a false prophet.[41] Though we no longer encounter prophets, concerns about focusing attention on holy individuals more than on God remain very relevant.

EPISTEMOLOGY

Rav Saadia outlines four sources of knowledge: sense experience, direct apprehension of the intellect, logical derivations, and reliable traditions.[42] The first refers to information gained through our five senses and the second to our intuitive appreciation of the importance of truth and the evils of falsehood. The third makes derivations based on the earlier sources of information. We might not empirically sense our soul and its intellectual capacity but we experience its functioning and can therefore derive its existence. We see animals eating and giving out waste and can infer that they have some kind of digestive system. The real innovation of Rav Saadia is his fourth category. Maimonides, our frequent foil, champions arriving at truths through metaphysical reasoning but does not emphasize information acquired via tradition. Indeed, a person could think that relying on others reflects some kind of epistemological failure and that the truly independent thinker would accept only truths he personally verified. Rav Saadia notes that no one actually functions that way. We accept what we are told about our family lineage and our property as true. We rely on the advice of others to determine which courses of action are worthy and rewarding and which are foolhardy and dangerous.[43] Obviously, we exercise some judgment regarding whom to rely upon and we try to determine if they have a decent track record of reporting. That being said, we justifiably rely on others in our pursuit of knowledge.

---

41. Ibid., 3:8.
42. Ibid., Introduction: 5.
43. Ibid., 3:6.

Some scholars think that the idea of a reliable tradition applies only to the Jewish tradition but Rav Saadia's examples indicate that the idea has broader purview. Even in our skeptical age, we still function this way. Science progresses because scientists rely on the results of their predecessors; they do not feel a need to reproduce every experiment. Literature students can safely assume that Shakespeare is a more significant writer than Danielle Steele before they read those two writers for themselves. Alasdaire MacIntyre[44] and Charles Taylor[45] argue that our ethical knowledge is transmitted in the context of a community with its stories and values.[46] Thus, reliance on a community's traditions may very well be a part of the modern experience. Perhaps the basis for our religious beliefs is our religious experience but our communal traditions enable us to formulate a coherent structure and language for those experiences.

RESPONSE TO SKEPTICISM

As mentioned at the outset, the medieval world was certainly more confident than we are about the human ability to establish truths through logical reasoning. We might think that medieval thinkers would have nothing to contribute toward facing the contemporary challenge of radical skepticism. Yet Rav Saadia Gaon has a few important passages of relevance. He cites the view of those who maintain that they can create their own reality. He asks them whether they solve various problems of life in this way. Do they deal with hunger by imagining themselves full, with poverty by asserting that they are wealthy, or with advancing age by declaring their youth?[47] In other words, even with all our modern skepticism, we encounter the harsh contours of reality and it is not simply pliable to our desires and declarations. This critique resembles

---

44. Alasdair MacIntyre, *After Virtue: A Study in Moral Theory* (Notre Dame, 1984).
45. Charles Taylor, *The Ethics of Authenticity* (Cambridge, 1992).
46. Admittedly, this analogy is imprecise because MacIntyre and Taylor focus more on the narrative that bolsters a society's values whereas Rav Saadia emphasizes reliability and truth content. Nonetheless, I do not believe truth is irrelevant to Taylor and MacIntyre.
47. *EV* Introduction: 4.

Alvin Plantinga's criticism of Richard Rorty's idea that truth is "what our peers will let us get away with saying."[48]

Another passage deals with those totally skeptical about the results of human thinking. Rav Saadia points out that they use thought to argue against thinking.[49] If they truly adhered to their position, they could not be in favor of skepticism either. In fact, they bring thought-based arguments in favor of skepticism about human thought. This is akin to arguing against arguments or proving that there are no such things as proofs. Furthermore, they rely on human analysis when they turn to professional doctors, engineers, and craftsmen. The complete skeptic would not be able to assume that these experts have any greater knowledge than others. In other words, no one truly lives a life of total skepticism about human thought. The very act of thinking about these issues begins by granting credence to our admittedly limited human analysis.

FREE WILL

Rav Saadia affirms our belief in free will and offers many of the classic arguments in favor. Determinism would render commandments as well as rewards and punishments pointless.[50] Furthermore, we experience ourselves as free beings making choices.[51] We decide either to lie in bed pretending to still be asleep while waiting for our spouse to hear the baby or to get up ourselves and take care of our child before our spouse wakes up. As Dr. Samuel Johnson, the eminent eighteenth-century writer, said: "All theory is against the freedom of the will; all experience for it." Rav Saadia addresses the classic conundrum of reconciling divine foreknowledge with human freedom and offers an intriguing answer that may simply move the problem without truly solving it. He writes that God can know of an event before it happens without causing that event to happen. I know that the sun will come up tomorrow but I am not a causal agent in its rising.[52] While it is true that this removes causality

---

48. Alvin Plantinga, *Warranted Christian Belief* (Oxford, 2000), 429–430.
49. *EV* 1:3.
50. Ibid., 4:3.
51. Ibid., 4:4.
52. Ibid.

from the equation, it remains a question whether a person is logically free to make either choice if God already knows what he will choose. Further work remains to be done regarding this problem.

CONCLUSION

As noted at the outset, it is not always easy to identify with medieval philosophical writings. Many of us experience this when studying the beginning of Maimonides' *Laws of the Foundations of the Torah*, four chapters based primarily on Aristotelian physics and metaphysics. At the same time, medieval insights into the balance between reason and revelation, the purpose of the commandments, ethical theory, and the nature of human freedom remain just as relevant today as when written over a thousand years ago. This essay argues that Rav Saadia even has what to contribute toward addressing contemporary issues of epistemology and skepticism. I hope that this effort inspires other writers to apply the wisdom of our impressive predecessors to the problems of today.[53]

FURTHER READING

Rav Saadia wrote *Emunot VeDeot* in Arabic and it was first translated into Hebrew by Yehuda ibn Tibbon in 1186. The famed Yemenite scholar Rabbi Yosef Kafih penned a new Hebrew translation in 1970. Samuel Rosenblatt produced the only complete English translation, which he entitled *Saadia Gaon: The Book of Beliefs and Opinions* (New Haven, 1948). Rabbi Yisrael Kitover, a nineteenth-century Ukrainian rabbi, wrote a running commentary entitled *Shvilei Emuna*. One contemporary Hebrew version is accompanied by a commentary by Rabbi David Cohen, the famed "Nazir" and student of Rav Kook. The commentary is called *Derekh Emuna*, and it is in *Sefer HaEmunot VeHaDeot* (Jerusalem, 5772). There is also a contemporary commentary written by Rav Shalom Hakohen published by the Machon of Yeshivat Ohr Etzion. The classic study of Rav Saadia's life and works is Henry Malter, *Saadia Gaon: His Life and Work* (Philadelphia, 1921). For a more up-to-date study, see Robert Brody, *Saadia Gaon*, trans. Betsy Rosenberg (Oxford, 2013).

---

53. The author would like to thank Rabbi Shalom Carmy, Dr. Yoel Finkelman, Noach Goldstein, and Dr. David Shatz for their helpful comments.

Jews, Japan, and Chosenness: The Extraordinary Universalism of Rabbi Judah Halevi's *Kuzari*

Rabbi Dr. Meir Y. Soloveichik

I.

In 1940, as the future of the world hung in the balance and the shadow of destruction was descending on European Jewry, one of the most surreal scenarios played a role in the development of halakhic literature. Fleeing from the Nazi hordes, hundreds of young Lithuanian *bokhrim* (yeshiva students) – most of them affiliated with the yeshivot of Mir and Ḥakhmei Lublin[1] – found salvation in the unlikely form of Chiune Sugihara, the Japanese acting consul in Kovno (Kaunas).[2] Sugihara provided visas allowing the Jews to travel to the Territory of Curaçao by way of Japan. Thus these shtetl Jews, who had traveled little, if at all, in their lives, crossed the vast Asian continent on the Trans-Siberian Railway and then spent three perilous days on a ferry sailing the Sea of Japan.

---

1. On the escape of the Mirrer Yeshiva, see A. Bernshtain et al., *Yeshivat Mir: HaZeriḥa BeFaatei Kedem*, 3 vols. (Benei Berak, 1999); on Ḥakhmei Lublin, see David Mandelboim, *Gibborei HaḤayil: Yeshivat Ḥakhmei Lublin BiTekufat HaShoah*, 2 vols. (Benei Berak, 2010).
2. See Gao Bei, *Shanghai Sanctuary: Chinese and Japanese Policy Toward European Jewish Refugees During World War II* (Oxford, 2013), 112–120.

By the time they had arrived in Kobe, Japan, the attack on Pearl Harbor had occurred, trapping them for the war's duration in Japanese territory.

Having escaped the German death camps, these Jews now faced a halakhic conundrum. When halakhically was Shabbat to be observed in Japan? Convention had it that Saturday began in Japan several hours ahead of Jerusalem, but did halakha agree? After all, where the first moment of the day begins is, for international timekeeping, purely a matter of convention, and it is not halakhically obvious whether Shabbat starts in Japan before or after it begins in Jerusalem. While the refugees in Kobe had the option of observing two days of Shabbat, the options were murkier when it came to Yom Kippur.

In a justifiably famous gathering that took place in the Jerusalem home of Rabbi Isser Zalman Meltzer (1870–1953), the most influential rabbis of the Holy Land gathered to discuss the question sent from the other side of the world. Some, most notably Rabbi Avraham Yeshayahu Karelitz (1878–1953), known by the title of his magnum opus, *Ḥazon Ish*, pointed out that the issue had been resolved almost one thousand years prior in one of the most well-known medieval works relating to Judaism: the *Kuzari* of Rabbi Judah Halevi (ca. 1075–1141).[3]

That this complex halakhic question was to be resolved by the *Kuzari* was surprising; it was not, first and foremost, a halakhic work, and the author was not known for his halakhic authority. Halevi's good friend Rabbi Joseph ibn Migash (1077–1141) was recognized as the supreme halakhic light of Andalusian Jewry at that time; Halevi was respected and admired primarily for the lyrical poetry that he had written for most of his life. Born in in Christian Spain in the last third of the eleventh century, Halevi went to seek his fortune in Muslim Andalusia, where his literary fame grew. He would shuttle back and forth between Christian and Muslim territory most of his life. While his writing lives on in his poetry – his *zemirot* are still sung and his *kinot* still recited – much of his literary production remained

---

3. An account of the historical unfolding of the halakhic debate, which conveniently includes the relevant citations from the *Kuzari* and *HaMaor* cited in this essay, can be found in Bernshtain, *Yeshivat Mir*, 2:487–511.

unknown until the discovery of the treasure trove called the Cairo Geniza.[4] Nevertheless, Halevi's most famous work today is his Judeo-Arabic *Kitāb Al-Khazarī*, or the *Kuzari*. He completed this work in 1140, toward the end of his life, dying one year later, perhaps, as legend has it, upon finally reaching the sacred soil of *Eretz Yisrael*. The *Kuzari* was composed not as a philosophical treatise but rather in the style of a Platonic dialogue. Halevi constructs a conversation in which one of the central figures – indeed, the hero of the story – is a convert. Halevi depicts an Asiatic king of the Khazars, a religious seeker who examines Christianity, Islam, and Aristotelian philosophy and finds all their worldviews wanting. The king then interviews a rabbi and becomes convinced that he has discovered the truth, leading to the conversion of the king and his entire people to Judaism.[5]

It is in the midst of these conversations that the discussion turns, unexpectedly, to an exceedingly technical talmudic passage in Tractate Rosh HaShana that discusses the *molad*, or lunar conjunction, the moment when the previous month's lunar cycle concludes and the new one begins. The conjunction is a halakhic construct that occurs all over the world simultaneously. The particular passage makes reference to what time in Jerusalem the *molad* occurs: "If the conjunction of the moon takes place before midday, the new moon becomes visible near sunset." The implications of this terse statement are not immediately clear, and so a variety of interpretations have been given by commentators. Rashi (1041–1105) explains it in a way that has absolutely no bearing on the issue of an international dateline. Halevi, however, understands the Talmud to be delineating the following rule: If the *molad* occurred before *hatzot* (midday) Jerusalem time, then the Sanhedrin is able to declare that day Rosh Hodesh. If, however, the *molad* occurs after noon

---

4. On the discovery of the Cairo Geniza, see Adina Hoffman and Peter Cole, *Sacred Trash: The Lost and Found World of the Cairo Geniza* (New York, 2011). The documentation related to Halevi found in the Geniza, including a number of holographs, was edited in Moshe Gil and Ezra Fleischer, *Yehuda Halevi and His Circle: 55 Genizah Documents* [Hebrew] (Jerusalem, 2001).

5. See *Kuzari* I:1–10.

in Jerusalem, then that day is treated as the last of the concluding month, with the day that followed to be deemed Rosh Ḥodesh.[6]

What is striking about this interpretation is not the halakhic ruling, but the theological reasoning behind it, as stressed by Halevi, and as elucidated several years later by Rabbi Zerahia HaLevi, known as Baal HaMaor (twelfth century[7]).[8] According to the approach of Halevi and Baal HaMaor, a day can be declared Rosh Ḥodesh in the Holy Land only if, *somewhere on earth*, it will still be Rosh Ḥodesh for twenty-four hours. To put it slightly differently, *the ability of Jews to declare a new month in their land is dependent, metaphysically and halakhically, on a location in the remotest ends of the earth*. This, Halevi and Baal HaMaor explain, is the meaning behind the talmudic dictum. As long as the new cycle of the moon begins before midday in the Land of Israel, with six hours left before sunset, then there is still one location on earth that is eighteen hours behind Jerusalem, where the day is just beginning, and a full twenty-four hours of Rosh Ḥodesh has yet to take place. This, Halevi writes, is a small sliver of the earth in what was then known as the Orient:

> Consequently Sabbath does not come in till the sun has set behind Sinai, and so on to the remote west, and round the globe to China, which is the extreme end of the inhabited earth. Sabbath begins in China eighteen hours later than in Palestine, since the latter lies in the center of the world. Sunset in Palestine, therefore, concurs with midnight in China, and midday in Palestine concurs with sunset in China. This is the problem of the system based on the eighteen hours in the [talmudic] rule: If the conjunction of the moon takes place before midday, the new moon becomes visible near sunset.[9]

---

6. *Kuzari* II:18–20. See also Shlomo Yosef Zevin, "*HaKuzari BaHalakha*," in *LeOr HaHalakha* (Jerusalem, 2004), 358–365.

7. The dating regarding his lifetime is subject to dispute. See Israel M. Ta-Shma, *Rabbi Zerahia HaLevi Baal HaMaor UVenei Ḥugo* (Jerusalem, 1992).

8. Baal HaMaor's comments are printed in the standard Vilna edition of the Talmud on Rosh HaShana 20b.

9. *Kuzari* II:20. All translations from the *Kuzari* are taken from Hartwig Hirschfeld's translation from the Judeo-Arabic, which has been reprinted a number of times and is available on the internet.

It was based on these words, cited by Baal HaMaor, that Ḥazon Ish insisted that the halakhic dateline lay six hours – or ninety degrees – east of Jerusalem, with just a bit of the easternmost territory of China – as well as Japan – on the other side of the dateline. It is this small slice of territory that is actually eighteen hours behind Jerusalem, and whose experience of the sanctity of Rosh Ḥodesh for twenty-four hours determined the declaration of the new month in Jerusalem. This would mean that Japan is actually eighteen hours *behind* Jerusalem, with Yom Kippur occurring in Japan the day after the date one might have assumed.

Ḥazon Ish's argument was disputed by many of those participating in the colloquium, led by Rabbi Yechiel Michel Tukachinsky (1872–1955).[10] Rabbi Tukachinsky stressed that though cited by Baal HaMaor, Halevi's interpretation was rejected by many subsequent *Rishonim*, most notably Rabad of Posquières (ca. 1125–1198), the renowned interlocutor of Baal HaMaor. Rabad argued that Halevi predicated his interpretation of the passage in Rosh HaShana on a religious contention whose logic is ludicrous: that the chosen nation, in setting its divinely dictated calendar in its chosen land, should be impacted in any way by whether those who dwell in the Far East experience twenty-four hours of Rosh Ḥodesh:

> After these words, and after this entire gloss, the scent [Baal HaMaor] followed is from the *Kuzari* and the works of Rabbi Abraham the son of Rabbi Ḥiyya the Spaniard, for they explained these laws in this very manner, and he is bedecking himself with adornments that are not his. We should not learn from the words of those who are not scholars of the Talmud, for they turn the face of the halakha to accord with their own words, when it is in truth not so. And we have already heard that the *Nasi*, Rabbi Isaac the son of Rabbi Barukh [Albalia], of blessed memory, who was an

---

10. For halakhic analyses of the various positions, see, *inter alia*, Menachem Kasher, *Sefer Kav HaTaarikh HaYisraeli* (Jerusalem, 1977); Yisroel Taplin, *Sefer Taarikh Yisrael* (Lakewood, 1999); and Yochanan HaKohen Schwadron, *"BeInyan Kav HaTaarikh,"* *Kovetz Beit Aharon VeYisrael* 25:3 (147): 99–121; 25:4 (148): 103–114; 25:5 (149): 99–103; 27:1 (157): 141–153.

expert in this discipline and an expert in halakha, smashed these ideas, and all honor is due him for doing so. For we should not follow those who dwell in China, who live at the eastern extremity, and ignore those who live in the Land of Israel, for they are *Ikkar HaMo'adot*, the most relevant to the holidays.[11]

Rabad's question is clear, and obvious: Why in the world (no pun intended) does Halevi link the determination of Jewish sacred time – perhaps the ultimate embodiment of particularism – to non-Jews who live on the other side of the earth?

Rabad's challenge is not merely an intriguing attempt at halakhic refutation; it cuts to the core of our understanding of Halevi's theology. In what way are Jews and non-Jews linked? How can the election of Israel actually be understood as something that occurred for the sake of all humanity? The question is particularly intriguing to the author of this essay, himself a grandson of Jews saved by Sugihara, Jews who were simultaneously committed to the chosenness implied by the particularism of Jewish chosenness, yet lived forever indebted to the extraordinary sacrifice of a Japanese consul. Rabad's question, in other words, has led me to ponder the extraordinary universalism at the heart of the great defender of God's unique relationship with the chosen people: the role of all humanity in the particularistic theology of the *Kuzari*.

II.

To read the *Kuzari* carefully is to consider how it defies all stereotypes that circulate about the work. Let us begin with what is well known and indubitable: Halevi's aim is, as he writes, to defend the "despised faith,"[12] and to assert that the bond between God and Israel, and the link between God and the Land of Israel, remain unbroken. How Halevi does this is

---

11. His comment can be found in his *Katuv Sham* on Rosh HaShana 20b, conveniently reprinted at the back of the *Oz VeHadar* edition of the Babylonian Talmud together with the comments of Baal HaMaor.

12. *Al-Kitāb Al-Khazarī* is also titled *Kitāb Al-Radd wa-'l-Dalīl fī 'l-Dīn al-Dhalīl* (The Book of Refutation and Proof on Behalf of the Despised Religion).

all too often misunderstood, and many stereotypes exist in the public imagination about the *Kuzari*'s approach to the Jewish people and the world. For example, the *Kuzari* is often cited as a proto-Zionist work,[13] e.g., that the Rabbi in the story ultimately departs for the Holy Land, as Halevi himself reportedly did at the end of his life.[14] There are few who loved the Holy Land more than Halevi. Yet the *Kuzari*, in a striking passage, emphasizes that Jewish powerlessness is part of the divine plan, and that had the Jews had power, they would have wielded it unethically:

> The Rabbi: I see thee reproaching us with our degradation and poverty, but the best of other religions boast of both. Do they not glorify him who said: He who smites thee on the right cheek, turn to him the left also; and he who takes away thy coat, let him have thy shirt also. He and his friends and followers, after hundreds of years of contumely, flogging, and slaying, attained their well-known success, and just in these things they glorify. This is also the history of the founder of Islam and his friends, who eventually prevailed, and became powerful. The nations boast of these, but not of these kings whose power and might are great, whose walls are strong, and whose chariots are terrible. Yet our relation to God is a closer one than if we had reached greatness already on earth.
>
> Al Khazari: This might be so, if your humility were voluntary; but it is involuntary, and if you had power you would slay.
>
> The Rabbi: Thou hast touched our weak spot, O King of the Khazars. If the majority of us, as thou sayest, would learn humility towards God and His law from our low station, Providence would not have forced us to bear it for such a long period. Only the smallest portion thinks thus. Yet the majority may expect a reward, because they bear their degradation partly from

13. See Lawrence J. Kaplan, "'The Starling's Caw': Judah Halevi as Philosopher, Poet, and Pilgrim," *JQR* 101:1 (Winter 2011): 123–130 with notes.
14. Much has been written about Halevi's final journey. Most recently, see Hillel Halkin, *Yehuda Halevi* (New York, 2010), and Raymond Scheindlin, *The Song of the Distant Dove: Judah Halevi's Pilgrimage* (Oxford, 2008), together with Kaplan, "'The Starling's Caw,'" 97–132.

necessity, partly of their own free will. For whoever wishes to do so can become the friend and equal of his oppressor by uttering one word, and without any difficulty. Such conduct does not escape the just Judge. If we bear our exile and degradation for God's sake, as is meet, we shall be the pride of the generation which will come with the Messiah, and accelerate the day of the deliverance we hope for.[15]

Modern Zionists (such as myself), then, would be right to draw inspiration from Halevi's love of Israel, but to find political Zionism in the *Kuzari* would be to engage in an anachronism.

It is with this in mind that we may turn to another common trope about Halevi: that he presents a theology of Judaism that is intensely particularistic, with little interest in non-Jews. Here too we must first study the kernel of truth in this overgeneralization. Halevi locates the source of Jewish chosenness in a biological faculty that allows Jews unique access to, and a unique connection with, the divine influence on this world, termed in medieval Hebrew the *inyan HaElohi*. It is this faculty, he writes, that allows Jews access to prophecy, as well as to mediate the relationship between heaven and earth through their performance of the mitzvot. While Adam, the first man, was blessed with this faculty, not all of his children inherited it; only Seth received the capacity for prophecy, and it devolved ultimately to the twelve sons of Jacob:

> The essence of Seth, then, passed to Enosh, and in this way the divine influence was inherited by isolated individuals down to Noah. They are compared to the heart; they resembled Adam, and were styled sons of God. They were perfect outwardly and inwardly, their lives, knowledge, and ability being likewise faultless. Their lives fix the chronology from Adam to Noah, as well as from Noah to Abraham. There were some, however, among them who did not come under divine influence, as Terah, but his son Abraham was the disciple of his grandfather Eber, and was

---

15. *Kuzari* I:113–115.

born in the lifetime of Noah. Thus the divine spirit descended from the grandfather to the grandchildren....[16]

Al Khazari: Would it not have been better or more commensurate with divine wisdom, if all mankind had been guided in the true path?

The Rabbi: Or would it not have been best for all animals to have been reasonable beings? Thou hast, apparently, forgotten what we said previously concerning the genealogy of Adam's progeny, and how the spirit of divine prophecy rested on one person, who was chosen from his brethren, and the essence of his father. It was he in whom this divine light was concentrated. He was the kernel, whilst the others were as shells which had no share in it. The sons of Jacob were, however, distinguished from other people by godly qualities, which made them, so to speak, an angelic caste. Each of them, being permeated by the divine essence, endeavoured to attain the degree of prophecy, and most of them succeeded in so doing.[17]

In today's egalitarian age – especially coming as it does on the heels of terrors fueled by the belief in the biological superiority of one nation over another – this passage from Halevi does not fail to disturb, even shock. It is this passage that is often cited to show that Halevi gives a profoundly particularistic theology of chosenness, while Maimonides, who locates Jewishness first and foremost in the cognizing of philosophical truths, maintains a more universalistic worldview.[18] Halevi's words, however, must be placed in their proper context, both chronologically and within Halevi's own book. Menachem Kellner's statement on Halevi's notion of election bears quoting:

---

16. *Kuzari* I:95.

17. *Kuzari* I:102–103.

18. Among others, see Harry Austryn Wolfson, "Halevi and Maimonides on Prophecy," *JQR* 32 (1942): 345–370, and Warren Zev Harvey, "The First Commandment and the God of History: Halevi and Crescas versus Ibn Ezra and Maimonides" [Hebrew], *Tarbiz* 57:2 (1988): 203–216.

Fairness to Halevi demands that we take note of the special circumstances surrounding the adoption of his position, and that
we do not accuse him of nor blame him for twentieth-century
racism. Halevi flourished in a place and time in which conflicting
national and religious groupings each advanced its own claims
to nobility and belittled the character of its opponents. Christian
Spaniards affirmed their superiority over Jews and Muslims; Muslims affirmed their superiority over Jews and Christians; Muslim
Arabs affirmed their superiority over non-Arab Muslims; Halevi
affirmed the superiority of the Jews over the Spaniards, Arabs,
and North Africans.[19]

This allows us to place the quote in historical context; once we
do so, we understand that his biological notions of prophecy notwithstanding, a careful reading of the entire book shows Halevi to be one of
the most intriguingly universalist thinkers of the age. In order to see why
this is so, we must return to the opening passage of the *Kuzari*. Halevi
describes a pagan king whose devotion to religious observance inspires
the intervention of the one true God in a way that changes his life forever:

I was asked to state what arguments and replies I could bring to
bear against the attacks of philosophers and followers of other
religions, and also against [Jewish] sectarians who attacked the
rest of Israel. This reminded me of something I had once heard
concerning the arguments of a Rabbi who sojourned with the
King of the Khazars. The latter, as we know from historical records,
became a convert to Judaism about four hundred years ago. To
him came a dream, and it appeared as if an angel addressed him,
saying: "Thy way of thinking is indeed pleasing to the Creator,
but not thy way of acting." Yet he was so zealous in the performance of the Khazar religion, that he devoted himself with a
perfect heart to the service of the Temple and sacrifices. Notwithstanding this devotion, the angel came again at night and

19. Menachem Kellner, *Maimonides on Judaism and the Jewish People* (Albany, 1991),
110 n. 16.

repeated: "Thy way of thinking is pleasing to God, but not thy way of acting." This caused him to ponder over the different beliefs and religions, and finally become a convert to Judaism together with many other Khazars. As I found among the arguments of the Rabbi, many which appealed to me, and were in harmony with my own opinions, I resolved to write them down exactly as they had been spoken.[20]

"Thy way of thinking" – meaning, the intentions of the king of the Khazars – *"is pleasing to God*, but not thy way of acting." We must pause to ponder how extraordinary it is that such words were written one thousand years ago by a devout Jew about a devout pagan. One has to return to the talmudic tales of Rabbi Yehuda the Prince and his Roman friend Antoninus[21] to find anything remotely like this: the notion that while the actions of *avoda zara* (foreign worship) are to be condemned, the religious devotion motivating those actions by this individual, the religious searching that drives him – is pleasing to God. It is impossible to imagine anything like this written by Maimonides – for whom the cognition of truth is all that matters, and for whom even those who observe the Noahide laws but are unaware of their foundation in Mosaic law are excluded from the category of *ḥasidei umot haolam* (righteous gentiles), and therefore, presumably excluded from a portion in the World to Come as well.[22] It is Halevi who not only begins his book with praise of a pagan, but actually *makes him the hero of his story.*

There is something else that is striking here. While gentiles are, for Halevi, precluded from prophecy, the *Kuzari* begins with a divine message delivered directly to a non-Jew. Moreover, it is a providential intervention on behalf of a man engaged in pagan devotion. Here too, God's affection – love is not too strong a word – for this devout pagan in Halevi's narrative must be contrasted with the worldview of Maimonides. It is *The Guide of the Perplexed* that emphasizes that providence for individuals is linked to a person's cognition of the truth:

---

20. *Kuzari* Introduction.
21. See, *inter alia*, Avoda Zara 10a–11a.
22. *Mishneh Torah, Laws of Kings* 8:11.

We have already stated in the chapters which treat of Divine Providence, that Providence watches over every rational being according to the amount of intellect which that being possesses. Those who are perfect in their perception of God, whose mind is never separated from Him, enjoy always the influence of Providence. But those who, perfect in their knowledge of God, turn their mind sometimes away from God, enjoy the presence of Divine Providence only when they meditate on God; when their thoughts are engaged in other matters, Divine Providence departs from them.[23]

The *Kuzari*, in contrast, begins with a man who could not be further from the philosophical truth, who nevertheless draws the delight of the divine, Who providentially inspires a religious journey to Judaism. The *Kuzari*, then, makes manifest at least one form of universalism that is not fully evident in the Maimonidean oeuvre.

III.

For any theologian who is impacted by Halevi – Franz Rosenzweig is the most obvious example – Jewish thought begins with pondering the paradoxical dialectic between the fact of Jewish eternity and the fact of Jewish suffering. Israel, the Bible stresses, is guaranteed to be eternal but is also subject to divine punishment for its actions, and will be judged more severely than other peoples. In explaining this, Halevi develops a remarkable metaphor, one in which the purpose of the People of Israel is to serve as the means by which the Divine Presence, and the divine influence, spreads through the world:

> The Rabbi: Israel amidst the nations is like the heart amidst the organs of the body; it is at one and the same time the most sick and the most healthy of them.
> Al Khazari: Make this a little clearer.

---

23. *Guide* III:51. All translations of the *Guide* are from the Michael Friedländer translation, which is in the public domain.

The Rabbi: The heart is exposed to all sorts of diseases, and frequently visited by them, such as sadness, anxiety, wrath, envy, enmity, love, hate, and fear. Its temperament changes continually, undulating between excess and deficiency, and moreover influenced by inferior nourishment, by movement, exertion, sleep, or wakefulness. They all affect the heart whilst the limbs rest.

Al Khazari: Now I understand how it can be the most sick and most healthy of all organs simultaneously. ... [24]

The Rabbi: Our relation to the Divine Influence is the same as that of the soul to the heart. For this reason it is said: "You only have I known of all the families of the earth, therefore I will punish you for all your iniquities" (Amos 3:2). These are the illnesses. As regards its health, it is alluded to in the words of the sages: He forgives the sins of His people, causing the first of them to vanish first. He does not allow our sins to become overwhelming, or they would destroy us completely by their multitude.[25]

Jews, for Halevi, are akin to a heart in a body. If so, by implication, just as the heart circulates blood, the very life force, throughout the body, Jews are the medium through which God Himself has His presence made manifest throughout the whole world.[26] But the heart's significance to a person *is due only to the preciousness of the body*; it is the body's preciousness that lends the heart its purpose. Halevi, then, insists on God's desire to impact, and indeed sanctify, the entire world, and the uniqueness of the Jewish election is the medium by which this end goal is achieved. It is Hillel Halkin who noted that just as every intellectual might be termed a Platonist or an Aristotelian, every Jewish intellectual might be termed a Maimonidean or a Halevian:

He either believes that Judaism can and needs to be harmonized with the advanced thought of his age, or he doesn't. He considers

---

24. *Kuzari* II:36–39.
25. *Kuzari* II:44.
26. *Kuzari* IV:23.

the highest level of Jewish self-realization to lie either in the inward or the outward life. He regards the notion that one can be born with a Jewish soul as either fanciful nonsense or an intuitive truth. He thinks of himself as belonging first to the species of Jew and then to the genus of man or vice versa.[27]

This is true, but Halevi would add that it is in understanding the election of the Jews that a Jew can truly comprehend how important the whole world is, and how profoundly linked he or she is to all humanity. For the theologian Michael Wyschogrod, chosenness expresses to everyone – Jew and gentile – "that God also stands in relationship with them:"[28]

> When we grasp that the election of Israel flows from the fatherhood that extends to all created in God's image, we find ourselves tied to all men in brotherhood, as Joseph, favored by his human father, ultimately found himself tied to his brothers. And when man contemplates this mystery, that the Eternal One, the Creator of heaven and earth, chose to become the father of his creatures instead of remaining self-sufficient unto himself, as is the Absolute of the philosophers, there wells up in man that praise that has become so rare yet remains so natural.[29]

Here, again, we must contrast Halevi, who sees the Jews as elected by God to serve as the heart of the world, with Maimonides, who rejects all matters of the heart as unworthy of the divine, who rejects the notion of God's passionate love for humans as an anthropomorphism. In his *Guide of the Perplexed*, Maimonides insists that when the Bible describes God's love, "such instances do not imply that God is influenced by a feeling of mercy."[30]

One other point here remains to be made. We have noted that rather than showing a lack of interest in humanity, Rabbi Judah Halevi, in

---

27. Halkin, *Yehuda Halevi*, 247.
28. Michael Wyschogrod, *The Body of Faith: God in the People Israel* (Northvale, 1996), 64.
29. Ibid., 65.
30. *Guide* I:54.

casting the king of the Khazars as the central hero of his book, was making manifest a universalist foundation to his thought. Yet a question raised by Leo Strauss deserves addressing: Why did Halevi choose to make the Rabbi's interlocutor a philosophical neophyte, albeit a royal one? Would it not have been more effective had the Rabbi debated, and defeated, the philosopher? Would that not have made for a more powerful tale to tell?[31]

Strauss offers an answer of his own; yet I would suggest that had Halevi structured his story this way, had the one who discovered the truth been a member of the intellectual elite, then the message conveyed might have been that only those truly sophisticated in their thinking can discover the theological truth. Halevi, in contrast, wished to illustrate that the chosenness of Israel is something that any seeker could discover. To remain loyal to Halevi's theological insights today, we need not adopt his linking of biology and prophecy; but we do need to grasp that the extraordinary impact of one small nation on the earth is a truth accessible not only to the elite, but to every one of us – intellectual or not, Jew or non-Jew. The *Kuzari*, composed before the Maimonidean corpus, often seems as if it were written in response to Maimonides, and Halevi emphasizes that the first of the Ten Commandments is not, as Maimonides would later insist, an obligation to know the existence of God through Aristotle's proof for the Unmoved Mover; rather, as the verse itself stresses, it is to discern the existence of the Almighty through the salvation of the people that God took out of the Land of Egypt:

> In the same way God commenced His speech to the assembled People of Israel: "I am the God whom you worship, who has led you out of the land of Egypt," but He did not say: "I am the Creator of the world and your Creator." Now in the same style I spoke to thee, a Prince of the Khazars, when thou didst ask me about my creed. I answered thee as was fitting, and is fitting for the whole of Israel who knew these things, first from personal experience, and afterwards through uninterrupted tradition, which is equal to the former.[32]

---

31. Leo Strauss, "The Law of Reason in the *Kuzari*," *PAAJR* 13 (1943): 57.
32. *Kuzari* I:25.

What this means is that God is not to be found through philosophy but through history, and one need not have read Aristotle to be emotionally inspired, and religiously moved, by the question posed by the southern American writer Walker Percy:

> Why does no one find it remarkable that in most world cities today there are Jews but not one single Hittite, even though the Hittites had a great flourishing civilization while the Jews nearby were a weak and obscure people? When one meets a Jew in New York or New Orleans or Paris or Melbourne, it is remarkable that no one considers the event remarkable. What are they doing here? But it is even more remarkable to wonder, if the Jews are here, why are there not Hittites here?[33]

Percy, of course, was a Christian rather than a Jew, and a Christian might still assume that the Jews are eternal, as Augustine argued, in order to illustrate their rejection by God. Yet Halevi might stress that one need not be a sophisticated theologian like Augustine to see the problem with this approach. All one need ask is whether a good God is faithful to His promises. This was a profound Halevian point made by Michael Wyschogrod to Karl Barth, the most important Protestant theologian of the twentieth century:

> At one point he [Barth] said, "You Jews have the promise but not the fulfillment; we Christians have both promise and fulfill-ment." Influenced by the banking atmosphere of Basel, I replied: "With human promise, one can have the promise but not the ful-fillment. But a promise of God is like money in the bank. If we have His promise, we have His fulfillment, and if we do not have the fulfillment we do not have the promise." There was a period of silence and then he said, "You know, I never thought of it that way." I will never forget that meeting.[34]

---

33. Walker Percy, *Message in the Bottle: How Queer Man Is, How Queer Language Is, and What One Has to Do with the Other* (New York, 1975), 6.
34. Michael Wyschogrod, *Abraham's Promise: Judaism and Jewish-Christian Relations*, ed. R. Kendall Soulen (Grand Rapids, 2004), 211.

If the truth of Judaism is ultimately discovered not by the philosopher but by the Khazar king, it is because the chosenness of the Jewish people is something that anyone could discover. Here, too, we find in Halevi an impressive universalism that cannot be found in most medieval versions of Jewish philosophy.

IV.

We are now able to understand how, whatever one may think of Halevi's interpretation of the talmudic passage cited above, his notion of Rosh Ḥodesh is the ultimate embodiment of the complexity, the balance between the particular and the universal, that lies at the heart of his theology. It is true, as Hillel Halkin puts it, that the whole of the *Kuzari* is "a grappling with the question of why the infinite Creator of all things would choose to limit His revelation of Himself to a particular people such as the Jews, in a particular place such as the Land of Israel, in a particular form such as Judaism."[35] This, however, is only part of the story. Yes, Jews have a land of their own in which they are meant to make their election manifest, observing the Torah that is theirs alone, and continuing a calendar that is theirs alone; yet they do so as the heart of humanity, so that God's choosing of the Jews can lead, in a way that we cannot fully predict or comprehend, to the spread of divinity around the world. If the Sanhedrin can sanctify Rosh Ḥodesh only if one location on earth that may well be devoid of Jews will experience twenty-four hours of the sanctity of Rosh Ḥodesh, it is because Jews are the heart of humanity, and live uniquely Jewish lives for the sake of humanity.

It is a striking fact of history that nothing illustrates this more than the story of the Jews of Kobe in 1941. A Jew alive in that era might have been forgiven if he adopted an utterly essentialist approach to the divide between Jew and non-Jew, and assumed a literal reading of "*halakha beyadua sheEsav soneh leYaakov,*" "it is a well-known law that Esau hates Jacob."[36] Yet it is precisely at this point, when so much of the world embraced evil and so much more of the world embraced silence, that certain individuals, revered today in Israel as "righteous gentiles,"

---

35. Halkin, *Yehuda Halevi,* 93.
36. *Sifrei Bemidbar,* sec. 69 (Num. 9:10).

illustrated a profound courage and goodness for which God's chosen people are indebted to this day. This includes a fascinating fellow who happened to be a Japanese consul in, of all places, Kovno, and helped ensure the survival of hundreds of Jews and of the Torah of Jewish Lithuania. To be a Jew is to ponder how stories such as these embody the eternity of the Jewish people, the Jewish devotion to the Torah, and the metaphysical link binding them to humanity in ways we cannot quite understand, and it is Halevi who, more than anyone else in the medieval period, pondered this question.

When the Jews arrived in Kobe, their rabbis were summoned to Tokyo to meet with Japanese leadership, who were already allied with the Nazis. The Japanese asked the rabbis, in all earnestness, what the Jews had done to deserve the enmity of the Germans; why, asked the Japanese, do the Nazis hate you so much? The response of one of the rabbis, the Amshinover Rebbe, is famous: "The Germans," he said, "hate us because we are Asians." The Japanese were flummoxed by this response. "But we are Asians!" they cried in response. "Indeed you are," replied the Rebbe, "and you are also on the list."[37] No nation has suffered at the hands of humanity more than the Jews, yet the Jews stubbornly refused to write humanity off, insisting that through them the nations of the world will be blessed. The journalist Yossi Klein Halevi, living in a Jerusalem of which Judah Halevi could only have dreamed, writes that at times he does not feel as if he is living anywhere special. And then, he adds:

> I suddenly remember where I am. I feel myself, then, like one of those barefoot and wide-eyed Ethiopian immigrants, silently stepping off the plane at Ben Gurion Airport into Zion. I recall, too, my father's wonder at the Wall, whose fragile and improbable endurance he saw as a metaphor for the Jewish people. Like him, I ask myself what it is about this strange little people that continually finds itself at the center of international attention, repeatedly on the front lines against totalitarian forces of evil – Nazism, Soviet Communism, now jihadism – all of which [have]

---

37. See, for example, Bernshtain, *Yeshivat Mir*, 2:478–480.

marked the Jews as their primary obstacle to achieving world domination. At those moments, I feel gratitude for having found my place in this story.[38]

It is thinking seriously about this point that is an essential task of Jewish thought; and all who do so earnestly, embracing the reality of Jewish chosenness without relinquishing the profound Jewish connection to the rest of the world, are walking in the footsteps of Rabbi Judah Halevi.

FURTHER READING

Introduction/Commentary:

Rosenberg, Shalom. *In the Footsteps of the Kuzari: An Introduction to Jewish Philosophy.* Edited by Joel Linsider from a translation by Gila Weinberg. 2 vols. (New York, 2007–2008).

Critical Edition of the Original Judaeo-Arabic:

Halevi, Judah. *Kitāb al-Radd wa-'l-Dalīl fi 'l-Dīn al-Dhalīl.* Edited by David H. Baneth and prepared for publication by Haggai Ben-Shammai (Jerusalem, 1977).

Most Popular Edition:

The Hebrew translation by Judah ibn Tibbon is the standard edition used by Jews throughout the ages. It has been reprinted many times and is conveniently available together with an English translation (based on the classic commentaries) in *The Kuzari: In Defense of the Despised Faith*, newly translated and annotated by Rabbi N. Daniel Korobkin (Jerusalem, 2009).

Medieval Commentary on the Kuzari:

An Early Commentary on the Kuzari: *Ḥeshek Shlomo* by R. Shlomo ben Yehuda of Lunel, annotated critical edition with introduction by Dov Schwartz [Hebrew] (Ramat Gan, 2007).

---

38. Yossi Klein Halevi, "The Photograph: A Search for June 1967," *Azure* 29 (Summer 5767/2007): 27.

Modern Commentary on the Kuzari:
Cohen, David. *The Kuzari Elucidated* [Hebrew]. Edited by Dov Schwartz. 3 vols. (Jerusalem, 1997–2002).

Reception History of the Kuzari:
Shear, Adam. *The Kuzari and the Shaping of Jewish Identity, 1167–1900* (Cambridge, 2008).

Modern Discussion of the Kuzari:
Goodman, Micah. *The King's Dream* [Hebrew] (Or Yehuda, 2012).

Maimonides' *Guide of the Perplexed*:
An Enchanted Book of Puzzles

Dr. Warren Zev Harvey

Rabbi Moses ben Maimon, known as Maimonides or Rambam (1138–1204), the renowned jurist, philosopher, and physician, was born in Cordoba. Owing to the Almohad persecutions, his family was forced to leave Andalusia when he was in his early teens. He lived for a while in Morocco, visited the Land of Israel, and finally settled in Egypt around 1165, where he served as a physician in the court of King Saladin.

His *Guide of the Perplexed*, written in Arabic (*Dalālat al-Ḥā'irīn*), was the most influential book in the history of Jewish philosophy. Jewish philosophers like Rabbi Levi Gersonides, Rabbi Ḥasdai Crescas, Rabbi Isaac Abrabanel, Baruch Spinoza, and Moses Mendelssohn, read the *Guide* in Rabbi Samuel ibn Tibbon's admirably literal Hebrew translation, known as *Moreh HaNevukhim* (completed in 1204). Some Jewish philosophers followed Maimonides loyally, others criticized him, but none could ignore him. The *Guide* wrought a revolution in Jewish philosophy. It changed its character in two main senses: first, it established Aristotelianism as the prominent medieval Jewish philosophy, in place of neo-Platonism; second, it turned Jewish philosophy into a tradition of questions, puzzles, and perplexities, not answers or doctrines.

The *Guide* was also an important book in the history of Western philosophy in general. Christian philosophers, like Albert the Great, Thomas Aquinas, and Maester Eckhardt, read it in the anonymous thirteenth-century Latin translation (*Dux Neutrorum*). Later European philosophers, like Leibniz and Hegel, read it in Johann Buxtorf's seventeenth-century Latin translation (*Doctor Perplexorum*).

The *Guide* stands at the center of the medieval Aristotelian tradition, and thus also at the center of the history of Western philosophy. The medieval Aristotelian tradition was historically and geographically divided into two periods: the first took place in the Islamic world, beginning with Alfarabi in the tenth century and ending with Averroes and Maimonides at the turn of the thirteenth century; the second took place in the Christian world, beginning in the thirteenth century with Albert the Great and Thomas Aquinas, and continuing until the end of the Middle Ages. The Muslim Averroes and the Jew Maimonides, both Cordobans, represented the culmination of the Arabic Aristotelian tradition, but also provided the foundation for the construction of the Aristotelian tradition in Christian Europe. Averroes, the great commentator on Aristotle, taught the philosophers in Christian Europe how to read the Stagirite Aristotle, and Rabbi Moses, the author of the *Guide*, taught them how Aristotelianism may be successfully integrated with Scripture.

The transfer of the Aristotelian tradition from the Islamic world to the Christian world at the turn of the thirteenth century was one of the most remarkable and fateful events in the history of Western philosophy. When philosophers in the Islamic world, like Alfarabi, Avicenna, and Rabbi Solomon ibn Gabirol, were assiduously studying the works of Plato and Aristotle, Christian Europe was still in the Dark Ages and the only works by Plato and Aristotle available in Latin were Plato's *Timaeus* (partial) and *Republic* (partial), and Aristotle's *Categories* and *On Interpretation*. Beginning in the middle of the twelfth century, the major philosophic works began to be translated from Greek and Arabic into Latin. Just when fundamentalism brought the Arabic Aristotelian tradition to an abrupt end, Aristotelian philosophy amazingly began to come to life in Christian Europe. In this transference of the Aristotelian tradition from the Islamic world to the Christian world, Maimonides' *Guide* played a vital role.[1]

WHAT KIND OF A BOOK IS THE *GUIDE*?

The *Guide* is a very strange book. Each chapter is written in a different style. There are pentateuchal chapters, prophetic chapters, and hagiographic chapters; talmudic chapters and midrashic chapters; orthodox Aristotelian chapters and radical Aristotelian chapters; Avicennian[2] chapters; Platonic chapters and neo-Platonic chapters; and even one mystical chapter with arcane allusions to *Merkava, Heikhalot,* and Sufi concepts.

What kind of a book is the *Guide*? What is its subject matter? To what genre does it belong? Many answers have been given to this question, since the *Guide* treats of many and diverse subjects in many and diverse ways. Some have said that it's a book of metaphysics, others that it's a book of theology. Some say that its subject matter is politics or ethics. Others say that its subject matter is Bible commentary or Midrash. Some claim its theme to be anthropology, sociology, or the philosophy of religion. Others say it's the philosophy of science. Surely the most prudent answer is that the *Guide* is *sui generis*. As for me, I believe that the main subject of the *Guide* is the philosophy of law or the philosophy of halakha. Maimonides, in the *Guide*, is primarily interested in determining why human beings need law, in defining the difference between a "divine law" and a regular political law, and in explaining the advantages of a divine law.

Leo Strauss, in his magisterial essay, "How to Begin to Study *The Guide of the Perplexed*," refers to the *Guide* as "an enchanted forest" and "an enchanting forest," in which grows the tree of life.[3] Indeed, the *Guide* is an enchanted and enchanting book. Part of its enchantment

---

1. See my "Maimonides' Place in the History of Philosophy," in Benny Kraut, ed., *Moses Maimonides: Communal Impact, Historic Legacy* (New York, 2005), 27–35.
2. Avicenna (980–1037) was the most influential philosopher in the Islamic world. His Aristotelianism was colored by neo-Platonism and mysticism, and was more amenable to traditional religion than were most other interpretations of Aristotle. Maimonides generally preferred Alfarabi (872–950) and Averroes (1126–1198) to him, but in metaphysics he often followed Avicenna.
3. Maimonides, *The Guide of the Perplexed*, trans. Shlomo Pines, with introductions by Pines and Leo Strauss (Chicago, 1963), xiv (henceforth, *Guide*).

derives from its bold spirit of open-ended philosophic adventure; part from the changing styles of its chapters, which keep the reader on his or her toes; and part from the fact that it is written in the form of puzzles and riddles. Maimonides gives two reasons why he has written the book in such a curious form: first, it is necessary to use literary ruses in order to hide radical teachings from those not equipped to understand them and who might be psychologically hurt by them; second, and more basic, metaphysical truth by its very nature cannot be formulated in discursive propositions but can be apprehended only in "lightning flashes," and such flashes can be sparked by puzzles and riddles. In teaching that metaphysical truth can be apprehended only in lighting flashes, Maimonides adumbrated – or perhaps influenced – a famous teaching of the twentieth-century German Jewish philosopher, Walter Benjamin.[4]

Ever the pedagogue, Maimonides composed the *Guide* in such a way that he addressed different audiences simultaneously. Leo Strauss, in several studies, taught that the *Guide* was written on two different levels: one exoteric and religious, which he called "Jerusalem"; and one esoteric and philosophic, which he called "Athens." According to this view, Maimonides had in mind two different kinds of readers: a pious religionist and a hard-nosed philosopher. Shlomo Pines, the distinguished Israeli historian of philosophy and translator of the *Guide* into English, revised Strauss' approach and spoke about *four* different levels in the *Guide*. According to this view, Maimonides had in mind not two but four different kinds of readers, which may be described as follows in order of increasing profundity: the dogmatic or dialectical theologian (including representatives of the Kalām), the orthodox Aristotelian, the critical Aristotelian ("critical" in the Kantian sense), and the intellectualist mystic.[5] Pines is certainly closer to the truth than was Strauss. However, in point of fact, the number of levels in the *Guide* is much

---

4. *Guide*, I: Introduction, 8, 18. Cf. Walter Benjamin, *The Arcades Project*, trans. H. Eiland and K. McLaughlin (Cambridge, 1999), 456: "Knowledge comes only in lightning flashes." See my "Maimonides' *Guide*: A System-Lover's Critique of Systematic Philosophy," in H. Wiedebach, ed., *Die Denkfigur des Systems* (Berlin, 2013), 196–197.
5. See my "Maimonides' Critical Epistemology and *Guide*, II, 24," *Aleph* 8 (2008): 213–214. The term "Kalām" refers primarily to Islamic dialectical theology. However,

more than two or four. Maimonides does not have in mind only one or two kinds of religionists and only one or two kinds of philosophers. He has in mind many different kinds of religionists and philosophers. The best description of the multileveled nature of the *Guide* is that of the French historian Sylvie-Anne Goldberg. "The *Guide*," she said," is a *millefeuille*."[6]

Maimonides writes simultaneously to different readers, encouraging each to think that he agrees with him or her, but then criticizing each trenchantly. Sometimes Maimonides writes as if he were a Kalām theologian, sometimes as if he were an orthodox Aristotelian, sometimes as if he were a radical Aristotelian, sometimes as if he were an Avicennian, sometimes as if he were a Platonist or a neo-Platonist, sometimes as if he were a mystic. What is his true view? Scholars have been arguing about this ever since the book appeared, and will surely continue to do so even after the coming of the Tishbite. I am convinced, however, that Maimonides was more interested in getting us readers to debate the problems than in giving us his definitive doctrines on each subject. He didn't want to give us dogmas. He wanted to give us perplexities! He didn't write a "Guide for the *Dogmatic*" but a "Guide for the *Perplexed*"! Needless to say, had Maimonides wanted to set down univocal doctrines, he could have done so very easily. After all, he demonstrated in his *Mishneh Torah* and in other works that he has a superb ability to express the most difficult ideas in the most lucid language. If in the *Mishneh Torah*, his monumental fourteen-volume code of Jewish Law, he sought to make everything crystal clear, in the *Guide*, his philosophic masterwork, he sought to make everything perplexing.

As part of his efforts to make the *Guide* as perplexing as possible, Maimonides peppers the book with intentional contradictions. He tells us in his Introduction that two kinds of contradictions are found in the book. One is the *pedagogical* contradiction, where an author oversimplifies a subject in order to make it comprehensible to beginners, but

---

there are also Jewish and Christian thinkers who were considered to belong to the Kalām. Rabbi Saadia Gaon, for example, is commonly considered a representative of "Jewish Kalām."

6. Quoted in ibid., 214–215.

later presents it precisely, thus causing a contradiction between the oversimplified and precise versions; the other kind of contradiction is the *esoteric* one, where an author presents contradictory theses in order to conceal obscure teachings from vulgar readers. Maimonides remarks that the pedagogical contradiction is found in philosophic books, while the esoteric contradiction is found in the Midrash.[7] In a sense, therefore, the *Guide* is a combination of a philosophic book and a midrashic book.

WHO ARE THE INTENDED READERS OF THE *GUIDE*?

The *Guide* begins with an Epistle Dedicatory, addressed to Maimonides' student, Joseph ben Judah ibn Simeon. Maimonides says in the Epistle that the book was written for him and those like him.[8] Thus, if we look carefully at Maimonides' description of Joseph ben Judah, we can get an idea of who are the intended readers of the *Guide*.

The Epistle begins with Maimonides' recalling how young Joseph had first been accepted by him as his student:

> My honored pupil, Rabbi Joseph, may the Rock guard you, son of Rabbi Judah, may his repose be in Paradise.
>
> When you came to me, having journeyed from afar to read texts under my guidance, I had a high opinion of you because of…what I had observed in your poems of your powerful longing for speculative matters. This was based on your letters and compositions in rhymed prose [*maqāmāt*] that were sent to me from Alexandria, before your grasp was put to the test. I thought, however: perhaps his longing is greater than his grasp.[9]

From young Joseph's poems, Maimonides learned of his strong desire for philosophy, but was not sure about his ability. Although he had doubts about his academic potential, Maimonides, who lived in Old Cairo, invited Joseph, who lived in Alexandria, to come to study with him.

---

7. *Guide* I: Introduction, 17–20.
8. Ibid., Epistle, 4.
9. Ibid., 3.

In the continuation of the Epistle, Maimonides writes of how Joseph began his studies with him in an impressive way:

> When you read under my guidance texts on astronomy and before that texts on mathematics, which is necessary as an introduction to astronomy, my joy in you increased because of … the quickness of your grasp. I saw your longing for mathematics was great, and let you train yourself in that science…. When, next, you read under my guidance texts dealing with the art of logic, my hopes fastened upon you, and I saw that you are one worthy to have the secrets of the prophetic books revealed to you so that you might consider in them that which excellent individuals ought to consider.[10]

Maimonides is pleased with Joseph's "quickness of grasp," and teaches him mathematics, astronomy, and logic. In Maimonides' comment about the relationship of mathematics to astronomy, we see an important principle in his theory of education: one must study subjects in their proper order. For example, subjects that are prerequisites for other subjects must be studied before them: mathematics before astronomy, physics before metaphysics, Bible before Mishna, and Mishna before Gemara. Maimonides judges that Joseph is an "excellent individual," worthy to have revealed to him "the secrets of the prophetic books." It is striking that Maimonides decides to reveal to Joseph "the secrets of the prophetic books" not because Joseph prays with great fervor, is meticulous in his observance of the kosher laws, or wears his phylacteries all day, but because he has excelled in logic, mathematics, and astronomy.

Maimonides, the Epistle continues, began to reveal to Joseph the secrets of the prophetic books, but encountered problems:

> I began to let you see flashes and to give you hints. You demanded of me additional knowledge and asked me to make clear to you some things pertaining to divine matters, to inform you of the intentions of the Mutakallimūn[11] … and to let you know whether

---

10. Ibid.
11. I.e., the Kalām theologians.

their methods were demonstrative and, if not, to what art they belonged. I saw you had already acquired a smattering of this subject from people other than myself. You were perplexed (*ḥā'ir*), as stupefaction had overcome you. Your noble soul demanded of you to "find out acceptable words" (Eccl. 12:10). Yet I did not cease dissuading you … and enjoining you to approach matters in an orderly manner. My purpose in this was that the truth should be established in your mind according to the proper methods, and that certainty should not come to you by accident.[12]

In accordance with his view, mentioned above, that metaphysical truths can be learned only by means of "lightning flashes," Maimonides began to let Joseph see such flashes. However, Joseph was impatient. He demanded to be told about "divine matters," even though he had studied only logic, mathematics, and some astronomy, but had not yet undertaken natural science, which in the medieval curriculum was studied after astronomy. Joseph, it seems, wanted to be told the secrets of metaphysics before he had mastered the basics of physics.

Moreover, Joseph seems to have been confused by the teachings of the dialectical theologians who belonged to the Kalām. He had studied the doctrines of the Kalām with teachers other than Maimonides. That Joseph should have been tempted by the Kalām must have been disappointing to Maimonides. The Aristotelian philosophers generally considered the Kalām theologians to be sophists. Maimonides had a visceral dislike for the Kalām, whose arguments, in his view, were tendentious and jeopardized the intellectual integrity of Judaism. Philosophers, Maimonides taught, seek to make their ideas conform to the world, while the Kalām theologians seek to make the world conform to their ideas.[13]

We see here also the first use of the word "perplexed" in the book. It seems that Joseph's perplexity derived from his strong desire to know things that he did not have the required preparation to know. Maimonides, it emerges from the Epistle, tried to restrain Joseph, and sought to get him to pursue his studies in an orderly way. The rash desire

---

12. *Guide*, Epistle, 3–4.
13. Cf. *Guide* I:71, 179.

to know things for which one does not have the required preparation was called by Maimonides *"harisa"* (breaking ahead), after Exodus 19:21, "lest they *break ahead* unto the Lord to gaze."[14]

Nonetheless, the Epistle relates, Maimonides continued to reveal "the secrets of the prophetic books" to Joseph:

> Whenever during your association with me a biblical verse or some text of the sages was mentioned in which there was a pointer to some strange notion, I did not refrain from explaining it to you. Then … God decreed our separation and you betook yourself elsewhere … . Your absence moved me to compose this treatise … for you and those like you, however few they are.[15]

Joseph left Maimonides in the middle of his studies, apparently to pursue a business opportunity. Maimonides, thus, writes the *Guide* for Joseph as a means of continuing his education from afar.

What can we say about Joseph? What kind of a student is he? He is a talented student, but one whose fervid lust for knowledge sometimes leads him to be guilty of "breaking ahead." He is also a student who is allured by the Kalām, a fact which may indicate that his critical faculties are not as sharp as they should be. His craving to know what he is not prepared to know frustrates him and leaves him *perplexed*. His discontinuing his studies for the sake of a business endeavor may be a sign that he was not profoundly committed to them.

However, the most important thing we learn from the Epistle about Joseph is the stage of his academic development. He is a young man whose academic status parallels that of a first- or second-year undergraduate student today. He has studied logic, mathematics, and astronomy, but not physics or metaphysics. Maimonides, in other words, is addressing the *Guide* to college frosh and sophomores, not to accomplished philosophers. This is important. It is often said that Maimonides was

---

14. In his Letter to Rabbi Samuel ibn Tibbon, Maimonides advises him to use *harisa* as the Hebrew translation of the Arabic *"tahāfut."* See also Ibn Tibbon's *Glossary of Technical Terms*, appended to his translation of the *Guide*.

15. *Guide*, Epistle, 4.

an "elitist." Now, it is true that he respected only those who developed their intellects, and had contempt for those who did not; and so in one sense he was an intellectual elitist. However, in a more significant sense he was the opposite of an elitist. He wrote his great philosophic book, the *Guide*, not for professional philosophers in their ivory towers, but for young perplexed students at a critical stage in their personal development. Similarly, his great legal code, the *Mishneh Torah*, was written for all the people, not only for superior talmudists. Indeed, almost everything that Maimonides wrote – whether legal, philosophic, or medical – was written with a pedagogical or practical intent and with an eye to spreading knowledge and enlightenment. The Hebrew title of the *Guide*, *Moreh HaNevukhim*, may be translated "The Teacher of the Perplexed." In consideration of this title, the medievals often called Maimonides simply *HaMoreh*, the Teacher par excellence. This was a most appropriate name for him.

WHAT DOES "PERPLEXITY" MEAN?

Maimonides named his book "The Guide of the Perplexed." Who are "the perplexed"? What does it mean to be perplexed?[16] The Arabic term "*ḥayra*" (perplexity) has two distinct senses. First, it may mean straying from the straight path, wandering, meandering, being lost. In this sense, the term is synonymous with the Hebrew "*toeh*" (cf. Gen. 37:15). Second, it may mean reaching an impasse, being in a state of indecision, being disoriented, confused, or stymied. In this sense, the term is a standard translation of the technical Greek philosophic term "*aporia*" (from *a-poros*, no passage, no way out). These two senses of *ḥayra* present two different images. According to the first sense, the perplexed individual is moving, but not on the right path; according to the second sense, the perplexed individual is not moving at all, but has come to a halt, unable to go in any direction. The preeminent Maimonidean scholar Salomon Munk understood Maimonides' use of *ḥayra* in the first sense, and named his 1866 French translation of the *Guide*, *Le guide des égarés* (*The Guide of Those Who Go Astray*). Shlomo Pines understood

---

16. See my "Maimonides on the Meaning of Perplexity," in *CISMOR Proceedings* 7 (2013), 68–82.

Maimonides' use of the term in the second sense. In criticizing Munk's title, he suggested a supposedly more exact one, *Le guide des désorientés* (*The Guide of the Disoriented*),[17] although he himself conservatively entitled his 1963 English translation, "The Guide of the Perplexed." In point of fact, Maimonides understood *ḥayra* in both senses. The perplexed individuals mentioned in Maimonides' title are *both* wandering astray *and* stymied.

Although Maimonides wrote the *Guide* in Arabic, he opened and closed it with short Hebrew poems. In the opening poem, he writes: "My knowledge goes forth to point out the straight way, to pave its road. / Lo, everyone who goes astray (*hatoeh*) in the field of Torah, / Come and follow its path."[18] In the closing poem, he writes: "[God] is found by every seeker who searches for Him, / If he marches toward Him and goes not astray (*velo yiteh*)."[19] In these two poems, which serve as bookends for the *Guide*, it emerges that Maimonides seeks in the book to guide those who have gone astray by pointing out the straight path to God and paving it. It would thus seem that the best Hebrew translation of the *Guide* is *Moreh HaTo'im* (*The Guide of Those Who Go Astray*).

However, in the Introduction to the *Guide*, Maimonides gives two examples of perplexed individuals: one is perplexed by a contradiction between the literal meaning of biblical *words* (e.g., "the *hand* of the Lord") and Reason; the other is perplexed by a contradiction between the external meaning of biblical *stories* (e.g., the talking serpent in the Garden of Eden) and Reason. In both cases, the individual is in a state of *aporia*, unable to decide between the biblical text and Reason; and in both cases, the perplexity is dispelled when the individual is made aware that the biblical texts have to be interpreted figuratively or allegorically. If in the opening and closing poems perplexity was understood in the sense of going astray, in these two examples it is understood in the sense of *aporia*.

By far the most significant use of the term "perplexity" in the *Guide* is found in part II, chapter 24. Maimonides calls this perplexity "the true perplexity." It is the perplexity caused by a contradiction

---

17. Ibid., 82, n. 2.
18. *Guide*, 2.
19. Ibid., 638.

between Ptolemaic astronomy and Aristotelian physics. Ptolemaic astronomy gives a precise mathematical description of the motion of the heavenly bodies, but in order to do so it uses epicycles and eccentric orbits, which make no sense in Aristotelian physics.[20] In other words, twelfth-century science had no physical theory to explain the motions of the heavenly bodies. Indeed, it was not until Galileo and Newton that such a physical theory was developed. In Maimonides' day, the contradiction between Ptolemaic astronomy and Aristotelian physics was definitely a "true perplexity." Regarding this perplexity, Maimonides remarks that Aristotle did not know enough mathematics in order to recognize the problem, but had it been explained to him, "he would have become most perplexed." Maimonides concludes the chapter with the confession: "The extreme predilection that I have for investigating the truth is evidenced by the fact that I have explicitly stated and reported my *perplexity* regarding these matters."[21] Maimonides is not speaking here about an *aporia* that can be facilely resolved (like the two examples concerning biblical texts), but one whose resolution is unknown.

We see here that perplexity is found not only among literalistic or simplistic readers of the Bible. The great Aristotle himself was saved from perplexity only because his insufficient mathematics did not allow him to understand the problem. And Maimonides, the Guide of the perplexed, admits to his own perplexity (or, perhaps, boasts of it). Rabbi Aharon Lichtenstein once observed that the title of Maimonides' book is correctly "The Guide *of* the Perplexed" not "The Guide *for* the Perplexed"; for the former title properly includes Maimonides among "the rank of the perplexed," while the latter erroneously removes him from it. Perplexity, explained Rabbi Lichtenstein, is not a contradiction to faith and leadership.[22] Maimonides, I think, would say that it is a *necessary condition* of true faith and true leadership. Only those who lack understanding are not perplexed.

---

20. Ibid., II:24, 322–327. The phrase "true perplexity" appears on p. 326.
21. Ibid., 326–327.
22. Menachem Genack, "Rav Aharon Lichtenstein: A Personal Reminiscence," *Orthodox Union*, 23 April 2015: https://www.ou.org/life/inspiration/rav-aharon-lichtenstein-a-personal-reminiscence.

THE GARDEN OF EDEN

In the opening chapters of the *Guide*, Maimonides presents a fascinating interpretation of the biblical Garden of Eden story. He treats the story as a state-of-nature parable, which concerns the foundations of ethics, and illustrates why human beings need laws.

According to his interpretation in part I, chapters 1–2, Adam's being created in "the divine image" means that he was created with a perfect intellect, capable of knowing the true and the false:

> The intellect that God made overflow unto the human being and that is the latter's ultimate perfection was that with which Adam had been provided before he disobeyed. It was because of this that it was said of him that he was created "in the image of God and in His likeness" (cf. Gen. 1:26–27).... Through the intellect one distinguishes between truth and falsehood, and that was found in [Adam] in its perfection.... Good and bad, on the other hand, belong to the things generally accepted as known, not to those cognized by the intellect. For one does not say "it is good that heaven is spherical" or "it is bad that the earth is flat," but one says "true" and "false" respectively with regard to these assertions.... Now, the human being, by virtue of his intellect, knows truth from falsehood.... Accordingly, when he was in his most excellent state...he had no faculty that was engaged in any way in the consideration of generally accepted things, and did not apprehend them. So among these generally accepted things even that which is most manifestly bad, namely, uncovering the genitals, was not bad according to him.[23]

Maimonides distinguishes here between "things cognized by the intellect" and "things generally accepted as known." The distinction is that between objective knowledge and subjective knowledge. Things cognized by the intellect are said to be "true" or "false," whereas things generally accepted as known are said to be "good" or "bad." Maimonides defines "true" as corresponding to reality, and "false" as not corresponding it. He defines

---

23. *Guide* I:2, 24–25.

"good" as corresponding to one's intentions, and "bad" as not corresponding to them. "True" and "false" are common to all. The proposition "$2 + 3 = 5$" is true for everyone, everywhere, anytime, and the proposition "the earth is flat" is false for everyone, everywhere, anytime. Judgments of "good" and "bad," however, are not common to all. The proposition "the government's economic policy is good" may be affirmed by some and denied by others, depending on their values and priorities. Similarly, the proposition "the film is bad" may be affirmed by some and denied by others, depending on their cinematographic taste. Adam and Eve, before disobeying the divine commandment and eating of the fruit of the Tree of Knowledge of Good and Evil, had, according to Maimonides, perfect rational knowledge; that is, all their judgments were objective and scientific. They lived the perfectly rational life: sleeping no more but no less than their bodies required, eating in accordance with the science of nutrition, and regulating their sexual relations in accordance with their combined needs. Everything they did was in accordance with their true needs, not their imaginary desires. They enjoyed the necessities of life, and shunned luxuries. However, given human physiology and psychology, such a purely rational existence could not last long. The rule of Reason is unstable. Adam and Eve soon gave in to their imaginary desires, disobeyed the commandment, and ate of the fruit of the Tree of Knowledge of Good and Evil.[24]

Maimonides continues:

> When he disobeyed and inclined toward his imaginary desires…
> he was punished by being deprived of that intellectual apprehension. He…disobeyed the commandment that was imposed upon him on account of his intellect…and became absorbed in judging things to be "bad" or "good".… Hence it is said, "And ye shall be like *elohim* [judges and rulers] knowing good and evil" (Gen. 3:5), and not "knowing the false and the true".… "And the eyes of them

---

24. The idea that the Edenic condition is unstable is already found in rabbinic literature. Adam "could not obey his commandment even for one hour" (Genesis Rabba 21:7); "in the ninth [hour] he was commanded, in the tenth he transgressed" (Leviticus Rabba 29:1).

both were opened, and they knew they were naked" (Gen. 3:7) ....
[Adam] entered upon another state in which he considered as "bad"
things that he had not thought of in that way before.[25]

Adam disobeyed the one divine commandment he had been given: Do
not eat of the fruit of the Tree of Knowledge of Good and Evil! This
commandment is equal to "Do not forsake your intellect," "Do not go
after your imaginary desires," or "Thou shalt have no other gods before
Me" (Ex. 20:3; Deut. 5:7). Having rejected the rational life, Adam was
punished by having to live the irrational life – the life ruled not by Reason but by the imaginary desires. Unlike purely rational human beings,
human beings living in accordance with their egotistic impulses need
rules of "good" and "bad." Adam and Eve became like judges and rulers knowing good and evil. Following Onkelos, Maimonides parses
the word "*elohim*" in Genesis 3:5 as referring to judges and rulers, not
God. The first moral rule Adam and Eve adopted was that of the fig
leaf. When they had lived rationally and had regulated their sexual relations in accordance with their combined needs, they did not need rules
to restrain their sexual desires. Reason controlled their desires. Their
nakedness was no problem. When they had been truly rational beings,
Adam could never have raped Eve or harassed her, and, for that matter,
Eve could never have raped or harassed him. Once they forsook Reason and followed their imaginary desires, they became a threat to each
other. The rule of the fig leaf was adopted to restrain their self-centered
passions, which were no longer controlled by Reason. The rule of the fig
leaf, the first moral rule, is a symbol for all moral rules: they all come to
help human beings restrain their passions and live more in accordance
with Reason.

What was the change that Adam and Eve underwent? Maimonides
writes:

> Now, concerning its dictum with regard to Adam, "He changeth
> his face, and Thou sendest him forth (*vateshaleḥehu*)" (Job 14:20),
> the interpretation...is as follows: when the direction toward

---

> which the human being tended changed, he was sent forth.... His punishment was...measure for measure.... He had been given license to eat good things and to enjoy ease and tranquility. When however... he became greedy, followed his imaginary desires, and ate what he had been forbidden to eat, he was deprived of every-thing, and had to eat the meanest kinds of foods... and only after toil and labor [cf. Gen. 3:18–19].... "And the Lord sent them forth [*vayeshaleḥehu*] from the Garden of Eden" (v. 23).[26]

Adam changed his direction. He had been marching happily on the straight path of the intellect, but now he changed his direction and pursued the path of his imaginary desires. In interpreting Job 14:20 as referring to Adam, Maimonides followed Genesis Rabba 21:4 (cf. 16:1): "'He changeth his face, and Thou sendest him forth'.... Adam forsook the knowledge (*daat*) of the Holy One, blessed be He, and went after the knowledge (*daat*) of the Serpent." In Maimonides' adaptation of the midrash, Adam forsook the *intellectual* knowledge of the Holy One, blessed be He, and went after the *imaginary* knowledge of the Serpent – or, in other words, he forsook the knowledge of true and false, and went after that of good and bad. The midrash is able to connect Job 14:20 with the Garden of Eden story because of two reasons: first, Job 14, like the Garden of Eden story, treats of the human condition; second, the word "*vateshaleḥehu*" recalls "*vayeshaleḥehu*" (Gen. 3:23). Maimonides adopts the midrashic interpretation but adds the identification of God's knowl-edge with the intellect and the Serpent's knowledge with the imagina-tion. Adam's punishment was "measure for measure": the punishment for living irrationally is living irrationally.

Maimonides' interpretation of the Garden of Eden story is based firmly on the midrashic tradition. However, it presents a radical philo-sophic teaching. Maimonides was the first philosopher in the history of Western philosophy to teach that the perfectly rational human being cannot comprehend the concepts of "good" and "bad," and, moreover, God cannot comprehend them! Maimonides' extraordinary teach-ing was a development of various Aristotelian views concerning the

---

26. Ibid., 25–26.

distinction between "theory" and "practice," but it radicalizes them and pushes them to their logical conclusion. Maimonides' radical view was later enunciated by Spinoza in his own interpretation of the Garden of Eden story, which was indebted to Maimonides (see Spinoza, *Ethics*, IV:68, scholium).

There are two verses which, on the face of it, say that God knows good and evil and thus appear to contradict Maimonides' interpretation. One is Genesis 3:5, "And ye shall be like *elohim* knowing good and evil." As already mentioned, Maimonides, citing Onkelos, interprets the word "*elohim*" here as referring not to God but to judges and rulers. The other problematic verse is Genesis 3:22, "And the Lord God said, 'Behold, Adam is become as one of us, to know good and evil.'" This verse is also interpreted by Maimonides in accordance with Onkelos: "And the Lord God said, 'Behold, Adam is become unique, of himself he knows good and evil.'" This odd reading of the verse is made possible by the equivocal meaning of the Hebrew preposition "*mimenu*" ("of us," "of himself") which may designate either first person plural or the third person singular (see *Mishneh Torah, Laws of Repentance* 5:1).

THE DIVINE LAW

The ancient Greek philosophers taught that human beings are social animals, that is, they must live together with other human beings in order to satisfy their physical and emotional needs. If human beings lived according to Reason, they would of course have no problem living together, working together, and sharing goods. However, as we learn from the Garden of Eden story as interpreted by Maimonides, human beings tend not to live in accordance with Reason but to pursue their egotistical desires. If rational human beings know how to divide a cake fairly between them, egotistical human beings, pursuing their imaginings, will try to get the whole cake for themselves by hook or by crook. Since human beings tend to live in accordance with their egotistical desires, Maimonides explains, they quarrel and fight, and thus government, laws, and police become necessary in order to protect the weak, impose order, and establish peace. An ordinary political law or a "nomic law" (after the Greek word "*nomos*," law) thus takes as its goal the physical welfare of the people. However, Maimonides observes, a nomic law, whose goal is entirely physical, has no incentive to advance true human excellence, that is, knowledge of the sciences and knowledge of God. In fact, it may well see free inquiry and critical investigation as a threat to law and order. Thus, continues Maimonides, the divine law becomes necessary. A divine law is a political law that considers physical welfare to be only an intermediate goal, but takes as its final goal the welfare of the soul, that is, intellectual perfection, the knowledge of the sciences and knowledge of God. A nomic law is interested only in peace; a divine law is interested in peace and enlightenment, where peace is the intermediate goal and enlightenment the ultimate goal. The divine law is willing to risk the dangers of free inquiry and critical investigation only because it is absolutely committed to promoting the true human perfection. The Law of Moses perfectly fits the definition of a divine law, and is its original paradigm.[27]

The Law of Moses, Maimonides exposits, does not only teach true beliefs (e.g., the existence and unity of God) but also "necessary beliefs" (e.g., that God becomes violently angry with the disobedient), that is, beliefs that, while not literally true, are "necessary for the sake of political welfare... for the abolition of reciprocal wrongdoing or for the acquisition of a noble moral quality."[28] In explaining the function of these "necessary beliefs," Maimonides follows the political philosophy of Plato (*Republic*, II, 377d–e; III, 389b–c; 414b–415d). Nonetheless, although he interprets the text "My wrath shall wax hot, and I will kill you with the sword" (Ex. 22:23) in the Platonic manner and although he seems to hold here that in biblical times it was permissible for the multitude to understand the text literally,[29] he elsewhere in the *Guide* teaches emphatically that all such texts which attribute emotions to God are metaphors and examples of the rabbinical rule "The Torah speaks according to the language of human beings" (Yevamot 71a and elsewhere), that is, "according to the imagination of the multitude."[30]

---

27. See *Guide* II:40, 381–385; III:27–28, 510–514.
28. Ibid., III:28, 512, 514.
29. Ibid., 514.
30. Ibid., I:26, 56. Cf. I:36, 82–83.

The divine law, in short, seeks to create a community of peace and enlightenment. In a sense, therefore, it seeks to return human beings to the Garden of Eden, that is, to enable them to live rational lives as much as humanly possible. Many commentators on the *Guide,* beginning with Rabbi Abraham Abulafia in the thirteenth century, have noted that the number of chapters in the *Guide* numerologically equals *gan eden* (177), the Garden of Eden. However, like all things concerning the *Guide,* even the number of its chapters is perplexing. In the manuscripts of the Arabic original, the chapters are not numbered and it is unclear how many there are. According to Rabbi Samuel ibn Tibbon's Hebrew translation, there are 178 chapters, and according to Rabbi Judah Alharizi's Hebrew translation, there are 177. The various manuscripts of the thirteenth-century Latin translation have several different chapter numberings. That Alharizi's numbering equals *gan eden* may be a reason for preferring it to Ibn Tibbon's. However, to my mind, the *Guide* does *not* try to return us to the ideal or utopian Garden of Eden, with no government, no laws, and no police, but rather it holds out the realistic hope of a relatively rational society, which has government, laws, and police. I would, thus, have expected the number of chapters in the *Guide* to be 176, that is, *almost* the Garden of Eden.

There is one messianic chapter in the *Guide.* It is part III, chapter 11. In this remarkable little chapter, Maimonides speculates about a world in which "They shall not hurt nor destroy in all My holy mountain, for the earth shall be full of the knowledge of the Lord, as the waters cover the sea" (Is. 11:9). He explains that the second clause of the verse gives the reason for the first clause. When people are rational and know God, they do not hurt others or try to destroy them. Maimonides considers the Messianic Era to be a realistic goal. Indeed, the Messianic Era, for him, is simply the time in world history when the divine law succeeds in creating a rational community. In the Messianic Era, according to him, the laws of the Torah will continue to be in force, since human beings will continue to be human beings, and will therefore need government, laws, and police. Thus, the Messianic Era is not a literal return to the utopian Garden of Eden. Maimonides' messianic vision, however, is of a world that comes as close as is realistically possible to the Garden of Eden. Owing to their knowledge of God, human beings will cooperate with each other, will not exploit others, and will not hoard goods; and therefore Nature will provide abundantly for all. The more human beings pursue luxuries, the less Nature is able to provide for their needs; and the more human beings satisfy themselves only with the necessities of life, the more Nature is able to provide abundantly for all.[31]

LOVE OF GOD

The *Guide* is an Aristotelian book containing difficult technical philosophic discussions. However, as already mentioned, it has one mystical chapter. The mystical chapter is part III, chapter 51, and its subject is the intellectual love of God.[32] It has also been mentioned that according to the view of Shlomo Pines, the deepest level of the *Guide* is intellectual mysticism. Given these mystical elements in the *Guide*, the book, despite its rugged Aristotelianism, has throughout the ages been a favorite of the most creative mystics, like Rabbi Abraham Abulafia, Nahmanides, and Maester Eckhardt.

Nonetheless, the main focus of the *Guide* is the philosophy of law. Even when Maimonides discusses the mystical intellectual love of God, he discusses it in the context of law. How, he asks, does one fulfil the legal obligation to serve God "with all your heart" (Deut. 11:13)? He gives three answers to this question: (1) animal sacrifices, (2) statutory prayer, and (3) intellectual contemplation. Historically, in ancient Israel, when the Temple was standing in Jerusalem, the commandment was fulfilled by animal sacrifices. Today, the commandment is legally fulfilled by statutory prayer. Optimally, the commandment is fulfilled by intellectual contemplation without words.[33] Here is Maimonides' description of the optimal or ideal "service in the heart" (*avoda shebalev*):

> If you have apprehended God and His acts in accordance with what is required by the intellect, you should afterwards engage

---

31. Ibid., III:11, 440–441. Cf. *Mishneh Torah, Laws of Kings* 11–12.
32. See Steven Harvey, "Maimonides in the Sultan's Palace," in Joel Kraemer, ed., *Perspectives on Maimonides* (Oxford, 1991), 47–75.
33. *Guide* I:59, 137–143; III:32, 525–531; 51, 618–628. Cf. Maimonides, *Book of the Commandments*, positive commandment 5.

in totally devoting yourself to Him, endeavor to come closer to Him, and strengthen the bond between you and Him, that is, the intellect.... The Torah has made it clear that this last worship... can be engaged in only after apprehension has been achieved. It says, "to love the Lord your God and to serve Him with all your heart" (Deut. 11:13).... This love is proportionate to apprehension. After love comes this worship to which attention has been drawn by the sages, may their memory be blessed, who said "This is the service in the heart" (Taanit 2a; Y. Berakhot 4:1). In my opinion, it consists in setting thought to work on the first intelligible and in devoting oneself exclusively to this, as far as it is within human capacity.... Thus... after apprehension total devotion to Him should be the aim. Mostly this is achieved in solitude.[34]

Maimonides makes it clear that the commandment to serve God in one's heart can be optimally observed only *after* one has achieved the knowledge and love of God, and that this service in the heart is an intense mystical exercise best achieved in solitude, not in the commotion of the synagogue.

The intellect is described here as neither divine nor human, but "the bond" (Hebrew: *hadibuk*; Arabic: *al-wuṣla*) between the divine and the human. A similar expression is found in *Guide* III:52.[35] Elsewhere, Maimonides describes the intellect as something "foreign," "strange," or "remarkable."[36] It sometimes seems to be human and sometimes divine. However, in truth, it does not belong to the human being and it is not God, but it enables us to have a connection with Him. It is "the bond."

The rabbinical phrase "service in the heart" refers commonly to statutory prayer. Maimonides, however, gives here his own distinctive interpretation of the phrase ("in my opinion") according to which it refers to intellectual contemplation ("setting thought to work on the

---

34. *Guide* III:51, 620–621.
35. Ibid., 629.
36. Ibid., I:1, 23.

first intelligible"). In his discussion of Deuteronomy 11:13 and the rabbinical phrase "service in the heart" in his *Mishneh Torah, Laws of Prayer* 1:1, Maimonides rules that the commandment to pray is biblical (*min haTorah*) but the "times" and "text" of the prayers are only rabbinical. In the light of his statement in the *Guide*, it appears that this means that there is a rabbinical obligation to recite certain prayers at certain times, but the biblical obligation has no prescribed time or text but is optimally performed by "setting thought to work on the first intelligible." By "first intelligible" Maimonides seems to mean the first created intellect, the prime mover of the heavens, which he identifies with the angelic class of *ḥayyot hakodesh* (see *Mishneh Torah, Laws of the Foundations of the Torah* 2:7; 3:1; 7:1).

In the continuation of his discussion of the love of God in *Guide* III:51, Maimonides goes further and states that the ultimate love of God is not merely "love" (Hebrew: *ahava*; Arabic: *mahabba*) but "*passionate* love" (Hebrew: *ḥeshek*; Arabic: *'ishq*). He defines "passionate love" as "an excess of love so that no thought remains that is directed toward a thing other than the beloved" (see *Mishneh Torah, Laws of Repentance* 10:3).[37]

The law, for Maimonides, does not only seek to bring about a peaceful and enlightened community living together rationally, but also seeks to direct each individual to the most passionate love of God. Maimonides knew no contradiction between intellect and passion.

CONCLUSION

I have said that Maimonides' *Guide of the Perplexed* addresses different readers in different ways. In truth, it also addresses the same reader in different ways. Every time I pick up this amazing book, it speaks to me in a different way, challenges me in a different way, teaches me something surprising, and perplexes me anew. I have tried in this brief chapter to give the reader a taste of this enchanting philosophic book. I am aware, of course, that the *Guide* could have been presented in many other ways.

---

37. Ibid., 627.

My hope is that this chapter will encourage the reader to open the *Guide* and to grapple with its perplexities.

FURTHER READING

Arabic text:

Dalālat al-Ḥā'irīn. Edited by Salomon Munk and Issachar Joël (Jerusalem, 1929). Arabic text in Hebrew letters. This is the standard critical edition.

Dalālat al-Ḥā'irīn/Moreh HaNevukhim. Edited and translated into Hebrew by Rabbi Joseph Kafih (Jerusalem, 1972). Arabic text in Hebrew letters. Kafih made use of Yemenite manuscripts unknown to Munk and Joël.

Dalālat al-Ḥā'irīn. Edited by Hüseyin Atay (Ankara, 1974). Arabic text in Arabic letters.

Samuel ibn Tibbon's Medieval Hebrew Translation:

Moreh HaNevukhim, with commentaries of Ephodi, Shem Tov ben Joseph ibn Shem Tov, Asher Crescas, and Isaac Abrabanel (Warsaw, 1872). This edition has many mistakes, but has important medieval commentaries.

Moreh HaNevukhim. Edited (with punctuation and vocalization) by Yehuda Even-Shmuel (Jerusalem, 1981). This is the best edition of Ibn Tibbon's translation.

English Translations:

The Guide of the Perplexed. Translated and annotated by Michael Friedländer (London, 1881, 1885). Popular edition (without annotations) printed in 1904, and reprinted often.

The Guide of the Perplexed. Translated by Shlomo Pines, with introductions by Pines and by Leo Strauss (Chicago, 1963). This is the most accurate English translation, but Friedländer is often more readable. The introductions by Pines (on Maimonides' sources) and Strauss (on the argument of the *Guide*) are very important.

Modern Hebrew Translations:

Moreh HaNevukhim. Translated by Rabbi Joseph Kafih (see above under "Arabic text"). Kafih's translation is printed alongside the Arabic text.

Moreh HaNevukhim. Translated and annotated by Michael Schwartz (Tel Aviv, 2002). This translation into contemporary philosophic Hebrew is the favorite of Israelis.

Two Popular Introductions to the *Guide*:

Goodman, Micah. *Maimonides and the Book That Changed Judaism: Secrets of "The Guide for the Perplexed."* Translated from Hebrew by Y. Sinclair (Philadelphia, 2015).

Hartman, David. *Maimonides: Torah and Philosophic Quest* (Philadelphia, 1976; revised edition, 2009).

Sefer HaIkkarim: Rabbi Joseph Albo's Exposition of Jewish Dogma

Dr. Shira Weiss

Rabbi Joseph Albo composed one of the most popular Hebrew works within the corpus of medieval Jewish philosophy, accessible and relevant not only to his generation, but to the modern reader as well. Albo's *Sefer HaIkkarim* (*Book of Principles*), his iteration of Jewish dogma, attempted to defend the authenticity of the Jewish faith and create a uniform set of Jewish doctrine. He artfully integrated exegetical interpretations which convey theological lessons within his philosophical discussions of principles of faith.

BIOGRAPHY

Few details are known about Albo's life. Born in Monreal, a town in the kingdom of Aragon (the northeast of modern Spain) sometime before 1380, Albo studied with Ḥasdai Crescas of Saragossa, to whom he refers in his book as his teacher. Albo served as rabbi and preacher in the community of Daroca in Christian Spain and played a significant role in a particularly turbulent time in Jewish history. He moved to a rabbinic role in Soria, in Castile, possibly as a result of the destruction of his community in Daroca in 1415, and there completed his major treatise, *Sefer HaIkkarim*. Well aware of the hardships facing his generation until his death in approximately 1444, Albo sought to lead his own, as well as the larger Jewish community, in the preservation of their religious commitments amid persecution and hostility.

HISTORICAL CONTEXT

Living at the end of the medieval era, Albo witnessed the culmination of a long period of Christian persecution of the Jews. In the early summer of 1391, anti-Jewish riots destroyed the communities in Andalusia, Castile, Navarre, and the Balearic Islands; their citizens were massacred or forced to convert to Christianity to escape death or slavery. Forced conversions continued throughout the fifteenth century, by which time the New Christians (later referred to as Marranos) outnumbered the Jews.

Albo's *Sefer HaIkkarim* was completed in 1425 and reflects his historical context – a time in which the Christians attempted to denigrate Judaism and force Jews to acknowledge the truth of Christianity as having superseded the Jewish tradition. The Christian attacks were not only physical, but philosophical as well. For two centuries, the Church held compulsory religious disputations, intended to publicly demonstrate the inferiority of Judaism and disparage its anti-Christian sentiments. Since these demonstrations were conducted with no regard for justice, Jewish scholars were invited to participate under threat of punishment and were not afforded free speech to defend their values. The pope was the arbiter and the Jews were forced to accept his conclusion of Christianity's superiority in order to escape punishment. The goal of these propagandist attacks by the Christians was to intimidate and coerce the Jews to submit to their adversaries' arguments.

In the first disputation, held in Paris in 1240, Nicholas Donin, a Jewish apostate, argued against Judaism, while Rabbi Jehiel ben Joseph represented the Jewish community. This disputation resulted in the burning of the Talmud. In 1263, a disputation was held in Barcelona, wherein Pablo Christiani, a converted Jew, engaged in a confrontation against Nahmanides. With these disputations as precedent, Albo was called upon to defend the Talmud and Judaism against Gerónimo de Santa Fe in a third major disputation, in Tortosa (Feb. 7, 1413–Nov. 13, 1414), inaugurated by Antipope

Benedict XIII. Albo's opponent had converted from Judaism in 1412 and was originally known as Joshua Lorki. He had earlier defended Judaism against his former master, Solomon Halevi of Burgos, who had converted and adopted the name Pablo de Santa Maria (and later became bishop of Burgos). Lorki's own faith, however, began to erode; as he engaged in religious struggles, he sought guidance from Pablo de Santa Maria to "solve for me a multitude of doubts."[1] Through his preaching and written work, Albo set out to combat such theological confusion, which had become common among many Jews in his generation who had suffered religious persecution and who were unprepared to defend their beliefs.

Albo's historical context had a significant impact upon his philosophy. Following the precedent of Ḥasdai Crescas – who also lived under Christian Spain's severe oppression in the late medieval period and whose historical context was evident in his *Refutation of Christian Dogmas* (1397–1398) – Albo similarly addressed the needs of his suffering generation. As a result, a plethora of allusions to Albo's political circumstances can be found throughout *Sefer HaIkkarim* (many, however, have been omitted in publication due to the objection of the censor). Albo's participation in the Tortosa Disputation and his exposure to Christian philosophical propaganda and polemics, in addition to his study of Christian philosophical literature, such as that of Thomas Aquinas, motivated him to counteract his opponents' arguments by teaching his community the truths of Judaism, the exclusive divine law. During the Disputation, Albo responded to Lorki's argument that the Messiah had already come by arguing that there were two possible times for the arrival of the Messiah according to Jewish tradition: either the time foretold by God or when Israel reached a state of readiness and repentance. He encouraged his coreligionists to uphold their Jewish faith in order to merit redemption.

The Tortosa Disputation revealed to Albo the difference of opinion among the rabbis called upon to defend Judaism. Albo felt he was not afforded an opportunity to adequately respond to his accuser during the Disputation, and Jewish scholars had not yet succeeded in formulating a commonly accepted opinion regarding Jewish dogma. As

---

1. Joshua Lorki, *Ketav Divrei Ḥakhamim*, ed. Eliezer Ashkenazi (Metz, 1849), 42.

a political and rabbinic leader and preacher, Albo wished to compose a comprehensive philosophical formulation of Jewish belief that would earn the widespread approval of the Jewish community and would enable his coreligionists to uniformly respond to their attackers and withstand Christian religious coercion. Albo sought to restore Jewish resolve by proving Judaism's authenticity against other religions. In doing so, he incorporated philosophical and exegetical innovation into an apologetic work in which he examined fundamental questions of dogma.

VALUE OF *SEFER HAIKKARIM*

Albo had a broad knowledge of the philosophical tradition, as he alludes to both explicitly and, far more often, implicitly many of his predecessors' ideas, including those of Rav Saadia Gaon, Rabbi Judah Halevi, Maimonides, Nahmanides, Gersonides, Crescas, and Simeon ben Zemah Duran as well as Aristotle, Averroes, and Aquinas.[2] The chief objective of Albo's work was to defend Jewish dogma. Collette Sirat argues:

---

2. Despite his book's appeal and his rabbinic stature, modern scholars have considered Albo to be an unoriginal philosopher who merely synthesized the views of his predecessors in an accessible style. His work has been criticized for neglecting to offer the type of philosophical innovation comparable to others in the genre. (See Zev Diesendruck, "Review of Book of Principles," trans. Isaac Husik, *Journal of Philosophy* 28:19 [1931], 526; Isaac Husik, *A History of Medieval Jewish Philosophy* [New York, 1966]; Julius Guttmann, *Philosophies of Judaism: The History of Jewish Philosophy from Biblical Times to Franz Rosenzweig* [New York, 1964]; *Encyclopedia Judaica*, 1st ed., s.v. "Albo, Joseph." Eliezer Schweid, "The Polemic Against Christianity as a Factor in Shaping Joseph Albo's Doctrines" [Hebrew], *Proceedings of the Fourth World Congress for Jewish Studies* 2 [1968], 309–312.) While much of Albo's work does reference the ideas of his predecessors, his critics' objections can be refuted. Upon closer examination, philosophical originality can, in fact, be uncovered in his exegetical homilies in *Sefer HaIkkarim* and in his halakhic responsa which reflect his unique view of free choice, a topic that was highly debated in the medieval period and continues to be of interest in contemporary philosophy. Thus, Albo innovatively utilizes the Bible as a source which demonstrates the philosophical truth of free choice at a time which was plagued by persecution and coercion. (See my, *Joseph Albo on Free Choice: Exegetical Innovation in Medieval Jewish Philosophy* [New York, 2017].)

[*Sefer HaIkkarim*] perfectly accomplishes the task for which it was conceived ... namely, to show that the Law of Moses was the only one that corresponds to the definition of divine law, and therefore to establish its particularism in the larger context of the universal laws that tie man to God.[3]

The accessible style in which Albo composed his work contributed to the achievement of his goal. Albo, a renowned preacher in fifteenth-century Spain, wrote *Sefer HaIkkarim* as a series of philosophical homilies that conveyed theological doctrine to a wide audience. As a result of the publication of his work, Albo was able to provide a large and diverse audience with an understanding of Jewish doctrine. *Sefer HaIkkarim* had wide-ranging appeal both in Jewish and non-Jewish contexts. The work has been classified as the last of the philosophical and theological classics of medieval Judaism, belonging to the same genre of literary works as *Emunot VeDeot, Ḥovot HaLevavot, Kuzari, Emuna Rama, Moreh HaNevukhim, Milḥamot Hashem,* and *Or Hashem.* Described by Menachem Kellner as "one of the most enduringly popular works of medieval Jewish philosophical theology," the first edition of Albo's work was published in 1485. Over seventeen editions of Albo's Hebrew text were subsequently published and translated into Latin, English, German, and Italian in order to accommodate the demand of readers unable to understand the original. Additionally, the work was abridged and commented upon, and it continues to be analyzed by modern scholars. Albo's work not only had prolonged success in Jewish circles, but Christian theologians, including Hugo Grotius, Joseph de Voisin, and Bernardo de Rossi, also held *Sefer HaIkkarim* in high esteem. Sixteenth- and seventeenth-century Christian theologians viewed Albo's work as representing a comprehensive Jewish theology. Albo's arguments in his work were often appropriated by Christian thinkers as they engaged in polemics with Jews and with fellow scholars of other Christian denominations.

Albo ascertained the strengths and weaknesses of divergent philosophical sources and developed an insightful philosophical work. His

---

3. Collete Sirat, *A History of Jewish Philosophy in the Middle Ages* (Cambridge, 1990), 381.

thought, as articulated in *Sefer HaIkkarim*, is informed by the impact of his particularly turbulent historical environment and is characterized by unique exegetical interpretations integrated with logical and conceptual analyses that teach metaphysical, ethical, psychological, and theological lessons. Sensitive to the religious coercion experienced by his coreligionists, Albo composed an accessible work that would fulfill the needs of the Jews in his generation and fortify Judaism against attacks in the future. His dogmatic text was intended to afford all of his coreligionists with a uniform defense of the Jewish faith in a precarious time.

Albo encouraged his generation to engage in an investigation of divine law by comparing the Torah to other sciences. He argued that just as it is necessary for a doctor to know the principles of medicine, so too, an adherent of religion must understand its laws:

> All the people that we know of in the world today possess a law, and it is inconceivable that a person should be subject to or identified with a law without knowing its principles or having some notion of them sufficient to induce belief in them, as we do not call a person a physician who does not know the principles of medicine.[4]

In his introduction to *Sefer HaIkkarim*, Albo articulates his objective of explicating principles of divine law and identifies the divine character of the Law of Moses:

> I have composed this book and called it *The Book of Principles*, because it investigates the principles of laws generally, and especially the principles of divine law.... Then it investigates the principles of the Law of Moses, concerning the divine character of which all agree, and shows that it has general principles, appertaining to it in virtue of its character as divine, and special principles, appertaining to it as being the particular divine law that it is.[5]

---

4. Joseph Albo, "Introduction," *Sefer ha-'Iqqarim: Book of Principles*, trans. Isaac Husik (Philadelphia, 1930), 35. All subsequent translations are taken from this edition (henceforth, *SH*).

5. Ibid., 37.

Albo's goal to redefine the principles of Judaism in the context of philosophy was due to the internal conflict regarding Jewish dogma during his time. No other Jewish philosophical work, according to Albo, had adequately dealt with the general principles of religion. There was no universally accepted work on dogma; rather, numerous works were composed which varied with regard to the nature and number of the principles:

> For while they all agree that it [the Law of Moses] is divine, they differ not a little concerning the number of its basic principles, some saying they are thirteen (Maimonides), some that they are twenty-six (David bar Yom Tov ben Bila), and some that they are only six (Crescas). But there is not one of these learned men who made any effort to explain those principles which pertain to a divine law generally... nor to whether there can be only one divine law.[6]

Albo was not satisfied with his predecessors' failure to make distinctions between the principles common to all religions that pertain to divine legislation, and special principles unique to a particular religion. He wanted to offer the Jews of his generation a rationalistic defense of Judaism by proving that the Law of Moses is the only law that corresponds to the definition of divine law in general, thereby demonstrating its uniqueness within the context of the universal law that connects man with God.

Albo, following Duran, conceptualizes religion as a science with fundamental premises. By identifying a universal common denominator as a basis for all religions, one can establish criteria by which one can examine and deduce which religion claiming exclusive truth demonstrates its unique authenticity. Therefore, in the *Sefer HaIkkarim*, Albo attempts to integrate the Law of Moses within the larger framework of divine law and political laws of human society before deducing its superiority. Additionally, he refutes the doctrines of Christianity in order to combat the pressures of conversion and raise the declined spiritual level among Jews in Christian Spain. Thus, Albo's work reflects the impact

---

6. Ibid., 36.

of the public disputations and persecution against Jews taking place at the time.

In *Sefer HaIkkarim*, Albo begins his introduction by distinguishing divine law from human law and explaining the need for divine law altogether. He then proceeds to prove that Judaism is the uniquely genuine divine law. He explains the limitation of the human mind in ascertaining the true and the good and, therefore, argues that only divine guidance can define the true and the good beyond doubt. Albo seeks to delineate the principles of divine law in order to demonstrate how the Law of Moses is the authentic divine law, which teaches the true and the good:

> It is incumbent therefore upon every person to know that out of all laws, there is one divine law which gives this guidance. This is impossible unless we know the basic principles without which a divine law cannot exist. Accordingly the purpose of this work is to explain the essential principles of a divine law.[7]

In days of religious challenge and debate, Albo wanted to address an issue of tremendous concern for his people: Whether or not it was proper, or perhaps obligatory, to analyze the fundamental principles of one's religion in order to determine their truth. Such a concern demonstrates the difference between the focus of the age in which Albo lived and the focus of the age of Maimonides, for whom inquiry about the truth of one's beliefs was not only permitted, but expected. Albo's generation stood on the threshold of apostasy, and this question was raised by both Jews and those Christians who did not trust Jewish intentions to convert. Albo was aware of the danger of the potential of finding a seemingly superior religion and the continuous pursuit of a truer religion that prevents the affirmation of steadfast religious convictions. Nevertheless, Albo encouraged his coreligionists to investigate and arrive at the truth of Judaism and cajoled his community to preserve their faith at any cost in order to merit eternal life.

Albo responded to these threats by attesting, similar to Judah Halevi in the *Kuzari*, that all religions agree that one faith is divine, but

---

7. Ibid., 2.

they claim that it has been superseded. Halevi argues that the superiority of Judaism over other religions is demonstrated by the fact that the Jews were the only nation to experience a history in which God providentially intervened through public miraculous revelations that have been recounted throughout the generations by an unbroken chain of tradition, which Halevi equates with experience. The chosenness of the Jews cannot be disputed because it was experienced and transmitted without dissent by thousands of people, as opposed to the more private revelatory experiences of the other major contending faiths, in which there were few (if any) witnesses. Everyone, including Christians and Muslims, concedes that God participated in the history and redemption of the Jewish people, despite their subsequent claims of God's rejection of Israel. Albo advised, therefore, that every non-Jewish religionist should investigate his religion to see if he is justified in opposing the religion which is acknowledged to be divine. Similarly, every Jew should investigate whether his divine religion is temporary (as the Christians and Muslims claimed) or eternal. In such an investigation, he must first determine whether his religion conforms to the principles of divine religion and leads its devotees to justice and human perfection.

Albo explains that a divine law is recognized as genuine if it fulfills two criteria: (1) it is in accordance with three principles (God's existence, revelation, and reward and punishment) that are integral to the evaluation of such laws, and (2) it has been proven that it was transmitted by a genuine divine messenger in a direct manner from God (namely, revelation). The test of the prophet must be as direct as it was in Moses' revelation, wherein the Israelites actually saw that he was addressed by God and commissioned with a message for them. Albo rejects the pretensions of the two great religions to be divine: the Catholic religion's doctrine of the Trinity contradicts divine unity which is essential to the principle of the existence of God, whereas Islam's messenger does not fulfill the criteria necessary for transmission of divine law, in that it was not proven that Mohammed was directly addressed by God and commissioned with a divine message. Furthermore, a mass revelation comparable to that of Moses was not achieved by Jesus or Mohammed, who both claimed to have superseded Judaism:

The fact that a person claiming to be a prophet can walk on the water, or divide a river and walk through it, or walk through fire without being burned, or can cure the sick or the lepers, is evidence of the fact that he is a worthy instrument for the performance of miracles. But it is not a direct proof that he is a prophet, much less is it evidence that he was chosen to give a law.[8]

In his work, Albo shows that the Law of Moses is the only law that corresponds to the definition of divine law, thereby proving its particularity in the context of the universal laws. He argues that God revealed Himself to Israel in order to "prove to them directly the reality of prophecy, and also that Moses was sent by Me [God] to give them the Torah."[9] Albo describes God's choice of Israel and the miraculous nature of such revelations. Albo appeals to the coerced and afflicted Jews of his generation by reminding them of God's revelation and salvation throughout history in an effort to reassure them that they would continue to be saved by the power of the miraculous.

ALBO'S DELINEATION OF DOGMA

Albo enumerates the three general *ikkarim* (principles) of all divine law, distinctive from natural and conventional law, without which divine law could not exist: existence of God, revelation, and retribution. Albo's delineation reflects the influence of his contemporary Duran, who lists the same three essential beliefs in his philosophical work, *Ohev Mishpat*:

> The fundamental principles are three and no more. Belief in God and what follows [from that belief] is one principle. [The consequences of this principle are:] existence, unity, eternity a parte ante, incorporeality, and that one ought to worship God and no other. Belief in the Torah and the necessary corollary beliefs constitute one principle, which is that God, through the intermediation of the Separate Intellects, causes a divine overflow to extend to those who cleave to Him so that they become prophets

---

8. Ibid., I:18, 155–6.
9. Ibid., 158.

of various ranks. Included in the principle are four [derivative] principles: prophecy, Mosaic prophecy, Torah from heaven, and that the Torah will never be changed or altered, for divine activity is perfect, enduring, and eternal. Belief in retribution and its necessary corollary beliefs constitute one principle which is that God knows the deeds of men and rewards and punishes them according to their deeds.... Included in this principle are four [derivative] principles: God's knowledge and retribution, the coming of the Messiah, and the resurrection of the dead.[10]

Duran essentially divides Maimonides' thirteen principles into three hierarchical categories, in which his derivative principles comprise the remaining ten Maimonidean principles. Duran maintains that the individual achieves a share in the World to Come through purity of the soul and observance of all of the divine commandments. His delineation of three fundamental beliefs aims to group all of the revealed beliefs around what he considers to be three essential themes of the Jewish religion. Duran, like Albo, conceives of his principles as chapter headings introducing the entire traditional divine law. Albo uses the same three categories, but reworks Maimonides' delineation in a new way.

Albo's three principles can be traced back further to Averroes' *Decisive Treatise on the Harmony of Religion and Philosophy*:

> Acknowledgment of God, Blessed and Exalted, of the prophetic missions, and of happiness and misery in the next life; for these three principles are attainable by the three classes of indication, by which everyone without exception can come to assent to what he is obliged to know: I mean the rhetorical, dialectical, and demonstrative indications.[11]

Albo's derivation of the three basic dogmas from the concept of revelation was influenced by Averroes. However, unlike in *Sefer*

---

10. Simeon Duran, *Oheb Mishpat*, ch. 8, trans. Menachem Kellner, *Dogma in Medieval Jewish Thought: from Maimonides to Abravanel* (New York, 1986), 86–87.

11. Averroes, *On the Harmony of Religion and Philosophy* (London, 1976), 58.

HaIkkarim, Averroes' conception has no exclusive significance, since he believes that prophecy was a widespread natural occurrence, and therefore, the many historic faiths are all of divine origin. Albo, by contrast, argues that only Judaism achieves the three criteria necessary to constitute authentic divine law.

According to Albo, the criteria for a believer are not solely acceptance of the three principles, but also inclusion of the derivative principles, *shorashim* (roots), which follow them. From his first *ikkar,* existence of God, Albo derives God's unity, incorporeality, independence from time, and freedom from defects. From his second *ikkar,* revelation, he derives God's knowledge, prophecy, and authenticity of God's messenger. From his third *ikkar,* reward and punishment, he derives divine providence. In addition to the three fundamental and eight derivative principles of divine legislation, Albo specifies six dogmas of lesser status, *anafim* (branches), which must be believed by every Jew: creation ex nihilo, superiority of the prophet Moses, immutability of Torah, the possible achievement of human perfection by any one of the Torah's commandments, resurrection, and Messiah.

Several of the *anafim* were anti-Christian in their intent and may reflect the influence of Albo's hostile times. For instance, belief in the immutability of the Torah enabled Jews to counteract the Christian claim that Christianity superseded the Jewish tradition and that the New Testament had supplanted the Torah. Belief in the coming of the Messiah allowed Jews to counteract the Christian claim of the past arrival of the Messiah.

Avi Kadish argues that the overall preoccupation with the principles of the Torah in Jewish philosophy and the development of hierarchical systems began with, and was the hallmark of, Gerondi's school.[12] Rabbi Nissim ben Reuben Gerondi (ca. 1320–1380), author of *Derashot HaRan,* taught Ḥasdai Crescas and had a profound influence upon him and his students. Albo's hierarchical structure of dogma reflects the influence of Crescas, and his fellow disciple Rabbi Abraham ben Judah, author of the *Arbaa Turim* (*Four Rows*), which was composed in 1378, prior to

---

12. Avi (Seth) Kadish, "The Book of Abraham: Rabbi Shimon Ben Zemah Duran and the School of Rabbenu Nissim Gerondi" (PhD diss., University of Haifa, 2011), ch. 4, 111, 114.

Albo's composition, as well as his contemporary, Duran.[13] Albo, a homilist in addition to a philosopher, integrates philosophical exegesis within the delineation of his hierarchical system of dogma in order to illustrate his philosophical doctrine in an innovative manner for his audience.

Albo may have been motivated to compose such a philosophical work even though Maimonides had already delineated thirteen articles of faith because Maimonides made no mention of such a creed in his philosophical work, *The Guide of the Perplexed*, but rather included his dogma in his *Commentary on the Mishna*, a work intended for the masses, in an attempt to prevent the uneducated of his time from arriving at erroneous theological conceptions. Albo may have felt it necessary to focus on a comprehensive explanation of Jewish dogma and related concepts in a *philosophical* text that reflected and expanded upon the influence of Maimonides and others.

Despite numerous innovations, Albo's delineation of dogma does not oppose the systems of his predecessors, but rather reflects their significant influence. In fact, he writes how his three *ikkarim* can be viewed as a condensed version of Maimonides' thirteen:

> It may be that Maimonides has the same idea concerning the number of fundamental principles as the one we have just indicated, and that his list consists of the three chief principles that we have mentioned, plus the derivative dogmas issuing from them, being all called by him principles.[14]

While Albo seems to assert the fundamental nature of free choice on numerous occasions throughout his work, he, like Maimonides, does not enumerate it as an essential principle of divine law, since free choice is not exclusive to divine law, but pertains to conventional law as well. Conventional legal codes are founded on justice, rewarding and punishing the individual on the basis of his free decisions. Although Albo does not identify free choice as an *ikkar*, he does assert the Torah's allusion

---

13. Shalom Rosenberg, "The *Arbaa Turim* of Rabbi Abraham bar Judah, Disciple of Don Ḥasdai Crescas" [Hebrew], *Jerusalem Studies in Jewish Thought* 3 (1985), 525–621.

14. *SH* I:4, 69.

to freedom – "See I have set before thee this day life ... therefore choose life" – in order to refute those deterministic opinions that deny free choice. These, Albo argues, are "obviously unsound, because they nullify all human acts and human purpose, not to speak of undermining all laws."[15] Albo explicitly states his agreement with Maimonides' assertion of human freedom while maintaining belief in divine omniscience, a topic of significant debate among Albo's predecessors.

Even though Albo may have been in general agreement with Maimonides, he does take issue with some particulars:

> The question still remains, however, why he [Maimonides] did not include under existence of God life and power and other attributes, seeing that he included eternity and other attributes. The same criticism applies to the dogmas he derives from the other fundamental principles.[16]

Albo takes into consideration all thirteen of Maimonides' articles of faith, but places them into three categories of descending rank. Albo's first *ikkar*, the existence of God, and its derivative principles, parallel Maimonides' first five principles. His *shoresh* regarding freedom from defects is implied in Maimonides' fifth principle that God alone should be worshiped. Albo excludes from his *ikkarim* and *shorashim* Maimonides' seventh principle of the superiority of Moses' prophecy and the ninth principle of the immutability of Torah because he does not consider them to be essential to divine law, but rather like branches (*anafim*) issuing from the belief in the authenticity of a prophet's mission. Unlike Maimonides, Albo includes God's knowledge in his *shorashim*, since he argues that if God does not know the world, prophecy and the Torah could not have been revealed to man. Additionally, unlike Maimonides, Albo does not consider the Messiah or the resurrection of the dead to be essential to divine law. He excludes them from his *ikkarim* as a response to the Christian affirmation during the Tortosa Disputation that the Messiah had already come. Albo responded to his opponent, De Santa

---

15. Ibid., I:9, 96.
16. Ibid., I:4, 70.

Fe, in the Disputation: "Even if it were proved to me that the Messiah had already come, I would not consider myself a worse Jew for all that." Although not a fundamental principle of divine law, Albo does regard belief in the Messiah, similar to creation ex nihilo, as a dogma which "it behooves every one professing a divine law to believe."[17]

While Albo does not consider the *anafim* to be essential to divine law, he does regard them as critical for Jewish law, and denial of any one of them constitutes heresy and loss of one's portion in the World to Come. Therefore, he concludes that he is in general agreement with Maimonides' conception of dogma, even though he disagrees with various details.

Regarding such particulars, Albo not only differs from Maimonides in the number of obligatory beliefs, but in the status of his tenets as well. Maimonides taught that anyone who does not accept any one of his thirteen articles of faith is punished by being deprived of a share in the World to Come. Maimonides' rationale behind the consequence was to motivate the masses to acknowledge these cognitive beliefs, the integral prerequisites for the intellectual perfection necessary for the afterlife. As a result, even an individual who mistakenly arrived at a false belief that contradicted one of the Thirteen Principles is subject to such punishment, as he would be intellectually unprepared for existence in the World to Come. Albo rejects Maimonides' position with regard to accidental heretics and argues for a less intellectual approach in which intentions are considered.

Albo, echoing Duran's position on accidental heresy, considers an individual who was led to a belief that violates an *ikkar* as guilty of error and in need of forgiveness, but not a heretic who deserves to be punished. Since man's rational capacity is limited, he argues that an individual who is accidentally misled by his speculation to a misinterpretation of a principle is considered among the pious and simply needs to atone for his error. Albo elaborates upon four ways that an accidental heretic may arrive at his erroneous beliefs:

---

17. Sirat, *A History of Jewish Philosophy in the Middle Ages*, 380.

When he undertakes to investigate these matters with his reason and scrutinizes the texts, he (a) is misled by his speculation and interprets a given principle otherwise than it is taken to mean at first sight; or (b) denies the principle because he thinks that it does not represent a sound theory which the Torah obliges us to believe; or (c) erroneously denies that a given belief is a fundamental principle, which, however, he believes as he believes the other dogmas of the Torah which are not fundamental principles; or (d) entertains a certain notion in relation to one of the miracles of the Torah because he thinks that he is not thereby denying any of the doctrines which it is obligatory upon us to believe by the authority of the Torah. A person of this sort is not an unbeliever. He is classed with the sages and pious men of Israel, though he holds erroneous theories. His sin is due to error and requires atonement.[18]

Albo brings support for his view from Rabbi Abraham ben David of Posquières who, in his glosses on Maimonides' *Mishneh Torah*, rejects Maimonides' opinion that one who, due to insufficient knowledge, interprets biblical texts literally and arrives at belief in a corporeal God is to be considered a heretic. Albo's lenient attitude toward unintentional heresy seems consistent with his view on the limits of human rationality. After all, if he argues that the human mind is limited, how can he then condemn those who arrive at false beliefs due to speculative errors? Additionally, Albo's ruling of an accidental heretic may reflect the mood of his generation. As a public religious preacher and political leader, Albo was trying to dissuade the oppressed Jewish community from succumbing to the pressures of the Christians. Albo may have wanted to articulate to those who had been persuaded or coerced by other religions that they have the free choice to repent and that the erroneous beliefs to which they may have been led do not constitute heresy.

Albo's deviation from Maimonides' extreme rationalism, which emphasized the role of theoretical speculation over other religious

---

18. *SH* I:2, 49.

values, was characteristic of the prevailing currents that marked the end of the Middle Ages. Late medieval Jewish philosophers were deeply involved in defending "conservative" theistic doctrines expressed in rabbinic tradition in an effort to combat the attacks of Christian theologians and the criticism of radical philosophers at the time. In search of philosophical confirmation of their theistic doctrines, fifteenth-century Jewish philosophers, such as Albo, returned to the less radical, more moderate rationalistic conclusions of many earlier medieval Jewish philosophers, such as Saadia Gaon and Judah Halevi, in their defense of Judaism.

Albo and his philosophical contemporaries stress the limits of human knowledge and object to the Maimonidean notions that rational speculation constitutes the purpose of Torah and can lead an individual to human success and perfection. Instead, Albo argues that faith, performance of commandments, proper intention, and fear of God – not intellectual development – can merit the reward of miracles, divine union, immortality, and prophecy. Whereas Aristotle (and thus Maimonides) argues that the (unaided) individual can develop his intellect to grasp theoretical truths which is the ultimate human end, Albo argues that the human intellect's limited capacity requires divine law to guide the individual to both proper truth and conduct. Albo rejects Aristotle and Maimonides' conclusion that human perfection is defined in intellectual terms, since, he argues, such perfection would not be attainable by the majority of humanity, whose lives would then be in vain. God, he asserts, would never make the desired purpose of man only achievable by a small minority. Thus, according to Albo, individuals of every intellectual capacity have the ability to reach spiritual perfection; after all, the entire nation of Israel achieved prophecy at Mount Sinai.

While fifteenth-century Jewish philosophers in Spain opposed the radical (Aristotelian) trends that had emerged from southern French and Iberian Jewish philosophers, they were unwilling, despite their theologically conservative leanings, to adopt an antirationalist approach that denied the propriety of philosophical study, as advocated by some Christian theologians. Albo felt the need to deviate from the extreme views that emerged from the Maimonidean school, which brought him closer to the position that blurs the distinction between Judaism and other religions. However, the need to oppose Christian thought returned him closer to the Aristotelianism of Maimonides. Thus, Albo integrates a dialectical approach in *Sefer HaIkkarim*, as he attempts to deviate from Maimonides' focus on rationalism, while also opposing the irrationality of Christianity.

Such dual objectives are not unique to Albo. They are also espoused by his (theologically conservative) teacher, Hasdai Crescas, albeit in two separate works. In *Or Hashem* (*Light of the Lord*), Crescas consistently challenges Aristotelian metaphysics and the Maimonidean view of rationality, as he attempts to replace Maimonides' *Guide* with a less radical theological work that suits the needs of his generation. Yet in his anti-Christian polemical work, *Bitul Ikkarei HaNotzerim* (*The Refutation of the Christian Principles*), Crescas utilizes Aristotelian arguments to attack the irrationality of Christian theology. Following his teacher's model, Albo also develops a theology that deviates from radical rationalism, as well as a philosophical polemical treatise, but incorporates both within his *Sefer HaIkkarim*, in which his rational polemical critique of Christianity (III:35) is at the heart of his theological work.

Numerous points in which Albo departs from Maimonidean dogma within *Sefer HaIkkarim* reflect Crescas' influence. In *Or Hashem*, Crescas, as an anti-Aristotelian opponent of Maimonides, develops his own list of dogma and criticizes Maimonides for neglecting to distinguish between fundamental and derivative tenets. Crescas modifies Maimonides' enumeration of dogma by delineating a hierarchy of six principles (*shorashim*) of divine law – God's omniscience, providence, and omnipotence; prophecy; freedom of will; and the purpose of revelation – in addition to the three principles that Maimonides proved scientifically – the existence, unity, and incorporeality of God – as well as eight true beliefs of lesser status. Albo concurs with Crescas' stated need to present a hierarchy of creed, but deviates from his teacher's set of dogma. Crescas, in Albo's opinion, failed to include other principles unique to the Law of Moses, neglecting to incorporate general principles by which the genuine divine law may be distinguished from the spurious and omitting revelation from his explicit dogma. Albo, like Crescas, also rejects Maimonides' basis of human perfection upon the intellect and argues, like his teacher, that performance of the commandments, coupled with spiritual intention of fulfilling the divine will, leads to human perfection. Although profoundly influenced by Crescas, Albo most significantly departs from his teacher with respect to his view of free choice, as Crescas maintains a deterministic position.

In light of these influences, Albo's general philosophic approach is perceived to lie somewhere between that of the rationalists (most notably Maimonides) and that of philosophers such as Halevi and Crescas, who focus on man's spiritual, rather than intellectual, worship of God. Albo agrees with the rationalists that man is the noblest form of creation in the sublunar world and the purpose of his existence is to perfect himself, thus reflecting the influence of Aristotle's thought and that of Maimonides, and Gersonides, within the Jewish Aristotelian movement. Albo does not, however, conceive of such perfection in terms of theoretical understanding, but rather in terms of finding favor with God. Albo maintains that only the Torah can give man full knowledge of the means of obeying God's will and achieving human perfection, representing the Jewish anti-Aristotelian school of thought of Halevi, Nahmanides, Rashba, Ritva, and Rabbi Nissim, as well as Ḥasdai Crescas. Albo's philosophical work, *Sefer HaIkkarim*, reflects his moderate philosophical stance which, perhaps, contributes to its popularity among its diverse audience.

HOMILETIC INTERPRETATION

Albo, a medieval preacher and homilist, combines sermonic exegesis within his philosophical argumentation. In one of his most well-known biblical teachings, within his exposition of his third *ikkar*, retribution, Albo innovatively interprets biblical narrative to expound upon theological lessons. Drawing upon the commentaries of his predecessors, Albo creatively reads the text in a unique way, thereby conveying important messages for his suffering generation.

During the Exodus narrative, the Bible states that God "hardened Pharaoh's heart" following the plagues so that he would not agree to allow the Israelites to leave his land. The literal meaning of the narrative implies that God restrained Pharaoh's free will, as argued by

Maimonides.[19] Such an interpretation, however, calls God's justice into question since Pharaoh is held morally responsible for his divinely coerced refusal to liberate the Israelites. In an effort to reconcile the seeming conflict, Albo innovatively interprets the development of this enigmatic narrative, concluding that God did not deprive Pharaoh of his free choice, but rather preserved his volitional will, thereby maintaining divine justice.

After God's introductory statements to Moses foretelling the divine hardening, the narrative of the plagues unfolds. Moses appears before Pharaoh prior to the onset of each of the first five plagues, but despite the afflictions Pharaoh endures, he obstinately refuses to heed Moses' request. After each of the first five plagues, we read: "And Pharaoh's heart was hardened (*vayeḥezak lev Paro*)," or, "And Pharaoh hardened his heart (*vayakhbed Paro et libo*)." Following the sixth plague, a literary shift appears in the text. Instead of Pharaoh hardening his own heart, God is explicitly mentioned as hardening Pharaoh's heart: "*Vayeḥazek Hashem et lev Paro.*" God continues to harden Pharaoh's heart in the later plagues, as well as on two additional occasions following Israel's exodus from Egypt.

Albo argues that despite the implication of the literal meaning of the text – that Pharaoh's free will was restrained – God's hardening of Pharaoh's heart must not be understood as God's coercion of Pharaoh. Rather, God preserved Pharaoh's free will in order to allow him the opportunity to freely repent from his wrongdoings and not be forced into liberating the Jews as a result of his suffering caused by the plagues. God maintained Pharaoh's free will by giving him the fortitude to withstand his afflictions and suggesting to him alternative explanations for the cause of the plagues. Accordingly, Pharaoh was morally responsible for his ultimate free choice of attributing the plagues to natural causes and refusing to let the Jews go, and he was therefore deserving of punishment. According to Albo's theory, God does desire

---

19. Maimonides, *Mishneh Torah, Laws of Repentance* 6:3. Maimonides argues that God deprived Pharaoh of his free will and opportunity to repent as a punishment for initially freely enslaving and afflicting the Israelites and then hardening his own heart after the first five plagues, thus refusing to allow them to worship God in the desert.

that sinners repent; He hardened Pharaoh's heart in order to give him a free opportunity to do so.

Albo seems to reject Maimonides' approach and instead draws upon Nahmanides' influence, but focuses his view around the concept of free will and develops his analysis in order to demonstrate its direct opposition to Maimonides' theory. Whereas Nahmanides does not mention free will, Albo makes it the focal point of his analysis. Such an innovation is characteristic of the time during which Albo lived and of the philosophical school to which Albo belonged. In fifteenth-century Spain, Albo was more willing to study and incorporate philosophy into his biblical interpretation than was Nahmanides. Albo argues that God's hardening of Pharaoh's heart was not the deprivation of Pharaoh's free will, as Maimonides suggests, but rather the preservation of his free will, thereby transforming a narrative that is philosophically problematic with regard to free will into an interpretation that preserves free will.

Albo's exposition of the hardening of Pharaoh's heart is found in *Sefer HaIkkarim* IV:25, which he begins with a discussion about the nature of repentance (similar to Maimonides' discussion in the *Mishneh Torah*). There Albo distinguishes between repentance from love and repentance from fear. He further subdivides the latter category into repentance from fear of punishment and repentance from fear of the Lord. Repentance due to fear of punishment, he explains, is similar to a slave entreating his master while being beaten; as soon as his afflictions are relieved, he reverts back to his disobedience. A slave lacks fear when he is not being beaten; therefore, his repentance is the result of an episodic fear and not an abiding fear. Albo argues that such was the attitude of Pharaoh, and this does not constitute true repentance. For Albo, the penitent out of fear must be in a certain abiding cognitive and affective state, which was not true of Pharaoh.

The second type of repentance from fear is that of the man who has the fear of the Lord before him even in time of respite. He is afraid of God's punishment because he recognizes that all things come from God as reward and punishment, and he does not ascribe events to nature and chance. This is unlike Pharaoh, who associated each plague with a chance occurrence and then reverted back to his original bad behavior.

Albo seems to be original in his suggestion that the plagues caused cowardice, whereas choice requires courage. God thus hardened or emboldened Pharaoh's heart in order to afford him courage which would enable him to overcome the cowering effect of the plagues and arrive at a free decision whether or not to repent. Therefore, Albo writes, after the suffering from the plagues was alleviated, Pharaoh acted courageously and pursued the Israelites, thereby proving that his initial repentance (liberation of the Israelites) was due to the compulsion of his punishment and was not a result of free choice.

Albo's connection of courage to free choice is understandable from a historical perspective. Through his biblical interpretations in *Sefer HaIkkarim*, he sought to encourage his generation to be courageous in their resistance against the religious persecution that they were encountering. He insinuates that anyone who converts to Christianity under persecution is a coward. He preached that instead of acting cowardly through submission to such coercion, man must choose to preserve his Judaism.

Albo explains that God hardened Pharaoh's heart by allowing him to consider other possible sources for the plagues. In order for Pharaoh to achieve true repentance (the second type of repentance out of fear), he would have to recognize that his misfortunes were a punishment from God:

> Now, since this act is like one that is forced and not free, God hardens his heart, by suggesting to him other causes to which he can attribute the misfortune, accident – for example – rather than divine providence. This is done in order to remove from his heart the softening effect which came from the misfortune, so that he may return to his natural state and act freely without compulsion. Then it may be found out whether his repentance was free or not.[20]

---

20. *SH* IV:25, 227.

Relieved of the suffering from the plagues, Pharaoh had the ability to freely repent, but instead sought various excuses in order to make the plagues seem accidental, refusing to acknowledge God's providence.

The response of Pharaoh in the height of his fear, according to Albo, does not constitute repentance. However, one who repents as a result of fear that stems from recognition that every event is the result of divine providence, and does not seek pretexts and extraneous explanations for God's ways is considered a penitent. If Pharaoh were to have released the Jews due to fear that he would be punished for his past sins, and that fear were to remain with him and affect his future conduct, he would have achieved Albo's second type of repentance out of fear. Instead, Pharaoh reacted as would a slave who relents while being beaten; relenting, according to Albo, does not constitute repenting.

Just as Nahmanides' influence can be seen in Albo's free will preservation approach, Albo's influence is reflected in later biblical exegesis. In his commentary to Exodus 7:3, Rabbi Obadiah Seforno – although writing in Italy and therefore not suffering the same persecution as did the Jews in Spain – echoes Albo's (and Nahmanides') views. He explains that God does not desire the punishment of the wicked, but rather their repentance. God, therefore, increased His signs and wonders in order to bring the Egyptians to repentance and the Israelites to know God:

> Without a doubt, were it not for the hardening of Pharaoh's heart, he would have sent forth Israel, not because of repentance or submission to God, [nor because] he regretted his rebellion, recognizing God's greatness, but because he could no longer abide the anguish of the plagues, as his [own] servants said, "Do you not know that Egypt is lost?" (Ex. 10:7). Now this would not have been repentance. However, if Pharaoh would have [truly] wished to submit to God and return to Him in full repentance, there would have been no [divine] deterrent at all. Now, God states, "And I will harden Pharaoh's heart," granting him the courage to withstand the plagues; hence, he will not send forth Israel because he fears the plagues, "So that I might show My signs in their midst" (Ex. 10:1), through which they will perceive My greatness and repent to a degree, in sincerity.

Seforno reflects Albo's notion that repentance out of fear does not constitute true repentance. Through God's hardening of his heart, Pharaoh was given the strength and courage to withstand the suffering of the plagues and not feel compelled to liberate the Jews out of fear of the pain. The purpose of the anguish of the Egyptians was also intended so that Israel would learn that God affords man the opportunity to repent so long as he examines his deeds when misfortune befalls him.

Ascertaining the strengths and weaknesses of his predecessors' views, Albo assimilates and expands upon exegesis that is consistent with his perspective. Albo develops an interpretation of a biblical narrative that seems to conflict with the notion of free will by demonstrating how God's intervention actually preserved human freedom. In his homily, Albo may have intended to teach the theological lesson that man maintains free choice and has an eternal opportunity to repent. Even Pharaoh had the ability to freely choose to recognize God and liberate Israel. Similarly, the afflicted Jews of Albo's generation could learn from Pharaoh's example, despite the seeming coercion of their afflictions, that they also retain their free will; they need not succumb to their persecutors. Indeed, the opportunity to repent is eternal, even for those Jews who have already submitted to their Christian antagonists, thus innovatively teaching an important lesson about the nature of the principle of retribution.

MODERN RELEVANCE

Vastly popular in the medieval period, *Sefer HaIkkarim* maintains enduring relevance in contemporary times. Just as in the aftermath of the Tortosa Disputation when Albo's generation lacked a uniform Jewish dogma that could unite them as a nation and sustain them against persecution, modern Jews still do not share a defined and unifying system of beliefs. As the controversy over whether or not Judaism has a clear set of obligatory tenets persists in the modern day, Albo's objective to offer his reader an accessible and comprehensive articulation of the dogma of Judaism continues to be necessary. His integration of sermonic exegesis creatively conveys abstract philosophical lessons through the vivid illustration of biblical narrative. Such biblical analyses enable readers to benefit from learning lessons that emerge from the experience of biblical figures and draw connections between their own experiences and those of the characters. Albo's exposition of dogma enables modern Jews to achieve a uniform conception of God and Judaism which he believed had not been achieved by his predecessors, thereby enhancing Jews' personal and communal theological commitments while affording them the ability to defend their tenets against those who seek to threaten them.

FURTHER READING

Critical Edition:

Albo, Joseph. *Sefer Ha-Ikkarim (Book of Principles)*. Translated by Isaac Husik (Philadelphia, 1930).

Commentary:

Koppelmann, Jacob. *Ohel Yaakov (The Tent of Jacob)*. Commentary and explanation of Albo's *Sefer HaIkkarim* (Freiburg, 1584; second edition, Cracow, 1599).

Lipschuetz, Gedaliah ben Solomon. *Etz Shatul (A Planted Tree)* (Venice, 1618).

Modern Scholarship on Albo's *Sefer HaIkkarim*:

Ehrlich, Dror. "Philosophy and the Art of Writing in R. Joseph Albo's Book of Roots" (PhD diss., Bar Ilan University, 2004).

Weiss, Shira. *Joseph Albo on Free Choice: Exegetical Innovation in Medieval Jewish Philosophy* (New York, 2017).

Scholarship on Dogma:

Kellner, Menachem. *Dogma in Medieval Jewish Thought: From Maimonides to Abravanel* (New York, 1986).

Learning from Maharal: A Non-Mystical Approach with Illustrations from *Gevurot Hashem* and Other Works

Rabbi Shalom Carmy

I. INTRODUCTION

By the time I reached the age of thirteen, I knew two things about Maharal: One, he was an important rabbi and thinker; two, he had nothing to do with the Golem. I was not sure why he was important, other than that he was famous enough to be the subject of legends; as far as I recall, I had never seen any of his books. That was partially remedied at my bar mitzva, when a friend of the family presented me with Avraham Karib's anthology, *Kitvei Maharal MiPerag* (*The Writings of the Maharal of Prague*). Karib was an Israeli man of letters; I knew that he had returned to Orthodoxy and my elementary school had assigned his lively attack on anti-Jewish themes in recent (i.e., late nineteenth- and early twentieth-century) Hebrew literature. I later learned that his anthology, displaying judicious choice, abridgment, and often modernizing the Hebrew, had done much to promote general interest in Maharal. Not long afterwards, I tackled Karib's introduction and tried to wend my way through the selections. The results were not encouraging. I could not figure out what Maharal wanted and what I had to do in order to learn from him. The goal of this essay is to explain what I did to overcome my initial frustration and what I gained from the effort.

I don't know much more about Maharal's biography than I did fifty years ago. His birth date is variously given as 1512 or 1522, which would make him either 97 or 87 at the time of his death on 18 Elul 5369 (September 17, 1609). He occupied four rabbinic positions, in Moravia, Posen, and finally and most famously Prague (one post is not clearly identified). In fact, scholars have discussed why Maharal is exceptionally reticent about biographical details, compared with other illustrious contemporaries.[1] From the cases where he is cited as a halakhist, it is evident that his rulings were highly esteemed. His commentaries on the Talmud, like those of many prominent contemporaries, were not published in his lifetime, and began appearing long after his death. In his old age, Maharal had an audience with the Habsburg Emperor Rudolf II, content unreported. His students include Rabbi Yom Tov Lipmann Heller, author of *Tosefot Yom Tov* on Mishna and other standard works, and Rabbi Ephraim of Luntschitz, best known for his homiletical commentary on the Torah titled *Keli Yakar*. However, his ideas are rarely recorded by those who knew him personally.

The external background of Maharal's career is better known and worth keeping in mind. Living in Prague when it was a center of nascent modern science, he was aware of developments in astronomy and other fields. His lifetime spanned the Reformation that divided European Christendom and saw harbingers of modern national identity. Needless to say, he was a Jew when the status of Jews in Central Europe, even their right of residence, was labile. Though Maharal rarely alludes to these factors, they are not irrelevant to his literary production, and

---

1. See Yitzchak Yudlov, "Maharal of Prague, His Life and Oeuvre" [Hebrew], in E. Reiner, ed., *Maharal: Akdamot* (Jerusalem, 2015), 51–75, and Alexandr Putík and Daniel Polaković, "Judah Loew ben Bezalel Called Maharal: A Study on His Genealogy and Biography," in A. Putik, ed., *Path of Life: Rabbi Judah ben Bezalel, ca. 1525–1609* (Prague, 2009), 29–83. Another recent English-language volume on Maharal is Meir Seidler, ed., *Rabbinic Theology and Jewish Intellectual History: The Great Rabbi Loew of Prague* (London, 2013).

perhaps have bearing on his overall project as author of a unique and original system of Jewish thinking.

That project is contained in the books Maharal began publishing at a fairly advanced age and continued to put out steadily until the end of his life. By that time, he had evidently deliberated to his satisfaction on the shape and focus of his theological legacy. Hence, the order and structure of these works is itself a good clue to his distinctiveness as a thinker.

The first to appear was *Gur Aryeh* (1578), a supercommentary on Rashi to the Torah. Next came *Gevurot Hashem* (1582), which contains three prefaces, the last of which sketches an entire authorship comprising six books. These books were to be linked to the holy days of the Jewish calendar. *Gevurot Hashem* was devoted to Passover. It covered the narratives pertaining to Israel's sojourn in Egypt, beginning with Abraham, through the Exodus, and the laws relating to the holiday. Two other volumes in this series appeared in Maharal's lifetime: *Tiferet Yisrael* (1599) was the Shavuot book, devoted to the story of the Giving of the Torah and a variety of subjects connected to the nature of the Torah. *Netzah Yisrael* (1599–1600) corresponded to Tisha B'Av and dealt with exile and redemption. The three other promised books – on Shabbat, on Sukkot, and on Rosh HaShana and Yom Kippur – were never printed; as Maharal does not cross-reference to them, they were likely never written. Two shorter holiday-themed books – *Ner Mitzva* on Hanukka and *Torah Or* on the Book of Esther (1600) – are not mentioned in this plan. In these works, Maharal's standard point of departure is rabbinic commentary.

Maharal's other books are devoted explicitly to exegesis or defense of rabbinic literature. *Netivot Olam* (1596) surveys a number of virtues, such as humility, fear of God, but including Torah study and prayer. In his preface, Maharal claims, astonishingly, that this book is no more than an anthology of rabbinic passages. *Derekh HaHayim* is a commentary on Mishna Avot. *Be'er HaGola* (1598) is a systematic polemical interpretation of controversial issues in rabbinic literature. The massive commentary on talmudic Aggada was published posthumously.[2]

---

2. See Yudlov, "Maharal of Prague."

This thumbnail survey points to two original and distinctive aspects of Maharal's work. Although he is not averse to commenting directly on biblical passages, the subject of his exegesis is almost always rabbinic, talmudic Aggada and Midrash. *Gur Aryeh* is the exception that proves the rule, since Rashi himself is distinguished among the major medieval exegetes for the vast amount of rabbinic material he incorporates. In this respect, Maharal differs markedly from the entire tradition of medieval Jewish philosophy, where the primary text cited and interpreted is the Bible.

Maharal's anchor in *Hazal* is not only a quantitative departure from the medieval norm. When medieval Jewish thinkers gave methodical attention to rabbinic thought, it was generally to interpret the Aggada in conformity with their philosophical predilections and to forestall misinterpretation of these sources. This is true of Maimonides, who intended to write a commentary on Aggada in this vein, though in the end he did not do so, and true of his acolytes who undertook the task.[3] It was equally true of Rashba, counted as a non-rationalist, whose commentary on Aggada concentrated on removing the difficulty in those passages that seemed strange to rationalist ears. It was true of writers like Abrabanel who countered Christian readings of eschatological rabbinic texts with non-Christian alternatives.

Except for in *Be'er HaGola*, Maharal does not devote space to the methodological question of how to interpret rabbinic dicta in the face of external challenges. Instead he dedicates himself to extracting from *Hazal* a comprehensive account of Judaism. It is up to the reader to determine, in each case, whether his close reading, in which every detail is examined, uncovers the deeper sense of rabbinic dicta, or instead imposes an idiosyncratic, terminologically narrow, late-medieval system on the texts. In *Be'er HaGola* too, Maharal does not posit a standard of correct philosophical reading with which Aggada is to be harmonized. Rather he exhibits interpretive approaches that lay bare the distinctive logic of rabbinic narrative and logic. He engages in explicit polemic

---

3. See Yair Lorberbaum, "Maimonides on Aggada, Halakha and 'Divine Law'" [Hebrew], *Dine Israel* 26–27 (2009–2010): 253–297; Marc Saperstein, *Decoding the Rabbis: A Thirteenth-Century Commentary on the Aggadah* (Cambridge, 1980).

in his reaction to Rabbi Azariah de Rossi's *Meor Einayim* because that "historicizing" book fails to treat all rabbinic Aggada as a normative source of doctrine and fails to defer to rabbinic knowledge on historical and scientific questions. The conclusion is that rabbinic literature is theologically omnisignificant and therefore the ultimate ground for Jewish theology.

In Eastern and Central European Jewish thought of the sixteenth and seventeenth centuries, there is indeed an increased attention to Aggada: the famous talmudic commentary by Maharal's younger contemporary Rabbi Samuel Edels (Maharsha) is a parade example.[4] David Sorotzkin has recently argued at length that Maharal's rabbinic turn is foundational for the intellectual establishment of Orthodoxy in the modern period because it centers Jewish thought on the sources that separate Jews from other nations.[5] While the medieval Jewish philosopher, working from the Bible and sensitive to rationalist standards, comes closer to a "universal" philosophy, Maharal's system increases that distance. Leaving to one side the justice of that historical assessment, from our present-day perspective Maharal's highlighting the voice of Ḥazal facilitates a more comprehensive, multivocal Jewish theology. For me this is one of his abiding contributions.

Secondly, Maharal's topical books depart from the pattern set by medieval Jewish philosophy. The masterworks of the medieval world are organized by topics, such as the existence of God, creation, revelation, providence, foreknowledge, resurrection. Take, for example, Saadia Gaon's *Emunot VeDeot*, the progression of Maimonides' *Guide*, the six essays of Gersonides' *Milḥamot Hashem*. Or, particularly in the late Middle Ages, in the aftermath of Maimonides, there are books enumerating, elaborating on, and arguing about the principles of faith, such as Albo's *Sefer HaIkkarim*. Many of these problems are subjected to general (non-Jewish) logical and metaphysical argument.

---

4. See Yaakov Elbaum, *Openness and Insularity: Literary-Religious Production in Poland and the German Lands in Late Sixteenth Century* [Hebrew] (Jerusalem, 1990), 82–153, for survey.
5. "The Theology of the Different: Maharal of Prague and the Emergence of Early Modern Orthodox Thought," *Kabbalah* 14 (2006): 263–328.

Maharal, by contrast, works from the cycle of Jewish holidays. In effect, *Gevurot Hashem* is "about" the Exodus, *Tiferet Yisrael* about divine revelation, and *Netzaḥ Yisrael* about exile and redemption. These are not classic metaphysical subjects with a rich history of logical argumentation in Greek, Islamic, Christian, and Jewish philosophy. Rather they are themes that shape Jewish experience. By giving center stage to these ideas, and to the texts that enunciate them, Maharal is shifting Jewish thought from what he would consider peripheral problems requiring resolution to the core of Jewish existence.

One of Maharal's occasional discussions of a standard philosophical issue underlines his indifference to the medieval mode of argumentation. Miracles, as deviations from the created order of nature, presented an inconvenience for rationalists who are committed to the wisdom, and hence invariance, of the created order. Maimonides had proposed a theory that limited the miraculous and made it a part of the natural order; Gersonides had explained some of the more astonishing biblical miracles, such as Joshua stopping the sun, in naturalistic terms. Maharal strongly and explicitly objects to these approaches. He does so, at length, in the second preface to *Gevurot Hashem*, which is, as we have noted, the first of his topical books to be published. It is as if he wanted to declare his position conspicuously at the very outset.

All this establishes what is new and important in Maharal's project. Clearly, however, despite the preface to *Netivot Olam*, Maharal is not merely compiling an anthology of rabbinic statements. What remains enigmatic is what his detailed reinterpretation of the sources, and most notably the rabbinic sources, is supposed to accomplish, beyond calling attention to the texts and themes contained therein.

This is what defeated me on first looking into Karib's *Maharal*. The writing was heavy with the vocabulary of medieval philosophy, like matter and form (*ḥomer vetzura*), cause and effect (*sibba* and *alul*), and other ponderous terms like *sikhli* (intellectual), *nivdal* (separate). These words have technical import in medieval philosophy. For example, matter is that which remains when a substance undergoes change of form, but Maharal meant something else when he employed the pairing. I didn't see what this terminology added to the paraphrase of the sources. Furthermore, Maharal seemed unlike any exegetical work

I had ever encountered. He was not occupied with philological explication of rare or difficult words; he rarely addressed contradictions among various sources or debated other interpretations. It seemed that he was mainly rewriting the text using a recondite language he had devised from the medieval tradition, and that this re-description was meant to provide a profound plumbing of the depths. It occurred to me that Maharal's terminology may be a stand-in for the ideas of Kabbala, but whether this was true or not, it did nothing to gain me enlightenment.

It would take many years, and many hours of study, before I grasped that Maharal's terminology, as clumsy and obscure and unnecessary as it sometimes appeared, offered a kind of conceptual X-ray of the themes contained in the text, as he perceived them. We can best enter this approach to Maharal by studying his work rather than by general remarks.

II. THE NATURE OF SLAVERY IN EGYPT AND THE BIRTH OF A NATION

One element in Maharal's understanding of the Exodus is the nature of Jewish enslavement in Egypt and the nature of God's redeeming intervention.[6] He draws on a passage in *Midrash Tehillim*. The midrash meditates on two images found in Deuteronomy: God took Israel from the "iron furnace," and God took them "one nation from the midst of another." The first is that of a goldsmith who introduces his hand to the furnace to extract gold; the second is that of a shepherd putting his hand in an animal's womb to deliver the fetus. According to Maharal the two parables reflect two features of Israel's subjugation to Egypt.

The furnace image means that "the Egyptians overcame them forcefully so that Israel could not leave their power." The shepherd image means that "the nature of Israel is that they were connected to Egypt, as it were, subservient to them, without existence of their own (*metziut bifnei atzmo*)." In the furnace, the fire impedes the attempt to take the gold out. The bowels of the mother, by contrast, are accessible, but the fetus is bound to the mother so that extracting it requires the skill to

---

6. *Gevurot Hashem* 3.

sever the umbilical cord. In the furnace, Israel had no link (*hitztarefut*) to God because of Egyptian domination: God's work is to overcome that separation by stretching His hand, so to speak, into the fire. The shepherd image is about Israel being bound (*meḥubarim*) to Egypt, swallowed up and identified with Egypt, and God's deliverance is to enable them to realize an identity independent of Egypt.

Imagine that we were studying the midrash on our own. A sensitive reader would notice that the verses in Deuteronomy can be understood to imply two distinct images and would try to appreciate the difference between them. In the same manner one would notice the two parables and would ask what each parable adds to our understanding of the original images. Of course a reader might dismiss these questions and answer that the biblical imagery and rabbinic elaborations are mere stylistic adornments. The insensitive reader would think unnecessary Maharal's attempt to discover the "deeper" meaning of the text. We are sensitive readers if we accept Maharal's premise that the words of the rabbis are rich in meaning and cannot be relegated to mere aesthetics. We may also be sensitive readers if we have a good ear for literature and have been trained to notice such fine points. Either way we might, on our own, come up with an interpretation approximately like Maharal's: that slavery manifests itself in physical subservience that prevents the emergence into freedom and also in a spiritual inferiority that binds one to the enslaver.

Note the Hebrew words transliterated that belong to Maharal's standard jargon. What do they add to the exposition? I cannot be certain that my "literary" reading captures every nuance of Maharal's. Suffice it to say that Maharal apparently believed the terminology was useful, perhaps necessary. At a more general level it is worth considering that any interpretation of a text involves some degree of paraphrase, and that paraphrase often entails exchanging a rich poetic vocabulary for a fixed set of terms: the gain in abstract theological or philosophical significance requires a reduction in the original source of insight. In Maharal's case one may regret that the repertoire of key terms is so small, so that he is forced to make these few abstract words do such a wide variety of work. Nonetheless, our presentation of this example shows how much literary insight can be extracted from Maharal's formulations.

The shepherd analogy presupposes that Israel's emergence from Egypt resembles the process of birth. By that logic, the time of the Exodus is not accidental; it is the fullness of Israel's gestation period. Maharal identifies this moment with the growth of Israel to 600,000. For Maharal the number is not accidental. His derivation of the 600,000 combines ideas about the symbolic significance of numbers with ideas about the significance of the Hebrew language. Six represents six geometrical dimensions: up, down, east, west, north, and south. Six is multiplied by various decimal exponents: one hundred and one thousand. The tens are not counted because Hebrew has particular words for multiples of ten – *sheloshim* for thirty, *hamishim* for fifty, and so on – unlike the hundreds and the thousands, which Hebrew expresses as "three hundred" or "three thousand" rather than coining a separate word for the number. Ten thousands are not counted either, because the Hebrew word *ribbo* connotes vastness etymologically rather than delimiting a specific decimal place.

Some readers of Maharal are enamored of such numerical derivations. There is a flashiness about them that dazzles and that promotes the conviction that everything is as it is for a profound reason without requiring further analysis of the concepts involved. It is the kind of Torah nugget that spices up a slow news day.[7] What does the passage have for the reader who is not as preoccupied with number mysticism? Maharal's premise is that numbers matter with respect to the birth of the nation: before a certain point, embryo-Israel is not ready to be born; after that point it is time to emerge. In other words, after reaching the appropriate size, identified with the number 600,000, Israel is no longer a congeries of families descended from the patriarchs but a new metaphysical entity, namely a nation. Regardless of the exact numerical borderline, this notion itself – the difference between the nation and the prenational unit – has theological significance.

Rabbi Ahron Soloveichik once remarked that Maharal, in his way, anticipated the Hegelian dialectic. I am not sure what he meant by that, but I found his suggestion helpful. Just as Hegel struggled to convey something deep about the relations of ideas and great historical

---

7. See, for example, *New York Times*, August 8, 1988, B1 where a rabbi-scholar expounds on the mystical significance of the number eight according to Maharal.

phenomena, something that was especially hard to understand and explain because the ideas in question are in flux and change in the process of being experienced, so too Maharal was struggling with dynamic religious phenomena and their literary and historical expression. In this case, the Hegelian principle is that quantity generates quality. Up to a certain point one only has a set of individuals; beyond that point, the individuals interact as an organism with a logic and identity of its own. It seems to me that this is what one can learn from Maharal's insight about the crucial role of numerical increase for the formation of the Jewish people.

III. BIRTH OF MOSES

Chapter 16 of *Gevurot Hashem* deals with the birth of Moses. Let us note two aspects of the discussion which are representative of Maharal's approach. According to a rabbinic tradition Yokheved entered Egypt together with Jacob. Given the tradition that Israel sojourned in Egypt for 210 years and the biblical testimony that Moses was eighty years old at the Exodus, his mother was therefore 130 years old. Ibn Ezra was skeptical about this tradition: since the birth of Isaac when Sarah was ninety years old is recorded in the Torah as a marvel, he argues that a much older woman giving birth would surely merit being remarked on in the text of the Torah. Maharal rejects this skepticism vigorously, as we might expect. One set of arguments he deploys aims to establish that the occurrence was not as anomalous as Ibn Ezra thought. In addition, though, he claims that Ibn Ezra misunderstands the nature of Scripture:

> What is written in the Torah was not written for the sake of novelty, for many marvels happened and were not written in the Torah, for the Torah is not a story of marvels but a Torah given by God and when the miracle was worthy of being mentioned in the Torah in its own right it was written in the Torah.

Maharal's goal, as so often, is to defend rabbinic statements against their detractors. He is doing so here by presenting a general thesis about the literary nature of the Torah. Every detail is to be justified in terms of its theological meaning, for instruction in understanding the nature of the world and its history in religious terms, not in terms of profane storytelling. The competent reader looks for the religious substance rather than the miracle mongering, however entertaining to the scientifically curious. Insofar as the patriarchs in the Book of Genesis are the "foundations" of the world, the miraculous element in their procreation is worthy of explicit attention. This is not so in the case of Moses, and therefore the Author avoids mentioning the corresponding details about his birth.

In fact, Maharal continues, when the Torah narrates the birth of Moses in Exodus 2, it omits mentioning the names of his parents: an "anonymous" man from the house of Levi went and took a daughter of Levi. This silence is something that many careful readers of the text would notice. Maharal explains that Moses is separate (*nivdal*) from the rest of humanity by virtue of his unique prophetic standing. Father and mother are the cause (*siba*) of the child. With respect to Moses, denoting his parents with proper nouns would make them particular individuals; as individuals they would belong to the general (*klal*) which is not implied by the generic word "man." Moreover the particular partakes of matter and Moses was separate from the material. The Torah does refer to the parents as Levites and this alludes to the distinctive sanctity of the tribe of Levi that is separate from "matter," and so forth.

At one level, Maharal's emphasis on the significance of every stylistic nuance in the biblical and rabbinic texts works in the service of a certain kind of literalism, as he perceives it, usually through the eyes of rabbinic exegesis. His opposite would be a medieval rationalist like Ibn Ezra who was ready to set aside rabbinic statements that don't appeal to the literal mind and that do not appear necessary to interpret the unadorned text. Maharal, by contrast, is preaching to the maximalist who is compelled to subscribe to the plenitude of rabbinic Midrash. From another perspective, however, Maharal is defending the tradition by demonstrating that the Bible and Midrash are a different kind of literature than Ibn Ezra takes them to be. The age of Yokheved need not be highlighted because, unlike a story book, the Torah is not interested in her pregnancy, miraculous or not, for its own sake. For the typical literalist, a fact is a fact, and it doesn't matter whether the fact is known from the explicit text of the Torah or via rabbinic embellishment, whether the identity of Amram and Yokheved is revealed in the

birth narrative of Moses or later on. For Maharal, the Torah is a certain
kind of literary production: what information it contains, and how that
information is presented, is essential to proper interpretation. His writings are therefore a great resource for those who appreciate such variety.

IV. "WHAT BEFALLS THE SINNER?"

So far we have seen Maharal's attention to the different levels in rabbinic
literature and the nuances in the biblical text. An excellent example of
the way Maharal notices the multiple voices in the canonic literature is
his attention to Yerushalmi Makkot 2:6 in *Netiv HaTeshuva*, chapter 1:

> They asked wisdom: What is the punishment of the wicked?
> Wisdom answered: Sinners are pursued by evil. They asked
> prophecy: What is the punishment of the wicked? Prophecy
> answered: The sinner must die. They asked the Torah: What is
> the punishment of the wicked? The Torah said: Let him bring a
> sin offering and be atoned. They asked God: What is the punish-
> ment of the wicked? He answered: Let him repent and be atoned,
> as the verse states: "God is good (*tov*) and straight (*yashar*), there-
> fore He shows the sinner a path."[8]

From a conventional perspective this text is puzzling. It implies that there
are multiple voices in the Bible, denominated wisdom, prophecy, and
Torah, all of which are transcended by the voice of God. For Maharal
the statement indicates the existence of multiple considerations, all of
which have their place in the world, but none of which is absolute. His
approach here, as in his interpretation of countless rabbinic disputes on a
variety of subjects, is to give credence to multiple voices that are part of a
comprehensive symphony. Sin, in Maharal's terminology, is characterized
as a "deficiency in the world"; as the world has no place for deficiency,
it must be hounded and pursued. Nevertheless, adds Maharal, wisdom
does not speak of "death" for the sinner, insofar as evil does exist as part
of the world. Prophecy, by contrast, is the word of God – as God is pure

---

8. This is Maharal's text of Yerushalmi. For alternate texts, see Shelomo Wiedder,
   "A Fragment of Jerushalmi" [Hebrew], *Tarbiz* 17 (1945–46): 133.

(free of imperfection), so too His spoken word, His communication, must be free of evil; hence prophecy cannot tolerate the sinner's continuation: the sinner must die. Torah must provide a way out for the sinner, as the nature of Torah is to improve the human being (*tikkun haadam*). Therefore Torah says let him bring a sacrifice for atonement. But God calls for repentance, for God accepts the heart broken in remorse.

Offhand the assertions about prophecy and about Torah are open to challenge: the same chapter of Ezekiel that contains the verse "the one who sins shall die" also contains a call to repentance. The same Torah that lists the laws of sacrifice contains the commandment to repent. For a literalist the Yerushalmi is contradictory; for a rationalist, it introduces an unwelcome multiplicity of values and voices in Jewish thought in place of one unambiguous voice. Maharal is attracted to this passage precisely because it conveys the complexity of the judgment confronted by the sinner. Despite calls to repentance in prophets and in the Torah, the overall logic of the prophets is that of a pure uncompromising judgment, and the overall tone of the Torah implies that sin is to be atoned for through external halakhic action. God, as a personal being available to the sinner, is both good and straight, and Maharal devotes much of his analysis to the ways in which His beneficence and stringency offer a path for the sinner that complements but also transcends the partial approaches inscribed in biblical wisdom, prophecy, and Torah respectively.

V. ON JUDGING (1)

The Talmud teaches that when all members of a court in a capital case immediately judge the defendant culpable, without any argument to the contrary, the accused goes free (Sanhedrin 37a).[9] Taken at face value, this is one of the enigmatic laws that provoke pejorative views of talmudic law. It is therefore a fit subject for Maharal's defense in *Be'er*

---

9. For other interpretations of this text, see Rabbi Meir Abulafia, *Yad Ramah*, ad loc. and Maharatz Chajes, Sanhedrin 17a. For the latter, see my discussion, "Use It or Lose It: On the Moral Imagination of Free Will," in *Judaism, Science and Moral Responsibility*, Yitzhak Berger and David Shatz, eds. (Lanham, 2006), 104–154, 144–145.

HaGola, chapter 2. His treatment is instructive as an example of the way his method is applied to legal material.

To begin with, Maharal observes several times in his discourse that the Torah's law of punishment is addressed to a God-fearing, law-abiding society. In such a society, the strict standards of evidence and other barriers to inflicting capital punishment do not risk leading to the free reign of crime. In a culture of violence and indifference to law, the rabbis taught that courts may apply extrajudicial penalties not mandated by the Torah in order to secure public safety and the authority of law.

Underlying this argument is Maharal's conviction that the Torah is a supernatural corpus. In other words, to read the Torah exclusively, or even primarily, as a code intended to regulate the mundane affairs of a profane society fails to take into account the very essence of divine revelation. Rather, the Torah engages the transcendent spirit in man. Maharal's acknowledgment of extrajudicial remedies within the halakhic system makes religious law practicable in a less-than-ideal society, but it does not compromise the uniqueness of the Torah. In this respect, Maharal differs from the kind of literalism that would apply Torah law mechanically to deeply flawed societies without regard to their lack of a thorough religious orientation and he is likewise disinclined to rationalize Torah law in terms of its utility in governing a mundane polity as was proposed, to some degree, by some of the medieval authors. For them the divinity of the Torah is manifest in its applicability to a flawed world; Maharal prefers to recognize multiple planes – one spiritual, the other pragmatic.[10]

Thus the interpretations Maharal produces for not punishing the defendant in this case presuppose the divine nature of Torah law in the sense just adumbrated. Within that framework he must attempt to explain its peculiarity. The first explanation he offers is premised on the matter/intellect dichotomy. The court is composed of human beings, unable to exist immaterially and, for that reason, lacking the

---

10. One may discern some affinity between Maharal and the fourteenth-century Spanish talmudist Rabbi Nissim of Gerona. Rabbi Nissim, in his *Twelve Sermons* 11, speaks of a division of judicial labor between the halakhic courts, committed to the ideal truth of Torah law, and the king, who applies law adapted to mundane needs.

clarity of pure intellection. Consequently the Torah requires delay of judgment (*halanat hadin*), a process of deliberation and clarification in capital cases, where, as Maharal notes, an erroneous verdict cannot be undone: in such a situation, a hastily delivered judgment betrays the material limitations of the judges. Where the judges have reached unanimous opinion without deliberation, they are incapable of actualizing their intellectual powers. For that reason they cannot judge. They must withdraw and allow God to judge in their place.

The second explanation focuses not on the status of the human judges, but on the nature of judgment. Judgment must be exercised for righteousness and good. Eliminating evil from the world is good, says Maharal; therefore conviction of the guilty counts as realization of the righteous and the good. However, this is true only where there has been a quest for the good by seeking arguments for exoneration. Where this has not happened, the court cannot claim to be an agent of righteousness and goodness, and the court must therefore withdraw from judgment and consign the accused to the True Judge.

Many readers of my summary of this idea, and many students of the full text, will suspect Maharal of playing with words and contriving a fallacious argument. To get at his meaning it is necessary, in my opinion, to unpack the argument, to see what is confusing about it and how the argument can be straightened out.

Here is how I understand Maharal's reasoning, proceeding from my own intuitions and investigating how well they fit the import of his words: There is an ambiguity in the statement that judgment aims at the righteous and the good. In one sense, this means that the goal of judgment is righteous and beneficial. In this sense convicting and punishing the criminal is right and good because it eliminates evil from our midst. But there is a second sense in which being good is understood as being benign and affirmative. In that sense of good, a court that is good to the criminal means one that helps him to avoid punishment. This ambiguity pervades common discourse, where it leads to colliding perspectives: Whereas law and order people recognize the first meaning, and identify a good court with one that punishes those who deserve punishment for the benefit of society, liberals would define a benevolent court as one that sympathizes with and looks for ways to obtain results agreeable to the accused. From a purely logical perspective, these meanings of righteous and good are incompatible with each other.

If you want to understand Maharal, you must allow him to embrace both meanings. The first, of course, is the commonsense meaning and requires little if any justification. The second entails a thesis about the metaphysics of justice. The doing of justice by the court – which may result in either exculpation or punishment, in accordance with the first meaning of righteousness and good – must be accomplished through a procedure that is right and good in the second sense. Benevolence, which on this version means a willingness to examine the case from the viewpoint of the accused, is somehow fundamental to the judicial process mandated by the Torah. In other words, even punitive justice must proceed from a "warm" benevolence. Once the double meaning of righteous and good in Maharal's text is grasped, his argument becomes coherent and we are able to uncover a bold and original view about the quality of justice that speaks to contemporary thinking even if it cannot be applied routinely to present-day jurisprudence.

VI. ON JUDGING (2)

As we have noted, Maharal's terminology is often daunting. As we just saw, in struggling to articulate his insights, he often gives his words – both his technical vocabulary and more common words – multiple meanings, so that comprehension and appreciation require the effort of clarifying those meanings and their interrelationship within a particular discourse. These challenges are both compounded and made more exciting by the fact that Maharal's oeuvre contains thousands of discussions of this sort. Some are extended, some quite brief. Frequently he seems to repeat himself, even within the same passage, and it is the task of the student to determine whether the repetitions introduce additional nuance of description or argument.

With respect to Maharal's ideas about the phenomenology of divine and human judgment it is worthwhile to look at a very different passage, in *Gur Aryeh* to Genesis 18:1. God has come to visit Abraham after his circumcision; the Torah says that Abraham was "sitting" at the opening of the tent. According to Rashi, by having him sit while God stood He was giving a sign to Abraham that his sons would sit in judgment in the courts of law while God stood among them – "God stands in the congregation of God, among the judges He judges [rabbinic interpretation of Psalms 81:1]." What does God's standing while the judges sit signify about the nature of judgment?

Maharal's first explanation: Circumcision engenders a covenant and relation (*ḥibur*, a favorite term for Maharal) between Israel and their heavenly Father. God, for His part, so to speak, cannot sit in this inferior world, as the mundane world is not His place. It is not, however, an indignity for Him to be depicted as standing while the judges sit because the relationship of love inaugurated by the covenant of circumcision entails indifference to the positions of sitting and standing. With the coming of the covenant, God no longer insists on formalities: "The friend is not offended when his friend sits while he stands." This commentary explains the placement of the verse following the story of circumcision. It also makes a statement about the kind of etiquette, as it were, that is appropriate within the covenantal relationship.

Maharal's alternative reading concerns the status of the judges. Judgment, says Maharal, belongs to God. He gave over the power of judgment to the court. In effect, God has abdicated His power to determine law to the court. He thus becomes dependent on the disposition of the court. One who is dependent is properly portrayed as standing while the judges who exercise power are seated. One might add that it is as if God waits to execute whatever verdict the human court arrives at. Maharal considers the first approach primary, perhaps because it also addresses the place of the verse in the Book of Genesis, perhaps because the power invested in the human judge applying the Torah is itself dependent on the nature of the covenant.

If one juxtaposes the second explanation with the discussion in the previous section it yields a complex account of the relationship between the idea that all judgment belongs to God and that human judgment is therefore a derivative and hence humble institution, on the one hand, and the idea that God has entrusted the children of His covenant with enormous responsibility for the realization of His word in this world. Veteran students will naturally suggest other relevant passages elsewhere in Maharal, in the sources that guided him, and in the literature that continues to draw on themes in his thought.

VII. CONCLUSION

My approach to reading Maharal is avowedly geared to my own theological program. The examples we examined display Maharal's skill as a sensitive interpreter of Ḥazal and Tanakh at the micro level, as a thinker who distinguished carefully between what is stated explicitly in the text and what is found between the lines or underpinning the text, as a perspicuous observer and analyst of multiple voices within Tanakh, as a theologian aware of the difference between practical and divine appropriations of Torah, and as a phenomenologist of religious experience and institutions who himself authored texts that can become objects of complex analysis.

Among those who like to quote Maharal, some would complain that their Maharal is more committed to literalism in interpreting Ḥazal than I. They might rightly allege that I downplay, for example, Maharal's rejection of De Rossi's historical analysis of some rabbinic texts or Maharal's objections to rationalist views of miracles and other phenomena. It goes without saying that one has no right to "edit" the historical Maharal to our contemporary taste, allowing only the elements in his work that are helpful to us today. Yet for me the most vital and distinctive principle of Maharal's voluminous teaching is the idea that the rich content and form of rabbinic literature and the details of Jewish life are significant and worthy of painstaking attention. It is legitimate, in constructing our own theological approach, to draw on those elements that fortify and foster reverence for Ḥazal.

Maharal's approach, precisely because it takes seriously the details of biblical history and halakha, in all their particularity, tends, like many mystical apprehensions of Torah, to determinism and the reification of concepts. By this I mean that if the details are important, one is inclined to conclude that they could not possibly have been any different than they are, and that if concepts carry a certain symbolic weight, those to whom the concepts apply are judged to display those traits in a fairly rigid manner. Such an orientation, whether it is strictly entailed by Maharal or not, encourages a reading of biblical and later Jewish history that downplays free initiative on the part of man (or even declines to take account of the freedom of divine response). It encourages one to infer more rigid distinctions between gentiles and Jews, or between men and women, than are entailed by halakha or by less deterministic theological anthropologies or theologies of history. The deterministic strain in Maharal and other mystical outlooks, like that in hasidic teachings, has a place in Jewish thought: after all, there are strands in biblical literature (most notably apocalyptic) which preach a sense of inevitability about the outcome of Jewish history and cosmic eschatology. In the spirit of Maharal's own appropriation of the multivocal Yerushalmi Makkot, I would propose that a truly comprehensive Jewish thought must listen attentively to both the libertarian element in prophecy and Jewish philosophy and to the more deterministic themes sounded by the more mystical thinkers.

Our dialogue with the sources and with the giants of the past is always mediated through their influential successors. Maharal is an unusual figure in the history of Jewish thought. For that reason it may be even more important in his case to ponder later thinkers who were largely or partially molded by him. As a thinker, Maharal left little immediate impact on his generation and that which followed; his books were not reprinted until some of the hasidic masters adopted him as a resource.[11] In our own era, Rabbi Isaac Hutner identified himself as a twentieth-century disciple of Maharal. As a thinker who flourished in the modern milieu and struggled with many of the challenges of contemporary culture, Rabbi Hutner is an auspicious model for those of us who wish not only to quote Maharal but to learn from him how to do our own thinking. The way he updated themes in Maharal, how he selected particular elements in Maharal's exposition, emphasizing some, ignoring others, whether he cited Maharal overtly or not showed me how I could benefit from my own study. To those whose appetite for Maharal has been whetted by this introductory essay I recommend, side by side with the close reading of Maharal, an exposure to Rabbi Hutner as well.[12]

---

11. See Betzalel Safran, "Maharal and Early Hasidism," in *Hasidism: Continuity or Innovation?*, ed. Betzalel Safran (Cambridge, 1988), 47–91.

12. See the essay by Dr. Yaakov Elman in this volume.

FURTHER READING

Recent collections on Maharal include Elchanan Reiner, ed., *Maharal: Akdamot* [Hebrew] (Jerusalem, 2015); Alexandr Putík ed., *Path of Life: Rabbi Judah ben Bezalel, ca. 1525–1609* (Prague, 2009), 29–83; and in English, Meir Seidler, ed., *Rabbinic Theology and Jewish Intellectual History: The Great Rabbi Loew of Prague* (London, 2013).

Yaakov Elbaum, *Openness and Insularity: Literary-Religious Production in Poland and the German Lands in Late Sixteenth Century* [Hebrew] (Jerusalem, 1990) is the best overview of Maharal's literary productivity in its general historical context.

There are several sets of Maharal's writings: among them the New York 1969 edition and the Jerusalem 1971 edition. The Benei Berak edition of 1980 is the only one to include the books on Ḥanukka and the Book of Esther.

Rabbi Yehoshua Hartman has published editions of many major works by Maharal, including *Gur Aryeh, Be'er HaGola, Netzaḥ Yisrael, Or Ḥadash, Ner Mitzva, Tiferet Yisrael,* and parts of *Netivot Olam* and *Gevurot Hashem.* In addition to his textual work, Hartman's volumes are distinguished for copious annotation, cross-referencing Maharal's texts and alluding to their impact on later writers, and for extremely detailed indexes. Rabbi Yosef Kehat has recently done similar work on the *Ḥidushei Aggada.*

The Sacred Writ of Hasidism: *Tanya* and the Spiritual Vision of Rabbi Shneur Zalman of Liady

Rabbi Dr. Ariel Evan Mayse

The classical texts of hasidic literature represent many genres. They include collections of sermons on the weekly Torah reading, random assortments of hasidic teachings, compendia of stories told about – and by – hasidic leaders, lists of mystical and pietistic practices, and letters written by *tzaddikim*. A small number of hasidic books are well-ordered treatises intended to elucidate pivotal theological concepts or methodically describe an inner spiritual path. Rabbi Shneur Zalman of Liady's *Tanya* is one of these rare works. It is theologically profound, mystically inspiring, and philosophically sophisticated, presenting the author's spiritual vision and devotional path with utmost clarity and precision. The publication of *Tanya* was a foundational moment in the history of Chabad Ḥasidut. It came to serve as a collection of mystical first principles, a closely studied canonical text to which all other works of Chabad thought are intimately linked. *Tanya* itself has been the subject of numerous commentaries, some of which date to the movement's early history, and it has been subsequently translated into many languages. *Tanya* was so important to the Chabad community that it was eventually deemed the *Torah Shebikhtav shel Ḥasidut*, or the Written Torah of Hasidism.[1]

Tanya offers its readers the keys to spiritual growth by challenging two religious orientations that Rabbi Shneur Zalman finds unconscionable. The first is expressed in the author's emphatic struggle against rote observance, or the notion that religious practice alone is of exclusive importance. Performing the mitzvot, he says, must be accompanied by spiritual devotion. The second approach rejected by Rabbi Shneur Zalman is a purely contemplative model, whether intellectual or ecstatic, justified by the claim that deeds are far less significant than cultivating one's interior realms. Rabbi Shneur Zalman resists both of the extremes, demanding responsibility from his readers and calling upon them to balance the inner and exterior elements of their religious lives. His path includes intellectual contemplation, mystical love of God, and overwhelming awe before the divine, but he demands that this interior work must be expressed in concrete actions. Rabbi Shneur Zalman wrote *Tanya* in order to awaken and inspire his "slumbering" readership and inspire them to a higher mode of serving God, providing them with a structured path for transforming their understanding of the world, the Torah and its precepts, and ultimately their own inner worlds.[2]

---

1. For example, see Rabbi Yosef Yitzchak Schneersohn, *Iggerot Kodesh* (Brooklyn, 1983), vol. 4, 261. Tradition recalls that Rabbi Menachem Mendel Schneersohn, the third Rebbe of Chabad-Lubavitch, once sought to add vowels to *Tanya*, which followed the convention of most Hebrew books and had been printed without them. But Rabbi Schneersohn experienced a dream in which he was studying the laws of how to write a Torah scroll, coming to the rule asserting that vowels invalidate the scroll. Rabbi Menachem Mendel grasped the allusion and gave up his wish. Tales such as this are difficult to verify but are essential for understanding the canonical status of *Tanya*. See *Kitzurim VeHe'arot LeSefer Likutei Amarim* (Brooklyn, 1948), 125.

2. On this dialectic, see Rachel Elior, *The Paradoxical Ascent to God: The Kabbalistic Theosophy of Habad Hasidism*, trans. Jeffrey M. Green (Albany, 1993).

EARLY HASIDISM AND
RABBI SHNEUR ZALMAN OF LIADY

The hasidic movement emerged from the teachings of Rabbi Israel ben Eliezer of Medzhybizh, a charismatic religious figure better known as the Baal Shem Tov (Master of the Good Name) or by the Hebrew acronym Besht (d. 1760).[3] This enigmatic mystic lived in Podolia (modern Ukraine), near the Carpathian Mountains. We know very little about his life that does not come from internal hasidic sources, but legends tell of his humble beginnings, followed by a period of prolonged solitude and mystical study with heavenly teachers. Sometime in the 1730s he "revealed" himself and began to spread a new approach to religious life that foregrounded the values of joy and ecstatic prayer. Many earlier Jewish mystics tended toward asceticism and even self-mortification, but the Baal Shem Tov was quite alert to the dangers of religious guilt and the psychological and physical damage wrought by penitential practices. His spiritual path foregrounded *devekut,* or the radical experience of the Divine Presence. The Baal Shem Tov emphasized that one must be ever mindful of the divine vitality in all aspects of existence, often described as sparks of holiness trapped within the physical world.[4] Freeing these sparks is a crucial goal of religious service, one that may be accomplished through ordinary deeds such as eating, drinking, and dancing, and, of course, by performing the commandments.

Several of the Baal Shem Tov's students led communities after his death. Of these, Rabbi Dov Baer Friedman, better known as the great Maggid (preacher) of Mezritch, was the most important. The Maggid attracted a substantial number of followers to his study hall, many of whom were brilliant scholars from the most illustrious families in

---

3. See Immanuel Etkes, *The Besht: Magician, Mystic, and Leader,* trans. Saadya Sternberg (Waltham, 2005).

4. For many years, Martin Buber and Gershom Scholem debated Hasidism's complicated relationship with the material world. Buber underscored the hasidic masters' positive attitude toward physicality, while Scholem emphasized texts that articulate the movement's more otherworldly, even ascetic, impulse. For a nuanced analysis of this controversy and an insightful new reading of the hasidic sources, see Seth Brody, "'Open to Me the Gates of Righteousness': The Pursuit of Holiness and Non-Duality in Early Hasidic Teaching," *The Jewish Quarterly Review* 89 (1998): 3–44.

Eastern Europe. These disciples played a crucial role in the development of the hasidic movement. After the Maggid's death in 1772 (and perhaps even before), these talented leaders began to transform Hasidism from an elite ethos into a mass movement. The chorus of voices "around the Maggid's table" was polyphonic, for rarely do all of these hasidic masters speak with a single voice on any given issue. Yet the leaders of the movement were also united by a shared cluster of theological beliefs regarding the devotional life, including worshiping God with joy; striving for *devekut* in prayer and study; cultivating an awareness of God's immanence; recognizing that the initial *tzimtzum*, the withdrawal of the divine from the physical world, is but an illusion; raising up sparks of holiness by serving God in ordinary deeds; and reorienting all of one's *middot*, or emotional, intellectual, and ethical character traits, toward God.

Rabbi Shneur Zalman was one of the Maggid's youngest and most gifted students.[5] He was born and raised in White Russia, where he received an excellent education in traditional rabbinic texts, but at some point Rabbi Shneur Zalman went south to Mezritch. What attracted the young scholar to study with the Maggid? He may have been interested in the study of Kabbala, but Rabbi Shneur Zalman seems to have been attracted by the devotional style of the Maggid and his resolute emphasis on serving God through prayer as a complement to religious study.

The Maggid died in 1772, and Rabbi Shneur Zalman became a student of the older Rabbi Menachem Mendel of Vitebsk, another member of the Maggid's circle. But Rabbi Menachem Mendel immigrated to the Land of Israel in 1777 together with Rabbi Abraham of Kalisk. They tasked the reluctant Rabbi Shneur Zalman, who had remained in White Russia, to act as leader in their proxy, shepherding their students and overseeing fundraising to support hasidic life in the Holy Land. But it was increasingly clear that the Hasidim in White Russia could not maintain sole allegiance to the two absent leaders, and Rabbi Shneur Zalman established a powerful and centralized hasidic court over the course of the decade following Rabbi Menachem Mendel's death in 1788.

---

5. Immanuel Etkes, *Rabbi Shneur Zalman of Liady: The Origins of Chabad Hasidism* (Waltham, 2015).

Rabbi Shneur Zalman's court flourished in the 1790s. So many disciples came to hear him preach that Rabbi Shneur Zalman was forced to enact a series of decrees carefully regulating the frequency with which his Hasidim were allowed to visit. This meant that his homilies and teachings were passed along by word of mouth from student to student, but some were circulated in semiofficial written form. In part to cull erroneous copies or transcriptions, and in part to answer the call of disciples without access to private audiences with their teacher or the option to visit whenever they wished, Rabbi Shneur Zalman made the decision to put his theology into a systematically written treatise. The work known as *Tanya* was published in 1796, a watershed event in the history of Hasidism.[6]

Rabbi Shneur Zalman took an active part in the controversy with the *mitnagdim*, the Lithuanian scholars and students of the Gaon of Vilna, who banned the Hasidim for offenses both social and theological. As early as 1772 he participated in a public defense of Hasidism, to little success. Although his efforts toward reconciliation were apparently rebuffed, Rabbi Shneur Zalman never forfeited his respect for the Gaon of Vilna as a paragon of scholarship and piety. The charges of the *mitnagdim* led to Rabbi Shneur Zalman being imprisoned by the Russian authorities in 1798 and 1800 on suspicion of sedition and religious factionalism. The documents produced from his questioning and testimony reveal his understanding of the nature of Hasidism and the role and function of the *tzaddik*. Rabbi Shneur Zalman was released from his first period of incarceration on the nineteenth of Kislev, the anniversary the Maggid's death, and the Chabad community saw this moment as a turning point in his career. It is often suggested that after 1798 Rabbi Shneur Zalman's sermons became longer, more involved, and explicitly kabbalistic, and that he now saw the thrust of his public service as spreading the theology of Jewish mysticism to the farthest reaches.

After his second arrest, Rabbi Shneur Zalman moved his thriving court to the city of Liady. He died in 1812 as he was fleeing into Russia

---

6. See Nehemia Polen, "Charismatic Leader, Charismatic Book: Rabbi Shneur Zalman's *Tanya* and His Leadership," in *Rabbinic and Lay Communal Authority*, ed. Suzanne Last Stone (New York, 2006), 53–64.

in advance of Napoleon's invasion. His son Rabbi Dov Ber (1773–1827), known in later Chabad circles as the Mitteler Rebbe (the Middle Rebbe), led the community after his death, moving the court to the Russian city of Lubavitch. This direct succession from father to son was an important development, since at this early point in Hasidism the dynastic system was not yet the norm. Furthermore, one of Rabbi Shneur Zalman's talented and veteran students, Rabbi Aaron Halevi Horowitz of Staroselye (1766–1828), was also vying for position of leadership.[7] Rabbi Dov Ber was victorious, and his ascent marked the beginning of a familial dynasty which lasted until the death of Rabbi Menachem Mendel Schneerson, the seventh Lubavitcher Rebbe, in 1994.[8]

STRUCTURE AND THEMES

Tanya is one of the many works in Rabbi Shneur Zalman's sizable body of teachings, but it is in all respects unique.[9] It was first published anonymously in 1796, and Rabbi Shneur Zalman's name did not appear until the eighth printing, in Shklov in 1814, by which point *Tanya* reached its present form of five sections. The alternative title *Tanya* (*It Was Taught*)

---

7. See Naftali Loewental, *Communicating the Infinite: The Emergence of the Habad School* (Chicago, 1990); and Louis Jacobs, *Seeker of Unity: The Life and Works of Aaron of Starosselje* (New York, 1967).

8. On Rabbi Menachem Mendel Schneerson, see Elliot R. Wolfson, *Open Secret: Postmessianic Messianism and the Mystical Revision of Menahem Mendel Schneerson* (New York, 2009); and Chaim Miller, *Turning Judaism Outward: A Biography of Rabbi Menachem Mendel Schneerson, the Seventh Lubavitcher Rebbe* (New York, 2014).

9. Rabbi Shneur Zalman was a gifted homilist, and after his death two important volumes of his sermons were published as *Torah Or* (Kopust, 1836) and *Likutei Torah* (Zhitomir, 1848). A significant number of other homilies remained in manuscript form and were printed for the first time as the *Maamarei Admor HaZaken* series that began in 1957 and continues to the present day. Rabbi Shneur Zalman edited a version of the liturgy, later printed as *Nusaḥ HaAri*, which became the standard prayerbook for the Chabad community. But Rabbi Shneur Zalman of Liady was also a mighty scholar of Jewish law, and a compilation of halakha known as a *Shulḥan Arukh HaRav* was published after his death. See Levi Cooper, "Towards a Judicial Biography of Rabbi Shneur Zalman of Liady," *Journal of Law and Religion* 30.1 (2015): 107–135. For an overview of his thought as found in all of these works, see Roman A. Foxbrunner, *Habad: The Hasidism of Rabbi Shneur Zalman of Lyady* (Tuscaloosa, 1992).

is taken from first word of the opening chapter, but the work also circulated under the name *Likutei Amarim (Collected Sayings)*.[10]

The book weaves together ideas from the Zohar and Safed Kabbala, and especially the teachings of Rabbi Isaac Luria (known as the "Ari"), which are cited more frequently than traditions from the Maggid or even the Baal Shem Tov. Yet Rabbi Shneur Zalman reads these texts in the hasidic fashion, reinterpreting the anthropomorphic, mythic theology of earlier Kabbala through a devotional and psychological lens. Like his hasidic teachers, Rabbi Shneur Zalman employs the same vocabulary to describe both the Godhead and the inner spiritual structures of the human mind, revealing that the divine and human realms are intimately intertwined. However, Rabbi Shneur Zalman retains much more of the Lurianic terminology than other hasidic masters of his day, explaining the ideas of the Baal Shem Tov and his students by means of classical Kabbala.

We will now turn to each of the four primary sections of *Tanya* in turn, exploring the major theological issues as they arise.[11] The various parts of *Tanya* were addressed to different audiences across several decades, and thus differ in both emphasis and thematic focus. However, the text offers a largely cohesive spiritual vision, reinforced by the fact that the contemporary reader confronts *Tanya* as a single literary unit.

---

10. *Likutei Amarim* is a strange title for this book, since it is anything but a random assortment of teachings. Most hasidic works from this period are loose anthologies of homilies that follow the weekly Torah readings, but the primary sections of *Tanya* are a carefully constructed theological treatise. This title may have been chosen as a way of connecting Rabbi Shneur Zalman's book to the work *Likutei Amarim – Maggid Devarav LeYaakov* (Koretz, 1781). This highly influential book was the first published collection of teachings attributed to Rabbi Dov Baer of Mezritch, Rabbi Shneur Zalman's own spiritual teacher. My thanks to Professor Nehemia Polen for this insight.

11. The fifth and by far shortest section of *Tanya*, called *Kuntres Aharon*, includes a series of concise essays addressing topics in *Sefer Shel Beinonim* or difficulties arising in other kabbalistic works. Here too we find Rabbi Shneur Zalman returning to the similar themes of Torah study, mystical prayer, the key elements of human service, and the structures of the Godhead, but these short excursuses are quite complex. Few ideas appear in *Kuntres Aharon* that cannot be found elsewhere in *Tanya*, though many are treated in this section with greater detail.

Part 1: *Sefer Shel Beinonim*

The first and longest section of *Tanya*, called *Sefer Shel Beinonim* (*The Book of the Intermediate Person*), is the heart of Rabbi Shneur Zalman's book. This part, which spans some fifty-three chapters, opens by outlining a rigid social architecture of individuals with differing spiritual capabilities. These categories, which are relatively fixed, include the following:

- the complete *tzaddik*, who lacks an Evil Inclination because it has been transformed into a positive force;
- the incomplete *tzaddik*, who has utterly vanquished the Evil Inclination;
- the (often) wicked person, who is frequently bested by the Evil Inclination;
- the (completely) wicked person, who is entirely consumed by sin.

In addition to these four types of people, Rabbi Shneur Zalman presents a fifth category, the *beinoni*, who is the primary subject of *Tanya*. This "intermediate person" is forever locked in the struggle against the Evil Inclination, but has never been overcome and enticed into transgression.

Rabbi Shneur Zalman claims that *tzaddikim* are present in each generation. They are the spiritual elites, aspects, or even reincarnations of Moses reborn throughout Jewish history, including the hasidic leaders of Rabbi Shneur Zalman's own day. But these flawless *tzaddikim* are not the intended audience of *Sefer Shel Beinonim*, which is directed toward individuals for whom much of their spiritual work is yet undone. Rabbi Shneur Zalman sought to inspire these readers to rise above their natural state as one of the categories of "wicked" people, and to reach the station of the *beinoni*. This victory, though difficult, is theoretically available to all. Beginning *Tanya* with this hierarchy pushes most readers to abandon any false aspirations of becoming a *tzaddik*, thus allowing Rabbi Shneur Zalman's students to take up the inner work necessary and appropriate for their true rung and thereby strive to become a *beinoni*.

Rabbi Shneur Zalman then describes the nature of the human spirit. Jewish people, he suggests, have two souls. The first of these, the animal or vital-animating soul (*nefesh behemit* or *ḥiyunit*), comes from the *kelipot* – the "husks" of the material world that obscure the divinity within. It gives us material life, but it is also responsible for all negative character traits, compelling one to follow his banal instincts and become attached to the physical realm. The *nefesh behemit* can be uplifted and transformed into a godly instrument, but doing so is a heroic task. The second soul, however, is a pure aspect of God embodied within the human form (*ḥelek eloha mimaal*, see Job 31:2). This indwelling divine presence is the key to the spiritual life and the gateway for connecting to God. These two souls, the animal and the divine, are respectively housed in the left and right chambers of the heart. The divine soul, however, is also found in the mind, a cornerstone of the intellectual element of Rabbi Shneur Zalman's theology.

In these opening chapters, Rabbi Shneur Zalman claims that the souls of the gentile nations come from an even lower grade of the *kelipot*. For this reason and because they lack the indwelling of the divine soul that characterizes Israel, the souls of non-Jews cannot achieve the same kind of spiritual uplift. This weighty statement, to which we will return in the conclusion, is found throughout *Tanya*, and is far more central to Rabbi Shneur Zalman than for most other hasidic masters of his day.

The results of the stark, almost dualistic battle between the animal and divine souls in the *beinoni* is expressed through his physical actions. Rabbi Shneur Zalman teaches that the spirit is manifest through the three exterior "garments" (*levushim*) – thought, speech, and actions – all movements in each of these realms impact the cosmos as well as the individual. If the devoted worshiper follows God's will, his deeds increase the divine light in the world. The opposite is also true, for even minor transgressions distance a person from the divine and obscure God's illumination. They also extend the exile of the *Shekhina*, the feminine aspect of God that dwells within the world and accompanies Israel throughout all of their peregrinations.

Rabbi Shneur Zalman's portrait of the human soul(s) is linked to his dualistic vision of the world. All elements connected to God belong to the divine realm, and everything else comes from the Other Side (*Sitra Aḥra*), a domain of darkness that occludes God's presence. Rabbi Shneur Zalman inherited this binary theological structure from medieval Kabbala, but he reinterprets it according to a central hasidic notion: there is no place devoid of God, and evil is simply divine energy manifest in a negative form. The *Sitra Aḥra* has no real substance, either metaphysical or ontological, because everything in the cosmos is a part of God's infinite Being. The realm of darkness was granted permission to exist, but only in order for mankind to rise up and overcome it. This was the purpose of Creation, says Rabbi Shneur Zalman, and he constantly reminds the reader that our task is to reveal more of the divine light in the world.

The notion that God may be served through *all* elements of the world, including the physical, was central to the Baal Shem Tov. The Maggid was circumspect in his attitude toward the world, retaining some of the ascetic impulse and preoccupation with sexuality found in medieval Kabbala and Ashkenazic pietistic literature. Rabbi Shneur Zalman follows the Maggid, and throughout *Tanya* we find a distrust of the earthly realm. The cosmos is filled with God, but he argues that excessive engagement with the corporeal will distract people from their own spiritual work. Of course one cannot eat something prohibited or perform a deed that has been forbidden (*assur*) in the name of serving God, since its divine spark is too far "bound" (*assur*) up in the *kelipot*. But Rabbi Shneur Zalman also suggests that even an act that is not technically prohibited but is performed for one's personal benefit or pleasure is the work of the animal soul. He recommends vanquishing the Evil Inclination by postponing mealtimes and limiting oneself in all permissible matters.

This position stands in tension with the general hasidic ethos of raising up the holy sparks, and, more broadly, with our task of transforming the physical world by infusing it with divine light. Rabbi Shneur Zalman claims that these goals are to be accomplished first and foremost by performing the commandments, since in doing so the worshiper uses a physical object (an *etrog*, money for alms, a *shofar*, etc.) to effect the divine will. This holy purpose sanctifies something that had once appeared to be purely mundane. There is, however, one noteworthy passage in which Rabbi Shneur Zalman emphasizes that eating, drinking, and so forth are useful steps in illuminating the world with God's sacred light.

Rabbi Shneur Zalman also takes a cautious position regarding the controversial practice of lifting up "strange thoughts" (*maḥshavot zarot*) during prayer.[12] This notion is present in the teachings of the Baal Shem Tov, who claimed that all thoughts have a holy source and must therefore be "returned" to their divine origin. For example, lust for something physical should be transformed into desire for God. Rabbi Shneur Zalman felt that this practice was too dangerous for the *beinoni*, and suggests that worshipers cast off any distracting thoughts without tracing them back to their godly root. However, he adds that a *beinoni* should not interpret the presence of such thoughts as indicating a lack of spiritual progress; it is a sign that the Evil Inclination is simply redoubling its efforts in the face of his accomplishments.

Much of the devotional path outlined in *Tanya* emerges from a sustained interpretation of the following verse: "But this matter is very close to you, in your mouth and in your heart, that you may do it" (Deut. 30:14). Rabbi Shneur Zalman understands the "matter" (*davar*) as referring to the innate fear and love of God that are literally inborn within the heart of every Jew. The "hidden love" (*ahava mesuteret*) inherited from the patriarchs is the source of their capacity to connect to God. To articulate this love Rabbi Shneur Zalman offers a parable based on the verse "the candle of God is the soul of man (*nishmat adam*)" (Prov. 20:27):

> The souls of Israel ... are like the flame of a candle that constantly and naturally stretches upwards, since a flame from the fire longs to separate from the wick and become attached to its root above. ...
>
> So too does the soul of a person (*nishmat adam*), as well as [his] spirit and pneuma (*ruah venefesh*), intrinsically long to separate itself from the body in order to unite with its origin and source in God, the font of all life, even though it would thereby become totally negated, completely losing its own identity, with nothing remaining of its former essence and being.[13]

---

12. Here too, Rabbi Shneur Zalman differs from other hasidic thinkers, including his teachers and some of his colleagues. For example, see *Peri HaAretz*, translated in Arthur Green, *Speaking Torah: Spiritual Teachings from Around the Maggid's Table*, with Ebn Leader, Ariel Evan Mayse, and Or N. Rose (Woodstock, 2013), vol. 1, 153–155.

13. *Sefer Shel Beinonim*, ch. 19, fols. 24a–b. All citations to *Tanya* refer to *Likutei Amarim-Tanya, Bilingual Edition*, revised edition (Brooklyn, 1998), and the present translations are based on those that appear in that volume.

The essential, burning desire of the Jewish soul to become attached to the divine is so great that it overcomes any sense of self-preservation. Like the famous metaphor of the moth drawn to the flame, the soul's innate love for God draws it closer and closer until it is totally subsumed in the divine. But Rabbi Shneur Zalman asserts that the Jewish soul holds a corresponding "awe," or "fear" (both expressed by the word "*yira*") as well, which tempers this elated love for God. This innate awe is not expressed simply as natural aversion to sin, of course, but rather as an intense fear of becoming cut off from the divine. How to cultivate these natural faculties of love and awe is one of the most important themes of *Sefer Shel Beinonim*, although Rabbi Shneur Zalman emphasizes that the goal of such inner work is to serve God through performing the commandments.

This point, the call to action, is a second cardinal message proceeding from Rabbi Shneur Zalman's reading of Deuteronomy 30:14. The words "that you may do it" are a reminder that our inner spiritual world must become expressed through physical deeds. The commandments are the crystallization of God's will, and, when performed correctly, they fill the world with an additional measure of divine light. Only these sacred actions build a dwelling place for God in this world.

The tenor of *Sefer Shel Beinonim* changes in chapter 26, as we find Rabbi Shneur Zalman turning to another cardinal hasidic value: the power of joy in divine service. Happiness (*simḥa*) gives us energy and vitality, whereas sadness (*atzvut*) is so dangerous because it leads to torpor and paralysis, making one prey for the Evil Inclination. In one passage, Rabbi Shneur Zalman offers a practical method for overcoming despondency: contemplate divine unity, coming to know that you too are a part of God's infinite expanse. Be ever mindful of the fact that the world was created in order to become a home for the divine, and know that each person has a unique role in that process. This reassuring awareness defends against fear and absurdity by reminding us of the interdependence – and thus interconnectedness – of all beings as expressions of God.

But Rabbi Shneur Zalman allows for genuine feelings of contrition. He distinguishes between sadness stemming from mundane matters (*milei de'alma*) and that which comes from religious struggles (*milei dishmaya*). The former should be totally ignored, since even difficult things ultimately happen for the good. Sorrow about a lack of spiritual progress, however, can serve as a catalyst for positive growth. Yet the worshiper must not fall into sadness during his divine service or even throughout the day. Rather, one should set aside times to reflect upon his journey, an earnest confrontation that will bring one to a state of constructive contrition (*merirut*) and brokenheartedness (*lev nishbar*). This acknowledgment of one's distance from God allows for growth, thus leading him back to a state of joy and optimism.

The opening chapters of *Tanya* do not give the reader interpretive principles or abstract postulates about the nature of the divine. Rabbi Shneur Zalman focuses on human nature, the inner workings of the soul, and man's role in the sacred drama of overcoming the darkness. But theological reflection is a crucial element of *Tanya* from the very first page, for the realms of God and man are tightly interlocked. Transformations in one domain lead to changes in the other, and the same kabbalistic terms used to describe the divine and the human are not simply homonyms. This shared vocabulary reveals the essential affinity between the two regions, reflecting the deep-seated imbrication of God and man.

In describing God Rabbi Shneur Zalman seeks to maintain a very fine balance. Like many earlier kabbalists, Rabbi Shneur Zalman refers to the divine as possessing both static and dynamic characteristics. On one hand, Rabbi Shneur Zalman inherited Maimonides' unchanging God, the Prime Mover who is permanently unaffected by human deeds. This conception of God, called *Ein Sof*, is singular, unique, and infinitely indescribable. We may project our understandings onto the divine, but God is above all positive description or attribution. But *Tanya* also draws on kabbalistic traditions that describe the *sefirot* as fluid and constantly changing. Human worship and covenantal deeds *do* have an impact on some aspect of the divine, and our love and service awaken God's endless compassion. Furthermore, our actions draw sacred energy into the Godhead and physical world by uniting the *sefirot*, described in the remarkably anthropomorphic terms taken from the Zohar and Lurianic Kabbala. These two different understandings of God, the immutable and the ever-changing, must be held together.

There is another related paradox in Rabbi Shneur Zalman's theology that must be addressed. He refers to God as simultaneously transcendent and immanent, using the zoharic terms of "the One that surrounds the worlds" (*sovev kol almin*) and "the One that fills the worlds" (*memale kol almin*). This may sound like a medieval structure of the universe in which God is above – or beyond – the world, as well as immanently manifest in the temporal region below. However, Rabbi Shneur Zalman makes it clear that these metaphorical names refer to the degrees to which God's light is disclosed, not physical spaces. *Sovev kol almin* describes divine light that has not yet taken on any form, and is therefore beyond our threshold because it is too intense and abstract. *Memale kol almin* denotes God's energy as manifest in the worlds, an attenuated illumination refracted through the cosmos. All elements of the physical realm are embodiments of the divine, but there are aspects of God that are not restricted to the cosmos; the expanse of the sacred transcends the worlds at the same moment that God's divine vitality is manifest within them.

This notion of absolute divine omnipresence (coupled with God's simultaneous transcendence) is an important hasidic principle that is often linked to literal interpretations of the verse "His glory fills the entire earth" (Is. 6:3) and the claim made in *Tikkunei Zohar* that "there is no place devoid of Him." This raises the question of how, if God is so totally omnipresent, we can speak of a localized indwelling of the divine called *Shekhina*. Rabbi Shneur Zalman claims that this term refers to an intensified Divine Presence, the manifestation of *Ein Sof* in the world that implies neither a multiplicity of gods nor spatial exclusivity. He also describes *Shekhina* as the conduit through which sacred vitality is constantly delivered into each person and everything.

Any theological system must address the intertwined issues of the extent to which humanity can *know* God, and the degree to which we may even use language in reference to the divine. Rabbi Shneur Zalman understands these conundrums and often cites the maxim from the *Tikkunei Zohar* that "no thought can grasp Him at all." Indeed, he often drifts close to Maimonides' negative theology, claiming that we cannot even say that God is "beyond comprehension." To do so would imply that the divine is beyond the threshold of human understanding, but he argues that the term "comprehension" is irrelevant when applied to God. But there is an important difference between Maimonides' and

Rabbi Shneur Zalman's thinking on this subject. Rabbi Shneur Zalman claims that divine wisdom cannot be grasped – and indeed, God Himself cannot be known – because of His absolute immanence rather than the insurmountable otherness of the divine.

Yet Rabbi Shneur Zalman interprets the classical notion that "the Torah speaks the language of man" as suggesting that theological discourse is both permissible and necessary. It is enabled by the symbolic and metaphorical language of the Kabbala, understood by Rabbi Shneur Zalman as a revealed body of information. The kabbalists have access to the hidden depths of God's wisdom and can attain a greater knowledge of the divine than even Moses, who knew God "only" through direct vision. Moreover, Rabbi Shneur Zalman often uses metaphors and parables to illustrate God's nature. While he often reminds the reader that there is no essential comparison between the metaphors and their divine referent, he employs these stirring images as an evocative way of describing God. Metaphors and parables are linguistic gestures toward the God that is ineffable – and inconceivable – and they allow us to grasp something of a divine world that would otherwise remain beyond the cusp of articulation.

Our understanding of God will always be partial until absolute knowledge of the divine is revealed in the future. This is the heart of Rabbi Shneur Zalman's intellectual messianic vision. But the new awareness of the divine will be built through human effort, not be delivered unto us from on high:

> The culminating fulfillment of the Messianic Era and of the Resurrection of the Dead, which is the revelation of the light of the blessed *Ein Sof* in this material world, depends on our actions and service throughout the duration of the exile. For what causes the reward of a commandment is the commandment itself, because by virtue of performing it the person suffuses a flood of light of the blessed *Ein Sof* downward from above, to be clothed in the physical aspects of the world.[14]

---

14. *Sefer Shel Beinonim*, ch. 37, fol. 36b.

The reward for performing the commandments is neither metaphysical recompense nor an expanded portion in the World to Come. Each deed accomplishes some part of revealing God in *this* world. This process stretches forward into the Messianic Era, but our involvement in the process means that some of the future consciousness spills back and illuminates the present.[15]

These theological reflections are an essential part of Rabbi Shneur Zalman's conception of divine service. Together with the animal and divine souls, Rabbi Shneur Zalman bifurcates the attributes of the human psyche (the *middot*, based on the *sefirot* of the Godhead) into three primary intellectual faculties and the seven "lower" elements of one's emotive personality. The upper faculties of *ḥokhma* (wisdom), *bina* (understanding), and *daat* (knowledge) drive human intellection and fuel contemplative meditation. They are the focus of Rabbi Shneur Zalman's inner work, because they arouse and control the otherwise unpredictable seven lower *middot*:

> This is a great principle regarding divine service for the *beinonim*: the most important thing is to govern and rule the nature that is in the left ventricle [of the heart] by means of the divine light that illuminates the divine soul in the mind. That is, to rule the heart by means of meditation in the mind on the greatness of the blessed *Ein Sof*, whereby his understanding will bring forth a spirit of knowledge and fear of God in his mind, making him turn away from evil condemned by the Torah and the sages, even from a minor rabbinic prohibition, God forbid; and at the same time [inspiring] the love of God in his heart, in the right ventricle, with a fervor and desire to cleave to Him through the fulfillment

---

15. This is similar to Rabbi Shneur Zalman's description of the redemption from Egypt as a continuous process. In quoting the famous mishna that demands that we see ourselves as leaving Egypt anew in each and every generation, he adds the words "each and every day," transforming the one-time journey out of Egypt (*Mitzrayim*) into a daily struggle for liberation from the constricted boundaries of the sea of consciousness (*metzar yam*) and the base elements of human nature. See *Sefer Shel Beinonim*, ch. 47, fol. 66b.

of the commandments of the Torah and the sages, and through the study of Torah that is equivalent to them all.[16]

Contemplation of God begins in the intellectual faculties, which the *beinoni* focuses upon the nearly overwhelming expanse of divine unity. This cerebral meditation awakens the innate love and awe hidden within the *beinoni's* heart, which are then expressed through the seven lower *middot*.[17] These attributes can be manifest in either positive or negative forms, the result of the inner struggle of the *beinoni* to devote all aspects of the self to God. Although a *beinoni* will never permanently transform the *middot* into their most ennobled form and thus eliminate any possibility of transgression, he never fails to use them as a channel through which to manifest the inner stirrings of his heart and mind.

Thus, we should not mistake Rabbi Shneur Zalman's contemplation for dry or stultified intellection. He writes:

> The essence of knowledge is not the knowing alone, that people should know the greatness of God from authors and books; but the essential thing is to immerse one's mind deeply into the greatness of God and fix one's thought on God with all the strength and vigor of the heart and mind, until his thought is bound to God with a strong and mighty bond ... for it is known that "knowledge" (*daat*) connotes union, as in the verse, "And Adam knew (*yada*) Eve." (Gen. 4:1)[18]

Intellectual meditation leads to a contemplative bond with God that is passionate and even erotic. It is no accident that he describes mystical gnosis in such expressive terms. Love and awe, the dyadic pair aroused through contemplation, are the pillars of the devotional life. They are the "wings" of the spirit that together lift the worshiper into the higher – or

---

16. Ibid., ch. 16, fol. 21b.
17. These include *ḥesed* (loving-kindness) and *gevura* (power or sternness), often respectively associated with love and awe, but also *tiferet* (splendor), *netzaḥ* (victory), *hod* (beauty, but also admission), *yesod* (foundation), and *malkhut* (kingship).
18. *Sefer Shel Beinonim*, ch. 42, fols. 59a–b.

innermost – realms. Both are necessary, for each person must be like a humble servant and a beloved child to the King of Kings. Love and awe balance one another, linking amorous excitement with ardent discipline, and either aspect in isolation is destructive.

Two kinds of awe are rooted in the Jewish soul. The first type, a prerequisite for the next stage, is little more than fear of punishment. It is expressed by performing the precepts of Torah, since these acts show deference to God. But the higher type is an overwhelming experience that comes about when one understands that he is nothing but an element of God. This is accomplished by being mindful of God's sovereignty over the worlds, but also, and more importantly, His immanent presence within the cosmos. Looking past the physical exterior to the divine Presence within leads the mystic to tremendous awe, which then spurs him to action. Rabbi Shneur Zalman writes:

> The essential thing, however, is the training to habituate one's mind and thought continuously, that it ever remain fixed in his heart and mind, that everything one sees with one's eyes – the heavens and earth and all that is therein – constitutes the outer garments of the King, the blessed Holy One. In this way he will constantly be aware of their inwardness and vitality.[19]

This profound experience results from attuning oneself to the inner divine nature of the world, manifest through all aspects of the physical realm. But it is much more than an inner feeling, for awe galvanizes one to perform the commandments with new intensity and vigor.

Counterbalancing this awe is the hidden love for God present in the divine soul. When first aroused this love may be mild, but it can be developed into a passionate longing to cleave to the divine:

> The union of the soul with, and its absorption into, the light of God, making them one, this is what every member of Israel truly desires, utterly, with all his heart and all his soul, because of the natural love that is hidden in every Jewish heart to cleave to God

---

19. Ibid., ch. 42, fol. 61a.

and not, under any circumstances, to be parted or sundered or separated, God forbid, from His blessed Unity and oneness, even at the cost of his very life.[20]

This innate love of the Jewish soul can be transformed into a fierce yearning to be absorbed into God. In these higher stages it is manifest in two different forms: *ahavat olam* (eternal love) and *ahava raba* (abundant love). *Ahavat olam* is the result of intellectual contemplation of God, nurtured as the seeker deepens his awareness of God's omnipresence and transcendence, eventually grasping that his individual identity is really an illusion. His power of love begins to shed its earthly referents (i.e., longing for corporeal things), and turns exclusively toward the divine. *Ahava raba*, however, is yet another level of intensity. It is fiery, all-consuming love that is a gift from God, a divine answer to the devoted rapture of the mystic below. This kind of wondrous joy and pure delight in God cannot be earned; the highest form of longing is given to the *tzaddikim* alone. Yet both *ahavat olam* and *ahava raba* inspire a response from God, arousing divine love as a result of the worshiper's service below. Rabbi Shneur Zalman does not recommend focusing exclusively on this theurgic aspect of our service, and emphasizes that awareness of God's unceasing benevolence toward mankind should once more arouse our love for God.

These kinds of contemplative meditation and the task of cultivating love and awe before the divine do not lead the worshiper to retreat from or escape the world. Rabbi Shneur Zalman's spiritual path is deeply embodied in praxis, since, as he quotes, "thought alone accomplishes nothing."[21] He often reminds his readers that their task is to infuse this world with new light and vitality:

> The Zohar teaches that the blessed Holy One and the Torah are one, and the *Tikkunim* [i.e., *Tikkunei Zohar*] explains that the 248 commandments are the 248 limbs of the King. The commandments are the innermost Supreme Will and His true desire, which

---

20. Ibid., ch. 41, fol. 58a.
21. *Kuntres Aḥaron*, ch. 1, fol. 153b.

are embodied in all the upper and lower worlds, giving them life, for all of their vitality and sacred energy depends on the performance of the commandments down below, as is known.[22]

The commandments draw the light of *Ein Sof* into the physical realm, for these precepts are part of the divine will that animates the cosmos. They transform the individual worshiper, and the world around him, into vessels that can reveal divine blessing. They form a bridge between the transcendent and immanent aspects of God, unifying the blessed Holy One (*kudsha brikh hu*, or *tiferet*) and *shekhina* (*malkhut*), thus redeeming the exiled sparks and establishing a home for God in the cosmos. And, as we shall see, this also informs Rabbi Shneur Zalman's description of ethical precepts and love for others as essential parts of complete divine service.

The mystical process of performing the commandments has an experiential component, for the action allows one to grasp some measure of the otherwise invisible light of *Ein Sof*. The commandments bring the physical body close to the divine, even allowing the worshiper to become incorporated with the divine. Through performing these precepts, we become embodiments of the divine will; for example, a hand that gives alms is transformed into a "throne" for God's presence in the physical world. In a later section of *Tanya*, Rabbi Shneur Zalman offers a fascinating distinction between "inspiration" (*hashraa*) and "reward" (*sekhar*). The latter is an influx of divine light as one performs a commandment. But this reward is limited, because the receptacle of the human soul is limited in its ability to absorb the sacred energy. Inspiration, by contrast, means that one becomes totally surrounded by the embrace of God's light. This higher measure of divine illumination is actually *less* perceptible to us, because the human mind is also limited in its capacity to sense this bountiful light.

Hasidism attributes great importance to *kavana*, a heightened state of consciousness or intention when performing all religious precepts. One goal of this awareness is to attain the level of communion (or even union) with God called *devekut*. Rabbi Shneur Zalman writes:

---

22. *Sefer Shel Beinonim*, ch. 23, fol. 28a.

This should be one's *kavana* when occupying himself with the Torah or a certain commandment: one's divine soul as well as his vivifying [i.e., lower, animal] soul, together with their "garments" [of thought, speech, and deed], shall cleave to Him.[23]

Devekut means connection and attachment to God through heightened presence in one's deeds, but for Rabbi Shneur Zalman it can even entail total absorption into the divine through sacred study, contemplative prayer, and performing the precepts of the Torah. The natural capacity for achieving *devekut* is present in the heart of all Jews. It derives from their hidden love for God, though it is only actualized through careful consideration. Thus Rabbi Shneur Zalman recommends that love and awe be used to foster *kavana*:

> One must contemplate profoundly and at length on this thought according to the capacity of apprehension of his brain and thought and according to the time available to him, before he occupies himself with Torah or a commandment, such as prior to putting on his tallit or tefillin. He should also reflect on how the light of the *Ein Sof*, which encompasses all worlds and pervades all worlds, which is identical with the Higher Will, is clothed in the letters and wisdom of the Torah and in the tzitzit and the tefillin, and through his study or donning these latter he draws over himself His blessed light, that is, over "the portion of Godliness from above" which is within his body, that it may be absorbed and nullified in His blessed light....
>
> This union is attained through the drawing forth of the light of the *Ein Sof* here below by means of occupation in the Torah and the commandments wherein [the light of *Ein Sof*] is clothed. And he should intend to draw this light over the fount of his soul and of the souls of all Israel, to unite them. This is the meaning of, "for the sake of the union of the blessed Holy One and His *Shekhina*, in the name of all Israel."[24]

---

23. Ibid., ch. 41, fol. 57b.
24. Ibid., ch. 41, fols. 56a–56b, 57b.

The worshiper must contemplate the presence of God all around him, understanding that this divine light is expressed and increased through the deed he is about to perform. This provides the correct contemplative focus to accompany his action. But here we also see a communal aspect of the *kavana*: the souls of Israel are all interconnected, and therefore drawing forth the illumination of *Ein Sof* is a communal project. Elsewhere Rabbi Shneur Zalman notes that the Jewish people as a whole are united by their shared commitment to the commandments, because issues of the spirit – such as love, awe, and even some elements of *kavana* – are unique to every person.

For these reasons *kavana* is essential, and commandments performed without intention or awareness are deeply lacking, although even mindless deeds are better than sacred actions performed with a negative or self-centered intention. The precepts of Torah possess inherent power as vehicles for divine illumination even without heightened *kavana*; the commandments are God's will, and can therefore automatically inspire the love and awe concealed in the Jewish heart.

Rabbi Shneur Zalman is well aware that emphasizing the power of deeds even without *kavana* could lead to mechanical observance of the commandments. Therefore, he often stresses the centrality of avoiding habituation and rote. He demands that the commandments be performed with a perpetual sense of newness, and the worshiper always seek to transcend his comfort zone and surpass whatever achievements have already become commonplace. Rabbi Shneur Zalman draws a fascinating distinction between "worship" or "divine service" (*avoda*) and a simple "deed" (*maase*). *Avoda* requires tremendous effort and even overturning one's own will before God, whereas *maase* is a deed that may be performed automatically.

Rabbi Shneur Zalman devotes special attention to a few key commandments, but the study of Torah is the core of his mystical vision. He even suggests that there is an independent precept of *knowing* Torah (*mitzvat yediat haTorah*) in addition to the command of studying God's sacred writ. This prioritization reflects Rabbi Shneur Zalman's preference for the intellect above the emotive faculties of the soul, since the act of study allows the *beinoni* to rise above the coarse *middot* and connect directly to God. But the centrality of study is related to Rabbi Shneur Zalman's understanding of Scripture itself:

> The Zohar teaches that the Torah and the blessed Holy One are one.... [25] The blessed Holy One focused His Will and Wisdom into the six hundred and thirteen commandments of the Torah, their laws (*hilkhoteihen*) and the combinations of letters of the Bible, and their interpretations (*derashoteihen*) in the aggadot and midrashim of the sages. [God did this] so that every pneuma, spirit, and soul in the human body can attain it and fulfill them.[26]

The Torah came into existence by means of a "withdrawal" or "constriction" (*tzimtzum*) of divine light, attenuating the ineffable brilliance of the primordial divine wisdom. If the Torah had not taken on the form of words, thus becoming an embodiment of the divine through the medium of language, it would have been impossible to grasp the infinite expanse of the primordial Scripture, to understand God's essence, or even to perform the divine will. This process led to the genesis of the Torah as we know it, as a document composed of stories and law. But the revelation of Torah created a unique bridge between man and God, since for Rabbi Shneur Zalman, God cannot be understood without the Torah.

This conception of Torah shapes the experience of sacred study, for Scripture is the nexus through which the mystic unites with God:

> When a person is occupied with the words of the Torah, the Supreme Will, united as it is in perfect unity with the blessed *Ein Sof*, is completely manifest and in no way obscured in the divine soul and its innermost garments, i.e., thought and speech [of the scholar] – it follows that the soul and its garments are also at such a time truly united with the *Ein Sof* in perfect unity.[27]

---

25. Zohar I:24a.
26. *Sefer Shel Beinonim*, ch. 4, fols. 8a–b.
27. Ibid., ch. 23, fol. 29a.

Torah study is a way of cleaving to God and even a reenactment of divine revelation, since the divine comes to be known through the embodiment of His Will. In another chapter, Rabbi Shneur Zalman reinterprets the act of "reading Torah" (*koreh baTora*) as "calling out" (also *koreh*) to God, likening one who studies God's word to a child calling out his beloved parent's name. This awareness of the intimate subtext of sacred study should inspire the scholar to awe, trepidation, and ultimately to rapture.

Rabbi Shneur Zalman praises studying the inner dimensions of Torah, namely kabbalistic and hasidic texts, but he reserves a special place for the study of halakha as well. Of course, part of his concern is practical. Knowing the halakha is essential because it governs every aspect of Jewish life. But each person has a duty to master all areas of practical halakha because the detailed rules of the commandments govern their ability to impact the worlds; God's precepts cannot influence the cosmos if performed incorrectly.

Rabbi Shneur Zalman frequently refers to halakha as God's will and an expression of the divine Mind, manifest in the material world through an intricate web of legal details. In a classic passage from an early chapter in *Tanya*, we read:

> A particular halakha is the wisdom and will of God … therefore, when a person knows and comprehends with his intellect such a verdict in accordance with the law as it is set out in the Mishna, Talmud, or codes, he has thus comprehended, grasped, and encompassed with his intellect the will and wisdom of the blessed Holy One, whom no thought can grasp, nor His will and wisdom, except when they are clothed in the laws that have been set out for us …. This is a wondrous union, like none other and with no parallel in the material world.[28]

The 613 commandments correspond to the different elements of the human body, as well as to the aspects of the divine superstructure (the "limbs of the King" mentioned above). And, like a complex organism,

---

28. Ibid., ch. 5, fols. 9a–b. See ch. 23, fol. 28b; ch. 46, fol. 65b; and *Iggeret HaKodesh*, ch. 1, fol. 102b. In one passage, he refers to each and every word of halakha as a spark of *Shekhina*; see ibid., ch. 26, fol. 145a.

the commandments are composed of an elaborate network of interconnectivity. This system is the halakhot, laws that represent the ever-flowing complexity of the divine realm. Rabbi Shneur Zalman claims that these halakhot are rooted to *keter*, the first *sefira* that designates an unformed and unarticulated divine realm. The laws of the Oral Law and the system of halakha writ large explain *how* the commandments are to be performed, revealing the will of God with a clarity not found in the literal text of the Hebrew Bible. Thus the infinite and ever-changing spring of the Oral Torah crystallizes the latent potential of the Written Torah.[29]

There is no doctrine in *Tanya* comparable to *Torah Umadda* (*Torah and secular knowledge*). Rabbi Shneur Zalman, like many rabbinic leaders in Eastern Europe, used the suspicious kabbalistic term "external wisdoms" in reference to non-Jewish disciplines. In one passage, however, he claims that these outside ideas are destructive unless used correctly, either in order to earn one's livelihood, or, more impressively, for divine service (*avodat Hashem*), as was the case with Maimonides and Nahmanides. These two uses of non-Jewish thought are strikingly different. The first is a utilitarian approach that allows one to study certain fields in order to cultivate a trade. The second, however, suggests that it is possible to internalize the non-Jewish wisdom and use it to deepen one's connection to the divine.

Prayer is another commandment of great importance for Rabbi Shneur Zalman. He refers to worship as a time of sacred renewal in which one brings forth new intellectual and spiritual vitality (*moḥin*). More specifically, prayer is the ideal opportunity for contemplating the greatness of the infinite divine. A *tzaddik* serves God in such a way that he is incorporated into God and his entire being is transformed into a vehicle for God, manifest constantly in all of his deeds. For the *beinoni*, however, expanded consciousness and self-transcendence are a rare experience, coming only at heightened moments of spiritual uplift such as prayer.

Of course, this exaltation of mystical worship raises questions about petitionary prayer, which appears to focus on this-worldly rewards and physical needs. Rabbi Shneur Zalman compares an individual who

---

29. For more on the relationship between hasidic spirituality and halakha, see Ariel Evan Mayse, "The Ever-Changing Path: Visions of Legal Diversity in Hasidic Literature," *Conversations* 23 (2015): 84–115.

engages in *only* petitionary prayer to someone called by the king who steps into the royal presence but ignores the ruler and busies himself with his petty needs. Hasidic texts commonly explain that petitionary prayer must be undertaken only for the sake of *Shekhina* – the divine sparks exiled amid a fractured world. But this approach does not seem to have been favored by Rabbi Shneur Zalman, who instead recommends that the worshiper use petitionary prayer as an opportunity to underscore his own insignificance before the Divine. More subtly, and less pessimistically, this entails a radical awakening to the fact that one's own existence is naught; the hearts and souls from which we pour out our prayers are in truth filled with the divine.

It is worth noting that Torah study and prayer, the two devotional pillars of the hasidic religious life that lead to *devekut*, are both linguistic practices. For Rabbi Shneur Zalman, as for most other early hasidic mystics, language is a potent divine gift, a finite access point through which the worshiper comes into the presence of the infinite One; for this reason words are to be cherished rather than avoided. God is found in the words of study and prayer, and the worshiper must enter them with presence and contemplative focus. But the Talmud calls prayer "temporal life" (*ḥayei shaa*), contrasting it with the "eternal life" (*ḥayei olam*) of studying Torah. Rabbi Shneur Zalman reinterprets the former as indicating that worship is a moment of temporary spiritual uplift in which *Shekhina* is redeemed from exile. Prayer is particularly important for later generations, since lifting up the sparks is even more important in a time of heightened darkness. Doing so requires considerable effort and focus, and for this reason true prayer takes a significant amount of time each day. And worship has the power to accomplish things that study cannot. Most commandments cause an intensification of sacred energy within the material realm, but they do not change the physical structure of the world. Prayer transforms the vessels in which the divine light is garbed. Thus the worshiper can indeed work miracles, such as bringing rain or healing, elicited from God as a divine response to our human supplication.

Part 2: *Shaar HaYiḥud VeHaEmuna*
The second section of *Tanya* begins with *Ḥinukh Katan*, a short excursus echoing many of the themes in *Sefer Shel Beinonim*. These include

the importance of cultivating love and awe, and here too Rabbi Shneur Zalman reinforces that God's benevolence for mankind must inspire a similar love in us for the divine. This desire can indeed be commanded, he says, because love is the emotional and intellectual result of contemplating the divine unity. Rabbi Shneur Zalman suggests that the ideal time for meditating on this truth is while the worshiper recites the first two sentences of the *Shema* (Deut. 6:4 and the additional *barukh shem kevod malkhuto leolam va'ed*); these are respectively called the "upper" and "lower" unifications (*yihuda ilaa* and *yihuda tataa*) by the Zohar.

The subsequent chapters outline a sophisticated description of the relationship between the infinite God and the phenomenal world. It is one of the boldest articulations in early hasidic literature of a theology that may be called mystical panentheism, also described by scholars as acosmism. *Shaar HaYihud VeHaEmuna* is intricate and at times difficult, but the heart of the message is both simple and resoundingly clear: there is nothing in the cosmos but God. All existence is Divinity. Succinctly captured in the words commonly invoked in Chabad, *altz iz Gott* – everything is God. The world would return to its pre-Creation state of unity and hence total nothingness without the constant influx of God's energy. This sacred vitality is immanently present within the cosmos in order animate it.

Shaar HaYihud VeHaEmuna is anchored in an interpretation of the verse "Know this day and take into your heart that Y-H-V-H is God, in the heavens above and upon the earth below; there is no other" (Deut. 4:39). Rabbi Shneur Zalman takes this to mean that God literally fills the worlds with divine energy, a fact that must be contemplated long and hard in order to be taken to heart. He reads "there is no other" quite literally as "there is nothing other than Him," suggesting that our perception of a differentiated cosmos, as well as our own individual existence, is ultimately an illusion.

Rabbi Shneur Zalman boldly claims that God is the source of all being, and that everything in the universe is a manifestation of the divine. But why do we not see the cosmos as such? How can some things seem to be disconnected from God? And why do we encounter multiplicity? The answer, claims Rabbi Shneur Zalman, is *tzimtzum*, a concept taken from the Lurianic creation myth that may be translated as both "withdrawal" and "focusing." In creating the worlds as material reality from absolute nothing (*yesh me'ayin*), it was necessary for *Ein Sof* to attenuate the infinite divine light in order to make it perceivable and to allow space for the cosmos to come into being. *Tzimtzum* happened in progressive stages,[30] and although God surrounds the universe equally, the "higher" (more abstract) worlds reveal more divinity than the "lower" (more corporeal) worlds.[31] The purpose of *tzimtzum*, and Creation, was to allow for a *dira batahtonim* – a dwelling place for God's presence in the lower, physical realm. This ultimate goal can only be accomplished through the deeds of mankind. Born into the world, we are a sacred spark of divinity that has become incarnate within the human form, in order to uplift the physical and separate the negative from the good, drawing new vitality and divine light into the worlds through performing the commandments.

In this context Rabbi Shneur Zalman suggests a striking reading of the verse "For a sun and a shield is Y-H-V-H God" (Ps. 84:12). Y-H-V-H, the aspect of God that animates the cosmos and perpetually brings it into being (*mehaveh*), is too expansive to be withstood by human minds. Therefore God kindly restrained our vision of this divine animating force. Rabbi Shneur Zalman notes that "God" (*Elokim*) and "nature" (*hateva*) have the same numerical value (86), suggesting that the natural world represents the aspect of God that shields us from an overabundance of divine light. We are protected from the imperceptivity of the great divine by the multiplicity of the material world. Just as a person's true essence may only be grasped when projected through his thoughts, words, and deeds, Rabbi Shneur Zalman argues that the inner divine nature of the

---

30. As in classical Kabbala, Rabbi Shneur Zalman describes four different worlds, the first of which, *atzilut* (emanation), is united with God totally and imponderably. The following three worlds of *beria* (creation), *yetzira* (formation), and *asiya* (deed, the world of humanity) are further gradations of *tzimtzum*. Rabbi Shneur Zalman's spectrum of the four worlds is complicated by another tetrad embedded in each of those worlds: the four levels of existence – *domem* (the inanimate), *tzemah* (vegetation), *hai* (animal life), *medaber* (humanity, the speaking being). Each of these sets of four refers to degrees of revelation of God in addition to planes of existence. See *Sefer Shel Beinonim*, ch. 39, fol. 52b; and ibid., ch. 49, fol. 69b.
31. Ibid., ch. 40, fol. 54b. We may safely use quotation marks for these terms, because the vertical language of upper or lower, inherited from medieval Kabbala, is for Rabbi Shneur Zalman a metaphor that should not be read literally; see ibid., ch. 36, fol. 45b.

worlds can *only* be sensed through the mediating force of the *sefirot* and the cosmos. Without *tzimtzum* everything in the cosmos would become null, an overwhelming retreat into divine Nothing as the project of Creation melts back into God's unity.

Divine immanence via the protective filter of *tzimtzum* actually allows for a special type of unitive experience. The worshiper can retain a sense of individual identity, but at the same time hold an awareness that the worlds are infused with God:

> The rabbis, of blessed memory, have said that one should never separate himself from the community (*klal*).[32] Therefore he should intend to unite and attach to Him, blessed be He, the fount of his divine soul and the fount of the souls of all Israel... called by the name *Shekhina*, because it dwells and clothes itself in all worlds, animating them and giving them existence, and is that which imbues him with the power of speech to utter the words of Torah, or with the power of action to perform the particular commandment.[33]

Here Rabbi Shneur Zalman interprets the word *klal* not only as the spiritual community surrounding the worshiper, but as the entire network of material existence that is to be uplifted. The goal is not to forsake the physical or even to transcend it, because the corporeal realm itself is the unique opportunity for mystical experience.

It is important to note that *tzimtzum* was an act of God's love. The divine light was attenuated not in order to vindictively conceal God from mankind, but in order to show love for humanity by making room for them in the cosmos. Moreover, *tzimtzum* imbued mankind with agency, thereby ennobling and empowering us:

> "As water mirrors the reflection of a face" (Prov. 27:19): the blessed Holy One has, as it were, set aside His great infinite light and stored it away.... This is because of His love for lowly man, in

---

32. Berakhot 49b.
33. *Sefer Shel Beinonim*, ch. 41, fol. 57b.

order to raise him up to God, for "love moves aside the flesh" [i.e., God moved aside the light of the divine out of love for man].[34] It is infinitely more fitting that a man should relinquish and set aside all he possess, both spiritually and physically, and renounce everything in order to cleave to Him, may He be blessed, with attachment, desire, and longing.

God's love for mankind is another of Rabbi Shneur Zalman's interpretations of *ahavat olam*, which may be translated as "worldly love." He claims that, "God took on a garb of finitude, which is called *olam* [i.e., the world], for the sake of the love of His people Israel, in order to bring them near to Him, that they might be absorbed into His blessed Unity of oneness."[35] The phrase "love moves aside the flesh" thus works in both directions – God withdrew the infinite light of *Ein Sof* in order to make room for the cosmos, and mankind is invited to return the favor by turning aside from the vanities of the world and delving into the unity of the cosmos.

This is the meaning of the phrase "Y-H-V-H is God" (*hu HaElokim*) from our original verse. These two aspects of the divine are truly one and the same. Y-H-V-H represents Being as the origin of all existence, and *Elokim* alludes to the restricted expression of God through the physical world. Attunement to this ultimate unity thus brings one to the knowledge that "in the heavens above and in the earth below, there is nothing else." In other words, the cosmos has no existence of its own, for all is divinity. From our perspective we may see multiplicity and variety, and thus the verse must remind us, "Know and take into your heart" – be ever mindful God's true unity.

In *Shaar HaYihud VeHaEmuna* Rabbi Shneur Zalman gives several metaphors to illustrate the relationship between God and the cosmos. One is the way in which the soul fills the body and continuously

---

34. Bava Metzia 84a. The reader who looks this source up will be surprised by Rabbi Shneur Zalman's reinterpretation of the talmudic adage.
35. *Sefer Shel Beinonim*, ch. 49, fol. 69b. Rabbi Shneur Zalman's interpretation of the liturgy anchors this meditation on divine love in the devotional practice of reciting the *Shema*.

sustains it. But Rabbi Shneur Zalman admits that this is an imprecise analogy, since the body and the soul are two separate – if intertwined – entities. Their partial unity can only allude to God's immanent presence in the world. Another frequent metaphor is a ray of light as it is subsumed into the sun, where the individuated sunbeam is totally nullified by the intensity of its source. By extension, our perception of the material realm is true only from our perspective, since nothing truly exists from God's point of view. We remain fully incorporated within our divine source, and, like the ray of sun, our existence melts into the infinite light of the divine.

Rabbi Shneur Zalman's most sustained metaphor for God's unity within the world is based on the idea that Creation took place by means of language. In the opening lines of *Shaar HaYihud VeHaEmuna* he quotes a tradition from the Baal Shem Tov built upon a myth of creation through the Hebrew language that stretches back into antiquity. The Baal Shem Tov interpreted the biblical story of God forming the world through ten divine "utterances" as meaning that the letters of this speech remain within the physical world as its animating force. Rabbi Shneur Zalman develops this theme at length, describing the unfolding of the different aspects of the divine and God's continuous presence in the physical world as elements of divine speech. The infinite expanse of *Ein Sof* underwent a contraction (*tzimtzum*) into divine thought, and then into the concrete structures of embodied language and eventually the very letters undergirding the materiality of existence. This is an essentially linguistic as well as a metaphysical argument, for the Hebrew letters of each object's name are its true essence.

Rabbi Shneur Zalman adds more nuance to his description of the role of language in the revelation of the divine. He claims that the notion of words and letters is itself a metaphorical – or symbolic – way of referring to God. Thus the primordial utterances of Creation are called "speech" from our perspective, a fitting metaphor for us since we are, after all, fundamentally creatures of language. We must invest our thoughts into language in order to convey them to another person, and therefore the flow of divine energy is called a speech act composed of letters. Thus the letters of a Hebrew word may be described as the source of the vitality of their referent not because they exist as microscopic entities within it, but because they are a way of referring to the unique combination – or permutation – of pathways through which the energies are drawn in this case.

Rabbi Shneur Zalman squarely asserts that God's creation of being out of the infinite divine Naught (*yesh me'ayin*) cannot be understood by the human mind, nor can the resulting divine unity be expressed or even comprehended. There is a limit to what one can know with certainty, and this may only be witnessed through a type of faith that transcends intellectual apprehension. His readers are called upon to believe in the unity of God, the cosmos, and all of the *sefirot* with total faith.

Including *Shaar HaYiḥud VeHaEmuna* as the second part of *Tanya* means that the quest to attain the awareness of God's unity is not restricted to the *tzaddik*. Most of *Tanya* is explicitly directed to *beinonim*, and we should underscore that the printed introduction to *Shaar HaYiḥud VeHaEmuna* identifies the *Shema* as the ultimate unification with God. That means that this entire section of *Tanya* grounds the search for divine unity in a twice-daily practice upheld by everyone in Rabbi Shneur Zalman's community.

Part 3: *Iggeret HaTeshuva*

The third section of *Tanya*, entitled *Iggeret HaTeshuva*, was first published in 1799 and revised in 1806. The primary subject of these letters is, unsurprisingly, the various aspects of repentance (*teshuva*). This classical theme is found in many medieval works, both philosophical and kabbalistic, and repentance rituals suffused with an ethos of mystical piety (*tikkunei teshuva*) were popular in Eastern European moralistic literature. Rabbi Shneur Zalman understands repentance as far more than a moral or ethical imperative, though it is certainly these as well. It is rather a process of personal accounting, transformation, and action with cosmological – and theurgic – implications as well.

Rabbi Shneur Zalman highlights transgression as a damaging force that causes fracture within the Godhead. The soul is an embodiment of God, and therefore our performance of the commandments is crucial because these sacred deeds draw more divine illumination into the physical realm. When a person sins this potential energy is cast into exile and flows into the Other Side, feeding the forces that obscure God's presence in the material world. And, on a personal level, sin causes a defect of the soul. With this in mind, Rabbi Shneur Zalman interprets the word *teshuva* by splitting it into two: *teshuv heh* (restoring the *heh*). This means that repentance is returning the letter *heh*, a symbol for the exiled *Shekhina* and the element of God within man's soul, to its rightful place in the name Y-H-V-H.

Teshuva begins with internal transformation. The penitent must carefully reflect upon his deeds, leading to a sense of total contrition and a positive type of brokenheartedness that can overcome the negative infraction. But Rabbi Shneur Zalman underscores that this initial inner work must be followed by concrete action; thought alone cannot effect real change in one's self and in the world around him. This was the function of the sacrifices in the times of the Temple, but now fasting must fulfill this same role. Rabbi Shneur Zalman, as noted above, looks favorably on fasting and asceticism. He admits that a regimen of intensive fasting is only for the very robust, but a spiritually accomplished individual (*baal nefesh*) should fast. Those who cannot withstand such extreme asceticism must give alms in great abundance. True repentance starts in the heart, but it remains abstract and ineffectual until the penitent constructs a vessel – a physical deed – into which to draw the energy.

Rabbi Shneur Zalman outlines two basic models, or stages, of *teshuva*. The first level (*teshuva tataa*) is simply to refrain from sin. But the higher form of *teshuva* (*teshuva ilaa*) includes positive actions expressing love for the divine, which is then reciprocated by an arousal of love from God. He describes it thus:

> After the cleansing spirit passes over and purifies them [i.e., those who have sinned], then their souls are enabled to return unto God Himself, literally, to ascend the greatest heights, to their very source, and cleave to Him with a remarkable unity. This is the original unity, the ultimate in union, that existed before the soul was blown by the breath of His mouth to descend and be incorporated with the body of man.... This is the perfect return (*teshuva*).[36]

---

36. *Iggeret HaTeshuva*, ch. 8, fols. 98a–b.

The higher form of *teshuva* restores the unity of the soul to God, return-ing the element of the divine imbued within man to being in harmony with God. Indeed, as this passage goes on he cites a tradition that a penitent has some advantage over the perfect *tzaddik*, for his service is filled with a manifold longing for God, expressed in his desire to restore his intimacy with the divine.

In *Iggeret HaTeshuva* Rabbi Shneur Zalman once again describes a vision of careful balance between fostering the inner world and empha-sizing the power of physical deeds. The importance of the command-ments is highlighted throughout these chapters. One who sins and repents is certainly forgiven, but this cannot erase the missed oppor-tunity for bringing divine light into the worlds and into his soul. This underscores that deeds, as well as inaction, have lasting consequences beyond the simple categories of "transgression" or "atonement." Indeed, the final chapter of this section of *Tanya* concludes by underscoring the commandments' transformative power. Here we find Rabbi Shneur Zalman's interpretation of the blessing, "the One who has sanctified us with His commandments" (*asher kiddeshanu bemitzvotav*). We perform sacred deeds, says Rabbi Shneur Zalman, and God sanctifies us with an extra measure of holiness from "above." This is "the reward of a com-mandment is a commandment" – the flow of vital divine energy into the soul of the worshiper and the world itself is the greatest possible reward.

Part 4: *Iggeret HaKodesh*

The fourth section of Tanya is also composed of letters written by Rabbi Shneur Zalman over many years. Some are addressed to communities or particular individuals, and were included because they relate to matters of spiritual importance. The letters frequently refer to and expand upon other parts of *Tanya*. Some are excerpted from longer epistles, and most appear without dates or their addressees, which compels the reader to focus on their theological content rather than their historical context.

In these letters Rabbi Shneur Zalman repeatedly returns to the familiar theme of mystical prayer, but here we find him giving specific instructions about how to perform the services. Rabbi Shneur Zalman commands his followers to prevent individuals who must rush off to work from leading services, although anyone is allowed to lead the prayers on the Sabbath and Holidays. He openly informs his readers that he will send spies (*meragelim*) in order to see if they are conducting the services in line with his demands. Those who do not conform, Rabbi Shneur Zalman warns, will be punished by being distanced from his community. Obviously so much time is needed for prayer because of the great intensity, both emotional and intellectual, demanded by Rabbi Shneur Zalman's path.

The single most important theme throughout this section is the importance of *tzedaka* (alms). Rabbi Shneur Zalman has practical motivations for emphasizing this commandment, for he did not want his followers to be invested in the material. Giving *tzedaka* helps break attachment to the physical world, combating the craven natural instinct to hoard money. And of course, many of these letters were originally used to elicit funds for the hasidic communities of the Holy Land.

But distributing *tzedaka* is also a spiritual practice with cosmic implications. Helping the poor redeems the fallen divine sparks that have become trapped and literally impoverished in the material world. In one particularly moving formulation, Rabbi Shneur Zalman reminds his readers that the appearance of God and the experience of the divine in our own lives is an act of divine grace and metaphorical *tzedaka*.[37] Those who wish for a vision of the divine must therefore give alms, an act of *imitatio Dei* that reflects God's loving concern for man.

Giving *tzedaka* is a theological declaration, claims Rabbi Shneur Zalman, for sharing with others is the necessary moral outcome of belief in God and contemplation of His unity. Reciting the *Shema* and thus communing with the divine must be fulfilled through the spiritual-ethical mandate included therein: "And you will love Y-H-V-H your God ... with all your physical wealth" (Deut. 6:5) – cleave to God by aiding someone in need. This outpouring of human love then arouses God to express an extra measure of His love for man. This is a point he repeats with great frequency and vehemence: our compassion in this world inspires God's love and benevolence. This is the "reward" for any commandment – an effluence of bounty that manifests in different ways, including the material realm.

---

37. *Iggeret HaKodesh*, ch. 8, fol. 112b.

The act of giving alms transforms the mystic in a profound way. It brings about life, says Rabbi Shneur Zalman, not in the sense of literally prolonging one's days or averting a negative decree, but by eliciting forth a flow of new vitality from the Source of all life. We read:

> This is the meaning of "justice (*tzedek*) walks before Him" (Ps. 85:14). "Before him" (*lefanav*) is related to the word for "inwardness" (*penimiyut*), and "walks" (*yehalekh*) has a connotation of "bringing forth" (*holakha*). For it [i.e., *tzedek/tzedaka*] leads the innermost [element] of the heart to God, and then, "it sets his steps toward the way of Y-H-V-H," as it is written, "And you shall walk in His ways" (Deut. 28:9) ... with every performance of the commandments, and the study of Torah which is equivalent to them all. For they all ascend unto God through the inwardness of the heart with greater uplift, and exceedingly surpassing their ascent unto God through the externality of the heart, which is born of contemplation and knowledge alone, without an illumination of the face from above, but in a state of "concealment of the face." God's face (*panim*) only radiates downwards through an arousal from below, through the act of charity.[38]

Giving *tzedaka* highlights and cultivates the innermost nature of the Jewish soul, nurturing the innate love for God – and man – hidden within. It also directs one to walk a divine path, imitating the divine through the concrete act of sharing with others.

In *Iggeret HaKodesh* Rabbi Shneur Zalman also emphasizes the theological and social importance of humility, locating his discussion of this subject in these letters precisely because it is crucial for establishing community. Each person should become increasingly humble as he becomes more aware of the ever-present godly compassion. The closer one gets to the divine, the more his particular existence fades away in relation to the infinite expanse of God. Each seeker must also see his own identity as negated before his community, not raising himself above the beginners or depreciating himself below more advanced people.

---

38. Ibid., ch. 4, fols. 106a–b.

Humility is thus crucial to forging the bonds within the members' community so that it can serve God together as a single organic body. And, in the inverse, pride and the claim of exclusive self-identity is a form of idolatry, since the exercise of these traits suggests that there is something in the cosmos other than God. The Jewish people share a united origin in the divine, and one who looks at the different physical forms or identities cannot attain a true love for others grounded in the awareness of this enduring unity.

A few of the letters in *Iggeret HaKodesh* are addressed to specific individuals or refer to particular circumstances. In one such letter, written after the death in 1788 of Rabbi Menachem Mendel of Vitebsk, Rabbi Shneur Zalman explains why *tzaddikim* can still impact their communities after their death.[39] The presence of these great individuals remains a part of all those who were connected to them, because the lives of *tzaddikim* are purified and spiritualized through their total devotion to God. In fact, such people are no longer constricted by the physical world after death, and therefore their ability to give energy and inspiration to their students is unbounded.

Another of Rabbi Shneur Zalman's key letters explores the limits of free choice. The existence of free will is fundamental to the entire notion of the *beinoni*. One cannot choose to be a *tzaddik*, but the world (and the self) are full of a spiritual darkness that must be transformed through the positive actions of the *beinoni* as well as those of the *tzaddik*. However, in this letter Rabbi Shneur Zalman suggests a sweeping definition of divine providence in which nothing inherently negative comes from God, since the same sacred energy is included in all things and events. Everything must happen for a reason, even if it is not externally visible, and therefore we must have faith that Hasidism's theological fulcrum, "there is no place devoid of God," applies equally to sad and even tragic moments. One must never become depressed or angry, but rather have gratitude for his existence and the divine breath that courses through him. We are

---

39. Ibid., ch. 27, fols. 145b–147b. Similar themes appear in a letter addressed to Rabbi Levi Yitzchak of Berdichev after the death of the latter's son; see ibid., ch. 28, fol. 147b.

called to see the world with total equanimity, making no intrinsic distinction between good and bad. Our faith in this truth actually transforms the negative into positive by revealing the divinity held within all events or objects. Rabbi Shneur Zalman claims that many thinkers deny absolute providence and the possibility of miracles because they erroneously assume that God is separate from the world in the way that a human craftsman is distinguished from his works. Because God's language and divine energy remain forever within the created world, argues Rabbi Shneur Zalman, miracles are possible and providence is assured.

RECEPTION AND CONTROVERSY

Tanya was an immensely popular book, and it was frequently reprinted in the decades after its initial publication. For obvious reasons it quickly became a central religious text for Rabbi Shneur Zalman's followers, but *Tanya* also had a significant impact on the development of hasidic thought throughout White Russia and Poland. The influence of Rabbi Shneur Zalman extended to hasidic circles beyond the Chabad community both geographically and conceptually, a phenomenon that continues to the present day.

What accounts for the popularity of *Tanya*? It is not a simple book, and it assumes either a firm base in Kabbala or a good teacher (or perhaps both). Its popularity may come from the conceptual clarity, its vision and fearlessness, and the systematic manner in which the author lays out his arguments and description of the spirit, all of which set *Tanya* apart from other hasidic books of the 1780s and 1790s. *Tanya* is a powerful book that presents the author's theology with absolute confidence to scholars and seekers alike, for it includes lengthy discussions of the importance of Torah study as well as intellectual and emotive meditation. It is a deeply empowering work, for it translates the terminology of Lurianic Kabbala into a holistic psychological and spiritual system in which all deeds – and every moment – are opportunities for serving God. But *Tanya*'s popularity may also have been bolstered by a tempting element of Jewish triumphalism, manifest as an optimistic view of the latent potential of all Jews and underscored by the spiritual lack of all other peoples.

Not every chapter in the reception of *Tanya* has been sunny, and aspects of Rabbi Shneur Zalman's work were controversial from the moment it was printed. One of its early critics was Rabbi Abraham of Kalisk (d. 1810), a fellow student of the Maggid, who moved to the Land of Israel together with Rabbi Menachem Mendel of Vitebsk. Rabbi Abraham had once been a dear friend of Rabbi Shneur Zalman, but their relationship eroded into a series of controversies in the 1790s and the first decades of the nineteenth century. One issue between them involved the funds raised for the hasidic community in the Holy Land, a task with which Rabbi Shneur Zalman had been charged. But part of their disagreement is grounded in Rabbi Abraham's disapproval of Rabbi Shneur Zalman's style of leadership in setting up such a large, regimented court, which he saw as a departure from the model set by their teachers. Rabbi Abraham was also displeased with the extent to which Rabbi Shneur Zalman incorporated Lurianic Kabbala into *Tanya*, and he felt that the privileging of intellectual meditation rather than contemplative faith and transforming the emotive *middot* was similarly far afield from the path of the earlier hasidic masters.

Rabbi Abraham was not necessarily wrong in voicing his discontent with *Tanya* because of its discontinuity with other hasidic thinkers. *Tanya* is profoundly different from many other hasidic books, even those by fellow students of the Maggid, and Rabbi Shneur Zalman developed his teacher's theology in complicated and unique ways. Not only does *Tanya* stand apart from other hasidic works in terms of its distinctive structure and relative prolixity, it is also distinguished from its counterparts in theological and devotional areas such as the draconian vision of sin; the immutable, fixed, and natural identity of the *tzaddik*; the concentration on the intellectual faculties above and beyond the other elements of the soul; a tendency toward outward asceticism and denial of this-worldly things; and the absolute centrality of study – especially of legal subjects.

We noted above that Rabbi Shneur Zalman was actively involved in the debates and polemics with the *mitnagdim*. Many of these disagreements were sociological in nature, but their controversy held theological aspects as well. It is thus quite interesting that *Tanya* may have had an impact on the writings of Rabbi Chaim of Volozhin (1749–1821), one of the great Lithuanian thinkers and student of the Gaon of Vilna. The similarities between the descriptions of *tzimtzum* in the works of Rabbi Shneur Zalman and Rabbi Chaim are striking, and it has been suggested that the latter's *Nefesh HaHayim* is a response to hasidic theology, and Rabbi Shneur Zalman's thought in particular, but this is a matter of considerable debate.[40] Rabbi Shneur Zalman himself suggests that the correct interpretation of *tzimtzum* stands between the Hasidim and *mitnagdim*:

> In the light of what has been said above it is possible to understand the error of some, scholars in their own eyes, may God forgive them, who erred and misinterpreted in their study of the writings of the Ari, of blessed memory, and understood the doctrine of *tzimtzum*, which is mentioned therein, literally (*kifeshuto*) – that the blessed Holy One removed Himself and His essence, God forbid, from this world, and only guides from above, with individual providence.[41]

Rabbi Shneur Zalman attacks the "scholars," clearly a reference to the *mitnagdim*, on the basis of canonical texts claiming that God's immanent presence in the worlds is unchanging, a point that is a cornerstone of his theology. But he also attacks their position on rational grounds, arguing that to describe the divine as removed from the world paradoxically attributes a corporeal trait to God, namely that God can become divested from the world and thus occupies something akin to a temporal realm.

MODERN RECEPTION AND CONTEMPORARY RELEVANCE

The centrality of *Tanya* in the Chabad community is unchallenged. This book includes the foundations for so many of the ideas at the heart of modern Chabad life, such as love for other Jews, outreach, encouraging non-religious people to perform commandments, and a subtle – but

---

40. See Norman Lamm, *Torah Lishmah: Torah for Torah's Sake in the Works of Rabbi Hayyim of Volozhin and His Contemporaries* (New York, 1989), esp. 65–73, 99; Tamar Ross, "Rav Chaim of Volozhin and Rav Shneur Zalman of Liady: Two Interpretations of the Doctrine of *Tzimtzum*" [Hebrew], *Jerusalem Studies in Jewish Thought* 2 (1982), 153–169.
41. *Shaar HaYihud VeHaEmuna*, ch. 7, fols. 83a–b.

powerful – messianic vision. Chabad Hasidim view *Tanya* as a sacred book, and the huge number of editions printed across the world bear witness to its importance as a ritual object as well as a central theological text. Chabad has conducted one of the most successful outreach campaigns in Jewish history, and much of this has been fueled by the spiritual vision of *Tanya*. Eventually, this book was divided into a regimen of daily study to be completed over the course of the year, beginning and ending on the nineteenth of Kislev, the anniversary of the Maggid's death and the day on which Rabbi Shneur Zalman was released from prison.

Some contemporary Jewish thinkers have been impressed by *Tanya*'s clarity and conviction.[42] There are, however, at least three elements of *Tanya* that are particularly complicated and even problematic for modern readers. These issues must be frankly addressed if we are to find *Tanya*'s relevant voice for the twenty-first-century Jewish world.

The first obstacle is the presence of what appears to be a dated scientific and weighty medieval metaphysical system. The humors, the four elements, an anthropocentric universe, and especially the vastly complicated Lurianic cosmogony are all integral parts of the worldview. These can be confusing and even jarring to the modern reader, and it is quite problematic to interpret them as scientific facts, though there is no reason to assume that Rabbi Shneur Zalman would demand this of us.

The second issue is *Tanya*'s unwavering pro-Jewish and equally strong anti-gentile sentiments, which drift very close to xenophobia and perhaps even outright racism. While contextually understandable in the

---

42. It is often cited that Rabbi Joseph B. Soloveitchik (1903–1993) was exposed to *Tanya* in his childhood and continued to hold the work in high esteem. On the impact of Chabad upon his thought, see Elliot R. Wolfson, "Eternal Duration and Temporal Compresence: The Influence of Habad on Joseph B. Soloveitchik," in *The Value of the Particular: Lessons from Judaism and the Modern Jewish Experience – Festschrift for Steven T. Katz on the Occasion of His Seventieth Birthday*, ed. Michael Zank and Ingrid Anderson (Leiden, 2015), 195–238; and Miller, *Turning Judaism Outward*, 90–91 and fn. See also Yehudah Mirsky, *Rav Kook: Mystic in a Time of Revolution* (New Haven, 2014), 9–11, 220.

late eighteenth century, these attitudes are problematic in a world in which our relationships with non-Jews have moved beyond the medieval stigmas held by both parties. Where there is still anti-Semitic stereotyping in the world we condemn it as backward, and surely do not want to be guilty of the same. Notions of Jewish supremacy, which form a direct line from Rabbi Judah Halevi to Maharal and eventually to *Tanya*, are even more dangerous in a world where Jews have returned to power and must once more learn to wield it over others. It is not uncommon to see passages from *Tanya* and other such works sadly mobilized by extremists – most of whom are outside the core Chabad community – in an attempt to prove the inhumanity of the contemporary enemies of the Jewish people.

The final troublesome element is the inflexible model of the *tzaddik*, who is portrayed as qualitatively different from all other human beings. His (and for the author of *Tanya*, the *tzaddik* must always be a man) fate is determined by his conception and birth, and he will reach a spiritual level beyond the reach of even the most hard-working *beinoni*. Jewish modernity has included an awareness of the power of the individual and indeed a turn toward individualism, in terms of freedom, social mobility, and choices. Many contemporary Jews feel alienated from a religious system in which their spiritual growth is capped by a rigid caste system.

A reader may struggle with, reinterpret, and perhaps even reject these issues, but they cannot be elided. Given these difficulties, what does *Tanya* have to offer the broader Jewish world? Here I would like to highlight five foundational themes of this work that are of great relevance to the contemporary readers of *Tanya*. The first of these is Rabbi Shneur Zalman's unflagging focus on the importance of inwardness (*penimiyut*). This spiritual intensity must be expressed through concrete deeds, but he never allows for what is often called "orthopraxy" – religious commitment defined by action alone. For Rabbi Shneur Zalman, spiritual practice is an embodiment of theology; the deeds we perform, whether ritual, interpersonal, or ethical, reflect our spiritual center. He demands that his readers cultivate their inner worlds, understanding that awe and love for God are the axioms of uplift to the divine. This emotional work is grounded in intellectual contemplation of God, but even so it never privileges dry reason over the importance of faith. The divine unity may be experienced and witnessed, but it cannot ever be fully known or spoken aloud.

A second theme found throughout *Tanya* is the profound sense of religious obligation. This includes our duty to perform the commandments as defined by the halakha, but it also entails the constant inner work and regular spiritual development. The war against apathy and complacency is a difficult one indeed, and it must be fought on two fronts. One such battle is waged against the assumption that simply following God's commandments is enough, and the other is the struggle to rein in our desires for illuminated religious experiences without the hard regular work. Truly elevated spirituality, argues Rabbi Shneur Zalman, is a very difficult thing to achieve, and it cannot be attained without constant effort to effect inner transformation that is expressed through sacred deeds.

There is a positive aspect to *Tanya's* complicated metaphysical theology, which I believe is a third point of contemporary relevance. Rabbi Shneur Zalman's work provides a relatively approachable access point to the intricate symbolic language of Kabbala as refracted through the devotionally oriented hasidic lens. Furthermore, there is a very simple truth hiding within Rabbi Shneur Zalman's subtle and nuanced language: there is no existence other than God. All being is an aspect of the divine, and together with the cosmos itself we constitute a finite expression of the ineffable God.

A fourth idea, emerging from the third, is that Rabbi Shneur Zalman's theological vision generates an action-oriented life of service and devotional activism. Each of our deeds has the capacity to increase the divine light in the world, bringing the project of Creation one step closer to its telos of redemption. Rabbi Shneur Zalman's stirring descriptions of the power of *tzedaka* and kindness toward other Jews are unforgettable, and they have become one of the well-known hallmarks of contemporary Chabad. Rabbi Shneur Zalman's theological system is mystical to its very core, but his spirituality demands positive change in the world. Taking this paradigm one step further, David Seidenberg has recently argued that Rabbi Shneur Zalman's theology may be read as mandating environmental activism, since humanity has an obligation to protect the divine energy embodied in all elements of the material realm, including all forms of life and the natural world.[43]

Finally, regarding Rabbi Shneur Zalman's metaphysical assumptions about cosmology and the nature of the Jewish soul vis-à-vis that of non-Jews, there is a more universal message that must be extrapolated from *Tanya*. Here I argue that Rabbi Shneur Zalman's description of a natural capacity for love, an inborn spiritual faculty for altruism and self-transcendence, should be extended to all mankind and thus interpreted as an element of the human condition. This innate spiritual faculty in all people that manifests itself as the heartfelt quest for the divine, in theologies that call for moral courage, and, most broadly, in our ability to rise beyond the constraints of the ego and reach for the infinite, can be fostered through education or awoken through modes of contemplative awareness. We cannot fault Maimonides for the ways in which he was limited to an Aristotelian and geocentric universe. The writings of the Great Eagle are still compelling, powerful, wise, insightful, and profound in the modern era even as we shed some of his intellectual commitments in the process. This is true for all truly great thinkers, a category into which Rabbi Shneur Zalman of Liady must surely be placed. This type of reception history is a hermeneutical moment, and it requires that we emphasize such voices in *Tanya* over many others. But as contemporary readers of hasidic texts we are entitled, and indeed even obligated, to make precisely this sort of careful interpretive move.[44]

CONCLUSION

This thematic overview of *Tanya* has prepared us to ask an important meta-question: *Why* was the book written? Rabbi Shneur Zalman informs his readers that he was overwhelmed and too busy to attend to the crushing numbers of adherents and disciples who sought his counsel. He therefore wrote *Tanya* to replace personal audiences, trusting his Hasidim and their local teachers to further their spiritual journeys

---

43. See David Mevorach Seidenberg, *Kabbalah and Ecology: God's Image in the More-Than-Human World* (New York, 2015).
44. My thanks to Professor Polen for his help in formulating this essential point.

by absorbing his wisdom through the written word. Rabbi Shneur Zalman was also discontent with the imprecise copies already in circulation, and by printing *Tanya* he hoped to ensure the canonical status of his version of these texts.

Lurking behind the question of whether a book can truly replace a powerful and inspiring leader is an even deeper issue: Can the deepest spiritual truths be expressed through the medium of language whether spoken or written? The answer to both of these questions given by the leadership of Chabad, beginning with Rabbi Shneur Zalman, has always been resoundingly affirmative. Rabbi Shneur Zalman was one of the first hasidic masters to author a book in the proper sense of the term. Early Hasidism was primarily an oral movement, and teachings were transmitted by master to disciple (and from student to student) through the spoken word. But Rabbi Shneur Zalman clearly believed in the power of the written word to effect change and spiritual transformation within a reader.

But *Tanya* also represents the linguistic hybridity of early Hasidism, which was neither exclusively oral nor textual. *Tanya* was being taught by living teachers even within the author's lifetime. While it may have served as a substitute for Rabbi Shneur Zalman's personal instruction, it did not replace the spiritual community which studied its wisdom as a sacred text. Close disciples were meant to share their understanding of its content with others, thus establishing a network of associated groups all poring over its words and seeking its wisdom in the context of other Hasidim. This text was, in short, poised to become the sacred writ of Hasidism.

Nehemia Polen has argued convincingly that, "the initial purpose of *Tanya* was not the promulgation of mystical doctrines, much less the teaching of mystical techniques or practices, but the stratification and regimentation of the hasidic community and the assignment of appropriate roles."[45] Rabbi Shneur Zalman warns his readers that they should not deprecate their worth by thinking they are wicked, thereby pessimistically obfuscating their duty for inner growth, but nor should

---

45. Polen, "Charismatic Leader, Charismatic Book," 62.

they deceive themselves into thinking that they are *tzaddikim* and thus forgetting their place.[46]

However, changing the emphasis of this argument significantly alters the way that one approaches *Tanya*. It is not a treatise about the spiritual powers of the *tzaddik* meant to awe the humble *beinoni* into living his religious life by proxy, attaching himself to the *tzaddik* and attaining spiritual uplift through him alone. Time and time again, Rabbi Shneur Zalman emphasizes that everyone can, and should, become a *beinoni*. *Tanya* clarifies the differences between the ordinary seeker (the ḥasid who aspires to become a *beinoni*) and the extraordinary leader (the *tzaddik*), but it primarily addresses the spiritual work of the former. The superabundance of kabbalistic terminology in a book written for the *beinoni* means that Rabbi Shneur Zalman wants these concepts to become their spiritual vocabulary as well, not simply remaining the privilege of the elite. Finally, *Sefer Shel Beinonim* concludes with an exhortation to deed, underscoring that the *beinonim* have the great power in transforming darkness into light through their sacred actions. Rabbi Shneur Zalman repeats this point over and over again: each and every person who follows in his path must walk their own path.

Let us close our study of *Tanya* by noting that Rabbi Shneur Zalman, like so many Jewish mystics over the generations, reveals little about his own mystical experiences. The reader may sense Rabbi Shneur Zalman's spiritual life between the lines of *Tanya*, for surely there is a first-person voice hiding within his descriptions of the ecstatic love born of the *tzaddik*'s contemplation of God. But our understanding of this great leader and mystic is rounded out by stories and family traditions, some of which deal more explicitly with Rabbi Shneur Zalman's private spiritual quest. A particularly stirring example appears at the end of *HaYom Yom*, a Chabad calendar for daily study compiled by the seventh Lubavitcher Rebbe:

> Love of the type [found in the verse] "and beside You I want nothing [upon the earth]" (Ps. 73:25) means having no desire for anything except God. Not even heaven and earth, which are the

---

46. *Sefer Shel Beinonim*, ch. 13, fol. 18a.

upper and lower Gardens of Eden, for these were created with only the [letter] *yod*. One's love should be for God alone, for His very Being and Essence. This was expressed by my teacher and master (the *Alter Rebbe*, [Rabbi Shneur Zalman]) during his *devekut*, for he used to say as follows:[47] "I want nothing at all. I don't want Your Garden of Eden, I don't want Your World to Come. I want nothing more than You alone."[48]

FURTHER READING

Tanya has been reprinted countless times in locations across the world. The text and pagination of these myriad editions generally follow the Vilna 1900 printing, though a different edition based on a manuscript was recently published as *Likutei Amarim: Mahadura Kamma* (Brooklyn, 1982). The standard English version is *Likutei Amarim-Tanya, Bilingual Edition*, revised edition, translated by Nissan Mindel, with introductions by Nisen Mangel, Zalman I. Posner, and Jacob Immanuel Schochet (Brooklyn, 1998). The annotations, explanations, glossary, and various introductions included in this volume are tremendously helpful. Yosef Wineberg's *Lessons in Tanya: The Tanya of R. Shneur Zalman of Liadi*, 5 vols. (Brooklyn, 1987–1993), is a comprehensive explanation of the text from the traditional Chabad perspective.

The noted scholar Rabbi Adin Steinsaltz has produced a three-volume commentary to *Tanya* in English: *Opening the Tanya: Discovering the Moral and Mystical Teachings of a Classic Work of Kabbalah* (San Francisco, 2003); *Learning From the Tanya: Volume Two in the Definitive Commentary on the Moral and Mystical Teachings of a Classic Work of Kabbalah* (San Francisco, 2005); *Understanding the Tanya: Volume Three in the Definitive Commentary on a Classic Work of Kabbalah by the World's Foremost Authority* (San Francisco, 2007). The Hebrew reader is invited to turn to his more expansive *Biur Tanya*, 9 vols. (Jerusalem, 2012), a wonderfully rich commentary. Steinsaltz's teachings on *Tanya*

---

47. At this point the text switches from Hebrew into Yiddish, noting a shift from the language of scholarship to the language of the heart.
48. *HaYom Yom*, 18 Kislev.

are informed by Chabad, but are highly creative and display modern sensitivity to many of the issues that arise from the text.

The recent volume *Tanya, the Masterpiece of Hasidic Wisdom: Selections Annotated and Explained*, translation and commentary by Rami Shapiro, foreword by Zalman M. Schachter-Shalomi (Woodstock, 2010), offers an excellent survey of the key passages in *Tanya* aimed at the non-expert reader. The excerpts presented in this highly accessible English translation have been arranged in a poetic-line formation, emphasizing the devotional rhythms of *Tanya* that are sometimes lost in the work's complexity. All translations are accompanied by useful citations and illuminating explanatory notes. Finally, classes on and about *Tanya* are given by nearly all Chabad-Lubavitch centers across the globe. Many of these lessons, as well as those broadcast by the international Chabad headquarters (http://www.chabad.org/library/tanya/), are made available online in both audio and video formats.

On Rabbi Shneur Zalman's life and the religious thought of early Chabad, see Immanuel Etkes, *Rabbi Shneur Zalman of Liady: The Origins of Chabad Hasidism* (Waltham, 2015); Rachel Elior, *The Paradoxical Ascent to God: The Kabbalistic Theosophy of Habad Hasidism*, trans. Jeffrey M. Green (Albany, 1993); Naftali Loewental, *Communicating the Infinite: The Emergence of the Habad School* (Chicago, 1990); Roman A. Foxbrunner, *Habad: The Hasidism of R. Shneur Zalman of Lyady* (Tuscaloosa, 1992); Nehemia Polen, "Charismatic Leader, Charismatic Book: Rabbi Shneur Zalman's *Tanya* and His Leadership," in *Rabbinic and Lay Communal Authority*, ed. Suzanne Last Stone (New York, 2006), 53–64; Elliot R. Wolfson, *Open Secret: Postmessianic Messianism and the Mystical Revision of Menahem Mendel Schneerson* (New York, 2009).

The *Mayses* of Rabbi Nachman of Bratslav: What Makes a Hasidic Tale?

Dr. Jeremy Dauber

Ln the middle years of the first decade of the nineteenth century, the spiritual leader of a small community of Ukrainian Hasidim attempted to do something no less audacious than to force the heavenly hand and to bring about the messianic redemption. Nachman of Bratslav's failure in the task he had spent his life preparing for, and the disappointment and despair that followed in its wake, was transformed into a remarkable creative success: though he had previously composed theological and philosophical tracts, it was then that he began to tell the profound tales of struggle and of hope which assured him a place in the canon not only of spiritual leaders, but of literary masters.

Nachman ben Simcha was born into a family of great hasidic lineage, the movement's recency notwithstanding: he was the great-grandson of the Baal Shem Tov (Besht) on his mother's side, and the grandson of Rabbi Nachman of Horodenka, an important member of the Besht's circle, on his father's. The fact that he was born in Medzhybizh, the Besht's hometown, only accentuated his proximity to the movement's center – and the attention paid to him as a result.

Though the materials surrounding Nachman's childhood are fragmentary and generally hagiographic in nature, it's probably the case that despite a seemingly placid and happy exterior, Nachman was a sensitive child, given to acts of asceticism. It makes sense: given his family heritage, and the role genealogy was increasingly playing in the hasidic movement as a signal of incipient holiness and capacity for leadership, he was almost certainly constantly concerned about whether his youthful and adolescent struggles with doubt and sinful sentiment implied that he was unworthy of such a position, or characterization. The resulting struggles between pride and humility would later help shape many of Nachman's philosophical and literary efforts, the *Tales* very much among them. Such a unique, perhaps alienating, position also led to a sensibility which prized independence and a strong sense of the necessity for keeping close personal counsel; Nachman's later attraction to hidden messages, allegory, and deep secrets may have stemmed from this period.

Although most hagiographic accounts of Jewish rabbinic leaders feature displays of childhood genius, Nachman seems by general account to have been an undistinguished student. His education, which focused both on traditional texts such as the Talmud and the legal codices, and the mystical and kabbalistic literature which had been newly reemphasized in the hasidic movement, was noteworthy only in Nachman's interest in and familiarity with the Bible, then not a widely studied text among Jewish elites. Nachman's particular interest in the Book of Psalms complemented his dissatisfaction with the standard liturgy; and to try to express what he felt were his own uncategorizable feelings and situations, he composed his own prayers in Yiddish. Generally speaking, Yiddish prayer, in the form of *techines*, was located firmly within the women's sphere, so this was quite unusual; and, perhaps, it paved the way for later form-shattering literary experiments in that language.

Nachman married shortly after his bar mitzva; the conventions of the arranged marriage – and Nachman's lineage – meant he could make an excellent match, which, in that time and place, meant a woman from a wealthy family. Sosia was the daughter of a wealthy tax farmer from Usyatin, a village two hundred miles east of Medzhybizh. As was also customary, the couple began their married life at the bride's father's house; and the distance from the organized Jewish community and Nachman's hasidic family allowed the young man to commune with God in pastoral settings and indulge his sense of loneliness. In this isolated setting, Nachman's studies became more serious and his ascetic tendencies, never strongly encouraged in Medzhybizh, became more pronounced, growing to include acts of self-mortification and long periods of fasting.

Some of this change may have resulted from Nachman's increasing sexual awareness and the sense of sinfulness those sexual feelings almost certainly provoked. Though Nachman was eventually to pronounce himself the victor in the battle over sexual temptation, it is clear that similar concerns would occupy him for the rest of his life – and, perhaps, serve as the catalyst for much of his philosophical development, particularly the idea that the magnitude of the struggle was the truest proof of one's greatness as an individual.

Nachman left his father-in-law's house when he was around eighteen, and moved to the nearby town of Medvedevka. Though Nachman had previously been extremely ambivalent about taking a public role as a spiritual leader – perhaps because of the same spirit of doubt of his own self-worth – when the substantial dowry he'd received from his father-in-law ran out, he agreed to serve as the Medvedevka area's hasidic rebbe. Befitting his unconventional nature, he was an unconventional rebbe: many of his newly and loudly articulated ideas – including a de-emphasis on hasidic gatherings, his often abrupt dismissal of petitioners, and his preference for sincere gifts by the poor over large sums of money by wealthier supporters, to say nothing of his denunciation of "false" hasidic leaders who lacked the moral or spiritual qualifications for true leadership – left other rabbis decades older than he nettled, at best, and often irate.

Given Nachman's own struggles with self-doubt, it seems clear not all of Nachman's critiques were aimed only outward. That's even clearer from the aphorisms he began to write around that time, work that would become the alphabetical list of *Sefer HaMiddot*. Like almost all of Nachman's teachings, *Sefer HaMiddot* was edited by other hands and published posthumously, but it still provides an interesting window into Nachman's thought at an early period in his adult life. Nachman's preoccupations are certainly on display: the work is filled with concerns about sexual sin, both in thought and in deed, and inveighs against the false spiritual leader and delves into the requirements for the true leader. (It was pretty clear who Nachman thought the true leader was; and his transparent belief that he was, by far, the superior hasidic rabbi of his generation at such a young age didn't endear him to the hasidic leadership any further.) But Nachman wasn't a total philosophical rebel: much of the work remains connected to and continuous with the thought of other hasidic leaders, most notably the Besht.

The one subject treated deeply and originally in the book concerns faith, which will come to occupy the central place in Nachman's theology. Nachman's assertion of faith's importance seemingly stems from both his recognition of the existence of doubt even among the righteous; and his elevation of overcoming that doubt, and finding faith in and reconciliation with a seemingly distant and even absent God, into a grand, mythic struggle which is the most, perhaps the only, important task of the individual in general and the spiritual leader in particular. A related idea treated in Nachman's thought, the mystical notion that the leader might even need to enter into the depths of impurity to eventually reach the greatest heights, is certainly valuable in understanding the capacious empathy and understanding that has to, in its own way, characterize the greatest literature and fiction. It also helps to explain some of Nachman's next seemingly puzzling actions.

In 1798, when Nachman was twenty-six, he and his close friend and disciple Simeon ben Baer traveled to the Land of Israel. Such a trip, aside from any personal importance, had deep mystical and spiritual significance for Nachman. A number of hasidic leaders had previously taken such trips, including Nachman of Horodenka, Nachman's grandfather, who had settled there in 1764. The Besht himself had, famously, attempted to journey there, but had never completed the trip, for mysterious reasons, which remain the subject of much speculation. Nachman claimed that he went to visit his grandfather's grave, perhaps to receive mystical instruction. A clue to his other motives may have come in a preceding trip, both chronologically and conceptually speaking, to Kamenets-Podolsk, a city in the Ukraine, in the spring of 1798. The city was the former home of many leaders of the false messianic movement known as Frankism, and some have suggested that Nachman intended both to mystically purify the city of its sinful nature while simultaneously lowering himself into impurity in order to prepare the way for his eventual rise with his arrival in the Holy Land – perhaps, even, to take his place not only as a major hasidic leader, but something even more, mystically speaking.

Nachman and Simeon set out on their journey in May 1798, traveling from Medvedevka to Odessa, where they traveled by ship to Constantinople (Istanbul today). There, Nachman engaged in strange, childish behavior, annoying his companions and acquaintances and eliciting insults. This was, apparently, in order to exacerbate his state of degradation, in preparation for his elevation upon his arrival in the Land of Israel. Though Napoleon's invasion of Egypt had elicited a ban by Constantinople's Jewish community against any further pilgrimages to the Holy Land, Nachman refused to abide by the ban, and was reluctantly granted permission to sail for Jaffa. Though a storm threatened to capsize their boat, and Jaffa port officials refused to let him off the ship, seemingly worried that he was a spy, he eventually disembarked in Haifa on the day before Rosh HaShana of 1798. He spent the winter of 1798–1799 in and around Tiberias with the local Hasidim and their rabbi, Abraham Kalisker, and visited several holy places in the Galilee, including the gravesite of Shimon bar Yoḥai, at that time believed to be the creator of the Zohar, the most important work of Jewish mysticism (revealed by later scholarship to be the creation of the thirteenth-century Rabbi Moses de León).

With Napoleon's capture of the coast of Palestine and his impending siege of the port of Acre, Nachman and Simeon decided to return home immediately. They left, only to find themselves for all intents and purposes captives on a Turkish warship which first became engaged in a naval battle and then weathered a terrible storm. The ship landed at Rhodes; the local Jewish community ransomed the captives; and, after several other adventures, Nachman and Simeon returned to Medvedevka in the summer of 1799, about a year after they had set out.

Nachman's grand journey foreshadows the journeys that many of the protagonists of his stories will take in order to achieve their own goals – and certainly it gave him a perspective on adventure more common to the protagonists of the tales he tells than the conventional image of a spiritual leader might suggest. But far more importantly for Nachman – and for us – the journey was not merely adventurous but was perceived as an adventure, a journey, by the man himself for a specific reason and resulted in a specific prize: greater spiritual purity and deeper mystical understanding, as well as the opportunity to have communed with spirits Nachman believed to have managed to emerge victorious against the struggles of physical temptation that he himself continued to suffer. As will become clear, Nachman's tales are all allegories; and his self-consciousness about his own actions as symbolically meaningful and narratively significant means that he will be able to cast himself and his biographical experiences as central to a grand narrative – one no less grand, indeed, than that of all of human history as well as no less deep than the essential struggle of the human soul.

Nachman's successful return from his journey seems to have given him the confidence to become even more assertive in his claims as a major hasidic leader in Eastern Europe and particularly in Ukraine. By the year of Nachman's birth, 1772, Hasidism had sufficiently spread to occasion bans against its practice by conservative, traditionalist opponents, who became known as the *mitnagdim*; by the beginning of the nineteenth century, though, the Besht's original disciples had already generated disciples (and followers) of their own, and Hasidism had spread so broadly that opposition seemed to be futile. (Additionally, the hasidic movement had proven to be sufficiently conservative, in terms of its theologies and particularly its observances, to put to rest the specter of antinomianism that had originally animated its opponents.) Hasidism's spread, however, had also led to factionalism and power struggles within the hasidic community, and Nachman, upon his return, placed himself squarely in the middle of the arena, attempting to mediate between different hasidic rabbis, then starting a quarrel of his own.

The latter began in August 1800 with his move to Zlotopolye, still in eastern Ukraine but clearly violating the territorial authority of the local hasidic rabbi, Aryeh Leib of Shpole, known as the Shpoler Zeyde (Grandfather) because of his advanced age and his personal relationship with the now long-deceased Besht. Was Nachman's decision to take on the Zeyde as simple as a member of the younger generation pushing back against the old guard? A young revolutionary seeking to maintain the rebellious spirit of what had once been a protest movement against a representative of its rapid institutionalization, its ossification into more staid and conservative patterns? Or was there something more, something central to Nachman's increasingly grand sense of self, mission, and destiny? Scholars have never been able to definitively determine Nachman's reasoning; but it was probably – at least to some extent – strongly related to his thinking about his own greatness and unique nature.

Remember that for Nachman such greatness is defined by the quality of one's struggle: the constant alternation between pride and humility, between faith and doubt, both in one's God and in oneself. Given Nachman's own tendency to see parallels, and not just in metaphorical terms, between those struggles and the ones the righteous individual, the *tzaddik* (in both the moral sense and in its definition as a hasidic leader), encounters in the outside world, his progress can serve as a vindication of Nachman's true fitness for the role for which he has been destined. In other words, Nachman's role in creating and exacerbating struggle with other hasidic leaders isn't just a political search for the expansion of power and influence: it's a metaphysical necessity.

Of course, others didn't necessarily see it that way, and the Zeyde became a dedicated opponent, publicly denouncing Nachman and eventually attempting, in the summer of 1802, to acquire letters of denunciation against Nachman, perhaps with the aim of issuing a ban of excommunication against him. Among his charges, it seems, was the suggestion that Nachman's teachings contained traces of Frankism or Sabbateanism, another noted false messianic movement. (Given the increasingly messianic bent of Nachman's own self-perceptions, as well as his increasingly vocal and public statements about his own superiority to other *tzaddikim*, past and present – it was around this time that he said he was greater in stature than the Besht – perhaps this wasn't an entirely ridiculous charge.) Although the noted hasidic rabbi Levi Yitzchak of Berdichev managed to mediate between the two, and Nachman did leave Zlotopolye in the late summer of 1802, the Zeyde would remain hostile – as would his uncle, the hasidic rabbi Barukh of Medzhybizh, who may have been jealous of Nachman's growing success at attracting disciples at his expense. But the departure would lead to Nachman settling in the town of Bratslav, where he would remain for most of the rest of his life.

In the summer of 1802, around that same time, a man named Nathan Sternhartz joined Nachman's circle, and rapidly began to serve as his scribe and literary secretary. Sternhartz would serve as the editor and literary executor of most of Nachman's posthumously published works, and was intimately involved in taking down Nachman's theological teachings of the period, many of which were published in the *Likutei Moharan*. A brief discussion of them – particularly their complicated connections with his person, both as general *tzaddik* and as individual teacher and thinker – may help us make sense of Nachman's increasingly messianic statements, the controversy they engendered, and their effect on the rest of Nachman's life and literary production.

Building on the kabbalistic system articulated most famously by the sixteenth-century Jewish kabbalist Rabbi Isaac Luria, Nachman believed that the divine *Ein Sof*, the Infinite, out of a desire to display its nature of mercy, created the world, doing so by a process of retracting into itself called *tzimtzum* (retraction). The created world exists within the vacuum formed by the *Ein Sof*'s withdrawal – a fact which may help to explain the feeling that the Divine Presence is absent from the world; thus, generating the sense of doubt so pervasive in Nachman's own personal life. In this cosmology, though, this feeling of divine absence is neither the result of personal moral weakness or philosophical investigation: it is, instead, a deep and profound reflection of metaphysical reality.

Which is not to say that the Divine is entirely absent from Nachman's world. As the result of a catastrophic event known as the "breaking of the vessels" (*shevirat hakelim*), some sparks of the Divine Presence have made their way into the world, there to be covered by *kelipot* (husks or shells) of earthiness and materiality and thus to remain separated from the general Godhead. These husk-covered sparks exist in both the physical world (that is, objects and actions which are generally considered to be secular or earthy have holiness within them) and in the abstract world of speech and thought (secular ideas and even doubts bear within them the seed of holiness).

The job of the individual, then, is to remove the husks by engaging in a process of investing the everyday with holiness, a process called *tikkun* (correction or redemption). The object or thought so elevated – or, more properly, the spark of divinity within it so liberated – is then able to reunite with the Godhead. This paradoxical approach – of engaging in and with the secular, the everyday, even the degraded, in order to elevate both the actions and things engaged with and, in the process, oneself – is essential to understanding Nachman's seemingly strange and paradoxical behavior. It also accounts for the central role of faith and doubt in Nachman's theology: the concept of faith breaking free and rising out of the shell of doubt which imprisons it, elevating the believer to a perceived union with God when before all that was felt was absence, accords entirely with Nachman's metaphysical picture of the universe, his own personal feelings of alienation and doubt, and his desire for union with God.

This not only explains the important role of *hitbodedut* (private daily conversation with God) in Bratslav Hasidism, a practice which fit well with Nachman's own personal tendencies; it allows Nachman to elevate his struggles – both internal and external – to episodes in the never-ending struggle to achieve *tikkun*, a struggle in which faith plays a central role. Though questions of faith are firstly addressed in terms of the individual's faith in God, they're also expanded by Nachman to apply to faith in the *tzaddik* and, particularly, in himself. In part, this is because sometimes faith is necessary to accept the *tzaddik's* seemingly confusing and occasionally paradoxical actions: as it turns out, in this philosophy, what may seem inexplicable in truth has a deeper meaning, that the *tzaddik* is engaging in acts of *tikkun* whose secrets and complexities may lie beyond the comprehension of the untutored or uninitiated observer. Just as divine logic is ultimately incapable of being apprehended by the human, so too, analogously, is the *tzaddik's* logic incomprehensible to the follower: the only remedy is simply to believe. Which led, logically, to Nachman's insistence that his disciples and believers follow him in all things.

This was not merely to display adherence to the principle of faith. According to Nachman, the *tzaddik* is particularly capable of achieving *tikkun*, even with regard to others' actions (especially their prayers); Nachman once compared himself to a doctor and his disciples to patients, who have no need to understand how their medicine works in order for it to be efficacious. This doctor-patient metaphor also helps to illuminate the emphasis for Nachman's followers on confession to the *tzaddik*, rare among other hasidic communities. Nachman's role as receiver of confession highlights another of the paradoxical aspects of his thought. On the one hand, the ability to relate and to connect, which is a hallmark of the confessor-confessee relationship, stems from Nachman's own expressed sense that he'd struggled with the same problems as his followers, and differed from them not in kind, but only in degree. On the other hand, Nachman's elevated sense of his position as the *tzaddik* – and his increasing sense of his own position – cast him as essentially different from his followers.

It's clear that as early as Nachman's time in Zlotopolye, he was openly claiming himself to be the *tzaddik hador*, the righteous person of his generation; and after his move to Bratslav, which figured in his teachings as a new Jerusalem, a new *axis mundi*, the messianic aspect of this conception became more and more explicit. In the fall of 1804, Nachman asked his followers to begin saying a series of midnight prayers aimed at establishing the reunion of the Godhead crucial to the messianic redemption; half a year later, he instituted another series of extraliturgical prayers dedicated to atonement for physical and sexual desire, always conceptualized by Nachman as the ultimate hindrance to perfection; and in the fall of 1805, he asked them to observe a series of private fasts. Many materials relating to these years were censored or destroyed by the movement itself, but what is clear is that Nachman believed his soul to be the reincarnation of numerous great figures of the past: that he was the last link in a chain of reincarnated figures which included Moses, Shimon bar Yoḥai (whose grave he'd visited while in the Holy Land), Isaac Luria, and the Besht. As the last link in the chain, Nachman felt himself to contain the messianic soul, the figure who would usher in the redeemer himself; perhaps even to be the Messiah son of Joseph, who precedes the Messiah son of David, a figure Nachman may have believed would come from within his own family.

It's been suggested that the reason Nachman assigned himself the role of messianic harbinger, rather than actual Messiah, was that same feeling of ambivalence and doubt about his own fitness, particularly stemming from the sense that he'd never sufficiently transcended physical and sexual desire to merit the ultimate role in redemption. With the birth of his first son, Shlomo Ephraim, in the spring of 1805, Nachman seems to have become more and more convinced that the Messiah would be his son, and in May 1806, on the holiday of Shavuot, Nachman presented himself to his followers in white clothing, an unmistakable sign of expectant purification.

And when Shlomo Ephraim died a few weeks later, Nachman's messianic hopes lay in ashes. Not only was this a devastating personal tragedy, of course; it was compounded into a kind of universal devastation. In Nachman's mind, was this horrible event a punishment for attempting to hasten the redemption? For his hubris at arrogating to himself an overly elevated place in the divine scheme? Ultimately, we will never know exactly the tenor of his thoughts and considerations, but we do know two things. First, the messianic practices were discontinued fairly soon after his son's death. And second, it was soon after as well that Nachman began, for the first time, to tell the stories that assured him a foundational place in the history of Yiddish, Jewish, and hasidic literature.

Hasidic leaders more traditionally uttered philosophical teachings, or *toyres*; and although hasidic tales certainly existed, told by Hasidim as an attempt to pass the long Shabbat afternoons or to while away the time on market journeys, they were generally hagiographic tales of the remarkable lives, deeds, and sayings of their rebbes – of the kind collected in *Shivḥei HaBesht* (*Tales in Praise of the Baal Shem Tov*). But Nachman's tales were quite different. Although his emphasis on the stories made it clear to his disciples that they were meant to be perceived as equivalent to classical teachings, he told them in Yiddish – the natural language for tale-telling, true, being the vernacular, but not nearly as respected a vehicle for theological teaching as Hebrew.

The printed edition of Nachman's tales, first published in 1815, contained thirteen tales; other tales ascribed to Nachman are also recorded in other Bratslav writings, of varying degrees of authenticity. The book was published in a bilingual edition, with a Hebrew translation of the stories appearing above the Yiddish original. Though somewhat complicated, the reasoning behind the decision to do so was sensible: because of the crucial importance placed on every word spoken by the master, and the sense that deep secrets were hidden within the material as it was constituted, the stories were published in Yiddish; otherwise, there would be no hope of proper interpretation. However, to give the stories the status they deserved in a culture in which "serious" material was written in Hebrew, the stories were translated from the language of their composition into the latter. Bratslav followers, to this day, cherish both versions as sacred.

Though there's some evidence Nachman made preliminary notes on his teachings, and perhaps did so with his stories as well, the published stories, while clearly the result of careful contemplation and artful composition, also clearly maintain the hallmarks of an oral performance. Additionally, the Jewish restriction against writing on Shabbatot or Holidays meant that Nathan Sternhartz, as recording secretary, had to recall the rabbi's words from memory and write them down only after the holiday ended (though the printed edition of the stories, published with Nachman's partial approbation, were almost certainly the result of later consultations as well). And the stories would have certainly required careful attention: not simply because of respect for a *tzaddik*'s utterances, but because their form and detail were so unusual for the hasidic milieu; they had little external connection to traditional Jewish literature, instead boasting substantial continuities with fairy tales and similar secular genres.

Take, for example, Nachman's first and arguably simplest story, "The Tale of the Lost Princess" (1806), one of three we'll mention here. The tale tells of the youngest daughter of a king who, in a fit of anger, tells her that he wishes the devil (called in the tale, in typical Yiddish fashion, the "Not-good") would take her; the devil promptly does. The king himself does not search for the missing princess, but sends his second-in-command to do so. The journey of the second-in-command is a long one; though he encounters the princess on several occasions, including in the castle of the Not-good, she eludes his grasp; he is told to search and yearn for her for a year and then, on the last day, to fast, and he fails to do so, eating and drinking forbidden items which send him into a deep sleep. The second time this happens, he awakes with a handkerchief, on which a message written with the princess's tears tells him that she can be found in a pearly castle on a golden mountain. After consulting with a number of spirits and creatures, who deny the existence of such a place, he finally finds a wind that not only informs him of the existence of such a castle, but carries him there. Nachman ends the tale by telling the reader that the princess is freed by the second-in-command, but specifically refusing to elaborate on how the rescue takes place.

Nachman introduces the tale by noting that whoever heard it had thoughts of repentance, and on first (and perhaps second) glance it's difficult to see why. In fact, it's difficult to see exactly what the purpose of Nachman's telling this sort of story is at all. But with what we know of Nachman's theology, answering the latter will help clarify the former: the stories themselves, seemingly unrelated to Nachman's concerns and philosophies, upon careful inspection and interpretation, are revealed as deep allegories of hasidic philosophy, of *tzimtzum* and *tikkun*, of doubt, and of faith.

Recall that Nachman's mystical philosophy of *kelipa* and *tikkun*, of husk and elevation, was also applicable to abstract ideas, not just concrete objects, and thus to literature and stories wrapped in the *kelipot* of secularity just as items of the physical world were wrapped in earthiness. All stories, including – and given Nachman's conceptions of lowness and highness, perhaps especially – secular stories, contained within them sparks of holiness. The object of individuals, and particularly the *tzaddik*, was to perform an act of *tikkun* on these stories by means of telling the story in a particular way and having others engage in interpretive acts, seeking to understand the stories' depths.

Nachman's allegorical approach to action and to history – to see events in the narrative of life, and the life of narrative, as speaking to broader trends and understandings of the progress of the *tzaddik* and of Jewish history itself – can accordingly be the skeleton key to an interpretive approach, to understanding how the elements in the tale can be identified with an allegorical and kabbalistic reading of Jewish history.

And so: the princess is the lowest level of the Godhead, a level traditionally identified as feminine; the violent kidnapping of the princess can be seen as analogous to the *shevirat hakelim*, and thus this part of the Divine Presence has been captured in the "not-good" earthy world of impurity, imprisoned within the *kelipot*. The job of liberating this spark, however, is not up to God (the king), but rather is up to the second-in-command, who can be read complementarily both as the individual in general and as the *tzaddik* in particular, whose acts of *tikkun* will ultimately liberate the princess to reunite with her father. However, such liberation is far easier said than done: there is a long journey for the individual, a journey beset with obstacles. We've already spoken of Nachman's elevation of the notion of the struggle to the central role in Jewish theology, and it's certainly significant here. It's not only the act of eating and drinking, the satiation of physical desire, which figures so importantly in Nachman's thought as an obstacle, but that the particular items in question have symbolic significance in biblical episodes which conflate sexual behavior or knowledge and sin, such as Eve's apple and the wine of Lot's daughters, who inebriate their father to become incestuously impregnated by him. The individual's sleep, then, functions on many levels: it reflects post-coital slumber, the invention of post-Edenic death, or simply (and perhaps most powerfully), the alienation from God's presence after the degradation that necessarily takes place after sin.

Thankfully, the princess has given the man a means through which to find her: her handkerchief, with a message written in her tears. Given the place of the Torah, of God's law, in Jewish thought as both divine writ and as a blueprint for proper behavior to achieve closeness to God, the symbol seems particularly apt here. It provides evidence that God is indeed present, despite the individual's sense of a powerful, all-consuming absence. One needs faith, however, to accept the evidence for the definitive statement that it is, and this leads the man to face his final challenge: the skepticism of the world about his own faith. To make matters worse, that skepticism is once more complemented by the sense, so familiar to Nachman, that partially due to one's own sins, the distance between God and man is an unbridgeable gulf.

And yet, Nachman ends, the princess is indeed rescued. Despite the obstacles, despite the sense of futility – a sense which could never have been stronger for Nachman than that summer he first told the tale, when all his visions of how the redemption would take place had been so tragically shattered – the messianic redemption would indeed occur. God had promised it would. All that one could do was to continue and to rededicate oneself to the struggle, which meant a constant effort for perfecting the world, and for perfecting oneself. No wonder the tale, when properly told and understood, inspired thoughts of repentance in the listener: for what is self-perfection without the possibility of understanding that having erred, having sinned, is not an ending of one's narrative, a closing off of all possibility, but merely an opportunity to continue seeking and struggling?

Nachman continued telling stories from the summer of 1806 until 1810, the year of his death; the stories would grow in length and complexity, but would all lend themselves to deeper, allegorical interpretations, generally revolving around the grand struggle of human existence and the role of the *tzaddik* in particular. Nachman's stories were generally told on those occasions when his followers made pilgrimage to be with their rabbi: unlike many other hasidic rabbis of the period, Nachman discouraged the idea of a full-time hasidic court and encouraged his disciples to come only on the holidays of Rosh HaShana, Ḥanukka, and Shavuot.

However the number of those disciples was decreasing: many left him, particularly in 1806 and 1807, almost certainly disillusioned by the failure of his attempts to bring about the messianic redemption. (It couldn't have helped, either, that his messianic claims had also received wider circulation, and he and his followers became the subject of increasing criticism and isolation from other hasidic circles.) Nachman began to take a series of journeys around the Ukrainian countryside, perhaps as a means of atoning for his perceived sins which had prevented the redemption. These journeys were cut short when Nachman discovered that his wife was seriously ill from tuberculosis; though he joined her in Ostrog to consult a traditionalist physician, she died in the summer of 1807, and soon after Nachman, who had returned to Bratslav, discovered he too had contracted the disease.

Traveling to the cosmopolitan city of Lemberg, then the capital of Austro-Hungarian Galicia, to consult doctors about his illness in the fall of 1807, Nachman first came into significant contact with proponents of the new movement of the Jewish enlightenment, or Haskala. Their philosophical position privileging rationalism and scientism at least as highly, if not more so, than faith must have been anathema to Nachman; and the fact that he was consulting doctors – implying as it did only the partial efficacy of his own prayers, and his belief in them, to solve his problems – must have disturbed him still further. After his return to Bratslav in the summer of 1808, he strongly discouraged the seeking of medical advice, and he would transform his encounters with the modernizing figures of the Jewish Enlightenment into another of his stories, "The Tale of the Wise Man and the Simple Man" (1809), the tale which speaks most profoundly to how Nachman's theology and philosophy encountered the transitions and challenges of modernity.

The tale revolves around two townsmen, one wise and the other simple. The narrator takes great pains to emphasize that the simple man's simplicity is not identical to foolishness; rather, it consists of a joyful blindness to the world's imperfections and inequities. His poverty fails to bother him, and whatever he does satisfies him as what was meant to be. His faith is perfect. The wise man, however, is constantly seeking new worldly knowledge, particularly the mastery of crafts and techniques. His expertise, though prodigious, causes him pain: either it goes unrecognized by those around him, or, worse, his infinitesimal shortcomings loom large in his own self-perception. When a messenger from the king comes summoning both individuals, the simple man accepts the message and eventually rises to become the king's most trusted servant; the wise man, on the other hand, elevates the fact that he has never actually seen the king, only his message, to radical skepticism about the king's existence. Traveling the world proclaiming his new doctrine, the wise man outsmarts himself: he has become so convinced of the logical sense of his own arguments that he fails to see the evidence of the king's power when it is right before his eyes. The story ends with the wise man being beaten by demons, but refusing to see them because they ought not to exist.

The analogues here are clear, and Nachman does an excellent job anatomizing precisely both the distinctions between the man of faith and the man of reason, and the psychological complexities that constitute the neuroses of the modern individual. Nachman, of course, stands foursquare against modernity in the story: his wise man, who travels around the world and seems to master its methods, has lost the only thing that truly matters, his connection with the king. The simple man, who, as a shoemaker, is more connected to the simple, traditional ways of life, accepts the king, and so, in turn, the king accepts him.

Nachman's battle against the forces of modernity continued in 1810, when he moved from Bratslav to Uman, where he came into much greater and more sustained contact with representatives of the Haskala; in fact, he may have moved there precisely to make the effort to engage in what he saw as this ultimate struggle before his death. He died several months later, during Sukkot, and is buried in Uman. Unlike most hasidic circles which in the nineteenth century became dynasties, Nachman never provided for succession and the Bratslav Hasidim, who remain a group to this day, have never had another rabbi to take Nachman's place; as a result, they have become known as the "dead Hasidim" (*toyte* Hasidim), and were traditionally regarded with some skepticism in hasidic and non-hasidic circles. Some leadership, however, was provided after Nachman's death by Nathan Sternhartz, who, after a brief struggle with Rabbi Moshe Zvi of Safran, led the Bratslav community between 1810 and 1845; it was during this period that many of Nachman's works were first published.

Most of them were compilations of the master's teachings and speeches, but the *Tales* were the work that would secure his reputation outside of the hasidic community. Their flexible Hebrew style and their legitimization of Yiddish as a literary language would have lasting effect: later Hebrew and Yiddish writers were to draw lessons from both, and writers such as Isaac Leib Peretz and S. An-sky would, in the late nineteenth and early twentieth centuries, draw on Nachman's strategy of using apparently simple stories to discuss deeper allegorical matters in their own neo-folktales and plays. Even the figure of Nachman himself would become the grist for later Yiddish literary activity, figuring prominently in the poetic work of Jacob Glatstein, for example. It's not unreasonable to propose that in many ways the tradition of modern Yiddish literature begins with Nachman, sixty years before S. Y. Abramovitch, often considered the founder of modern Yiddish literature, published his first famous Yiddish novella in the pages of a literary supplement.

But ultimately, it's Nachman's sensibility – even if only partially grasped, its interpretation unfinished – that inspires and affects us. In his last, most complicated, and, significantly, unfinished tale, the tale of the Seven Beggars, he said:

> Now there is a mountain. On the mountain stands a rock. From the rock flows a spring. And everything has a heart. The world

taken as a whole has a heart. And the world's heart is of full stature, with a face, hands, and feet. Now the toenail of that heart is more heart-like than anyone else's heart. The mountain with a rock and spring are at one end of the world, and the world's heart stands at the other end. The world's heart stands opposite the spring and yearns and always longs to reach the spring. The yearning and longing of the heart for the spring is extraordinary. The spring also yearns and longs for the heart.

The interpretation of this passage – which can only be understood in the context of an interpretation of the story as a whole, which could take a book in itself – is less necessary, now, than the sense it provides, a sense that pervades Nachman's work and thought: that the essential fact of the world is longing, that deeply speaking all things are connected, and until the end of time, until the Messiah arrives, there will be separation which can only attempt to be broached through our efforts at *tikkun*. That in our act of trying to figure out what the story says – what its heart is, in other words – we ourselves become the spring, ever vital, ever creative. And, even more amazingly, that the story *itself* wants us to interpret it, to give it meaning; that it yearns for our *tikkun* as much as we yearn (or should yearn) to offer it.

Is there any work of thought, of literature, or philosophy that invests itself with such vitality? We're hard pressed to find it; which is a central reason why Nachman's work has remained so unforgettable, so powerful, in the two centuries since its creation.

Note: An earlier version of this piece was published in the *Dictionary of Literary Biography*, vol. 333, "Writers in Yiddish," ed. Joseph Sherman, under the title "Nachman of Bratslav (1772–1810)."

FURTHER READING

Kitzur Likutei Moharan (Mogilev, 1811).
Likutei Moharan (Ostrog, 1808).
Likutei Moharan Tanina (Ostrog, 1811).

Maggid Siḥot (Zolkiew, 1850). Later generally known as *Siḥot HaRan*. Large portions are translated in *Gems of Rabbi Nachman* (Jerusalem, 1980).

Sefer HaMiddot (Mogilev, 1811). Translated as *The Aleph-Bet Book (Sefer HaMiddot)* (Jerusalem, 1986).

Sipurei-Mayses (Ostrog, 1815). Translated as *Nahman of Bratslav: The Tales* (New York, 1978).

Editions in English:
Likutey Moharan by Rebbe Nachman of Breslov (Jerusalem, 1986–1993).

Selected Bibliography in English:

Band, Arnold. Introduction to *Nahman of Bratslav: The Tales* (New York, 1978), 5–48.

Band, Arnold. "The Function of the Enigmatic in Two Hasidic Tales." In *Studies in Jewish Mysticism*, edited by Joseph Dan and Frank Talmadge (Cambridge, 1978).

Encyclopedia Judaica, s. v. "Nahman (ben Simhah) of Bratzlav."

Green, Arthur. *Tormented Master: A Life of Rabbi Nahman of Bratslav* (Tuscaloosa, 1979).

Rapoport-Albert, Ada. "Hagiography with Footnotes: Edifying Tales and the Writing of History in Hasidism." *History and Theory* 27 (1988): 119–159.

Roskies, David. *A Bridge of Longing: The Lost Art of Yiddish Storytelling*, (Cambridge, 1995), 20–55.

Weiss, Joseph. "Sense and Nonsense in Defining Judaism: The Strange Case of Nahman of Brazlav." In Weiss, *Studies in Eastern European Jewish Mysticism* (Oxford, 1985).

Wiskind-Elper, Ora. *Tradition and Fantasy in the Tales of Reb Nahman of Bratslav* (New York, 1998).

Rabbi Samson Raphael Hirsch's *Nineteen Letters on Judaism*: Orthodoxy Confronts the Modern World

Rabbi Dr. Moshe Y. Miller

I n 1836, when a book called *The Nineteen Letters on Judaism* was published by one Ben Uziel in the German state of Oldenburg, Orthodox Judaism as we know it today did not exist. The book was published under a penname because its author, a young and idealistic German rabbi, did not want any attention drawn to himself that might detract from the cause to which he devoted his maiden literary effort. The book was an immediate success and subsequent editions were published with the author's name: Samson Raphael Hirsch (1808–1888). Why did Rabbi Hirsch write this book when he did? What are the main ideas of this book? What relation does the ideology expressed in it have to traditional Jewish thought, general thought, and contemporary Judaism? Over the course of this chapter, each of these issues will be treated.

I.

Prior to the nineteenth century, there were no denominations within Judaism. That is to say, there was no option for a Jew to identify as either

Reform, Conservative, or Orthodox (among other options). Instead, there was a traditional Jewish society that all Jews, by birth, belonged to. Some repudiated Judaism altogether in favor of another religion. Some, like Spinoza, expressed heretical ideas and were excommunicated from the traditional Jewish community. Others still remained within the fold of the Jewish community and gave lip service to its principles, but actually deviating from those principles in practice and thought, albeit clandestinely. The advent of the European Enlightenment and its Jewish counterpart, the Haskala, changed all of this.[1] The Haskala itself did not create any new Jewish denominations. It did, however, create a cadre of Jewish intellectuals who questioned many of the time-honored beliefs and practices of the traditionalists. Interestingly, the two most famous eighteenth-century *maskilim*, Moses Mendelssohn and Naphtali Herz Wessely, were strictly observant Jews their entire lives.[2]

The emphasis placed by the Enlightenment on human reason, which was accepted by the Haskala, proved detrimental for the preservation of traditional Judaism. At the turn of the nineteenth century, young Jewish intellectuals – and this was an intellectual era, in which young people took philosophical ideas seriously – began to reject many of the basic tenets of Jewish belief. Along with a desire for complete civic equality – what is known as Emancipation – many of these people

---

1. In characterizing the Haskala as the Jewish counterpart to the Enlightenment, I am following the regnant scholarly view, in opposition to Olga Litvak's intriguing revisionist study, *Haskalah: The Romantic Movement in Judaism* (New Brunswick, 2012). For the regnant view, see Shmuel Feiner, *The Jewish Enlightenment*, trans. Chaya Naor (Philadelphia, 2004). The above analysis is not intended to suggest that the changed intellectual orientation of German Jewry was the primary *cause* of weakened Jewish observance. For an excellent analysis of the social factors leading to a breakdown of observance in the city at the center of the Haskala, see Steven Lowenstein, *The Berlin Jewish Community: Enlightenment, Family and Crisis, 1770–1830* (Oxford, 1994). See also David Sorkin's classic study, *The Transformation of German Jewry, 1780–1840* (Detroit, 1999).

2. What may be surprising to many readers is that many of the *maskilim* were closer to Orthodox Judaism than to any of the more modernist denominations. Wessely in particular was quite traditional in outlook and, aside from a controversy engendered by one pamphlet that he wrote, was a respected rabbinic scholar who meets any contemporary definition of Orthodoxy.

abandoned Jewish observances in favor of a more secular lifestyle. At the same time, the most extreme elements were converting to Christianity, which granted them immediate social equality, something which many Jews, particularly in the pre-Emancipation period, desperately wanted. Into this breach, in the second decade of the nineteenth century, stepped the Reform movement. It sought to develop a version of Judaism that appealed to Germany's modernizing Jews, that would stem the tide of conversion, and that would retain a connection to Jewish identity among the masses of Jews to whom Orthodoxy appeared antiquated and irrelevant. Initially, the Reform movement was content with cosmetic changes to Jewish practices, such as reciting some of the prayers in German, deleting those prayers that seemed archaic, and having a non-Jew play an organ for Friday night synagogue services. These modifications, among others, were justified by the early Reform rabbis, who were learned and who wrote responsa in rabbinic Hebrew arguing for the halakhic validity of these practices. Although the lay founder of the Reform movement, Israel Jacobson, spearheaded several experimental Reform institutions in the early nineteenth century, the most successful was the Temple – this was the term used by the Reformers for their house of worship, as it was more universal than "synagogue" – that opened in Hamburg in 1818.

The earliest response of Orthodoxy – as the traditionalists came to be called – was the 1819 ban on the Hamburg Reform Temple, expressed in a Hebrew pamphlet titled *Eilu Divrei HaBrit (These are the Words of the Covenant)*. This pamphlet contained responsa by leading Orthodox rabbis condemning the early Reform movement's halakhic innovations. No attempt at dialogue with Reform leaders or an evaluation of Reform ideology was contained in this pamphlet. It consisted entirely of negation. Sensing the lacuna in this initial response of the Orthodox, the Hamburg Orthodox community decided that a new rabbi, who could disprove the Reform claim that only those Jews who repudiated the Orthodox interpretation of halakha could be genuinely modern, should be hired. They found their ideal candidate in Rabbi Isaac Bernays (1792–1849), who preferred the title *Ḥakham* over *Rabbiner* since the latter title was used by Reform rabbis. Rabbi Bernays, about whom the pioneering Jewish historian Heinrich Graetz stated that he was "the first to recognize in a much profounder manner than Mendelssohn the importance of Judaism in the history of the world,"[3] and who was university educated, preached in a polished German (as opposed to Yiddish or Judeo-German, which had been the norm), and donned modern clerical robes, could not be accused of naively and dogmatically following ancestral custom without due consideration of the values of modernity. Rabbi Bernays and his colleague and friend, Rabbi Jacob Ettlinger (1798–1871), author of the famed talmudic commentary *Arukh LaNer*, ushered in the emergence of what historians call neo-Orthodoxy. This does not mean that they created a new faction of Judaism but rather that their response to modernity charted a new course in traditional Judaism's relationship to the modern world,[4] one that differed markedly from that of, for example, the Ḥatam Sofer, whose most famous adage was that "anything new is biblically prohibited." Contemporary modern Orthodoxy owes much of its character to the pioneering work of rabbis such as Bernays, Ettlinger, and their students, Rabbi Hirsch and Rabbi Dr. Esriel Hildesheimer (1820–1899).

II.

Samson Raphael Hirsch was ten years old when the Hamburg Reform Temple opened in 1818, and his parental home was the site of meetings to discuss how Orthodoxy might confront the Reformers. Some historians have speculated that this imbued the young Hirsch with a sense of mission and a Pinḥas-like zeal to dedicate his life to rehabilitating Orthodox Judaism and making it relevant for modern Jews. Hirsch attended the philosophic lectures of Rabbi Bernays and, upon his suggestion, attended the yeshiva of Rabbi Ettlinger in Mannheim. After receiving rabbinic ordination from Rabbi Ettlinger, Hirsch attended the University of Bonn to study philology, history, science, and philosophy. Contrary

---

3. Heinrich Graetz, *Geschichte der Juden*, ed. M. Brann, 2nd ed. (Leipzig, 1900), vol. 11, 388.
4. For the now-classic scholarly thesis about the formation of Orthodoxy, see Jacob Katz, "Orthodoxy in Historical Perspective," *Studies in Contemporary Jewry* 2 (Bloomington, IN, 1986), 3–17. For critiques of Katz's position, see Yosef Salmon, Aviezer Ravitzky, and Adam S. Ferziger, eds., *Orthodox Judaism: New Perspectives* [Hebrew] (Jerusalem, 2006).

to popular misconception, Hirsch was never awarded a doctorate,[5] and he had spent hardly a year at the university when he received an offer for what turned out to be his first rabbinic post: the chief rabbinate of Oldenburg, made vacant by the recent departure of Rabbi Dr. Nathan Adler, who later became the first modern British chief rabbi. Rabbi Adler recommended Hirsch for the position in Oldenburg and it was there that Hirsch spent the next ten years of his life, during which time he married his wife, Hannah née Jüdel (1805–1882), and wrote his first two books.

The young chief rabbi of Oldenburg, still in his twenties, began work on a systematic classification of the mitzvot that describes both the details of their observance and their underlying rationale. This would eventually be published, in German,[6] as *Horeb: Essays on Israel's Duties in the Diaspora*, in 1837. However, Hirsch first brought the manuscript to the non-Jewish publisher that he knew. The publisher told him that the book was simply too long and therefore too risky for a first publication, and suggested Hirsch write a shorter synopsis of his main ideas to see if that sold well. Based on this suggestion, Hirsch began composing what would become his most famous and influential work, *The Nineteen Letters*, which was modeled, to some degree, on Rabbi Judah Halevi's twelfth-century work, the *Kuzari*. That work presented readers with a dialogue between a Jewish sage and an unlearned individual who was inquiring about Judaism. That Hirsch would choose the *Kuzari* as a model is no surprise given his expressed preference for Judah Halevi as a Torah-true thinker of the Middle Ages who avoided the extremes of both superrationalism and anti-intellectualism, as will be discussed below. Thus, Hirsch's work begins with a letter by a character named Benjamin, who is a young Jew, soon to be married. Though raised religious, he has completely abandoned all observance, regarding Jewish law as an obstacle to social integration, on the one hand, and intellectual enrichment, on

---

5. However, most of Hirsch's sons and sons-in-law did acquire doctorates.

6. Although today such texts are commonly published in the vernacular, it is notable that most of Hirsch's writings were published in German. Prior to this time, rabbinic texts were almost always published in Hebrew. Despite the reluctance of his own family, Hirsch persisted in writing in a language that the masses of German Jews could understand.

the other. Judaism, asserts Benjamin, stifles all creative and artistic tendencies that Jews may have, forbids them even the most innocent enjoyments, and makes social interaction with non-Jews in the modern world virtually impossible. Benjamin expresses his complaints to his childhood friend, Naphtali, who is now an Orthodox rabbi (and who clearly is a stand-in for Hirsch himself).

Here is an excerpt from Benjamin's complaint:

> As for our own religious literature (*Wissenschaft*), it perverts the mind and leads it astray into subtleties and the minutiae of petty distinctions, until it becomes incapable of entertaining simple and natural opinions, so that I have always wondered quite a bit how you, who have taste and understanding for the beauties of Virgil, Tasso, and Shakespeare, and who are able to penetrate into the consistent structures of Leibnitz or Kant, can find pleasure in the rude and tasteless writings of the Old Testament, or in the illogical disputations of the Talmud?
>
> And what effect has it, the Law, upon heart and life? The broad principles of universal morality are narrowed into anxious scrupulosity about insignificant trifles. Nothing is taught except to fear God. Everything, even the pettiest details of life, is referred directly to God. Life itself becomes a continuous monastic service, nothing but prayers and ceremonies. The most praiseworthy Jew is he who lives most secluded, and knows least of the world, though he permits it to support him, but wastes his time in fasting and praying, and the perusal of senseless writings.[7]

These are bold words! For the first time in the modern era, an Orthodox rabbi is putting pen to paper to express the point of view of non-believing, non-traditional Jews.

---

7. Samson Raphael Hirsch, *The Nineteen Letters*, 3. My citations from *The Nineteen Letters* are from the 2013 (Zurich: Verlag Morascha) reprint of the German original, which I have translated in conjunction with the Drachman and Elias English editions. Page numbers refer to this 2013 edition (henceforth, *TNL*). See below, Further Reading.

The initial response of Orthodoxy – the pamphlet issued in Hamburg in 1819, discussed above – did not attempt to engage in a dialogue with those Jews who could no longer uphold the tenets of Orthodoxy. It simply pointed out how they were wrong and described which halakhot were being violated by the early Reform innovations. A perplexed, university-educated young Jew certainly would not have been won over by any of the responsa contained in that pamphlet. With the publication of Hirsch's book, a new chapter in the history of Orthodoxy, one that insists that historic Judaism remain engaged with the modern world, began.

In terms of structure, only Letter One is written by Benjamin, the non-traditionalist. The remaining letters are all written by Naphtali (meaning, they present the views of Hirsch himself). While reviews written of the book by partisans of the Reform movement seized upon this fact and charged Hirsch with being disingenuous, this critique completely misses the point. Although Hirsch did wish to express the anti-Orthodox position in his book, he did not wish to carry on an equal dialogue between both points of view. His goal was to convince readers of the relevance of Orthodox Judaism to the nineteenth-century European world. Clearly, he had to devote the majority of his book to conveying this message. Subsequent letters contain references to the responses that Benjamin gave to Naphtali's ideas, and that was sufficient to achieve Hirsch's goals.

The first letter had ended with Benjamin asking Naphtali to respond to the former's questions about Judaism by forgetting his rabbinical office and telling Benjamin what Naphtali *really* believes. The second letter begins with Naphtali taking offense at this suggestion of professional bias. Naphtali maintains that he chose his career in the rabbinate *as a result* of his convictions. From an early age, he says, he had been reared by his "enlightened religious parents" (*erleuchtet religiösen Eltern*)[8] to study Tanakh and Talmud and to find the spirit of Judaism

---

8. Mordechai Breuer, review of Noah H. Rosenbloom, *Tradition in an Age of Reform*, *Tradition* 16:4 (Summer 1977): 140–149, expressing the dominant scholarly view, rejects the assertion of Rosenbloom that Hirsch's characterization of his parents as *erleuchtet* is an indication of their Haskala leanings. Hirsch's depiction of his parents this way should be viewed as synonymous with describing them as "openminded," in contemporary language.

in its texts.[9] Naphtali proceeds to address Benjamin's complaint that Judaism does not lead its adherents to happiness or perfection. Can the achievement of happiness truly be the barometer of a religion's success? How many people truly achieve it? Perhaps one of the most subjective attainments is that of happiness, defined differently by each individual. Perfection can only be obtained by those who have the truth, but "truth itself is conceived by a thousand thinkers in a thousand different ways."[10] Instead of exploring such hopeless pursuits, those investigating Judaism must determine what its own texts say about itself.

III.

The first teaching of Judaism, as the beginning of the Book of Genesis indicates, is that the entire world – everything that we can see and that which we cannot – is created by God. Everything in creation serves a purpose and no creations function in opposition to others; rather, all of creation functions in tandem to create a harmonious whole. "One immense bond of love, of receiving and giving, unites all creatures. None exists by itself and for itself." Thus, the first message conveyed to man by creation is that of love.[11] The next issues to be determined are the nature of man and his place in this world. Even if the Torah were silent on these points, says Naphtali, would they not be obvious? Man too is a creation of God and he too must somehow fulfill his role in this world just as everything else in creation does. But man is unique: he has been endowed with free will. What all other created beings, from plants to animals, planets to stars, do instinctively – that is, carrying out God's will – man must perform *of his own free will*.[12] The Torah describes man as created in the image of God, which Hirsch takes to be a calling, not

---

9. *TNL*, 5.

10. Ibid., 6.

11. Ibid., 17.

12. For examination of other aspects of this issue from the point of view of philosophers whose writings Hirsch was familiar with, see Michael H. Hoffheimer, "The Influence of Schiller's Theory of Nature on Hegel's Philosophical Development," *Journal of the History of Ideas* 46:2 (1985): 231–244. For a broader examination of this matter, see the excellent study by Gunther S. Stent, *Paradoxes of Free Will* (Philadelphia, 2002).

merely a description. Man is to be a likeness of God, that is, he is meant to emulate God's ways to the best of his ability.

Readers of *The Nineteen Letters* may not realize that Hirsch is here responding to critiques of Judaism that were made on the basis of the philosophy of the towering figure of the Enlightenment – and, in some respects, its most perspicacious critic – Immanuel Kant (1724–1804). Kant posited that no act that is performed out of compulsion – what he termed "heteronomously" – can be considered moral. A moral act is one that is carried out autonomously. But isn't Judaism predicated on a God who commands and forbids as He sees fit, with formidable punishments awaiting those who disobey His will? Does Judaism not, then, run afoul of Kant's moral theory? No, Hirsch avers, because Judaism expects man to *freely choose* to carry out God's will because he recognizes that this is his purpose in the world. The Mishna (Avot 2:4) calls upon man to "make His will as though it were your own will." In the traditional hierarchy of Jewish ethics, serving God out of love stands higher than serving God out of fear of punishment. Thus, Kant's critique is not applicable to traditional Judaism, as Hirsch understands it.[13]

Hirsch stresses the importance of history for the proper understanding of Judaism, which he considers the key to the salvation of all of mankind. The Torah is not a manual for how one nation fosters its unique relationship with its tribal god. Everything in it is predicated on the proper understanding of the role that all of humanity plays in God's world. The purpose of *Am Yisrael* from its inception was to serve as a model nation that would educate all of humanity to achieve its calling. This is how Hirsch understands the midrash cited by Rashi to Genesis 1:1 which states that the world was created "for the sake of Israel," that is, for the sake of a model nation that can inspire the rest of the world to strive to achieve its purpose – an inversion of the exclusivist reading of this midrash, to wit, that the whole world was created for the Jews.

---

13. Kant himself would probably not have been satisfied with Hirsch's response. See Immanuel Kant, *The Metaphysics of Morals*, trans. Mary Gregor (Cambridge, 1991), 185–213; Kant, *Critique of Practical Reason*, trans. Thomas Kingsmill Abbott (New York, 2008), 34.

Hirsch instead posits that the Jews were created to serve as benefactors for the whole world.

Why was it necessary for such a model nation to exist? Hirsch says this is because mankind, in its earliest stages, demonstrated that it was not fit to reach its calling unaided. The history of the earliest generations of man is the history of the consistent failings of people to live up to the divine task. From Adam to Noah to Abraham, only unique individuals succeeded in placing God's will at the center of their lives while the rest of mankind strove for materialism and pleasure. God therefore selected the descendants of Abraham, Isaac, and Jacob as those most fit to serve as a priestly nation since those men demonstrated in their lifetimes their commitment to carrying out God's will and to imbuing in their children a yearning to implement "benevolence and justice" in all their endeavors (Gen. 18:19). Immediately prior to the giving of the Torah, God tells Moses that the Jewish people will be "a kingdom of priests and a holy nation" (Ex. 19:6) which Hirsch, following Maimonides and Seforno, interprets to mean that the Jewish people are to be the spiritual regenerators of mankind.

Ironically, the German Reform movement adopted as a central tenet the so-called mission theory, the idea that the purpose of the Jewish people is to live scattered throughout the world and propagate their ideal of ethical monotheism to the gentiles. According to this view, the Return to Zion is a metaphor for a period during which Jews would be treated benignly by the non-Jewish nations, who would be inspired by the Jews' ethical zeal to grant human dignity to adherents of all creeds. The nineteenth century was seen as the dawn of that era by many Reform ideologues. Did Rabbi Hirsch simply advocate a slightly modified version of this theory? Although some writers have suggested that that is indeed the case, this view is difficult to sustain. The most pertinent question was, what is the content of the mission of the Jews? For the Reform movement, it consisted of promulgating monotheism while living ethical lives. If non-Jewish society adopted an ethical code that recognized God and the human dignity of all people, that would signal the success of the Jewish mission. But Hirsch's mission was a different one! He believed that the original purpose of Creation was not thwarted when mankind as a whole did not live up to its calling, leading to the selection of Abraham and his descendants.[14] Quite the contrary. That purpose was now to be achieved via a people uniquely qualified to inspire others, by their own example, to submit their *entire* lives to the divine will. The Jew cheerfully obeying the intricate laws of *kashrut*, for example, will demonstrate that there are indeed people who answer to a Higher Authority (as in the old Hebrew National commercials) even in their seemingly mundane affairs.

IV.

In subsequent letters, Naphtali introduces Benjamin to the history of the Jewish people and the fact that it failed to live up to its calling while it retained political sovereignty in *Eretz Yisrael*. It prized its possessions and military strength over its obligations to God, and thus it became necessary to exile the people from its land. In Letter Nine, Hirsch creatively translates Jeremiah 2:28 as "the number of your cities has become your god, O Judah."[15] (This verse is usually translated to mean that the Jews worshiped as many gods as the number of its cities.) Since the nation of Israel valued its material prosperity and its political security more than the spiritual values it was created to propagate, it had to be deprived of that which led to this situation. There was a short reunion in *Eretz Yisrael* under the leadership of Ezra. Then, on the eve of their second exile with the destruction of the Second Temple,[16] the mission of the Jews was further advanced by the creation of Christianity. This is because that new religion, though theologically flawed, did bring to the world knowledge of the One God (albeit in an adulterated fashion), the brotherhood of man, man's moral superiority over animals, and the

---

14. This is precisely the view of Rabbi Moshe Chaim Luzzatto (1707–1746); that is, that the selection of the Jewish people constituted a rejection of the salvific potential of the rest of mankind. See his *Derekh Hashem*, trans. Aryeh Kaplan (New York, 1997), 141.

15. *TNL*, 45.

16. Rabbi Hirsch, following a general view among medieval authorities, considers the return of some Jews to *Eretz Yisrael* during the period of Ezra to have been an incomplete redemption which ultimately served to fortify the spiritual bond of the people to the Torah in order to prepare it for the more extensive exile following the destruction of the Second Temple.

renunciation of wealth- and pleasure-worship. Later, the emergence of Islam, which was also heavily influenced by Judaism, further carried out Israel's mission of teaching mankind essential truths about man's purpose in this world.[17] Though Hirsch, throughout his writings, is scathing in his critique of certain doctrines of Christianity, his basic theory of religious tolerance is well captured in this short passage from *The Nineteen Letters* (even though those religions are not referred to by name).

"[The Jewish people] accomplished its task better in exile than while in possession of good fortune," writes Hirsch.[18] Jews, scattered throughout the world, demonstrated selfless dedication to the values of the Torah and were prepared to sacrifice even life itself when put to the challenge. Still, an exilic existence is not ideal, for it can contribute to the erosion of pure Jewish values and it makes the implementation of God's will on a national scale impossible. God will therefore gather the dispersed of *Klal Yisrael* once again in the Holy Land at a time that He sees fit, and they will then successfully dedicate their entire national lives to the fulfillment of God's will, and the other nations will seek inspiration from the reestablished Jewish national polity. Therefore, Hirsch opposed collectivist efforts at ending the exile, such as the program of Rabbi Zvi Hirsch Kalischer (1795–1874), the celebrated proto-Zionist author of *Derishat Tziyon*. Hirsch believed that God Himself will sound the Shofar of Redemption when the Jews are fit for it. Hirsch's approach to this issue was later adopted by the Agudat Yisrael organization that was founded by his descendants and disciples. This does not mean, however, that Hirsch would have had a negative view of Jewish statehood. The case of his grandson Rabbi Isaac Breuer, a founder of the Aguda, who favored the creation of a Torah-state, is instructive.[19]

---

17. *TNL*, 46.
18. Ibid.
19. Suggestions concerning how Hirsch would interpret the watershed events of the twentieth century, which climaxed in the creation of a sovereign Jewish state in *Eretz Yisrael* for the first time in nearly two thousand years, are merely speculative. However, Hirsch's insistence on seeing the hand of God at work in the developments of history suggests that he would have been averse to the theological anti-Zionism of the Satmar Hasidim, which is predicated on seeing the machinations of the Satan in the creation of *Medinat Yisrael* (the State of Israel). Isaac Breuer's unique

V.

The most significant issue for nineteenth-century Jewish thinkers was the authority of the Torah's legislation. While Mendelssohn had posited that in revealing the Torah, God had established a legal system that would remain in effect for all time, the next generation of German Jews gravitated more toward Spinoza's theory that the legal portions of the Torah ceased to have any authority when the Jews went into exile. In discussing Judaism with Benjamin, it became necessary for Naphtali to explain the significance of the mitzvot. Hirsch was strongly opposed to the medieval view that the mitzvot are to be divided between "rational" and "revelational" laws, that is, "those which are discovered by reason and those based on divine revelation only."[20] This view allows for a fundamental dichotomy to be suggested between those commands that humans readily understand as containing essential moral teachings, and which they are therefore likely to preserve for all time, and those which elude our understanding, and which therefore may come to be perceived as "ceremonies" that had spiritual potency for ancient Jews but are less relevant to modern Jews. It was precisely those mitzvot whose rationale the leaders of Reform did not discern or whose utility they questioned that were the first to be discarded. Hirsch developed a very creative system of classification of the mitzvot in which such a dichotomy is not possible.

Hirsch develops six categories of mitzvot: (1) *torot*: instructions or doctrines concerning God and man's place in His world; (2) *mishpatim*: precepts of justice toward creatures similar and equal to ourselves, i.e., fellow human beings;[21] (3) *ḥukkim*: precepts of justice toward those creatures subordinate to us, namely, animals and plants as well as

---

brand of Zionism may have appealed to Hirsch. See Moshe Y. Miller, "Between Frankfurt and Satmar: A Study of Two Schools of Orthodox Jewish Anti-Zionism" (MA thesis, Touro College, 2006).

20. The first medieval authority to posit such a distinction was Rav Saadia Gaon. See his *The Book of Doctrines and Beliefs*, trans. (from the Arabic original) Alexander Altmann, 94–102. (Quote from Altmann's commentary, 96 n. 4.)

21. Hirsch stresses fellow human beings and not merely fellow Jews. For discussion of this issue, see Moshe Y. Miller, "Rabbi Samson Raphael Hirsch and Nineteenth-Century German Orthodoxy on Judaism's Attitude toward Non-Jews" (PhD diss., Yeshiva University, 2014).

justice toward our own bodies; (4) *mitzvot*: precepts of love toward all beings (the most amorphous of Hirsch's six categories); (5) *edot*: observances which give symbolic testimony to fundamental truths about the nature of the Jewish people and its place in the world; and (6) *avoda*: divine worship which, today, consists primarily of prayer. The sequel to *The Nineteen Letters*, *Horeb*, was devoted to a discussion of those mitzvot that are still applicable in the absence of the *Beit HaMikdash* and the underlying symbolic meaning of each of those mitzvot. As Isaac Heinemann noted over half a century ago, Hirsch's work was the first of its kind to suggest as the motive for a particular mitzva an explanation that was in accord with the details of the halakha.[22] Instead of offering a general approach and treating the minutiae of the mitzva as the undecipherable will of God, Hirsch insisted that each rationale be based on the details; for example, the materials that render a sukka invalid for use according to the Talmud. For Hirsch, these details teach us a great deal about the meaning of this mitzva.[23]

VI.

After cursory sketches of the categories of mitzvot and primary examples from each category, in Letter Fifteen Hirsch discusses the suffering and isolation of the Jewish people. As for individuals, Hirsch takes strong exception to the view that the Torah interdicts pleasure. On the contrary, there is not one form of pleasure that it forbids; each is merely regulated by its laws so that it is properly utilized. Taking up a line of argument that is often cited by hedonists for a very different goal, Hirsch asks:

> Would God endow us with instincts only to have them proscribed by His law to the point of their eradication!! The highest form of serving God, according to this [Torah] teaching, is "to be joyful

---

22. Isaac Heinemann, *Taamei HaMitzvot BeSifrut Yisrael*, vol. 2 (Jerusalem, 1956), 91–92, 107–109. This view was expressed earlier in more partisan fashion by Hirsch's son, Dr. Mendel Hirsch. See his *Humanism and Judaism*, trans. J. Gilbert (London, 1928), 76–77.

23. The reader is encouraged to make use of Dayan Dr. I. Grunfeld's excellent English edition of the *Horeb*, which is both faithful to the original German and eminently readable.

before God," serene joyfulness in life based on our awareness that our life, thinking, feelings, speech, actions, our joys and our sorrows are all objects of God's attention.[24]

In this passage, Hirsch argues decisively against those currents within traditional Jewish thought that regard asceticism as a religious ideal.

As to the accomplishments of other nations which impressed Benjamin so much, Hirsch argues that, aside from the fact that these nations were merely seeking their own temporal happiness and not the enrichment of mankind when engaged in their endeavors, have not the Jewish people's achievements eclipsed those of other nations? After all, achievements in the realm of science, culture, art, and inventive skill only have value if they are subordinated to the spiritual purpose of human existence. The Jewish people can take pride in being the bearers of God's word for humanity. As for their isolation from other nations, how else could the Jews have preserved their spiritual identity but through isolation? Their task was to stand in opposition to the materialistic values of other civilizations, but this was never intended to foster chauvinistic attitudes toward non-Jews. The term that the Torah (Ex. 19:5) uses to describe the Jewish people, *segula*, does not mean that Israel has a monopoly on divine favor but rather that our God has a monopoly on *our* devotion; we must revere none but Him.[25] Hirsch here rejects the view, widely prevalent even to this day in many sectors of the Orthodox world, that Judaism's God has favor toward only one nation and is, at best, indifferent to the well-being of the rest of mankind. Hirsch, throughout his writings, consistently rejects this view as a distortion of Judaism.

Hirsch further notes that the entire purpose of human existence, a goal toward which we strive and for whose achievement we pray daily, is the unification of all human beings in the worship of God. The brotherhood of mankind is an ideal that the Jewish people has taught to the rest of humanity. Hirsch daringly suggests, in a footnote, that the well-known rabbinic adage that "*ḥasidei umot haolam yesh lahem ḥelek*

---

24. *TNL*, 76.
25. Hirsch, in a footnote, cites a passage in Tractate Bava Kamma 87a, as proof for this interpretation of the word *"segula."* Cf. Rabbi Obadiah Seforno to Exodus 19:5.

laOlam haBa," "the pious of the nations of the world have a share in the World to Come," that is, an afterlife in Paradise, can be understood to mean that the righteous of all nations will have a share in attaining the goal of all of human history, namely, advancing humanity toward the End of Days. This revolutionary reading of that rabbinic passage was noted by Abraham Geiger in one of his reviews of *The Nineteen Letters.*[26] Hirsch obviously felt justified in offering this creative rereading since its goal was to undergird his view that all nations play a role in advancing God's purposes for mankind over the course of history, though the Jews have been assigned the most prominent role in achieving that goal.

Hirsch continues the fifteenth letter by discussing Judaism's attitude toward dogma and speculation concerning faith. Following Mendelssohn, Hirsch argues that Judaism posits 613 commandments of faith but no dogmas. The truths that lie at the heart of Judaism are discernible to all who are open to perceiving them. The kind of speculation that is valuable, according to Judaism, is that which leads to greater understanding of the interrelationship between all of creation, man, and the world, and God's plan for the course of human history. The Torah discusses all of these things, and it should be studied as a guide to life.[27] For that reason, says Hirsch, the manner of Torah study that has come into vogue in the previous century – commonly known as *pilpul* (but which Hirsch calls *vorherrschend Grübelgeist,* or abstruse speculation) – is regrettable. Unlike the medieval codifiers of halakha and those who wrote the classic commentaries to the *Shulḥan Arukh* during the sixteenth and seventeenth centuries, the eighteenth-century pilpulists were not expanding the application of Jewish law to daily life, but were merely engaged in mental gymnastics.

But Hirsch goes further, and criticizes those who study Torah without due attention to its application to life. He notes that the reason the Talmud (Kiddushin 40b) concludes that "study" is greater than "action" is because the former necessarily leads to the latter. This indicates, in his view, that any Torah study which, by its nature, cannot be connected to real life, is misguided. Hirsch goes further and argues

---

26. Abraham Geiger, *Wissenschaftliche Zeitschrift für Jüdische Theologie* 3 (1837), 82ff.
27. *TNL*, 19.

that "scholarship has become an end [in itself] rather than a means [toward an end], and few have kept in mind its true objective."[28] This is a strong critique of what has become the hallmark of the Lithuanian yeshivot, an ideology based on Rabbi Chaim of Volozhin's definition of *Torah lishma*, in his classic work *Nefesh HaHayim*, as the study of Torah in order to know the Torah. According to Rabbi Chaim, any furtherance of our knowledge of any aspect of Torah is a fulfillment of the greatest mitzva in the Torah which, indeed, ought to be considered "an end in itself"! Although both Rabbi Chaim and Rabbi Hirsch have ample precedent among the *Rishonim* for their respective views, Rabbi Hirsch had to deal with the argument of Reformers that much of talmudic law had ceased to be relevant to the lives of modern Jews. In his view, part of the blame for that erroneous conclusion was the mistaken method of Torah study pursued in German academies in the century following the composition of the classic commentaries on the *Shulḥan Arukh* (though Hirsch was certainly not criticizing Rabbi Chaim's yeshiva in Volozhin, which had opened not long before Hirsch wrote *The Nineteen Letters* and about which he knew little).[29]

Though Hirsch disagrees with Rabbi Chaim's understanding of *Torah lishma*, he accords high merit to studying laws concerning the *Beit HaMikdash* or those treating ritual purity, since they are certainly in the category of being connected to life even if at the present, unfortunately, they are not practical. Hirsch writes further that people should spend time seeking out the spirit of Judaism in Tanakh. He was disappointed that this was not the method of advanced yeshivot, whose curriculums generally do not allot any time for Tanakh study.[30] In fact, Hirsch himself headed a large yeshiva in Nikolsburg during the four years that he served as the Moravian chief rabbi. There, he delivered lectures on Talmud – focusing on its plain meaning – and taught

---

28. Ibid., 80.
29. That Hirsch is decidedly *not* criticizing the Volozhin yeshiva, which opened in 1803, is made clear in a letter from 1835 (printed in the Grunfeld edition of *Horeb*, cxliii), wherein Hirsch criticizes the "mistaken method of Torah study" that has been pursued "for the last hundred years."
30. This critique was expressed as early as 1837 in Hirsch's *Horeb*. See the Grunfeld edition, 410 (par. 551).

the Book of Psalms in the synagogue. This unconventional approach led to sarcastic remarks that "formerly, we used to study the Talmud and say *Tehillim*; now we say the Talmud and study *Tehillim*." What is clear is that Hirsch did value Talmud study but he had formed definite opinions about its proper method and the position it occupies in the hierarchy of Jewish learning.

Hirsch ends this letter by discussing the halakhot which make social intercourse with non-Jews difficult. He affirms that such laws are necessary to preserve the purity of Judaism and to prevent assimilation and intermarriage. In the realm of ethics, however, Judaism does not distinguish between our obligations toward fellow Jews and gentiles:

> Be just in action, truthful in word, bear love in your heart for your non-Jewish brethren (*trage Liebe im Herzen gegen deinen nicht-jüdischen Bruder*), as your Torah teaches you. Feed their hungry... assist them by word and action. In short, display the whole noble breadth of your Jewishness.[31]

VII.

Letter Sixteen is devoted to the question of Emancipation. A Jew full of enthusiasm for the noble mission of Judaism may understandably quiver at the thought that Jews are now being granted civic rights and entering the world of European culture, as this may lead to assimilation. However, if properly utilized, the opportunities afforded by Emancipation for greater *kiddush Hashem* in our dealings with non-Jews can bring about an even more successful implementation of our mission. In Hirsch's words:

> I bless Emancipation when I see how excess oppression isolated Yisrael[32] from the [broader] life [of the surrounding world], has stunted the development of its spirit, has inhibited the free unfolding of its noble character.... For Yisrael, I bless Emancipa-

---

31. *TNL*, 84.
32. I have rendered the original German "Jissroel" as "Yisrael," which is simply Hirsch's way of saying "the Jewish people."

tion only if, concurrently, the proper spirit awakens in Yisrael ... [and we] strive to elevate and ennoble ourselves, to implant the spirit of Judaism in our souls in order to produce a life in which that spirit shall be reflected and realized. I bless it if Yisrael does not regard Emancipation as the goal of its mission but merely as a new facet of it, a new test, far more difficult than the test posed by oppression.[33]

But, Hirsch continues, he would grieve if Yisrael comes to regard Emancipation as the end of its exile, as the ultimate aim of its mission (as the German Reform movement would later claim). He would also grieve if Yisrael regarded Emancipation as nothing more than a way to lead a more comfortable, materialistic, and pleasurable life. Hirsch ends this letter by stating that only if we become true Jews, pervaded by the spirit of the Torah, would Judaism welcome Emancipation "as affording a greater opportunity for achieving its purpose, the realization of a noble [Torah] life."[34]

What is especially significant is that here is where Hirsch introduces his conception of *Torah im Derekh Eretz* (though not by name), which he understands to mean that the Torah is not intrinsically bound to any particular civilization, but is intended to serve as our guide for life in *any* civilization, and its values must be the yardstick by which we measure the values of the surrounding culture. This necessarily entails the involvement of the Jew in the wider, "non-Jewish" world. This ideology is thus opposed to the creation of spiritual ghettos wherein Jews will remain shut off from the influence of the surrounding culture. While Orthodox rabbis such as the Ḥatam Sofer preferred the cultural insularity of the ghetto for the spiritual fortification it provides, and therefore opposed Emancipation and encouraged Jews to shun all aspects of modern culture,[35] Hirsch disagreed. Though deeply concerned about

---

33. *TNL*, 89–90.

34. Ibid., 90.

35. On the Ḥatam Sofer, see Jacob Katz, "Towards a Biography of the Ḥatam Sofer," trans. David Ellenson, in Frances Malino and David Sorkin, eds., *Profiles in Diversity: Jews in a Changing Europe, 1750–1870* (Detroit, 1998), 223–266; Meir Hildesheimer,

the potential of Emancipation to upend traditional values, he boldly proclaimed that the change in the social and political context of the lives of European Jews called upon them to implement the Torah's vision for society rather than retreating from the broader world. A Jew who applies the Torah's values to inform *all* facets of his life, and who refuses to compartmentalize his Judaism to the private sphere, is someone who is trying to live up to the Hirschian ideal.

VIII.

In Letter Eighteen, Hirsch provides an ambitious overview of Jewish intellectual history from the destruction of the Second Temple until the nineteenth century. At the beginning of this synopsis, he provides a rational explanation of the well-known rabbinic statement attributing the destruction of the Second Temple to the fact that the Jews "did not first utter the blessing over the Torah":

> Yisrael's entire being rests upon the Torah: it is its basis and its goal; and its lifeblood. If our relationship to the Torah is proper, then Yisrael can suffer no ills. But if this relationship is not proper, then Yisrael cannot be healthy. There is no wrong development in Judaism which does not owe its origin to a flawed understanding of the Torah, or is at least perpetuated thereby. Our sages, with profound insight, point to this as the true cause of our first national catastrophe, *shelo berekhu baTorah tehila*, meaning that they did not study the Torah with the resolve to fulfill it in life and for the sake of living it. Life fled from the [study of] Jewish literature and that literature could not therefore properly pervade life, could not provide it light and warmth. If you search for the

---

"The German Language and Secular Studies: Attitudes Towards Them in the Thought of the Hatam Sofer and His Disciples," *Proceedings of the American Academy for Jewish Research* 62 (1996): 129–163; Marc B. Shapiro, "Aspects of Rabbi Moses Sofer's Intellectual Profile," in Jay M. Harris, ed., *Be'erot Yitzhak: Studies in Memory of Isadore Twersky* (Cambridge, 2005), 285–310; and the revisionist reading of Aaron M. Schreiber, "The Hatam Sofer's Nuanced Attitude Towards Secular Learning, *Maskilim* and Reformers," *Torah U-Madda Journal* 11 (2002–2003): 123–173.

cause of our present sickness, you will, again, find it only in this [misconception].[36]

Hirsch then goes on to present a synopsis of how the spirit of the Torah was developed over the course of the centuries from the beginning of the talmudic period. Hirsch says that only the legal aspect of the Oral Law was initially committed to writing. Later, due to the "pressure of the times," the various midrashim were written down but they contained the spirit of the Torah only in a "veiled form." This required students to make extra efforts to grasp the deeper meaning of the Torah. After a brief reference to the geonic period, Hirsch proceeds to the Golden Age of Muslim Spain. During that period, he says, Jews were drawn after Greek philosophy, as transmitted by Arabic sources. They began to accept Aristotle's view that the highest purpose of man is to achieve intellectual perfection. Thus, they did not conceive of Judaism as being primarily concerned with man's actions in this world, with knowledge serving only as a means toward the performance of good deeds.

The greatest thinker among these Jews was Maimonides:

> This great man to whom, and to whom alone, we owe the preservation of practical Judaism, is responsible, because he sought to reconcile Judaism with the difficulties which confronted it from without, instead of developing it creatively from within, for all the good and the evil born [subsequently].[37]

Although Maimonides is to be commended for the enormous work he did for the preservation of halakha by the writing of his Code, since his intellectual orientation was shaped by Greek philosophy, he developed an approach to the rationale for the mitzvot, says Hirsch, that is both untenable and spiritually dangerous. If the mitzvot are only means to the end of achieving intellectual perfection, as Maimonides writes, then perhaps, says Hirsch, if other methods of achieving such perfection can be found, the mitzvot will then become inessential. Furthermore,

---

36. *TNL*, 96.
37. Ibid., 97.

Maimonides' pragmatic rationales for many of the mitzvot render the Talmud's concern with the minutiae of the mitzvot incomprehensible. For example, if Shabbat was given to the Jews primarily so that they could acquire correct notions and rest their bodies (*Guide* II:31), then why does the Talmud devote many folios to determining what actions constitute *melakha* (work)? It even declares the writing of two letters – something that may well be part of intellectual activity – to be a capital crime while many acts that involve much physical exertion are free from penalty![38]

Hirsch then notes that other medieval authorities who had a more profound grasp of Judaism developed an opposition not only to Maimonides' philosophy but to all intellectual inquiry concerning Judaism. The passages in *Ḥazal* opposing being *dareish taama dikera* (investigating the reasons for biblical injunctions) were utilized as weapons to repel any efforts to elucidate the spirit behind the details of Jewish law. In studying the Talmud, the only legitimate question came to be, "What is stated here?" – that is, what does this halakha entail? The equally important question, "Why is it so stated?" – i.e., what is

---

38. Hirsch's critique of Maimonides is quite bold, and in his subsequent writings he omits this line of criticism and consistently adopts a reverential attitude toward Maimonides as a pillar of halakha. It should also be noted that these critical remarks were directed more at Reformers who justified their approach on the basis of Maimonidean ideas than at Maimonides himself. George Y. Kohler, *Reading Maimonides' Philosophy in 19th Century Germany: The Guide to Religious Reform* (Heidelberg, 2012), discusses how Maimonides was utilized by Reformers, and on p. 50 makes the following observation: "To Hirsch's credit, this description [of the legacy of Maimonides' philosophy in Letter Eighteen] is, in fact, more or less the lesson that the Reform movement learned from Maimonides' overall approach to the authority of Mosaic law." Hirsch himself notes this misuse of Maimonides' writings in the following passage: "It is true that Maimonides' *Moreh HaNevukhim* was burned. But Maimonides himself would have been the first to toss his book into the flames if he had lived to see how his book has been misused and is still misused today" (*The Collected Writings of Rabbi S. Raphael Hirsch*, vol. 6, 129). For the broader methodological issues that Hirsch had with Maimonides, see Michah Gottlieb, "Counter-Enlightenment in a Jewish Key: Anti-Maimonideanism in Nineteenth-Century Orthodoxy," in James T. Robinson, ed., *The Cultures of Maimonideanism: New Approaches to the History of Jewish Thought* (Leiden, 2009), 259–287.

the significance of this religious act? – was suppressed.[39] On the basis of a misunderstood passage of the *Tosafot*,[40] opposition to all study of Tanakh emerged, a mistaken approach, says Hirsch, about which *Ḥazal* themselves forewarned.[41]

During this entire period, asserts Hirsch, only a few Jewish thinkers found the proper balance between favoring intellectual inquiry and opposition to extreme philosophical rationalization. Hirsch singles out Nahmanides and Rabbi Judah Halevi, author of the *Kuzari*, as being the greatest of them. Hirsch also commends the *Ḥasidei Ashkenaz* (German Pietists of the twelfth and thirteenth centuries) for their selfless dedication of possessions and even life for the sake of God, though he notes that the persecutions that medieval German Jewry experienced robbed it of its intellectual vitality.

Around the same time, the Kabbala was introduced to the Jewish world when the Zohar was first circulated around 1290. This work is an invaluable repository of the genuine spirit of Judaism. However, it too was generally misunderstood by the masses, and what ought to have been guidance concerning the inner meaning of Judaism was instead turned into a "magical mechanism, a means of influencing or resisting theosophic worlds and anti-worlds."[42] That is, the supernatural aspects of the Kabbala became the primary appeal of this branch of Jewish wisdom instead of its elucidation of the true inner spirit of Judaism.[43]

The cumulative effect of the various Jewish intellectual trends that matured over the course of the Middle Ages which Hirsch regarded as

---

39. See Mosheh Lichtenstein, "'What' Hath Brisk Wrought: The Brisker Derekh Revisited," *The Torah U-Madda Journal* 9 (2000): 1–18.
40. To Sanhedrin 24a, s.v. "*belula.*"
41. Hirsch cites Masekhet Soferim 15:9.
42. *TNL*, 100–101.
43. Interestingly, Hirsch's use of Kabbala in his writings, especially *Horeb*, was criticized by reformist rabbis such as Hirsch B. Fassel, who was upset that Hirsch included the practice of gazing at one's fingernails through the light of the Havdala candle (par. 192 of *Horeb*). See Michael L. Miller, *Rabbis and Revolution: The Jews of Moravia in the Age of Emancipation* (Redwood City, 2010), 145. The details of this practice, as Hirsch describes them, accord with what the Rema writes (*Shulḥan Arukh, Oraḥ Ḥayim* 298:3) in the name of the Zohar. Hirsch not only made copious use of the Zohar in his notes that he used when preparing the writing of *Horeb* but, in one case at least

problematic led to a very serious vacuum in the intellectual state of the Jewish people precisely when such a situation posed the greatest danger: the European Enlightenment. When a Jewish manifestation of this movement emerged in mid-eighteenth-century Germany – the Haskala – its most gifted mind was Moses Mendelssohn (1729–1786). Unfortunately, in Hirsch's view, Mendelssohn was not up to the lofty task with which he was presented. The Jewish people needed a thinker who would creatively develop Jewish thought "from within," that is, based on its own sources. By contrast, Mendelssohn

> had not drawn his mental development from Judaism, was great chiefly in the philosophical disciplines of metaphysics and aesthetics... and did not build up Judaism as a science from itself but merely defended it against political stupidity and pietistic Christian audacity; who was personally a practicing religious Jew who showed his brethren and the world: one can be a religious Jew *and yet* shine, distinguished, as a German Plato! This "and yet" was decisive.[44]

Hirsch means that Mendelssohn never demonstrated the harmony, the congruence, between his Jewish identity and his achievements as a man of European culture. There was an unabated dichotomy between the two, and those who preferred European culture over being "a religious Jew" ultimately chose the former.[45]

By contrast, Hirsch's own ideal of *Torah im Derekh Eretz* calls for a synthesis of all aspects of life with the Torah. This would mean, after a strong foundation in Torah study, acquiring broad worldly knowledge and then examining the views thus acquired and deciding if they are in harmony with the Torah. If they are not, they must be rejected.

(the mitzva of *mila*), he utilized more passages from the Zohar than from the Talmud! See *Rabbi Shimshon Refael Hirsch: Mishnato VeShitato*, ed. Yona Emanuel (Jerusalem, 1989), 339–341. Any claim that Hirsch was fundamentally anti-Kabbala is untenable.

44. *TNL*, 101–102.

45. Hirsch's very strong critique of Mendelssohn's philosophy of Judaism does not preclude the possibility of Mendelssohn's having influenced Hirsch. Hirsch agreed, for example, with the assertion that "faith makes you into a man while the Law makes you into a Jew," a position with unmistakable Mendelssohnian undertones.

This is why, for example, Hirsch dedicated an oration to the memory of the German poet Friedrich von Schiller (1759–1805) on his centenary, because his ideas, Hirsch maintained, were drawn from Jewish truths as promulgated in the Bible. On the other hand, Hirsch told an acquaintance that had Goethe's (1749–1832) centenary occurred while Hirsch was in Frankfurt, he would have left Frankfurt just so as not to feel compelled to dignify Goethe with a tribute.[46] Goethe's eroticism and anti-Semitism were incompatible with Torah teachings; thus, there was no reason for Jews to peruse his writings. In fact, though Hirsch never issued a ban on the study of texts that conflict with Torah teachings, he considered heretical texts to be a grave danger to Judaism and waged battles against scholars such as Heinrich Graetz and Zechariah Frankel whose views concerning the Oral Law Hirsch considered unacceptable.

After discussing the challenges that his own generation found itself up against, Hirsch ends *The Nineteen Letters* with an appeal to go back to the sources of Judaism – specifically, Tanakh, Talmud, and Midrash – in order to determine what Judaism says about itself and how its vision may be realized in a post-Emancipation world.[47] This includes the foundation of schools that adhere to the *Torah im Derekh Eretz* educational program and which therefore teach secular subjects from a Torah point of view:

> With [King] Davidic sentiment should nature be studied, with the ear of [Prophet] Isaiah should history be heard, and then, with the eye thus aroused and the ear thus opened, the teaching concerning God, world, man, Yisrael, and Torah should be drawn from the Tanakh. Then, having formulated this basic conception of Judaism, let us study the Talmud in this spirit. In the halakha, only further elucidation of ideas already known from the Tanakh should be sought.

---

46. Heinemann, *Taamei HaMitzvot*, vol. 2, 267 n. 75.
47. Hirsch himself clearly grappled with the apparent tensions between certain rabbinic texts and humanistic ideals that he cherished and considered to be fundamental to Judaism. For an examination of this issue, see my dissertation, "Rabbi Samson Raphael Hirsch and Nineteenth-Century German Orthodoxy on Judaism's Attitude Toward Non-Jews."

Hirsch implores his readers to pursue this path without regard to the criticisms which it may engender – either from Reformers or from those Orthodox who value pilpulistic Talmud study above all else.[48]

IX.

One particularly striking aspect of Hirsch's presentation of Judaism in *The Nineteen Letters* is his willingness to criticize contemporary Orthodoxy. According to Hirsch, the blame for much of the misunderstanding of Judaism's true message and the subsequent development of the Reform movement, which sought to adapt Judaism to the times, lay at the feet of the Orthodox. While not naming any rabbis, Hirsch does state that

> today, two opposing generations confront each other: one of them has inherited uncomprehended (*unbegriffene*) Judaism, as mitzvot performed by mere habit, without their spirit, a holy mummy they bear [but are] afraid to rouse its spirit. The other [generation] is partly filled with noble enthusiasm for the welfare of the Jews but look upon Judaism as bereft of any life and spirit, a relic of an era long passed and buried, and tries to uncover its spirit and, not finding it, threatens through its well-intended efforts to sever the last life-nerve of Judaism – out of ignorance.... These [two opposing elements] are both mistaken.[49]

In this passage, Hirsch assigns equal blame to the older generation of the Orthodox as he does to the younger Reformers! It must be noted that in none of his later works does Hirsch express himself this way. Several factors may account for this. The one that seems the most compelling is the different posture of the Reform movement at these two periods. In the 1830s, during the composition of *The Nineteen Letters*, the Reform movement had not yet made drastic changes to halakha and had not yet established itself as the premiere faction of Judaism for German Jews. All this changed with the three Reform synods held in Brunswick, Frankfurt, and Breslau in the years 1844, 1845, and 1846.

---

48. *TNL*, 106–107.
49. Ibid., 105.

The overall purpose of these meetings was for the leaders of German Reform Judaism to discuss the direction their movement would take. Some of the key issues that were brought up were liturgical reforms, intermarriage, adjustments to observance of Shabbat and Jewish Holidays, and the status of the Hebrew language. These synods emboldened the German Reform movement and helped to create a veneer of legitimacy to its reforms of Jewish law among German Jews.

Hirsch penned a scathing Hebrew-language attack on the first Reform synod.[50] In it, Hirsch declares that the attendees at the conference were not rabbis and had no authority to modify the slightest jot of Jewish practice despite their pretensions to authority. Hirsch further declares that the time for zealotry has come, and that there can be no compromise between the Torah-true leaders and the Reform renegades. Strikingly, Hirsch writes that the only solution to his era's problems was the reintroduction of the educational program of *Torah im Derekh Eretz*, where Jewish schools would teach the youth Jewish and general subjects, with the latter being understood through the prism of the Torah, in which case the Torah has naught to fear from the study of what he calls *ḥokhma*, wisdom. What emerges from his remarks is a move away from his earlier conciliatory approach to Reform. The time for battle has come, and this militant approach to the Reform movement became Hirsch's consistent platform for the rest of his life.

If one is looking for a non-Jewish work that closely parallels Hirsch's *The Nineteen Letters*, it will not be found.[51] The roughly contemporaneous work whose stated goal was closest to Hirsch's may well be Friedrich Schleiermacher's *On Religion: Speeches to Its Cultured Despisers*, published in 1799 (revised several times, lastly in 1831). Schleiermacher was the most influential Protestant thinker of the nineteenth century,

---

50. This was originally published in *Sefer Torat HaKenaot* (Amsterdam, 1845), and has been reprinted in several works.

51. This is not intended to suggest that everything in *The Nineteen Letters* is strikingly original. Most of its central ideas are based on Hirsch's understanding of the classical texts of Judaism, and Hirsch's idiom owes much to that of philosophers from the school of German Idealism, though he borrowed their terminology and employed it for his own purposes, as noted by Pinchas Paul Grünewald, *Pédagogie, Esthétique et Ticoun Olam: Redressement du Monde – Samson Raphaël Hirsch* (Bern, 1986), 14.

deeply influenced by the Enlightenment and by Romanticism, and he is credited with ushering in the era of Liberal Protestant theology. Naturally, Hirsch and Schleiermacher disagreed not just about which religion will prove to be the salvation of mankind but also concerning the nature of religion and the manner in which it should be interpreted. In fact, Schleiermacher's views on religion were quite influential within German Reform Judaism. Still, their common goal was to inject religion with relevance at a time when its influence was waning and its truths being questioned due to Enlightenment thought.

x.

Contemporary readers may find the idiom of *The Nineteen Letters* to be slightly archaic but the ideas presented therein should strike a resonant chord with thinking Orthodox readers, unfamiliar with Hirsch's book, who have been thirsting for an intellectually compelling interpretation of the relevance of Orthodox Judaism for the modern world. Of the works on Jewish thought from the past two centuries, few have attempted a rational and systematic presentation of Judaism that insists on its essentially legal character and yet emphasizes the primarily ethical telos of its laws. Thus, Hirsch's *The Nineteen Letters* really does fill a vacuum. If you have ever pondered the relationship between the Jewish people and the other nations, particularly in the Diaspora lands today where Jews as individuals have been granted the same rights and responsibilities as their non-Jewish fellow citizens, this book will provide much food for thought. The book's treatment of this issue also has significant implications for the proper role in the international arena of the State of Israel – the Jewish state – which has ostensibly been granted full admission to the family of nations. If you have ever wondered why a perfect God "needs" people to sing His praises or to perform ritual acts that seem devoid of ethical content, *The Nineteen Letters* provides answers that will resonate. Readers who find *The Nineteen Letters* intriguing may well be spurred on to seek out Hirsch's other works, especially his monumental *Ḥumash* commentary which, aside from being a classic work of modern biblical exegesis, is a text that consistently brings out the lofty humane vision of the Torah.

The publication of *The Nineteen Letters* marked a turning point in the history of Judaism. The emergence of the Reform movement in previous decades provided Jews with a choice. They could cloister themselves within the spiritual ghetto of traditional Judaism as it was practiced until then, but in so doing, they would have to, effectively, renounce all aspects of modernity. As the Reform movement progressed, it provided an alternative, as it continued to incorporate modern sensibilities not only concerning externals like synagogue appearance but also concerning Judaism's values. A young educated Jew aware of recent European intellectual currents was gratified to find that Reform rabbis were not only cognizant of these currents but accepted many of their premises and evaluated traditional Jewish beliefs and practices on the basis of this knowledge. Slowly but steadily, those aspects of halakha that did not seem compatible with modern life were rejected as inapplicable in the present day. This presented a grave challenge to those who saw themselves as the guardians of tradition. The earliest reaction, that of the Hamburg *Beit Din* in 1819, was to simply excoriate the Reformers.

Samson Raphael Hirsch, guided by his teachers, Rabbis Bernays and Ettlinger, opted for a third course. He fervently believed that not only was traditional Judaism not rendered outdated by the dramatic changes in the European world, but that it was *precisely* this form of Judaism that provided solutions to the contemporary dilemma. The Torah was never intended to accept whatever values the changing times bring. The Torah had always stood in opposition to the varieties of paganism and hedonism that it encountered. Even in the "enlightened" nineteenth century, there were still values and ideas that were incompatible with the Torah, which Torah-true Jews therefore ought to oppose. But this spirited opposition is not to be conflated with obscurantism. Hirsch insists that the calling of the Jew never consisted of isolation from the world but engagement with it for the purpose of bringing to it the light of Torah.

The world of Orthodox Judaism as we know it today would not exist if not for Hirsch and his first-published work. *The Nineteen Letters* ushered in an era in which Orthodox rabbis could write in the vernacular language and borrow terminology from contemporary intellectual trends and even from ideological opponents (which Hirsch did quite often). Orthodox Jews could now be proud that their "version" of Judaism, the only one that could plausibly claim fidelity to the texts of the Torah, was not in any way outdated or archaic. Its spokespersons were highly educated and articulate individuals who were well informed about recent scientific and philosophical developments. They were capable of marshaling an array of sources to buttress the truths and practices upheld by Orthodox Judaism. The ideology of *Torah UMadda*, to which Yeshiva University is committed, could not have been conceived if not for the development of the *Torah im Derekh Eretz* ideology of Hirsch and his colleagues in the German Orthodox rabbinate (despite whatever differences may exist between these two ideologies). In fact, *Torah im Derekh Eretz* has, to varying degrees, become the educational model for schools across the spectrum of Orthodoxy. In short, the emergence of Rabbi Samson Raphael Hirsch in the leadership of German Jewry heralded the arrival of a self-confident and assertive Orthodox Judaism for the modern world.

FURTHER READING

Hirsch, Samson Raphael. *Die Neunzehn Briefe über Judentum* (*The Nineteen Letters on Judaism*). There is presently no annotated scholarly edition of this work in any language. The original German, in Gothic script, was first printed in 1836, and reprinted a number of times since. The 1889 edition is currently available free as an e-book from Google Books. There have been two subsequent reprintings of the original German albeit in the Latin script that became more predominant in printed German during the twentieth century, both by Verlag Morascha (a branch of Feldheim Publishers) in Zurich. The first was reprinted/printed in 1987 and an identical reprint, the one cited in this essay, in 2013.

Aside from Hebrew, French, and other languages, this work has been translated into English three times (there is also a partial fourth translation): Bernard Drachman's excellent 1899 edition published by Funk and Wagnalls, now available free as a Google e-book; Jacob Breuer's 1960 edition; and Rabbi Joseph Elias' 1995 edition. The 1960 edition is condensed and is not recommended for that reason. The 1995 edition contains erudite footnotes by Rabbi Elias and the English translation by Karin Paritzky is the most up-to-date in terms of the idiom. The issue with this edition is that Rabbi Elias' footnotes offer interpretations of Hirsch that align him with contemporary right-wing Orthodoxy in a manner that is not always compelling. For this reason, the Drachman edition remains the first recommendation.

Hirsch, Samson Raphael. *Horeb.* Translated by Dayan Dr. I. Grunfeld (London, 1962). This excellent English rendition of Hirsch's classic work on *taamei hamitzvot* is prefaced by Dayan Grunfeld's lengthy introductory essays, which are works of enormous erudition and scholarship. These essays have also been published separately as *Dayan Dr I. Grunfeld's Introduction to Samson Raphael Hirsch Horeb: A Comprehensive Study of Hirsch's Philosophy of Jewish Law.* In this writer's opinion, this remains the best introduction to Hirsch's thought.

Hirsch, Samson Raphael. *The Pentateuch, Translated and Explained by Samson Raphael Hirsch.* Translated by Isaac Levy (Gateshead, 1976). Although the newer Daniel Haberman English translation of Hirsch's Ḥumash commentary has become popular in the last several years, the earlier edition by Hirsch's grandson, Levy, is more faithful to the style and syntax of the original. Sure, we get some run-on sentences but that is the style of Hirsch's German, and despite a few errors and omissions, the Levy edition is very faithful to the original.

Hirsch, Samson Raphael. *The Collected Writings of Rabbi Samson Raphael Hirsch*, vols. 1–9 (New York, 1984–2012). This is the English edition of Hirsch's *Gesammelte Schriften*, containing the essays from Hirsch's journal *Jeschurun*, covering a wide range of topics in Jewish thought.

Breuer, Mordechai. *Modernity Within Tradition: The Social History of Orthodox Jewry in Imperial Germany.* Translated by Elizabeth Petuchowski (New York, 1992). This book, by the greatest scholar of German Orthodoxy, contains much incisive analysis of Hirsch's ideology and his role as a leader of German Jewry.

Grunewald, Pinchas Paul. *Pédagogie, Esthétique et Ticoun Olam – Redressement du Monde: Samson Raphaël Hirsch* (Bern, 1986). This French-language study of Hirsch is an excellent analysis of Hirsch's educational theory and worldview from an academic scholar who was well versed in rabbinic literature and the German philosophical tradition.

Klugman, Eliyahu Meir. *Rabbi Samson Raphael Hirsch: Architect of Torah Judaism for the Modern World* (New York, 1996). While some writers feel an almost ritual obligation to bash anything published by Artscroll, this is actually the most thorough and meticulously researched biography of Hirsch currently available. The late Prof. Mordechai Breuer, dean of Hirsch scholars, was heavily involved in the writing of this book, which provides footnotes for every assertion and which covers all the material in a respectful yet scholarly style. Dr. Shnayer Leiman has characterized Klugman's book as "magisterial" and even non-Jewish scholars of German Orthodoxy such as Dr. Matthias Morgenstern regularly cite it.

Liberles, Robert. *Religious Conflict in Social Context: The Resurgence of Orthodox Judaism in Frankfurt am Main, 1838–1877* (Westport, 1985). This classic study provides important social context to Hirsch's rabbinical position in Frankfurt.

Miller, Michael L. *Rabbis and Revolution: The Jews of Moravia in the Age of Emancipation* (Redwood City, 2010). Miller's study, based on his dissertation, closely examines, among other things, Hirsch's crucial four years in the Moravian rabbinate.

Morgenstern, Matthias. *From Frankfurt to Jerusalem: Isaac Breuer and the History of the Secession Dispute in Modern Jewish Orthodoxy* (Leiden, 2002). This expanded version of the original German is a brilliant study of the legacy of some of Hirsch's ideas on the succeeding generations and contains an excellent examination of Hirsch's rabbinic career.

Delving into the Matter: Rabbi Naftali Tzvi Yehuda Berlin's *Haamek Davar* as a Work of Jewish Thought

Rabbi Dr. Gil S. Perl

THE CASE FOR INCLUSION

Rabbi Naftali Tzvi Yehuda Berlin, better known by the acronym Netziv, was born in 1816 in the tiny countryside hamlet of Mir in a region that was then Czarist Russia, that is today Belarus, but which – in Jewish cultural memory – will forever be Lithuania. An aristocratic marriage was arranged for the young Naftali, the son of a successful merchant, at the age of thirteen. The bride was the twelve-year-old daughter of Rabbi Yitzchak "Itzele" of Volozhin, then the head of the famed Etz Chaim Yeshiva, and the granddaughter of Rabbi Chaim of Volozhin, the yeshiva's iconic founder and ideological father. A year later, the young groom left Mir for the even smaller town of Volozhin, where he would live, study, and teach for the remainder of his life.

Following the death of Rav Itzele in 1849, the Netziv's brother-in-law, Rabbi Eliezer Yitzchak Fried, was appointed *rosh yeshiva* in his stead. When Fried died prematurely only four years later, the Netziv, at the age of thirty-six, was chosen to take his place. For the next thirty-nine years, the Netziv served as the administrative, educational, and spiritual head of the world's largest and most highly regarded institution of Torah study. Over the course of his career he taught thousands of the Jewish community's most promising students, many of whom went on to positions of prominence in the Jewish rabbinic and intellectual world.

As much as he was a teacher and administrator, the Netziv was also a writer. From his earliest days writing commentaries on works of Midrash Halakha to his magnum opus – a commentary on the geonic halakhic compendium known as *She'iltot* – and from commentaries on the five books of the Torah, the Song of Songs, and the Haggada, to essays, glosses, and responsa, the Netziv was constantly writing, revising, and rewriting until shortly before his death in 1893. One thing the Netziv never wrote, though, was a work of Jewish thought.

The closest the Netziv came to penning a work which one might instinctively call a work of Jewish thought was the introduction he wrote to *Haamek She'ela*[1] and his essay on anti-Semitism entitled *She'ar Yisrael*.[2] The former is an intellectual history of Torah study through the ages based on the Netziv's critical and often creative reading of traditional biblical and rabbinic sources. The latter is a theological explanation and response to the suffering endured by the Jewish people in exile. While both clearly belong to the genre of Jewish thought, neither one quite fits the common definition of a "work." The introduction to *Haamek She'ela*, known as *Kidmat Haamek*, is, after all, just an introduction. And, the work it introduces squarely belongs to the world of talmudic and halakhic commentary. Similarly, *She'ar Yisrael* is but an extensive essay published at the end of the Netziv's commentary on the Song of Songs.

The inclusion in this volume of *Haamek Davar*, the Netziv's commentary on the five books of the Torah and the most widely read product of his prolific pen, may therefore seem a bit curious. To the Netziv, this work, which grew out of the daily lectures he gave to students in Volozhin on the weekly Torah reading, is a work of Bible commentary. He seeks to explain the meaning of the Torah text in a straightforward and systematic way. Yet, when viewed from ten thousand feet, what

---

1. Available in English as Naftali Tzvi Yehuda Berlin, *The Path of Torah*, trans. Elchanan Greenman (Jerusalem, 2009).
2. Available in English as Naphtali Zvi Yehuda Berlin, *Why Antisemitism? A Translation of "The Remnant of Israel,"* trans. Howard Joseph (Northvale, 1996).

emerges from this endeavor is a work that is undoubtedly much more than that. And, if we can apply Daniel Frank's analysis of the term "Jewish philosophy" to the term "Jewish thought," then it becomes a category to which *Haamek Davar* might well belong.

Frank, in his introduction to the *Routledge History of Jewish Philosophy*, argues that the very phrase "Jewish philosophy" is a grammatical misnomer as it suggests that there is a discipline called Jewish philosophy which exists as a subcategory of the discipline called philosophy. Even the greatest Jewish philosophers, according to Frank, did not see themselves as engaged in the discipline of philosophy:

> Neither Maimonides nor Gersonides nor even Mendelssohn, in the modern period, thought of himself as a Jewish philosopher. To the extent that they thought of themselves as philosophers, they imaged themselves as providing an interpretation of the biblical and rabbinic tradition according to universal, philosophical categories. For them, the Bible is a philosophical book, and they interpret it accordingly.[3]

Jewish philosophy, therefore, according to Frank, "must be parsed as 'philosophy of Judaism.'" If we apply the same reasoning to Jewish thought, we might argue that Jewish thought refers not to a genre that is subsumed under the larger, more universal disciplines of philosophy, theology, and epistemology, but to a distinct set of philosophical, theological, and epistemological questions that stand at the core of what it means to be Jewish.

Through the ages a relatively small group of rabbinic authors sought to dedicate whole works to these questions. In doing so, they marshaled innumerable biblical and rabbinic sources, along with their own insight and the influences of their contemporary culture, to proffer unique answers and original approaches. Equally as important, these works sought to bring some degree of systemization and order to the wholly unsystematized philosophical, theological, and epistemological

---

3. Daniel Frank, "What Is Jewish Philosophy?" in *History of Jewish Philosophy*, Daniel H. Frank and Oliver Leaman, eds. (New York, 1997), 3.

teachings scattered throughout the vast tomes of rabbinic literature. The Netziv, however, following the lead of Nahmanides and several other classical Torah commentators, took a different approach. To him, the answers to Judaism's core questions leapt out of the pages of the written Torah text, so long as the reader had the tools necessary to understand them. Borrowing Frank's phrase, the Bible is a philosophical, theological, and epistemological book, and the Netziv interprets it accordingly. What's more, the consistency of themes in the Torah's narratives, the choice of phrases in its legal passages, and the Netziv's steadfast belief that every single word is deeply significant provided the most powerful and the most authentic framework in which to systematize such ideas. So while the Netziv's project in writing *Haamek Davar* is not solely philosophical, theological, or epistemological in its objective – and while it isn't organized in a fashion akin to the more classical works of Jewish thought – a great number of the passages in the Netziv's commentary on the Torah do, in fact, wrestle with traditional Judaism's most essential questions in an effort to extract, elucidate, and systematize a rabbinic approach toward their answers. Seen in such a light, *Haamek Davar* does indeed deserve inclusion among the great works of Jewish thought.

THE SETTING

Like all great literary works, *Haamek Davar* is very much a product of its place and its time. Understanding the context, therefore, of when and where it was written provides invaluable insight into the nature of the project and its objectives.

Most importantly, *Haamek Davar* may represent the first work of Jewish thought that can be accurately called a product of the yeshiva. While *Nefesh HaHayim*, written by the Netziv's father-in-law's father, Rabbi Chaim of Volozhin, first outlines much of the theology behind the creation of the nineteenth century's yeshiva movement, the author was the founder of the first modern yeshiva and not a product of it. His worldview, shaped in the shadows of the Vilna Gaon, draws from a world where Torah study was done in small rooms, generally attached to the local synagogue, that lacked the feel and focus of the great yeshivot which emerged over the course of the nineteenth century. The Netziv, on the other hand, was raised in the study hall of Volozhin and its unique culture and ethos clearly shaped his interests, his passions, and his understanding of Judaism and its history. Thus, it is not surprising that the single most dominant theme in *Haamek Davar* is an exploration and elucidation of the act of Torah study: its roots, its form, its content, and its impact.

While the Netziv's total immersion in the world of the yeshiva separates *Haamek Davar* from works of Jewish thought which preceded it, the impact in his formative years of the unique intellectual milieu of the first half of the nineteenth century separates the Netziv's work from many of the later products of the yeshiva as well. As I have described elsewhere, Lithuanian rabbinic culture in the first half of the nineteenth century, prior both to the institutionalization of the yeshiva movement and to significant infiltration of the Haskala, was marked by extraordinary intellectual breadth. As a young man studying in Volozhin, therefore, the Netziv was not solely occupied with the study of Talmud, its commentaries, and its codes, as will largely be the case in later generations. In fact, his interests went well beyond Tanakh, Talmud Yerushalmi, Midrash Halakha, Midrash Aggada, and the works of the *Geonim* as well. As a young man, the Netziv actively studied the medieval philosophical works of Maimonides, Gersonides, Rabbi Judah Halevi, Rabbi Joseph Albo, and Rabbi Isaac Arama, among others. He read the works of Karaite scholars like Yehuda Hadassi and Renaissance writers such as Eliyahu Levita and Azariah de Rossi. Even modern Jewish thinkers such as Moses Mendelssohn and Naphtali Herz Wessely, and older enlightened contemporaries such as Tzvi Hirsch Katzenellenbogen, were objects of the Netziv's study.[4] This breathtakingly broad engagement with works of Jewish philosophy, theology, and history undoubtedly influenced the Netziv's own contributions to Jewish thought.[5]

---

4. For a thorough study of the Netziv's intellectual development and the breadth of early nineteenth-century rabbinic culture, see Gil S. Perl, *The Pillar of Volozhin: Rabbi Naftali Tzvi Yehuda Berlin and the World of Nineteenth-Century Lithuanian Torah Scholarship* (Boston, 2012).

5. While some would like to see the influence of Western European Haskala in the Netziv's breadth of intellectual interests and in his decision to write a *peshat*-oriented commentary, I have argued that both characteristics ought to be seen as rather natural outgrowths of the indigenous Lithuanian rabbinic culture of the early nineteenth century instead. See ibid., 61–89.

The fact, however, that the Netziv's *Haamek Davar* emerges from the lectures he gave to his students in the second half of the nineteenth century, and not from the culture which dominated the century's first few decades, is equally as important to the story. The Netziv ascended to the leadership of Volozhin in 1854, only one year before Alexander II ascended the throne of Czarist Russia, succeeding his father Nicholas I. Russia at the time was embroiled in the Crimean War, a humiliating exposure of Russia's military and technological inferiority compared to the burgeoning powers of the West. Alexander, therefore, set a very different course than that of his father by embarking on an ambitious program of Westernization and reform which came to dominate the first decades of his reign. In the Jewish world this relative embrace of the West not only eased some of the stifling oppression introduced by Nicholas, but also created social, economic, and intellectual space for Western-minded Jewish thinkers to carve out organizational and institutional footing within the traditional world of the Lithuanian Jewish community.

As a result, the world in which the Netziv pens *Haamek Davar* is quite different from the one out of which he, himself, emerged. Studying De Rossi and Mendelssohn in the 1860s and 1870s carried associations and stigmas that didn't exist in the 1830s and 1840s. In fact, even works like *The Guide of the Perplexed* and the *Kuzari* became associated with people, behaviors, and ideologies that were considered threatening to the traditional world of the yeshiva. Therefore, while the impact of such works on *Haamek Davar* is unmistakable, the Netziv makes no explicit mention of his considerable exposure to them in this work. What's more, the issues of the day – the authority of the Oral Torah, the nature of the Written Torah text, the motivation to sin, responses to "sinners," faulty theology, responsibilities of communal leadership, etc. – all play a central role in *Haamek Davar*.

What follows is not intended as a complete list of the philosophical, theological, and epistemological questions raised by the Netziv in his *Haamek Davar*, nor are the citations intended as an exhaustive list of all the places in the commentary where the issue is discussed. Instead, it is meant as an entry point for the reader into some of the most commonly occurring questions which implicitly dot the pages of the Netziv's Torah commentary and warrant its characterization as a work of Jewish thought.

THE NATURE OF THE TORAH TEXT

The Netziv dives immediately into this question in his introduction to *Haamek Davar*. In one of the work's more famous passages, he uses the Torah's self-description as *shira* to define the unique aspects of the Torah text as "poetic" in nature. This, he says, explains both the brevity of the text as well as its grammatical and syntactical "distortions." Whereas Maimonides interprets the talmudic dictum that "the Torah is written in the language of man" to mean that the Torah is written so as to be accessible to the masses, the Netziv seems to adopt a very different position. To him, the "poetic nature" of the Torah text makes it almost incomprehensible to the average reader. Indeed, the poetic diction which William Wordsworth rails against in the preface to the second edition of his *Lyrical Ballads* (1800), when he calls for modern poetry written in "language near to the language of men," is precisely the stuff of the biblical text according to the Netziv. The Torah is poetry in its highest form and thus its intricacies and insights are accessible only to the initiated:

> And behold, in Nedarim (38a) they explained the biblical phrase, "write for yourselves the song (*shira*)" (Deut. 31:19), as referring to the entire Torah.... Yet it remains for us to understand why the Torah is referred to as a song when it is not written in the language of songs. Rather it must be because it has both the nature (*teva*) and unique quality (*segula*) of songs, which is poetic language.
>
> For in a poem the issue at hand is not articulated as explicitly as it would be in prose and one, therefore, has to make notes on the side indicating that this stanza refers to this story and that stanza refers to that one. And this is not what we would call "*derush*," but rather it is the nature of poetry, even to the uninitiated. And it logically follows that for one who is well acquainted with the subject matter about which the poem is written, the language of the poem and its nuances are that much sweeter than for one who has no subject area knowledge and merely reads the poetry

superficially. For he is far more prone to make faulty assumptions that do not align with the intent of the author.

Such is the nature of the entire Torah – for the story within it is never fully articulated; rather one has to make notations and commentary on the intricacies of the language. And this is not called "*derush*"; rather such is the simple reading of the text (*peshat hamikra*). And it logically follows that one cannot fully understand the intricacies of God's word without the ability to reference a piece of halakha, *Musar*, or Aggada which we received via tradition through the words of our sages and that for him [who can], the light of [biblical] insight is sweetest.

For the unique quality (*segula*) of a poem is that one enhances it with allusions to that which is not germane to the subject of the poem itself, like the custom of aligning the first letter of every stanza to the letters of the *aleph-bet* or to the letters of the author's name. And this quality is unique to poetry as opposed to prose. And it's known that this quality often forces the author to distort the language somewhat in order to allow each stanza to begin with the requisite letter. And such is exactly the case with the entirety of the Torah: in addition to the subject matter conveyed in the simple reading of the text, every matter also contains many secrets and hidden subjects which frequently cause the text to be imprecise.[6]

Unlike human poetry, however, the divine poetry of the Torah text is perfect. Thus time and again the Netziv reminds the reader that "*ein davar reik,*" "there is no empty thing"[7] in the Torah text and, citing a passage in the Talmud Yerushalmi,[8] "*im reik hu, mikem hu reik,*" "if it is empty, its emptiness comes from you" – that is, it is your understanding that is deficient, not the text itself.[9] One such seeming deficiency in the Torah text is the numerous times in which instructions are relayed to Moses

---

6. Introduction to *Haamek Davar* (henceforth, *HD*).
7. Based on Deut. 32:47. See, e.g., *HD* Ex. 36:8.
8. Y. Shabbat 1:4.
9. See, e.g., *HD* Ex. 26:34.

followed, in turn, by a description of Moses carrying out God's command, followed then by a declarative clause stating that Moses acted "*kaasher tziva Hashem,*" "as God commanded." At the very least, the final clause seems to be extraneous. If the Torah relates God's command and details Moses' enactment of it, then the reader knows full well that Moses did it "as God commanded." What's worse, though, is that often Moses' actions don't follow God's instructions to a T. Sometimes the order of what to do when is reversed.[10] Sometimes Moses seems to leave elements of the command out or adds elements that God didn't command at all.[11] In one fell swoop, however, the Netziv resolves all such difficulties by explaining that the phrase "*kaasher tziva Hashem*" refers to additional oral instructions which Moses received and not to that which was written in the Torah text. Hence, the phrase is never extraneous and often indicates that God orally relayed a slight deviation from the written plan. Hence, the poetry of the Torah remains perfect and free of any "empty things."

Recognizing that oral instructions were given to Moses concurrently with those written in the Torah text is reflective of the Netziv's view of the general relationship between the Written Torah and the Oral Torah. Simply put, he maintains that the former is virtually incomprehensible,[12] and perhaps even dangerous, without the latter. Just as a reader of poetry who is unfamiliar with the objects of the poet's allusions fails to understand the author's true intent, so it is with a reader of the Written Torah who is ignorant of its Oral referents. In fact, such a reader is at risk of corrupting the text with his own misguided interpretations. Thus, when the rabbis compare a true Torah scholar to a bride who adorns herself with twenty-four ornaments, the Netziv takes the analogy one step further: "Just as one who is not a bride yet adorns herself with twenty-four ornaments is suspected to be a harlot, so too one who expounds upon the twenty-four books of Tanakh but is not a *talmid ḥakham* [i.e., is not proficient in the teachings of the Oral Torah], is suspected to be a heretic."[13]

---

10. *HD* Num. 27:22.

11. E.g., *HD* Gen. 7:5; Ex. 7:6, 20; 39:5.

12. *HD* Ex. 13:17; 19:19.

13. *Harḥev Davar* Ex. 32:2 (*hashmatot* in earlier editions). *Harḥev Davar* (henceforth, *HrD*) is a supercommentary on *Haamek Davar* written by the Netziv himself which appears

Rabbi Dr. Gil S. Perl

THE NATURE OF TORAH STUDY

In *Haamek Davar* one learns that Torah study, the primary vocation of the Netziv, his colleagues, and his students at the Etz Chaim Yeshiva in Volozhin, has a long and storied history. It began well before the Giving of the Written Torah with the forefathers who used reason and intuition to understand God's ways[14] and even innovated in the realm of Jewish law.[15] This process was embraced in earnest by Moses and Aaron who embodied two different approaches to engaging with the text. Like that of the forefathers before him, Aaron's method of Torah study centered around logic and reason as well as comparisons of one text to another. Moses, on the other hand, employed penetrating analysis and innovative exegesis (*pilpul* and *ḥidush*) in his approach to Torah study. While Aaron's approach was later reflected in the methods of the rabbinic sages living in the Land of Israel, rabbis who, like Aaron in the *Mishkan*, benefited from a certain proximity to God based on their location, the sages of Babylonia employed the methods of Moses.[16] While both are valid means of arriving at the divine will, the Netziv views the method of Aaron as requiring less effort and producing little of value other than the end product itself, while Moses' *pilpul* approach was more difficult but resulted in a process that was as valuable as the outcome. And, much as the Diaspora Jewish community adopted the Babylonian Talmud as its authoritative source for halakha, so too its exilic status necessitated the adoption of the Babylonian approach to Torah study as well.

The tools for this type of Torah study were given to Moses at Sinai and are repeatedly referred to in the biblical text, according to *Haamek Davar*, by the term "*ḥukim*." Whereas previous commentators interpreted this word as a reference to a legal category, to the Netziv "*ḥukim* are the rules by which Torah itself is legislated; [that is,] how to interpret and tease out previously unexplained laws from precise analysis of the

---

in all printed editions. The Netziv utilizes *Harḥev Davar* to expound upon themes and ideas connected to his comments in *Haamek Davar* but only loosely connected to the verse at hand. As such, it functions almost as footnotes do in contemporary literature.

14. *HrD* Gen. 4:9.
15. *HD* Gen. 26:5.
16. The Netziv elaborates on this dichotomy in his introduction to *Haamek She'ela* (henceforth, *HS*). See *HS Kidmat Haamek* 1:6–13.

biblical text."[17] And, while most classical Jewish thinkers ascribe a very different status to the "rules of interpretation" listed by Hillel and utilized by the talmudic sages than they do to their own exegetical tools, to the Netziv they are part and parcel of a singular evolutionary process: "*Kol shenehkar be'eize dor naase mishna ledor haba aharav*," "All that is studied in one generation becomes Mishna for the generation that follows."[18]

In this respect, the study of Torah as described in *Haamek Davar* shares much with the study of nature. Observable phenomena in both realms are guided by fixed laws, some of which are known and some of which still await discovery. In both realms the impetus for in-depth study is the observation of seemingly aberrant phenomena which do not fit the known rules. To the ignorant masses such phenomena in the scientific world are labeled as supernatural. As such, they represent one-time occurrences from which little can be learned and from which nothing can be applied. In the world of Torah study, the ignorant similarly attribute passages that seem to defy known rules of grammar, syntax, and the like, to singular instances either of divine poetic license or corruptions of the text. These too, therefore, add nothing to our understanding of other biblical passages.

Those highly trained in their respective disciplines, however, take a very different approach. Aberrations in nature to the scientist are simply indicators that our understanding of nature is deficient. Concerted study will ultimately lead to revisiting and revising nature's known laws so as to encompass the seemingly supernatural within it. This discovery, then, leads to knowledge that can – and must – be applied to many other contexts beyond that in which it was originally discovered. Likewise, the Torah scholar approaches aberrant passages as a call to further study – "*Haamek davar!*" "Delve into the matter!" – from which new understandings of biblical exegesis emerge. He describes the process as follows in his introduction to *Haamek Davar*:

> And it is written in Isaiah (34:4), "And all the host of heaven shall melt, and the heavens shall be rolled like a scroll, etc."

---

17. *HD* Ex. 27:20; Lev. 18:5; Num. 15:32.
18. *HD* Deut. 26:16.

The meaning of the verse is that the "scroll" is the Divine Writ which is compared to God's creation of the nature of both heaven and earth. For there are simple [laws of] nature that are known to all and many secrets of nature in which the power of each element, every animal, and every plant are [only] discovered by the scientists of that generation. And before such knowledge is discovered, if one observes a phenomenon which deviates from common understandings of nature, one is led to believe that it is supernatural and one does not delve deeply into the matter in an effort to learn anything that might be applied elsewhere. In contrast, after the matter is properly studied and it is understood that it is in fact a secret of nature – which is to say, the straight-forward understanding of creation – one can then extrapolate great amounts from it which can be of use to the entire world.

And so it is with the "scroll" of the Divine Writ. Before proper examination of the nature of the Torah's language and its principles, a verse whose language seems strange would be thought of as happenstance and "an empty thing," God forbid. And as such, one would not be able to learn anything from it which can be applied elsewhere. However, after proper study and the discovery that such is the nature of the language and the straightforward understanding of the Book, one can then learn a great deal for application to other verses and passages in halakha and Aggada....[19]

Just as the process of study in both Torah and science bear much in common, so does the nature of the truths they yield. Both fields must treat truth as derived from proper application of its methods as fact upon which to act and to build. Yet both fields must simultaneously recognize the possibility, or probability, that discoveries in future generations will force today's facts to be questioned, reexamined, and perhaps even undermined:

And it is easy to understand that just like no scientist could claim that he has discovered all of the secrets of nature [and

---

19. Introduction to *HD*. See also *HD* Deut. 16:12.

therefore, need not study any more]...and, what's more, [he realizes that] even that which he did study – if he doesn't have absolute certainty that it is true – is subject to reexamination in a future generation by someone who may demolish that which he has built, and yet, nonetheless, he has an obligation to study it as best he can. So too it is impossible for one who studies "the nature of Torah" to claim that he has discovered all of the nuances and peculiarities which require explanation and has understood them all. And even about that which he did offer an explanation there is no certainty that he arrived at the ultimate truth of the Torah. Nonetheless, we have to do what we can.[20]

While the by-product of such discoveries in the Torah text are more enhanced and more accurate rules of interpretation, the primary outcome is a more nuanced and deeper understanding of a particular biblical passage. These understandings, which may consist of heretofore unknown details of a biblical narrative or previously unknown biblical roots of halakhic norms,[21] represent the apex of Torah study. They are the *hidushim* to which the Torah beckons its readers each time it commands the Jewish people *laasot* (to do) the Torah's laws and statutes. It is not, *Haamek Davar* contends, a call for observance of Torah laws but a call for in-depth study and discovery of God's will.

In the Netziv's hierarchy of mitzvot, Torah study enjoys a hallowed and unique place at the very top. Service of God (sacrifices, prayer, etc.) and charitable works (*gemilut hasadim*) rank just below it, but the relationship between all three is symbiotic in nature. Service of God and charitable works are necessary prerequisites for Torah study. Without either one, authentic Torah study is impossible. Conversely, Torah study infuses proper form and higher value to both service of God and charitable works. Thus the Netziv sees the structure of a doorway, employed

---

20. *HD* Deut. 16:12. The limits of even the most highly qualified Torah scholar to arrive at ultimate truth in Torah study leads the Netziv to note on several occasions the importance of *siyata dishmaya* in arriving at correct halakhic decisions. See, e.g., *HD* Num. 4:6, 9; 27:18.
21. See *HD* Introduction to the Book of Leviticus for a detailed discussion of the contemporary Torah scholar's role in this process.

by God as part of the ritual around the original Passover sacrifice, as symbolic of this relationship. The two doorposts represent the spheres of *avoda* and *gemilut ḥasadim* while the lintel represents the sphere of *talmud Torah*. The latter is clearly elevated above the other two. However, take either of the posts away and the lintel will fall. Take the lintel away and the chances of either post remaining in place for posterity is greatly diminished.[22]

Along with the elevated status of Torah study in the taxonomy of mitzvot comes the unique power of this endeavor to protect its participants from harm. The biblical and rabbinic names used to describe Torah and its study reflect this protective nature, according to the Netziv. The Torah is referred to as *mishmeret*, because of its power of *shemira* (protection).[23] The Torah is referred to as a *ḥerev* (sword), because of the sword's ability to save human life.[24] The act of engaging in Torah study is referred to by the sages – and quite frequently by the Netziv – as *milḥamta shel Torah* not so much because of the intellectual sparring which takes place between study partners, but because the act of learning serves to ensure the welfare of the learner and of the Jewish people as a whole, much as a physical battle might.[25] It is for this reason that the Netziv suggests that had Joseph not stopped engaging in Torah study he would not have fallen prey to the wife of Potiphar.[26] Similarly, the Jubilee year, according to *Haamek Davar*, requires all Jewish families to reunite on their ancestral plots and work out any issues that may have caused them to drift apart. Doing so would necessarily leave the borders of Israel unprotected as soldiers headed home for their reunions. This extreme exposure and existential threat to the welfare of the Jewish state is mitigated by the fact that the Jubilee year is also supposed to be spent engaged in Torah study. Thus, the salvific power of Torah study will literally serve to protect the borders of the Land of Israel.[27]

---

22. *HD* Ex. 12:22. See also *HD* Ex. 40:20.
23. *HD* Gen. 12:17.
24. *HD* Gen. 12:13; Ex. 13:2; Deut. 11:18; 29:12; *HrD* Gen. 36:5.
25. *HD* Gen. 32:3; *HrD* Gen. 26:5; Ex. 13:16; Lev. 22:42; Deut. 28:10; 29:12.
26. *HD* Gen. 39:6; 41:51.
27. *HD* Lev. 25:18. It is ironic that the Netziv, who broke rank with nineteenth-century Eastern Europe's rabbinic establishment by vocally and ardently supporting the early

THE NATURE OF MITZVOT

From the very beginning of *Haamek Davar*, the reader learns of the Netziv's position that interpersonal ethics exist independent of mitzvot, though the Torah's mitzvot are inclusive of them. His well-known introduction to the Book of Genesis contends that the reason the sages refer to the book as *Sefer HaYashar* is because of its focus on the forefathers who were masters of *yashrut*, interpersonal ethics. In this pre-Sinaitic time, *yashrut* was the highest ideal around which one could organize one's life. For the non-Jewish world it remained so; hence, Balaam's request of God that he die a *mot yesharim* (death of the upright).[28] For the Jewish world interpersonal ethics becomes the baseline for all behavior, expected even of the faithless among the Jewish people.[29] Thus, when a generation arose during the times of the Second Temple in which Jews were excelling in "righteousness and charity" but were deficient in their interpersonal ethics, God brought about the Temple's destruction and the exile of the Jewish people because He "has no patience for *tzaddikim* such as these."[30]

The existence of natural morality is implied in the Netziv's famous interpretation of the Tower of Babel as well.[31] According to *Haamek Davar*, the sin of these pre-Abrahamic people was their desire to create a conformist community in which all people thought exactly alike. God, however, created a world in which "no two minds are exactly alike" and hence diversity of opinion is the natural and desired state.[32] When man failed to recognize or act on this, God had to intervene instead.

Natural ethics, according to *Haamek Davar*, are somewhat fluid and their details change with the passage of time. Thus they are not completely captured in either the Written or the Oral Torah. Mitzvot,

Zionist movement, is also the earliest explicit source I know for the idea that men who engage in full-time Torah study are doing as much, if not more, to protect the State of Israel as are those men who fight on the front lines.

28. *HD* Introduction to the Book of Genesis. See also *HD* Num. 23:10; Deut. 32:4.
29. *HD* Num. 23:10.
30. *HD* Introduction to the Book of Genesis.
31. *HD* Gen. 11:1–8.
32. *HD* Gen. 11:1.

however, are unchanging and though their details often require discovery and elucidation, they can be found within the Torah itself. God instructs the Jewish people to abide by both codes of conduct when He commands them to be both a "kingdom of priests," that is, upholders of morality, and a "holy nation," observers of mitzvot. By going beyond natural law to abide by Torah law as well, the Jewish people in turn merit divine providence and treatment that similarly extends beyond the laws of nature which govern all other people.[33]

While natural ethics have reasons and logic to them that are easily comprehended by the human mind, mitzvot, according to *Haamek Davar*, do not. Although classic Jewish thought often divides mitzvot into *mishpatim*, whose reasons are humanly knowable, and *ḥukkim*, whose reasons are not, the Netziv repeatedly argues throughout *Haamek Davar* that all mitzvot, at their core, are *ḥukkim*.[34] Thus he cautions his readers "not to praise honoring one's parents, which reflects the attribute of kindness, more than the commandment to wipe out Amalek or to decimate a wayward city, for both are no more than *ḥukkim* and edicts from the Giver of the Torah."[35] The fact that some mitzvot are aligned with human reason and our general moral compass is not for naught, however. Rather, the fact that honoring one's parents also accords with human reason means that there is a value which God wants one to learn for the purposes of applying it to other circumstances and other contexts. The Netziv compares it to the talmudic passage (Eiruvin 100b) which instructs one to learn modesty from a cat. It is not that a cat acts as he does because he is modest, but that by observing the behavior of the cat we can learn the value of modesty:

> And it is this way with all reasons ascribed to the mitzvot – they are also only [intended] to bring [a value] close to the mind – but, woe unto us, to think that this is the primary rationale of

---

33. *HD* Gen. 11:5.
34. *HD* Ex. 20:12; Deut. 5:16; 22:6, 7. Compare *Kuzari* III:7: "The social and rational laws are those generally known…. Even those social and rational laws are not quite known, and though one might know the gist of them, their scope remains unknown."
35. *HrD* Ex. 20:12.

the Giver of the Torah, blessed be He. For who comprehends
the secrets of God? And if God wished to arrive at human reason, He would not have brought the thunder, and the lightning,
and all this preparation. Rather, all of the Torah is no more than
hukkim beyond human comprehension.[36]

Taking his cue from Maimonides, and in accordance with what is today
known as legal formalism, the Netziv notes that the comprehensible reasons for mitzvot are often to be found only in a mitzva's most general
form. Once one drills down to the level of halakhic detail, however, the
rationale may no longer apply though the authority of the law remains
intact.[37] So, for example, he explains that the reason the Torah ascribes
a more severe punishment to a master who hits his slave than it does
to a freeman who strikes another freeman, is because physical fights
between equals generally arise as outgrowths of disputes over one matter or another. Between master and slave, however, there are no disputes.
If a master hits his slave, it is because the slave did not adequately fulfill
the wishes and desires of his master. The anger which results and which
prompts the blow reflects a far more nefarious character trait than that
which prompts a free person to strike at another free person. Hence,
the punishment is more severe. However, the Netziv notes that there
may be circumstances in which a master hits his slave for reasons other
than the anger of unrequited desire. The law in that case, however, does
not change. The stiffer penalty is still exacted even though the rationale
does not apply.[38]

The fact that all mitzvot in their essence belong to the category
of *hukkim* explains why Moses was reluctant to delegate his judicial
responsibilities among other judges. They, after all, would be inclined
toward using reason when human reason does not, in fact, lie at the
core of divine law.[39] This characteristic of mitzvot also helps the Netziv
to explain the harsh response of the Haggada to the question of the

---

36. *HrD* Ex. 20:12.
37. *HD* Num. 1:19; 3:47.
38. *HD* Ex. 21:26.
39. *HD* Ex. 18:16.

wicked son. The son, after all, was demanding reasons he could easily comprehend before agreeing to participate in the observance of Passover's laws. Doing so, according to *Haamek Davar*, runs contrary to the very nature of mitzvot and hence one has no choice but to "blunt his teeth."[40]

Although all mitzvot are "no more than *ḥukkim*" according to the Netziv, he does recognize that due to differences in personality and psyche different people will naturally be attracted to different mitzvot. Following one's personal predilection in the performance of mitzvot, writes the Netziv, is highly encouraged by the Torah. It was precisely this point that Solomon was making, according to *Haamek Davar*, when he wrote in Ecclesiastes (11:9), "And you shall walk in the ways of your heart." However, the Netziv is even more adamant in asserting that the mitzvot represent a finite and exclusive set of pathways to God. That is, following one's heart toward practices that are not within the defined set of mitzvot, even if motivated by nothing less than an overwhelming desire to draw close to God, is tantamount to heresy. This act of seeking God through non-sanctioned mechanisms led to the downfall of both Nadav and Avihu[41] as well as the 250 followers of Korah.[42] And in an effort to prevent future generations from following suit, God gives the people the mitzva of tzitzit and warns them not "to follow after your hearts."[43]

REWARD AND PUNISHMENT

Reward and punishment in *Haamek Davar* is described as belonging to the laws of nature.[44] Just as one would not blame God for "making his intestines curved" when something one shouldn't have eaten gets stuck

---

40. *HD* Ex. 12:27.
41. *HD* Lev. 10:1.
42. *HD* Lev. 16:1. The repeated reference to this extrahalakhic zeal for closeness to God as *ḥasidut* was undoubtedly intended to resonate as a contemporary social commentary among *Haamek Davar*'s nineteenth-century readers. While the *Kuzari* similarly warns against unbridled religious enthusiasm (III:49, 50), it is telling to note that the "*ḥasid*" in Rabbi Judah Halevi's work is the paradigmatic servant of God who walks the "middle path" and exemplifies self-control. The Netziv employs the term quite differently.
43. *HD* Lev. 15:41.
44. *HrD* Gen. 1:1.

in them, so too one cannot blame God when He punishes him for acting improperly.[45] The same holds true for rewards.

However, as noted above, the Netziv sees the Jewish people as being subject to a different, more intense form of divine providence than other people of the world. The nature of this relationship and its impact on reward and punishment is conveyed through an elaborate parable of a doctor and his patients:

> Reward and punishment for mitzvot are not like the [rewards and punishments that result from] the decrees of a king who decides at any time to do as his heart desires. Rather it is like a doctor who warns a person to stay away from certain foods that will harm him. For the matter is unrelated to his [the doctor's] desire; he simply informs him [the patient] of the way in which nature works.[46] And so it is with mitzvot and *aveirot* for which God established reward and punishment that results from their observance or violation. As it says in Deuteronomy Rabba in the beginning of *Parashat Re'eh*, "From the moment that the Holy One, blessed be He, said, 'Behold I put before you today the blessing and the curse' God no longer does anything. Rather the mitzvot act on their own and the *aveirot* act on their own, as it says (Lam. 3:38), 'The good and the bad do not emanate from the mouth on High.'" And this is like the "reward and punishment" of a doctor. For the doctor does not punish a person when finding out that he didn't heed his medical advice – rather the person is punished on his own. And it is not like the punishment of a king which comes about through the intention and the action of the punisher....
>
> Therefore, one would be warranted in asking whether God desires the fulfillment of His mitzvot or whether He is merely like

---

45. *HD* Deut. 32:6.

46. Compare *Kuzari* I:85: "The real cure was effected by the skill of the learned physician who prepared the medicines and explained the proper manner in which they were to be administered. He also taught the patients what food and drink, exercise, rest, etc., was necessary."

the doctor who warns and informs but has no inherent desire that a person follow his instruction. For what is it to him if a person helps or harms himself? But in truth it is different. For the Holy One, blessed be He, does desire the fulfillment of the mitzvot. And it is comparable to a doctor who gives [medical] advice to his son.[47] For he desires greatly that his son take the proper precautions so that he may live and sustain the world of his father, the [medical] advisor. And there is also a difference in the warning that a doctor gives his own son and the warning he would give someone else. Even though the essence of the warning is the same, nonetheless, there is a difference. [For when] the doctor warns his son, he promises him that if he heeds his warning not only will he be healthy, but he'll give him toys as well. Whereas when he warns another child he does not offer him any toys. And that is because of the fact that very existence of his [the doctor's] world is predicated on the son heeding his advice which is not the case with someone else's child.

And this is the essence of the difference between the reward received by Jews for the performance of mitzvot and that received by the nations of the world for the performance of their seven mitzvot. For Jews, in addition to receiving the reward inherent in the [performance of the] mitzvot, they also receive reward for upholding the world…whereas the sustenance of the world does not depend on the nations of the world and they, therefore, only receive the inherent reward of the mitzvot.[48]

While this mechanistic naturalistic approach to reward and punishment seems to allow for little deviation from strict retributive justice, other passages in *Haamek Davar* suggest the Netziv's view was a bit more complex. For example, he writes that when God wants to punish or reward someone but that person is not yet fully deserving, He will deliberately place opportunities before the person either for further merit or for further sin in order to bring the person to the point

---

47. Here the Netziv extends the metaphor beyond its use in the *Kuzari*.
48. HD Lev. 26:3.

necessary for the natural consequences to kick in.[49] He also writes that the natural consequences which result from sin can impact more people than just the sinner. The Netziv refers several times in *Haamek Davar* to the notion that God, at times, gets worked up into a state of violent wrath, an *idan deritha*. When that happens and God lashes out at the instigators, even innocent bystanders are at high risk of being harmed.[50]

MOTIVATION TO SIN

While God may occasionally entice a person to sin (never fully taking away his free will, of course), the motivation to sin, according to *Haamek Davar*, resides within the individual and generally falls into one of three categories. One is led to sin because of either a lack of faith, or overwhelming desire and lust, or anger. Each of these three avenues is personified in one of Judaism's three cardinal sins. Lack of faith reaches its climax in idol worship, the epitome of lust is adultery, and anger, at its worst, leads to murder.[51]

It is clear to the Netziv that sins which stem from philosophical mistakes or misgivings are worse than those that follow from lust or anger[52] and that proper *teshuva* for the former is more difficult as well.[53] Within this first category of sins caused by a deficiency in faith, *Haamek Davar* distinguishes between those driven to sin by an absence of faith and those driven by faulty theology. The Netziv maintains that a person of faith, even if that faith is misguided, is viewed more favorably than one who has none.[54] At the same time, he expresses grave concern over the potential impact that those with faulty theology can have on the greater Jewish community. Such people, he writes, are often passionate about convincing others that their approach is the correct one and can almost never be convinced of the error of their ways.[55] Therefore, it is incumbent upon those who have faith to avoid such people rather than

---

49. *HrD* Ex. 19:1.
50. *HD* Num. 31:2–3.
51. *HD* Deut. 25:17.
52. *HD* Num. 15:30.
53. *HD* Lev. 20:2.
54. *HD* Lev. 13:41; Deut. 29:17.
55. *HD* Lev. 13:44.

engage them.[56] In fact, even the *adam gadol*, the towering spiritual figures of a generation, ought not to take such risks, according to the Netziv.[57]

JEWISH LEADERSHIP

The capacities, privileges, and responsibilities of the *adam gadol* are another common theme in *Haamek Davar*. Terms which others have interpreted as references to the people as a whole, the Netziv, in his quest to demonstrate the omnisignificance of the Torah text, interprets as references to the people's religious and intellectual elite. Hence *Benei Yisrael* when contrasted with *Beit Yaakov* means "people of extraordinary minds" and excludes the "masses."[58] Similarly the word "*edah*" at times means not the congregation as a whole, but its leadership[59] and the word "*adam*" doesn't mean people, but rather means extraordinary people.[60]

This select cadre of *gedolei hador* exists on an elevated spiritual plane which allows them to live with fewer physical needs than the common folk[61] and to more readily influence God.[62] For this reason, commoners often seek out God's "beloved" in times of trouble and ask that they pray on their behalf.[63] The religious elite enjoy a certain intellectual prowess as well, which is reflected in the practice of setting out a fifth cup of wine at the Seder but not requiring that it be drunk. This optional cup, according to *Haamek Davar*, represents the fifth stage of redemption, which is (Ex. 6:7) "and you shall know God." The reason this cup doesn't have the same mandated status as the first four is because this stage of redemption – true knowledge of God – is attainable only by a special few. For the common folk, it remains out of reach.[64]

---

56. *HD* Deut. 29:17.
57. *HD* Lev. 13:44.
58. *HD* Ex. 19:3; Lev. 22:18.
59. *HD* Num. 23:9.
60. *HD* Lev. 1:1; 22:18.
61. *HD* Num. 20:5. It is worth considering whether the Netziv's consistent usage of the terms "*gedolei Yisrael*" and "*gedolei hador*" to describe the class of religious elite played a role in forming the "*gadol* culture" which blossomed in the yeshiva communities of the twentieth century.
62. *HD* Num. 23:9.
63. *HD* Num. 6:25.
64. *HD* Ex. 6:7.

Along with the benefits of membership in this leadership class comes a set of heightened expectations and responsibilities.[65] So, for example, the prohibition against eating the sciatic nerve, according to *Haamek Davar*, is intended to remind future generations of Jacob's failure to live up to his own elevated standards of conduct when he continued to wrestle with the angel even though the battle had already been won.[66] And, when Moses coronates Joshua as his successor he does so in front of Elazar the High Priest and the people. On the one hand this is intended to demonstrate Joshua's newly acquired authority, but the language of the text, according to the Netziv, indicates that the very purpose of his leadership position is to serve the needs of those before whom he is standing.[67] To the Netziv, then, servant leadership becomes the paradigm for all future Jewish leaders.

Saddling the religious elite with additional expectations, though, is not enough to ensure their proper conduct. The Netziv sees God as acutely aware of the danger that singling out such people for exalted status seems to bear. Therefore he explains that the Torah on several occasions issues warnings to Jewish leaders admonishing them not to allow their power to go to their head[68] and not to allow their positions to separate them from the people.[69]

JEWS AND NON-JEWS

Much as he conceives of Jewish leaders as being inherently different from the Jewish masses, the Netziv, in the parable of the doctor cited above, articulates an essentialist position regarding the status of the Jewish people as a whole vis-à-vis their non-Jewish brethren. Jews, to the Netziv, by virtue simply of their birth, are more "beloved" to God than are people of other faiths.[70] And, much as it does for those in the

---

65. *HD* Lev. 21:6; Deut. 29:9, 12.

66. *HD* Gen. 32:26.

67. *HD* Num. 27:19.

68. *HD* Ex. 28:2, 35.

69. *HrD* Num. 4:9.

70. One could argue, though, that the Netziv's position is actually less essentialist than that of the *Kuzari* as it is rooted not in the intrinsic composition of one's soul but in the extrinsic nature of each people's relationship with God.

leadership class, this elevated status also comes along with added respon-sibility. In the case of the Jewish people in relation to their non-Jewish neighbors, the responsibility is to teach and influence others to recog-nize God and understand His ways.

So, for example, when God tells Abraham that he will be an *"av hamon goyim,"* a "father of many nations," the meaning according to *Haamek Davar* is not that numerous peoples will descend from Abraham but that his descendants will be a father – a teacher, an influencer – to the nations of the world.[71] Similarly, when God refers to the observance of Shabbat as *"ot hi leolam"* (Ex. 31:17), the Netziv does not translate the word *"leolam"* as "for eternity" but rather with the equally correct but highly unique translation of "to the world." In his rendition, Shab-bat is not a sign for eternity that God created the world in six days and rested on the seventh, but a sign to the world that He did so. Likewise, the Netziv understands God's command to write the Torah on stones when the Jewish people first enter into the Land of Israel as reflective of this responsibility of the Jewish people to be a "light unto the nations." The commandment, according to the rabbis, was to do so in seventy lan-guages. To the Netziv, this was God's way of helping the Jewish people to spread the ideas found in His Torah throughout the rest of the world.[72]

Of course, learning to explain the essential ideas of the Torah in multiple languages is of little value when the Jewish people are living on their own in their own land. Thus the Netziv explains that the stone inscriptions they had to write upon entry to the Land of Israel were actually there for them to read upon exiting it. For it would only be in the Diaspora that they would fully actualize their mission to be an *or lagoyim.*[73] In fact, when God first informs Abraham that such is to be his progeny's mission and that such is to be their destiny, He quickly follows it with the mitzva of circumcision, the ultimate reminder for His people that even when they are living among others, they are to remain distinct.[74]

---

71. *HD* Gen. 17:4; 21:4.
72. *HD* Deut. 27:9.
73. *HD* Deut. 27:9. See also *HD* Deut. 29:1.
74. *HD* Gen. 17:9.

As critical as the Jewish people's mission of influencing the world is to the Netziv, the notion that they must always remain above and apart from their host society is equally as important. This characteristic was first demonstrated by Jacob, who insisted on camping outside the city of Shekhem and not entering it.[75] Hence, this Jewish proclivity toward isolationism is later referred to simply as *ein Yaakov*.[76] Joseph, according to *Haamek Davar*, knew that his father felt strongly about this issue. Joseph therefore makes a point of immediately informing Jacob, along with the fact that he is alive, that he is the "ruler of all of Egypt" and therefore can designate a land apart from the Egyptians in which Jacob and his family would feel comfortable settling.[77] The fact that the descendants of Jacob later move out of their designated space in the land of Goshen, as indicated according to *Haamek Davar* by the phrase "and the land was filled with them" (Ex. 1:7), ultimately results in the increased hatred which the Egyptians felt for them.[78] The notion that the Jewish people are safer and more secure when separated from their non-Jewish brethren is later noted by Balaam as well when he prophesies that they are "a nation destined to live apart" but that when they fail to do so "among the nations they are not respected."[79]

SENSITIVITY TO PSYCHOLOGY

One of the most unique contributions of *Haamek Davar* to the world of Jewish thought is his exploration of the nature of the human mind and its reflection in Torah and mitzvot. For example, in the Netziv's retelling of the passage about the Tower of Babel, the reader is first introduced to the fact that diversity of thought and multiplicity of opinions are basic characteristics of the human race. Indeed, the great sin of that generation was to try and forcefully curtail such diversity by limiting the environments in which people could live.[80] God, however, saw to it that they would not succeed.

---

75. *HD* Gen. 33:18.
76. *HD* Gen. 15:14; Deut. 33:28.
77. *HD* Gen. 45:9.
78. *HD* Ex. 1:7.
79. *HD* Num. 23:9.
80. *HD* Gen. 11:4.

These innate differences in the composition of human minds account also for differences in human learning. Not only are some people more intellectually capable than others,[81] but every person has an emotional proclivity toward certain vocations; and allowing people to pursue those passions results in extraordinary learning outcomes. The ability of the Jewish people to harness this capacity, which the Netziv understands to be the meaning of the Torah's phrase "*ḥokhmat halev,*" "wisdom of the heart," explains how a band of escaped slaves could have produced an engineering and artistic marvel such as the *Mishkan*:

> And it is certainly true that one's emotional inclination is relevant with regard to secular endeavors. For example, if one wanted to create a school for children to learn craftsmanship and he brought many children there and allowed them to choose the craft which they most desired, this one would say, "I want [to do] this one!" and that one would say, "I want [to do] that one!" And the act of choosing would help them advance in their learning for however many years they remained engaged in their selected craft. And so it was in the building of the *Mishkan*. Allowing people to choose their area of artisanship allowed them to perform without any [formal] training whatsoever, but rather only with success from God [granted] to "that which a person's heart is inclined."[82]

In addition to recognizing the capacities of the human mind, the Netziv was equally sensitive to its limitations. The mind, after all, is not easily changed. Therefore the Jewish people had to slowly proceed through several stages of redemption before they were psychologically fit to stand as a free people before God at Mount Sinai.[83]

Sometimes exceptional events will jolt the human mind into adopting a certain stance and moving beyond it becomes nearly impossible. The Netziv famously uses this idea to explain the relationship between Rebecca and Isaac. As a young girl, venturing on her own to a

---

81. See fn. 64 above.
82. *HD* Ex. 36:2.
83. *HD* Ex. 6:6.

strange land a long way from home in order to marry a strange man from a strange culture, Rebecca encounters a frightening sight upon her entry into Canaan. There, in an open field, was a person visibly engulfed in a state of spiritual rapture with no object of his worship anywhere to be seen. In a state of panic she turns to her guide, the servant Eliezer, and asks who that man is. When he replies that this was the man she was to marry, Rebecca's anxiety is so overwhelming that she falls from her saddle and hides her face behind her veil. Her trauma from this initial interaction creates permanent scars that inform the way in which she engages with her husband – or, more accurately, the way in which she doesn't engage her husband – throughout her lifetime.[84]

Earlier in the Book of Genesis, *Haamek Davar* sees the Torah distinguishing between what we might call extreme disappointment (*ḥaron*) and depression (*nefilat panim*). *Ḥaron*, an emotion caused by events in the past, manifests itself as a feverish pain caused internally by haughtiness and externally by unfulfilled desires. *Nefilat panim*, however, is caused by a bleak forecast of the future caused internally by low self-esteem and externally by the scorn and ridicule of others. Cain, in the moments leading up to the murder of his brother, suffered from both. He was gravely disappointed over having misunderstood God's will, and he was depressed by the notion that he'd be forever relegated to second class status vis-à-vis his brother Abel.[85]

The psychological dynamics which played out between Cain and Abel, and between Rebecca and Isaac, were mere examples of what life has in store for everyone, according to the Netziv. Families consist of human beings, each of whom has a mind of his own, and hence the dynamics are complicated and often unruly. Therefore, the Torah commands that once every fifty years all members of the Jewish community must (Lev. 25:10) "return to their ancestral plot and to their families they shall return." *Haamek Davar* explains the seeming repetition in the verse as follows:

> The straightforward meaning is that the first return (i.e., to one's ancestral plot) might suggest that a person could go for that

---

84. *HD* Gen. 24:65.
85. *HD* Gen. 4:5.

year to their land, visit with their family, and then return to their original place. Therefore it repeats "they shall return." [Meaning,] they shall return completely to their families. For the fact that the entire family returns to their birthplace causes them to work out the issues which led to their separation and permanently reestablish themselves as a family.[86]

Here too, then, the Torah reflects deep understanding into human psychology and even offers therapeutic approaches to overcoming some of its most difficult challenges.

This is just the beginning. Turning the pages of *Haamek Davar*, the reader will discover that the biblical text opines on the place of secular studies in the life a Jew,[87] on the benefits of a life lived religiously,[88] on the definition of holiness,[89] what constitutes nature and what belongs to the realm of supernatural.[90] To the Netziv, then, the Written Torah was a repository of ideas, insights, and instruction regarding the most essential questions of Jewish life. One only needs the proper training and the proper tools to "delve into the matter." That is the project to which the Netziv devotes himself in his *Haamek Davar.*

FURTHER READING

First printing of *Haamek Davar* (Vilna, 1879).
Annotated Edition: *Ḥumash Haamek Davar: Mevo'ar UMeforash* (Jerusalem, 2004).

Biographical Information:
Bar-Ilan, Meir. *Rabban Shel Yisrael* (New York, 1943).
Etkes, Immanuel, and Shlomo Tikochinsky, eds. *Yeshivot Lita: Pirkei Zikhronot* (Jerusalem, 2004).

---

86. *HD* Lev. 25:10.
87. See, e.g., *HD* Ex. 27:20; 37:19; *HrD* Gen. 45:16; *HD* Num. 8:2.
88. See, e.g., *HD* Gen. 2:7; 23:1; Deut. 4:1, 4; 30:6, 15, 19.
89. See, e.g., *HD* Ex. 19:6; 35:2; Lev. 19:2; 25:26.
90. See, e.g., *HD* Gen. 1:2; 6:12; 7:23; 18:12; Deut. 2:3.

Stampfer, Shaul. *Lithuanian Yeshivas of the Nineteenth Century: Creating a Tradition of Learning* (Jerusalem, 2014).
Zevin, Shlomo Yosef. *Ishim VeShitot* (Tel Aviv, 1952).

Critical Text Studies:
Eliakim, Nissim. *Haamek Davar LaNetziv: Middot VeKelim BeParshanut HaPeshat* (Rehovot, 2003).
Kets (Kehat), Hannah. *Mishnat HaNetziv* (Israel, 1990).
Perl, Gil. *The Pillar of Volozhin: Rabbi Naftali Zvi Yehuda Berlin and the World of Nineteenth-Century Lithuanian Torah Scholarship* (Brighton, 2012).

Rav Abraham Isaac Kook's *Orot HaTeshuva*: Repentance as Cosmology

Dr. Daniel Rynhold

Repentance is a uniquely religious concept. Morality may dictate that there are occasions when we ought to apologize to our fellows and even seek their forgiveness when we have wronged them. But the specific cluster of ideas that surround the concept of repentance, such as sinning against God, atonement, and divine punishment, along with the idea that repentance is the culmination of a lengthy spiritual exercise, for want of a better term, is specifically religious. Repentance, as generally conceived, is also a particularly personal matter, something that we engage in as individuals. As Ephraim Urbach noted in relation to the rabbinic view, repentance is "entirely a matter for the individual: he is both its subject and object."[1]

---

1. Ephraim Urbach, "Redemption and Repentance in Talmudic Judaism," in *Collected Writings in Jewish Studies*, Robert Brody and Moshe D. Herr, eds. (Jerusalem, 1999), 264.

Yet alongside this pointedly individual conception of repentance, the rabbinic tradition also contains a number of grandiose statements linking repentance to more cosmic concerns. Thus, "R. Yonatan said: Great is repentance, because it brings about redemption, as it is said, 'And a redeemer will come to Zion, and unto them that turn from transgression in Jacob (Is. 49:20)'" (Yoma 86a–b).

The precise nature of the relationship between repentance and redemption is admittedly a matter of rabbinic dispute (see Sanhedrin 97b–98a). Everyone agrees, however, that there *is* a fundamental relationship between the concepts, so it comes as no surprise to find rabbinic texts in which repentance takes on even greater cosmic weight. Take, for example, the following *baraita*:

> Seven things were created before the world was created, and these are they: The Torah, repentance, the Garden of Eden, Gehenna, the Throne of Glory, the Temple, and the name of the Messiah.... Repentance, for it is written, "Before the mountains were brought forth" (Ps. 90:2), and it is written, "Thou turnest man to contrition, and sayest, 'Repent, ye children of men'" (v. 3). (Pesaḥim 54a)

Repentance is here presented as one of the foundations of Creation – before the mountains were created, we are told, God told humanity to repent, a claim that for all its grandeur is not easy to understand. Note that the claim here is no longer simply that everyone repents, but the rather more sensational claim that repentance was instituted prior to Creation, before there were any human beings to repent. So is this just an example of rabbinic overstatement, or should it be understood as a genuine claim about the role of repentance in the universe?

In 1925, Rabbi Zvi Yehuda Kook, the son of Rabbi Abraham Isaac Kook (better known simply as Rav Kook), edited a short work culled from his father's writings called *Orot HaTeshuva* (*The Lights of Repentance*). In the introduction, Rav Kook writes that particularly for us moderns "this subject [of repentance] is still a closed book and is in need of clarification."[2] Some will find this claim surprising, and point to the many references to repentance throughout Jewish literature, and to extended discussions such as Rabbi Jonah ben Abraham Gerondi's (1180–1263) *Shaarei Teshuva* (*The Gates of Repentance*), or Moses Maimonides' (1138–1204) *Laws of Repentance* in his *Mishneh Torah*. But it might be that Rav Kook has one eye here on the neglect of these cosmic aspects of repentance, at least popularly (it is certainly a theme in the Zohar), and is concerned that they should reclaim their rightful place in Jewish accounts of repentance. Maybe this is what he meant when he wrote that despite repentance being a central concern of both the Bible and the rabbis, "our literature, which explores every area where there is manifest the poetry of life, did not probe at all into this wonderful treasure of life."[3] Rav Kook's eclectic combination of mysticism and modernity was uniquely placed to revive these elements of repentance for the modern Jew, and in *Orot HaTeshuva*, the cosmic claims are taken very seriously. Repentance is placed both literally and figuratively at the very epicenter of Rav Kook's universe.

RAV KOOK'S LIFE AND WORKS

Rav Kook was born on September 7, 1865 (10 Elul 5625), in Grieva, Latvia, the first child of a father, Shlomo Zalman, schooled at the famous Volozhin Yeshiva, and a mother, Perel Zlota, brought up in the world of Chabad Hasidism, a cultural mix that with hindsight can be seen as setting a precedent for the broad-based combination of influences that would eventually inform Rav Kook's own worldview. After being schooled by a succession of rabbis in the first two decades of his life – an education that did not prevent him from also being exposed to maskilic

---

2. Abraham Isaac Kook, *Orot HaTeshuva* (Jerusalem, 1985), 9 (henceforth, *OHT*). References to the Hebrew text are to the version reprinted in a volume together with *Orot HaTorah, Musar Avikha*, and two other works. Translations, which I have sometimes modified, are based on Ben Zion Bokser, ed., *Abraham Isaac Kook: The Lights of Penitence, Lights of Holiness, The Moral Principles, Essays, Letters and Poems* (Mahwah, 1978), 41–128. References first give the page numbers for the Hebrew text and then the corresponding page number in this English translation.

3. *OHT*, 9; 41.

literature – Rav Kook spent a year and a half studying in Volozhin under the Netziv (Rabbi Naftali Tzvi Yehuda Berlin), while continuing to absorb all manner of other formative influences. Following a move to Ponevezh in 1886, where he married Batsheva Rabinowitz-Teomim, the daughter of the Aderet (Rabbi Eliyahu David Rabinowitz-Teomim), he became increasingly steeped in the study of Kabbala, an interest that continued to deepen when, as a matter of economic necessity, he had to take up appointments as a communal rabbi. His first appointment in 1888 was in the small Lithuanian town of Zeimel, and it was here in the following year that Rav Kook's life took a tragic turn with the death of his first wife, though with the Aderet's encouragement he would remarry her cousin Raiza Rivka Rabinowitz within the year. Subsequently, in 1896, Rav Kook became the rabbi of Boisk, a community larger than that of Zeimel. His most significant geographical move, though, came on May 13, 1904, when, with the support of the Aderet, who was now the deputy chief rabbi of Jerusalem, Rav Kook moved to what was then Ottoman Palestine to take up the position of chief rabbi of Jaffa.

Rav Kook had not been, up to this point, a Zionist himself, at least not in any formal capacity. He had opposed the formation of the "separatist" Mizrachi camp in 1902 and had not joined the Eastern European Ḥibbat Zion movement. This all changed, however, when he was faced with the reality of life in Israel, where he often found himself caught in the crossfire between the Old Yishuv, with whom he shared a deep commitment to Torah and tradition, and the New Yishuv, whose critique of the traditionalists also resonated with Rav Kook's more expansive soul, a soul that quickly developed a growing appreciation for the redemptive qualities of the apparent "heresies" of secular Zionism and chafed against the confined view of Judaism put forward by his rabbinic colleagues. Indeed, imparting some of this acquired wisdom was part of the motivation behind Rav Kook fatefully setting sail in 1914 for Frankfurt, Germany, for the worldwide conference of Agudat Yisrael, a journey that stranded him in Europe for five years as a result of the outbreak of the First World War. After spending some time living in St. Gallen, Switzerland, in 1916 he moved to London to become rabbi of the Machzikei Hadas Synagogue in the East End of London, a period during which he would clash with the English Jewish establishment over his support for the Balfour Declaration, Foreign Secretary Arthur Balfour's statement of British support for the establishment of a Jewish homeland in Palestine.

Rav Kook eventually returned to Israel in 1919 when a cohort of influential rabbis made him a formal offer to be chief rabbi of Jerusalem, despite the reservations of one of the leading rabbis of the Old Yishuv in Jerusalem, Rabbi Yosef Chaim Sonnenfeld. Rav Kook subsequently became the first chief rabbi of British Mandatory Palestine in 1921, a year in which he also set up a beit midrash adjacent to his residence called the *Merkaz*, which would eventually evolve into Merkaz HaRav Yeshiva. Renowned for his gentle and tolerant nature, Rav Kook ironically spent much of his life embroiled in communal controversies, from his early support in 1907 for the Tachkemoni school of Jaffa in opposition to the Jerusalem rabbis, to his deeply unpopular defense of Avraham Stavsky in the case of the murder of the Zionist leader Chaim Arlosoroff in 1933. On the one hand, he came into conflict with the traditionalists over, for example, his permissive ruling on *Shemitta*, while on the other, his later opposition to women's suffrage alienated the modernists. And he managed to offend all sides simultaneously with his 1925 speech at the inauguration of the Hebrew University of Jerusalem; his very participation was anathema to the ultra-Orthodox, yet his defense of tradition as the measure of scholarly integrity proved too much for the academics. A man of peace, his life was rife with conflict, and there is a sad irony to the fact that on September 1, 1935 (3 Elul 5695), the day he eventually succumbed to cancer, the newspapers were reporting the sentencing of four members of the Histadrut for their part in violent summer conflicts occasioned by a labor dispute in Haifa.

Even in death, controversy continues to rage around Rav Kook's contributions to Jewish modernity. While he composed (though did not always publish) various works and articles as early as his time in Zeimel, including *Ḥavash Pe'er* (published in 1891, a short work extolling the mitzva of tefillin, which for many years Rav Kook would wear all day), *Midbar Shur* (a collection of his Zeimel sermons of 1894–1896), and *Musar Avikha* (the first work written in what would become his signature style – the spiritual diary), it was the edited collections drawn from his intense spiritual diaries on which his reputation was built, for good and ill. In particular, the 1920 publication of selections from these diaries under the title *Orot*, pieced together by his son Rabbi Zvi Yehuda, precipitated a very public controversy. A ban of excommunication claiming that *Orot* contained "all manner of poison" was put out by a group of zealots devoted to the leading rabbis of the Old Yishuv – the aforementioned Rabbi Sonnenfeld and Rabbi Yitzhak Yeruham Diskin – whose signatures were appended to the ban.

The only two other books edited from his diaries and seen through to publication during his lifetime came out in 1925. *Orot HaKodesh* (*Lights of Holiness*) – a three-volume magnum opus composed between 1910 and 1919 and edited by Rabbi David HaKohen ("the Nazir") from eight notebooks – is a majestic but diffuse collection best suited to sustained study by scholars. In contrast, *Orot HaTeshuva*, edited again by Rabbi Zvi Yehuda, is a concentrated study of a single topic – repentance – which, as the focus of the High Holy Days, has both the appeal and the occasion for mass annual study.

Even from this brief account though, one immediately becomes aware of a methodological issue with the study of Rav Kook's works. Other than the challenge of the often poetic and unsystematic form of the original diaries, which were not written with publication in mind, the three major works mentioned were not published by Rav Kook himself but were all edited from these diaries by other hands, and there is certainly evidence that Rav Kook and his son were sometimes at odds regarding what ought to be included for publication. Shai Agnon writes that he heard Rabbi Zvi Yehuda counsel his father to remove one of the passages in *Orot* that went on to cause much of the ensuing controversy[4] – section 34 of *Orot HaTehiya*, in which he writes that the physical exercise of Israel's youth "raises up the *Shekhina* (Divine Presence) just as it rises through songs and praises uttered by David, King of Israel, in the Book of Psalms."[5] We also know that the one diary notebook that Rav Kook himself prepared for publication in 1914 as *Arpelei Tohar*, the printing of which was halted with Rav Kook exiled in Europe after only eighty pages had been typeset, never saw the light of day in its full form,

---

4. See Shai Agnon, *Sefer, Sofer, VeSippur* (Tel Aviv, 1978), 352.

5. Abraham Isaac Kook, *Orot* (Jerusalem, 2005), 80. The translation is taken from *Orot*, trans. Bezalel Naor (Jerusalem, 2015), 233.

partly because of pressure from Rabbi Zvi Yehuda, concerned to save his father from himself given some of the bold views expressed in its unedited pages.[6] The nature of the editorial input is therefore a key question for Rav Kook scholars, though we now at least have access to the unedited diaries of 1910–1919, published as *Shemona Kevatzim* (*Eight Files*).[7] Our interest, however, is in the content of *Orot HaTeshuva*, and the picture of repentance it paints. Our primary purpose is to describe a book which has had an influence due to its revolutionary content, rather than reconstruct the precise original words of the man who was its (edited) author. Even if the original passages have a slightly different flavor, or even contain some significant particulars missing in the edited versions, there is little question that the analysis below broadly reflects the general philosophy of Rav Kook himself.

THE CONTEXT

We have already mentioned that, as far as Rav Kook was concerned, the context for his work on repentance was the very *lack* of context in his eyes. On the basis of what we will present of the book itself, we have conjectured that his dissatisfaction with the existing literature may have stemmed from its failure to take the cosmic significance of repentance, clearly signaled in the talmudic era, sufficiently seriously. From that perspective, the concept of repentance had not been adequately clarified, and thus his work was filling a lacuna. But, again based on evidence that

---

6. Some unbound 1914 versions of the eighty-page printing did find their way into certain hands – one was put up for auction in 2015 – and the full but edited version was published in 1983. Professor Rivka Schatz had a verbal agreement with Rabbi Zvi Yehuda prior to his death to publish the work in its original form, an agreement made within earshot of his students according to Schatz. After Rabbi Zvi Yehuda died, illness prevented her from publishing immediately, and upon her recovery, her intention to publish was thwarted by the rush by Mossad HaRav Kook to publish an "approved" edition, much to her immense displeasure. See her interview in Haggai Siegel, "*Orot BeOfel*," *Nekudah* 113 (September 28, 1987), 20–21.

7. See Avinoam Rosenak, "Hidden Diaries and New Discoveries: The Life and Thought of Rabbi A. I. Kook," *Shofar* 25:3 (2007): 111–147, for discussion of the publication of these key volumes. See also Marc B. Shapiro, *Changing the Immutable: How Orthodox Judaism Rewrites Its History* (Oxford, 2015), ch. 5, for further discussion of the editing of Rav Kook's works.

emerges from *Orot HaTeshuva* to be discussed, I want to suggest an additional concern that Rav Kook may have had with the existing literature.

Of that literature, to this day Rabbenu Yona's (Rabbi Jonah ben Abraham Gerondi, 1180–1263) *Shaarei Teshuva* (*The Gates of Repentance*) is probably one of the few works that competes for contemporary readers with *Orot HaTeshuva* when the month of Elul comes around, though the latter is likely prevalent in Modern Orthodox circles, along with Rav Soloveitchik's *On Repentance*.[8] As the first major theological monograph focused exclusively on repentance – Maimonides' *Laws of Repentance* of course is a single part of a much larger halakhic work – Rabbenu Yona's work has been, and continues to be hugely influential. Yet one cannot help but notice that his description of repentance is at odds with some key modern virtues. Thus, one of Rabbenu Yona's central principles of repentance is sorrow, or *yagon*, and he tells us that "the levels and degrees of repentance correspond to the magnitude of bitterness and the intensity of sorrow."[9] This would be relatively unremarkable were it not for the fact that this sorrow appears to be inescapable when combined with a further principle that he terms *daaga* (worry). Worry seems to be sorrow's mirror image. While sorrow pertains to the past, worry pertains to the future. The repentant person, we are told,

> must worry too, lest he has fallen short in repentance; in suffering, bitterness, fasting, and weeping. And although he may have suffered and wept much, he must tremble and fear that he may have sinned over and against this and that with all of his suffering, weeping, and fasting, he has not paid his debt.[10]

So for Rabbenu Yona, not only must we be sorrowful over the past and worry about the future, but we must also worry that we have not been sorrowful enough about the past, leading to a cycle of psychological

---

8. Pinchas Peli, *On Repentance: The Thought and Oral Discourses of Rabbi Joseph B. Soloveitchik* (Ramsey, 1984).

9. Rabbi Jonah ben Abraham Gerondi, *The Gates of Repentance*, trans. S. Silverstein (Jerusalem, 1967), I:13, 21. (Henceforth, *ST*, followed by gate, chapter, and page number.)

10. *ST*, I:16, 23–24.

torment that is never-ending. Similarly negative themes are emphasized throughout his treatise, with Rabbenu Yona keen to highlight the
links between sin, guilt, and punishment so as to drive one's fears to
an extreme and motivate one to repent. The third Gate of the book is
entitled "The Stringency of Mitzvot, the Exhortations, and the Different
Kinds of Punishments," and is there precisely so that one can "investigate, know, and recognize the magnitude of the punishment for each of
his transgressions ... so that he may be aware of the greatness of his sin
when he confesses it."[11]

One could expound at length on the bleak account of repentance exemplified by Rabbenu Yona and found in much of medieval
Judaism, though doing so here would take us too far afield.[12] What is
significant is that the level of psychological distress required, indeed
encouraged, by this view of repentance is the target of sustained modern critique, particularly at the hands of two of modernity's most
significant thinkers.

The first of these is Baruch Spinoza, who tells us in proposition
54 of Part IV of *The Ethics* that repentance cannot be a virtue since it
arises from passion rather than from reason. More importantly for our
purposes, he writes that "he who repents what he has done is twice
wretched" since he "suffers himself to be conquered first by an evil desire,
and then by sadness."[13] While Spinoza thinks that repentance can be useful for keeping the masses in check, guided as they are by their passions
rather than by their reason, for Spinoza its "wretchedness" is revealed
in the way it manifests this irrational foundation by preying on the sort
of fear and distress on which Rabbenu Yona focuses.

A similar line of attack is developed further in the latter part of the
nineteenth century by Friedrich Nietzsche, for whom guilt, as a feeling
of inadequacy stemming from the sentiment that one has transgressed
ethical or religious norms, yields feelings of self-loathing that he believes

---

11. Ibid., I:37, 51.
12. For some further discussion see Daniel Rynhold and Michael J. Harris, "Modernity
    and Jewish Orthodoxy: Nietzsche and Soloveitchik on Life-Affirmation, Asceticism,
    and Repentance," *Harvard Theological Review*, 101:2 (2008): 253–284, esp. 269–272.
13. Baruch Spinoza, *The Ethics*, in *A Spinoza Reader: The Ethics and Other Works*,
    ed. E. Curley (Princeton, 1994), 228.

are taken to depraved depths when placed within a religious context. Repentance is, for Nietzsche, a concept that is deeply damaging, of a piece with a worldview that not only serves those who are too weak to face their suffering honestly, but that also creates conditions that hamper the development of the type of great individuals that would, once upon a time, have elicited our admiration. It is a prime manifestation of modern man's disgust with himself, and one that is psychologically injurious to an alarming degree:

> One need only ask psychiatrists what happens to patients who are methodically subjected to the torments of repentance, states of contrition, and fits of redemption…. In the wake of repentance and redemption *training* we find tremendous epileptic epidemics…; as another aftereffect we encounter terrible paralyses and protracted states of depression.[14]

It is clear that Rabbenu Yona's account of repentance would have done Nietzsche proud – or rather, would have made him nauseated.

It is important to note that both Spinoza and Nietzsche begin with the idea that guilt for one's sins is a concept that does not answer to any external religious reality, given that they do not believe in the sort of objective values that could underpin any religious reality in the first place. So it might be thought that a religious thinker like Rav Kook would have limited sympathy for their views. And yet, what will emerge from our discussion is that whether or not one agrees with these critiques in all of their details, like Spinoza and Nietzsche, Rav Kook has little time for the weak and servile traits expressed in certain religious forms of self-abnegation and their accompanying accounts of repentance that paint it as a form of backward-looking psychological torture. We find him instead echoing their interest in promoting the more modern virtues that stress human adequacy, self-assertion, and strength.

It is impossible to know the extent of Rav Kook's knowledge of Spinoza and Nietzsche given that he did not have the type of formal

---

14. Friedrich Nietzsche, *On the Genealogy of Morals*, trans. W. Kaufmann and R. J. Hollingdale (New York, 1967), 142.

secular education where he would have studied them systematically; any knowledge he did have was likely from secondary sources. Nonetheless, we are aware of his admiration for Spinoza, whom even in the published writings Rav Kook describes, despite his faults, as a person "in whose soul the thought of God's unity had planted such deep roots" that his ideas concerning God, albeit "in a broken and crooked manner," still reflected – or in this case maybe refracted – "the great light."[15] There is also evidence of his acquaintance with Nietzsche's work, and even of his sympathy with some of that infamous German atheist's more penetrating psychological insights. As Benjamin Ish-Shalom has written, "Rather than rejecting Nietzsche's claims, [Rav Kook] accepted some of his seemingly basic assumptions."[16] In what follows, therefore, I suggest that in addition to his concern at the neglect of the cosmic significance of repentance, Rav Kook was also troubled by the psychology lurking in the background of some the most influential medieval Jewish accounts of individual repentance.[17] As we will see, whether or not directly influenced by Spinoza and Nietzsche, conceptually speaking there is no question that Rav Kook's account of repentance reflects their concerns and counters the life-negating accounts of his medieval Jewish forebears.

MONISM AND RAV KOOK'S THEORY OF REPENTANCE

Rav Kook is probably one the most mystically inclined modern Jewish thinkers to be taken seriously by those with little sympathy for mysticism. When it comes to *Orot HaTeshuva*, both the mystical and modern strands are prominent, which allows Rav Kook to deal with both of the

15. Rabbi Kook, "*Ikvei HaTzon*," in *Eder HaYekar* (Jerusalem, 1985), 134. For discussion of censored passages containing more fulsome praise, see Shapiro, *Changing the Immutable*, 168–170.

16. Benjamin Ish-Shalom, *Rav Avraham Itzhak HaCohen Kook: Between Rationalism and Mysticism*, trans. Ora Wiskind-Elper (Albany, 1993), 77. See also Naor's aforementioned English edition of *Orot*, 61–64 with the corresponding notes, and Yehudah Mirsky, *Rav Kook: Mystic in a Time of Revolution* (New Haven, 2014), 39–40.

17. Not to mention more modern ones, such as those found in the *Musar* movement. See Mordechai Pachter, "Repentance in the Thought of Rav Yisrael Salanter and the Musar Movement," in Benjamin Ish-Shalom and Shalom Rosenberg, eds., *The World of Rav Kook's Thought*, trans. Shalom Carmy (New York, 1991), 322–348.

deficiencies in prior theories of repentance that we have suggested may have been at the back of his mind when writing on repentance.

The cosmological foundations of repentance first emerge in only the second chapter of *Orot HaTeshuva*; it is worth noting that the opening three chapters are directly from the pen of Rav Kook himself. There Rav Kook writes that "the good and nobility in ourselves [is] but an expression of our relatedness to the All,"[18] giving us an early indication of the foundational role that a view known as monism plays in Rav Kook's theology generally, and his theory of repentance specifically.

For Rav Kook, Spinoza's pantheism contained an important kernel of truth. God, for Rav Kook, is the only true reality, so our world is, in a sense, identical with God. But while Spinoza identified God with nature, for Rav Kook, the world is merely one "element" of God's nature, so to speak. The basic idea found in the *Shema* that "God is One" is not simply a statement that when speaking of God we are speaking of a set with only one member. The point, rather, is about the nature of God as a perfect indivisible unity. While every existent can be split into parts, whether in a literal physical sense or by being broken down into its conceptual ingredients, God is not made up of parts at all. Moreover, in accordance with the kabbalistic concept of God as the *Ein Sof*, this unified being is also an infinite being without limits. The implication of this for Rav Kook (though those familiar with modern theories of infinity might balk at this) is that God, since He is infinite, must encompass all of reality and is therefore the "place of the world." Combining this with the idea of God's unity, he is led to conclude that reality must actually in some sense be one. This view, known as monism, leads Rav Kook to assert that "all of being is divine, that there is nothing at all other than God."[19]

The idea that everything is somehow divine has a number of very significant ramifications, not least that our natural perception of the world as having an independent existence and being composed of innumerable individual things – ourselves included – is somehow an illusion. So Rav Kook states:

---

18. *OHT*, 12; 45–46.
19. *Orot HaKodesh* (Jerusalem, 1985), vol. 2, 396. (Henceforth, *OHK*.)

True reality is the divine, and all existence that descends from God's ultimate transcendence is no more than the descent of will in its imperfect choice, which causes yet more deficiency until, at last, all impurity will perish, and the will in its freedom shall rise to the absolute good, and the Lord will be one and His Name one. The return of all to the Divine is the highest perfection of existence, and one cannot conceive its worth.[20]

When, therefore, Rav Kook writes that "through repentance all things return to God,"[21] he is literally speaking of the act of repentance – a word that in Hebrew is drawn from the root meaning "to return" – as returning the world to this original unity in God, to its foundation in holiness. As we see it, the world is a fragmented multiplicity of conflicting ideas and ideologies, but in its "natural" divine state, the world is perfect and unified. Repentance, therefore, is "an effort to return to one's original status, to the source of life and higher being in their perfection."[22]

It is unquestionable that Rav Kook means this in a literal sense. There truly is no reality independent of God. There are questions, however, of what this actually means, especially regarding its implications for our full "return" to this divinity. There are those who argue that Rav Kook is arguing for the explanatory dependence of all existence on God, but this is an extremely common view among Jewish thinkers that would amount to the simple search for an underlying religious "theory of everything" analogous to the type of theory that physicists seek. As we will see, at times Rav Kook clearly presents a more radical acosmic view whereby God is the only reality and any form of independent existence is illusory in a more significant sense, such that in a full return to God, our individuality will in some literal sense "dissolve" back into this divine unity – not an uncommon idea in kabbalistic texts.

While we will have cause to return to this controversial issue, what matters to us for the moment is that on his monistic account, repentance reflects an inbuilt "yearning of all existence to be better, purer, more

---

20. Ibid., 395–396.
21. *OHT*, 15; 49.
22. Ibid., 37; 87.

vigorous, and on a higher plane than it is,"[23] a yearning that manifests itself at every level. It is not just repentant individuals who have a will that yearns for this return to unity; the divine lights contained in all existence mean that there is a cosmic yearning in every existent that is as dynamic as that expressed in the will of human beings. Everything is a refraction of God's will, and the various forms of repentance in which everything engages "all constitute one essence"[24] – the will to return to their source in the divine will.

Significantly, therefore, the talmudic idea with which we began, quoted by Rav Kook – "Repentance preceded the creation of the world, and it is for this reason the foundation of the world"[25] – has a literal truth to it that he clearly believes has not been sufficiently brought to the fore in writings on repentance, even if the monistic metaphysical view it reflects is relatively common in mystical thought. The idea here would be that repentance must have been created "first" as it is a necessary condition for seeing creation as it truly is: as an element of the unified reality of God. Creation represents a "fall from unity," since the created world is seen as existing independently of God. But it *must* eventually return to its divine origins, otherwise God would remain forever in disunity, which would presumably be impossible. So repentance, on this account, is a logical condition of creation. Without it, God is not a unity, which would contradict the very definition of God.

Maimonides famously writes:

> A person should *look at himself* throughout the year as equally balanced between merit and sin, and the world as equally balanced between merit and sin. If he performs one sin, he decides the balance for himself and for the entire world on the side of guilt and causes their destruction. If he performs one mitzva, he decides the balance for himself and that of the entire world to the side of merit and causes their deliverance and salvation.[26]

23. *OHT*, 20; 56.
24. Ibid., 15; 49.
25. Ibid., 18; 55.
26. *Mishneh Torah, Laws of Repentance* 3:4.

For Rav Kook, it is not a matter of seeing oneself *as if* this were so. For Rav Kook, it genuinely is the case.

THE NATURE OF SIN AND HOW TO CORRECT IT

Given the monistic view outlined in the previous section, whereby everything is in some sense divine, it is inevitable that Rav Kook would ultimately have to see sin as a form of illusion, or at least a distortion of what really exists. It is no surprise, therefore, when he writes, "Existence, in its overall character, is sinless. Sin appears only in the evaluation of particulars. In the perspective of the whole everything is related in eternal harmony."[27]

This, however, has radical implications both for Rav Kook's understanding of sin as it appears in our lives, and for how we ought to go about rectifying it.

The first point to make is that sin now has to be seen as an unnatural state for man to be in. Given the divine nature of the All, and our yearning to return to it, at the individual level it must be that sin "oppresses the heart because it disrupts the unity between the individual person and all existence."[28] Basically, sin obstructs the healthy functioning of an individual. Sin disturbs the unity that underlies all existence, and this malfunctioning can be recognized, Rav Kook writes, through "marks on the face, in gestures, in the voice, in behavior, in the handwriting, in the manner of communication, in speech, and especially in the style of writing, in the way one develops one's thoughts and arranges them"[29] – though I'm obviously hoping that the last two don't manifest themselves too clearly.

Note that there seems to be an ambiguity here in Rav Kook's use of the term "natural." On the one hand, if everything is divine, then at some level, at least descriptively, everything, including sin, is "natural" for man – though of course for Rav Kook everything is in actual fact "(super) natural" – since, in a quasi-Spinozan sense, everything man does reflects God and is therefore an element of our divinely created human "nature."

---

27. *OHT*, 37; 87.
28. Ibid., 24; 63.
29. Ibid., 26; 67.

It must be, then, that when Rav Kook speaks of sin as unnatural, he uses the term "natural" in a normative sense, to indicate the perfected unity of God for which we strive. This sense of "natural" is teleological, referring to the ultimate perfection of man, and rendering all "deviations" from this unity unnatural.[30] The idea of sin as unnatural, therefore, would refer to the fact that it is primarily a deviance from our ideal telos, or purpose.

This view is further confirmed by the first in a list of three levels of repentance with which Rav Kook opens the book: repentance according to nature, repentance according to faith, and repentance according to reason.[31] The first, repentance according to nature, he then splits into its physical and spiritual manifestations. The former, defined somewhat cryptically as being "related to all transgressions against the laws of nature, and such laws of morals and the Torah as are linked to the laws of nature,"[32] appears in part to be a function of literal physical damage given that he mentions that "the science of medicine concerns itself a good deal with this."[33] One presumes that smoking could be seen as such a transgression that requires "repentance" to restore us to physical well-being. Thus, while the damage caused by smoking is perfectly "natural," it is something that impedes healthy human functioning, and is therefore "unnatural" in the normative sense. While, as we will discuss, there are further levels of repentance, this underlying idea of the "natural" disturbance that is a consequence of sin is a recurrent theme.

How, then, is repentance achieved? Rav Kook's third level of repentance from the listing in the opening chapter is "repentance according to reason," which, we are told, "represents the peak of penitential expression" and *includes* previously defined forms of repentance. What it adds to them is "a comprehensive outlook on life … [that] transforms all past sins into spiritual assets."[34] As Rav Kook puts it later, "the deeds of the

---

30. I am indebted to Dr. David Shatz for pointing out this distinction.
31. Rav Kook makes various overlapping but non-equivalent distinctions between types of repentance throughout *Orot HaTeshuva*. I should note here that it is not my intention in this essay to précis the work and map out these variations, but rather to give a more thematic account of what strikes me as most significant about the work.
32. *OHT*, 11; 43.
33. Ibid.
34. Ibid,. 11; 44.

past ... are not eliminated from the thrust of life" for instead "the will can impose a special configuration on past actions."[35]

What is most notable about this "configuration" is the transformation of the very nature of an act from a sin to a "spiritual asset," presumably in line with the saying of Resh Lakish that "great is repentance for because of it premeditated sins are accounted as merits" (Yoma 86a). The manner in which repentance effects this is by allowing the individual to learn from past sins and utilize them as a springboard for an ascent to greater "spiritual heights." When a person sins he has separated himself from God, "entered the world of fragmentation, and then every particular being stands by itself, and evil is evil in and of itself."[36] Through repentance out of love, however, "there at once shines on him the light from the world of unity" and therefore "the evil is joined with the good ... the willful wrongs become transformed into real virtues."[37]

This is not an unusual view in itself. Rav Joseph B. Soloveitchik writes similarly of repentance from love in which we can transform prior sins to merits through a reinterpretation of the narrative of our lives, a view in which

> sin is not to be forgotten, blotted out or cast into the depths of the sea. On the contrary, sin has to be remembered. It is the memory of sin that releases the power within the inner depths of the soul of the penitent to do greater things than ever before.[38]

For Rav Kook, however, this is not the end of the process, for the transformation must run deeper given the cosmic background that we have set up. Rav Kook puts the contrast above between the worlds inhabited by the sinner and the repentant individual respectively in the language of the Zohar, distinguishing between the *alma deperuda* and the *alma deyiḥuda*. When he goes on to say that "any action

---

35. Ibid., 21; 58.
36. Ibid., 36; 85.
37. Ibid.
38. Peli, *On Repentance*, 276–277. For a fuller comparison between Rav Soloveitchik's and Rav Kook's views on repentance, see Reuven Ziegler, *Majesty and Humility: The Thought of Rabbi Joseph B. Soloveitchik* (New York, 2012), ch. 22.

that deviates from the norm, that is not oriented toward its source, is reoriented to its source when the will is mended,"[39] the change he is speaking about is not, therefore, simply one whereby the sin becomes a virtue from a psychological standpoint. Rav Kook's view is that "the perception of truth is the basis of penitence,"[40] and the truth in question is that of the divine nature of all existence. Repentance comes "from the depths of being…in which the individual stands not as a separate entity, but rather as a continuation of the vastness of universal existence."[41] The movement between the two "worlds" must then be a matter of cognizing this truth, though cognition here is bound up with the will as much as it is with reason.

What, though, is the nature of this cognitive shift? Pure rational reflection deals with the type of analysis and conceptualization that for Rav Kook simply cannot grasp the underlying unity of reality. Rav Kook is speaking here of a more mystical reparative vision based on the perception that "all existence…must be seen from one comprehensive perspective, as one essence constituent of many particularities."[42] Since at its root this unified essence is God, and God cannot be evil, correctly reconfiguring one's individual existence as part of a greater harmonious whole in this way presumably means that one no longer sees the act for which one is repenting as evil, and inasmuch as we are able to make sense of this, it might be explained by contrasting our temporal grasp of reality with God's atemporal perspective. Our perception of sin is entirely a function of our limited temporal view of reality. From our perspective, sins take place at a certain point in time, and even if we do manage to repent, the balancing out of the sin takes place at a different time, meaning that the sin still has its own independent existence at the point at which it was done. Given, however, that a God's-eye-view is not subject to such temporal limitations and that He sees reality from the perspective of a timeless eternity, as if it were all set out simultaneously – what Spinoza refers to as *sub specie aeternitatis* –

---

39. *OHT*, 37; 86.
40. Ibid., 50; 112.
41. Ibid., 20; 56.
42. Ibid., 15; 50.

sin never stands uncorrected, as a discrete moment unconnected to its counterbalancing act of repentance. To God, the "sin" is simultaneous with the repentance that counteracts it, and thus sin never really exists as such. The challenge is for us to gain this mystical perspective on reality where repentance is equivalent to understanding the divinity inherent in all of reality, even human sin.

This suggests, returning to Rav Kook's cosmic concerns, that there is a symbiotic relationship between the various levels of repentance. Individual repentance is necessary to repair the world, but at its highest levels, absolute individual repentance comes about only through our ability to see the world as it really is, that is, as already repaired, so to speak, with its apparent independence (however we understand that) just the result of a veil of illusion, which is the evil that we must address. If we can reconfigure the manner in which we understand our place in the cosmos correctly "the vision of penitence transforms all sins and their resultant confusion...to concepts of delight and satisfaction."[43] So, if we repent, the world will be repaired; but at the same time, seeing the world in its unified "repaired" state is the highest form of individual repentance.

THE PSYCHOLOGY OF THE REPENTANT MAN

The discussion so far might have begun fulfilling the task of giving repentance its appropriate redemptive and metaphysical due, but how does Rav Kook's discussion relate to the type of repentance of the individual that is our annual focus on Rosh HaShana and Yom Kippur?

In the view sketched above, we mentioned that given our metaphysical relation to the Divine, repentance is primarily seen as a natural reaction to sin. Rav Kook's monism renders the separation from the All through sin an unnatural state that presumably cannot be a stable form of existence. His is a dynamic universe in which the constant yearning for return at every level of existence means that "the world must inevitably come to full penitence."[44] Repentance therefore is "always present in the heart."[45] But as a result it also, unavoidably, is a spur to health, given

43. Ibid., 22; 60.
44. Ibid., 18; 54.
45. Ibid., 20; 57.

that "the nature of the will that is forged by repentance is an expression of the will immanent in the depth of life…[and] represents the most basic essence for the foundation of life."[46]

Thus, rather than seeing repentance as a function of an unhealthy obsessing over our moral guilt, Rav Kook writes that at the individual level repentance "is the healthiest feeling of a person."[47] Since we all participate in God's divinity, the desire to return from sin becomes a natural desire to return to psychological health, contrasting starkly with the psychically tortured soul that is the target of modern critiques of repentance. This takes on practical significance for the individual since rather than focusing on the guilt of one's past actions, Rav Kook counsels that we need to start with the future, and only then turn to the past; our focus "must always be directed toward improving the future…. If he should immediately begin by mending the past he will encounter many obstacles, and the ways of repentance and the nearness of God will seem too hard for him." We are, for Rav Kook, to work on the future first, at which point "it is certain that divine help will also be granted him to mend the past."[48]

This future-oriented approach to repentance is a recurring theme for Rav Kook, and seems primarily intended to guard against precisely the sort of psychological self-flagellation and extreme moral guilt that reaches such tortuous levels in Rabbenu Yona's account. Agonizing over the past is simply not in the driver's seat for Rav Kook, who tells us instead that we must take care "not to fall into depression to the extent that it will inhibit the light of repentance from penetrating to the depths of the soul."[49] And the notion that one should worry in case one has not been sorrowful enough about the past is directly opposed when Rav Kook writes, "Let him not become depressed because of the portion of offenses he has not yet managed to rectify. Instead let him hold firm to the pursuit of the Torah and the service of God with a full heart in joy, reverence, and in love."[50] Indeed, Rav Kook points out that

---

46. Ibid., 27; 69.
47. Ibid., 18; 53.
48. Ibid., 42; 95. It is unclear how directly he believes such divine help manifests itself. There is very little talk in the work of direct divine help or "grace."
49. Ibid., 26; 67.
50. Ibid., 23; 62.

even concerning the sins that are more difficult to redress, a person must "always anticipate that he will redress them."[51]

That is certainly not to say that there is no place for moral guilt or for suffering in repentance. The repentance according to nature mentioned earlier deals, in its spiritual manifestation, with transgressions against nature that trouble our conscience, clearly appealing to some form of moral guilt at transgressing against natural law, a guilt that spiritually disturbs a person and will "cause him disquiet"[52] thereby motivating him to repent. And the second level of repentance that he mentions – repentance according to faith – is the particularly religious form of repentance that we generally associate with the term; in Rav Kook's words it is the form of repentance with which "all the admonitions of the Torah deal."[53] Guilt certainly has an important role to play then, as does suffering. Sinners have an "anger with the whole world...the bitter melancholy that consumes spirit and flesh."[54] In the last of the three chapters from Rav Kook's own hand, he distinguishes between repentance that is focused on a particular sin or sins and a more generalized repentance which is not focused on any particular deficiency but instead is precipitated by the experience of being "embittered against oneself; ... [and] his whole being is as though in a torture chamber."[55] So repentance is far from easy. There is suffering and struggle involved, particularly since "the more resolute he becomes in pursuing the upright way and the more committed he becomes to the service of God, the stronger the evil impulse becomes in him."[56] Indeed, at certain points, Rav Kook seems to say that the more struggle the better,[57] though at the same time, the pain felt through the process can be one of the reasons we are discomfited by the thought of repentance and delay doing it.[58]

---

51. Ibid., 41; 99.
52. Ibid., 11; 44.
53. Ibid.
54. Ibid., 24; 64.
55. Ibid., 13; 47.
56. Ibid., 46; 105.
57. See, for example, ibid., 51; 115–116.
58. Ibid., 59: 128.

So repentance, understood as the navigation of our passage back to harmony with self and God, is a challenging skill to master. But even so, it is always portrayed as a natural result of the pain engendered by leaving one's native state. Guilt is a natural feeling of alienation from our true nature which "emanates from the source of repentance"[59] – the higher lights of divine illumination. Rather than driving one's thought of sin to depths of depravity then, for Rav Kook even the mere thought of repentance makes one "happier and more at peace with himself than he was before."[60] Given that we are in some sense a manifestation of God, whatever suffering is involved does not come from an inordinate fear of punishment or the concern that one's sins can never be forgiven. What we experience is a "natural remorse that burns in the heart as an expression of repentance."[61] Consequently, while we are currently in an imperfect state, as a result of what seems to be for Rav Kook a form of cognitive error, it is natural that we constantly strive for perfection. We do not find the sort of obsession with unhealthy levels of moralizing prevalent in those earlier accounts that so disturb Spinoza and Nietzsche, though Rav Kook is clearly more comfortable with some level of guilt than is Nietzsche.

In this context, it is interesting to note just how much Rav Kook equivocates even regarding the reduced levels of psychological anguish that he does invoke. Thus, at times he discusses lower and higher forms of repentance that are distinguished precisely by their relation to negative emotional content. Of the lower form, despite the fact that anguish plays a role in the subsequent joy at one's release from it, he nonetheless writes that it "weakens a person's will and thereby damages his personality."[62] Indeed, Rav Kook believes that in all forms of repentance there is at least initially a "weakening of the will related to the remorse felt for past misdeeds"[63] and that at the individual level repentance "necessarily bears within itself a certain weakness that even the most heroic

---

59. Ibid., 51; 114.
60. Ibid., 22; 62.
61. Ibid., 52; 113.
62. Ibid., 28; 71.
63. Ibid., 32; 79.

spirits cannot escape."[64] His point here is that "when one restrains the life force through inner withdrawal and the inclination to avoid any kind of sin…the vitality of the virtuous life is also weakened."[65] This is why, in his view, the High Holy Days are followed by a period of unfettered joy, to "restore the will for the good and the innocent vitality of life."[66]

Echoing Nietzsche then, Rav Kook seems concerned that the weakening of our more powerful drives that can result from repentance may block our ability to "identify the good that is embodied in the depth of evil."[67] But he goes even further than this when speaking of the highest levels of repentance that transcend the anguish of prior depression altogether. Such repentance is seen as a form of pure light that does not require a contrast with prior pain for its identity. The anguish is entirely submerged by the new orientation provided by repentance. This sort of repentance from "the perspective of wisdom (*bina*)…was never involved in the weakening pain of remorse,"[68] since "everything has been converted to virtue, from the very beginning, through the manifestation of discernment in the soul."[69] The use of *bina* here no doubt alludes to the third of the *sefirot*, which is often seen as the object of repentance in kabbalistic texts.

Yet beyond even this level, Rav Kook's very highest degree, which refers to the highest of the kabbalistic *sefirot* – the crown (*keter*) – takes us back to our discussion at the end of the previous section, and appears to barely be a form of repentance at all given that it is "the manifestation of the light of the 'universal crown,'" which is "the mysterious vision of the All," according to which "there is no deficiency or darkness at all."[70] While the prior forms of repentance all deal in their differing ways with the sin that motivates the entire process, this form, we are told, is "beyond the action of discernment that voids [the wrongs, through

---

64. Ibid., 29; 73.
65. Ibid.
66. Ibid.
67. Ibid., 28: 71.
68. Ibid., 33; 79.
69. Ibid.
70. Ibid.

penitence]."[71] As such, though, it seems to almost render repentance otiose. If there is no darkness, there is no need for repair. While this startling account of repentance could be understood to reflect the taking up of the "eternal" perspective on sin discussed earlier, there is no question that it verges on an antinomian view whereby there is no real sin to be atoned for.

At its heights then, Rav Kook's view of repentance takes us into the realms of the perfect mystical vision of the original unity, to which we all strive to return, one in which "death loses its name… [and] individual identity continues to expand, it becomes part of the general being of the people in a very real fusion, and from there it is absorbed in the general existence of the whole world."[72] Given that he here explicitly references the *sefira* of *keter*, which is also known as *ayin* (nothingness), we seem here to have a picture from which particularity has disappeared altogether. While there might be no sin in such a picture, there are no individuals either.

While Rav Kook does at times speak of this type of elimination of particularity, which is the implication of the most literal reading of his monism whereby all is God, it is difficult to see how to practically assimilate such an approach into our own temporal lives, and Rav Kook often struggles with this tension between the universal and the particular. As human beings, one would imagine that we cannot achieve actual unity with God, at least not if we are to remain individuals. The apex of human achievement would seem to have to be a level below this, the level of the rare *tzaddikim* who are able to maintain their awareness of the divine essence unifying all of reality without collapsing into it.

Regardless of these tensions, the unavoidable takeaway of all of this is that in general Rav Kook's phenomenology of repentance could hardly be more opposed to that described by Rabbenu Yona. In direct contrast to his view that the level of repentance is proportional to the degree of sorrow and bitterness one experiences, for Rav Kook the level of repentance is in inverse proportion to such emotions. Rather

---

71. Ibid.
72. Ibid., 33; 80.

than expressing despair and sorrow, "the degree of penitence is also the degree of the soul's freedom."[73] Echoing Hegel, Rav Kook writes that repentance "restores the world and life to its original character precisely by focusing on the basis of their highest attribute, the dimension of freedom,"[74] though this is a freedom that can only manifest itself in one way – as the realization of one's inherent holiness. While his mysticism would be anathema to Spinoza and Nietzsche, Rav Kook's alignment with their psychological critique of traditional theories of repentance nonetheless emerges very clearly. His higher form of repentance aims "to strengthen [man's] will and to heighten his self-esteem."[75] As Benjamin Ish-Shalom notes, "Nietzsche's basic interest, the aggrandizement of selfhood, becomes Rav Kook's own, yet he [Rav Kook] proposed a truly alternative view."[76] The irony is that the endpoint of this alternative aggrandizement of selfhood recalls the early Chabad idea of *avoda bebittul*, "the annihilation of being into nothingness, the effacement of each person's separate being and its reinclusion within the Divine,"[77] an idea that we have seen Rav Kook occasionally toying with. Saying that though, Rav Kook is nothing if not a dialectical thinker.

REPENTANCE, MYSTICISM, AND TORAH

One thing that has been barely mentioned in our discussion so far is Judaism. Up to this point, the theory of repentance outlined could be used in any religion. In a sense, this is no surprise. Given the divine origins of all of creation, there must be an element of truth in every manifestation of the religious impulse, so that even with specific regard to repentance:

---

73. Ibid., 22; 61.

74. Ibid., 19; 55.

75. Ibid., 28; 71.

76. Ish-Shalom, *Rav Avraham Itzhak HaCohen Kook*, 77. The contrast between Rav Kook's view and theories that stress self-degradation has also been noted in Lawrence A. Englander, "On Repentance," in Ezra Gellman, ed., *Essays on the Thought and Philosophy of Rabbi Kook* (New York, 1991), 121–132. See also Shalom Carmy, "On Optimism and Freedom," in ibid., 114–120.

77. Rachel Elior, *The Paradoxical Ascent to God: The Kabbalistic Theosophy of Habad Hasidism*, trans. Jeffrey M. Green (Albany, NY, 1993), 143. Of course, Rav Kook's emphasis on the more joyous and assertive elements of repentance are likely also of hasidic descent.

Everything helps to elevate the spirit, to achieve a higher level of repentance: all one's knowledge of Torah, all one's general culture, all one's energies, everything one knows about the world and about life, every contact with people, every disposition to equity and justice.[78]

But while, in this sense, all religious expressions are therefore equal, some are more equal than others, and there is no question that the Torah is the superior expression of divinity. As Rav Kook writes:

Morality, the impulse for equity and good, represents the central direction of the will of existence.... In the Torah, this moral conformity in all its manifestations is represented in the light of holiness, adapted to each community according to its stature, and to the Jewish people in its most authentic form.[79]

Thus the Jewish people play a pivotal role in redeeming the world and restoring it to its divine essence, and their Torah observance is the axis around which everything revolves: repentance "necessitates full penitence for all the detailed acts of wrongdoing and transgression, on the basis of the Written and Oral Torah, all of which express the divine soul embodied in the Jew."[80]

At the first level then, it is through the repentance of the *tzaddik* that "the whole world is renewed in a new light."[81] In Rav Kook's understanding, the righteous person "by looking at the basic nature of existence with an eye for the good...exerts an influence on existence and on the complicated processes of life that they emerge from their deficiencies."[82] But the Jew who repents in this manner must attach to the universal soul of the nation of Israel if he is to exert a cosmic influence. A person must unite himself with "the divine good in the soul

---

78. *OHT*, 47; 107.
79. Ibid., 37; 86.
80. Ibid., 40; 92.
81. Ibid., 24; 65.
82. Ibid., 27; 69.

of the community of Israel,"[83] for it is only nationally, through Israel, that the transformation through repentance of the world as a whole is mediated – "the community of Israel holds within itself the divine good, not for itself alone, but for the whole world,"[84] since Israel in its very essence aspires to universality. Rav Kook has an essentialist account of the chosen people who as a result "of their added spiritual sensitivity, will be the first with regard to penitence,"[85] though such sensitivity also means that among them, those "noble spirits who seek the light of God suffer because of the sins of society as a whole."[86]

There is, then, a clear emphasis on the national agenda over that of the individual in his theory of repentance. This national revival is the "foundation of the great repentance...and the repentance of the world that will follow it,"[87] drawing a clear line between his theory of repentance and his famously messianic understanding of Zionism, which is therefore the foundation of this ultimate repentance.[88]

For all the grandiose talk of this cosmic influence, Rav Kook initially describes the nuts and bolts of such repentance in a relatively prosaic manner, spending a few paragraphs on one of the mundane activities best known as being a focus of Jewish law – that of eating, which features prominently in mystical literature and practice. Rav Kook here discusses, in far from mundane fashion, how the wrong motivations when eating are a barrier to repentance in their inability to raise the holy sparks in

---

83. Ibid., 40; 92.
84. Ibid.
85. Ibid., 19; 55.
86. Ibid., 36; 85.
87. Ibid., 58; 126.
88. Jonathan Garb argues that this use of kabbalistic mysticism in the service of historical and nationalistic forms of redemption reflects a general trend that began with Rabbi Moshe Chaim Luzzatto (the Ramḥal) in the eighteenth century and was picked up by the Vilna Gaon and his students. Secular Zionism was particularly fertile ground for Rav Kook's application of this idea. See Jonathan Garb, "Rabbi Kook and His Sources: From Kabbalistic Historiosophy to National Mysticism," in Moshe Sharon, ed., *Studies in Modern Religions, Religious Movements and the Babi-Baha'i Faiths* (Leiden, Neth., 2004), 77–96.

the meal.[89] In addition, he also emphasizes on a number of occasions straightforward civil matters: "The most original and the best approach to repentance, which is inspired by the light of the Torah in the world, consists in the study of civil law…the *Ḥoshen Mishpat.*"[90]

At the same time, he adds that "one must always sensitize the heart and the mind through the other branches of the Torah,"[91] and notes that once such broadened study instills the desire for justice, it raises one's observance of those very same civil laws to an even higher spiritual level which in turn reinforces "a special love for the study of those laws that define man's obligations to his neighbor, and the largest section of the Torah, the laws dealing with money matters."[92] Study and practice here seem to be mutually supportive. We study in order to spread justice, while the love of justice this engenders leads to further study and ennobled practice.

Nonetheless, the tensions that grow out of Rav Kook's monism reemerge even here in his attitude toward Torah. While writing, on the one hand, of the need to study and practice Torah in what seems to be its most exoteric sense, on the other hand, Rav Kook often expresses reservations about the external level of understanding Torah, reservations that are best approached by looking at what he says of those who rebel against Torah altogether.

When Rav Kook speaks of the motivations for repentance, a primary stimulant, indeed a "special factor in this process will be the anguish felt over the humiliation visited on the great spiritual treasure of our ancestral heritage."[93] Though such anguish is a primary motivation to repentance, Rav Kook also believes that from such religious denials "positive elements may be garnered from the different paths of straying on which they stumbled."[94] Rebellion against religion has to be valuable to Rav Kook given his monism – after all, every phenomenon is at some level divine – but it is the claim that such a revolt indicates a defect in

---

89. *OHT,* 44; 101.
90. Ibid., 40; 93.
91. Ibid.
92. Ibid., 41; 93–94.
93. Ibid., 16; 51.
94. Ibid.

our Torah observance that marks out his approach. The "chutzpah" of the rebels is grounded in the holy sparks of divinity and indicates a lack in *our* understanding of the world, and indeed in our approach to Torah, specifically, our inability to see all particulars as part of the universal spiritual whole. As he tells us elsewhere, heresy "is needed to purge away the aberrations that attached themselves to religious faith because of a deficiency in understanding and divine service."[95] Thus, despite writing that the "rebellion against the divine law is a frightful moral regression,"[96] a simple rejection of those who rebel against the Torah fails to see that in their rebellion lies an idealistic yearning for perfection, or at least a dissatisfaction with the status quo, which, in Rav Kook's eyes, can only find a voice if our ideologies are indeed unsatisfying and lacking perfection. There is a clear tension here between, on the one hand, the sinfulness of religious rebellion, and on the other, the necessity for such rebellion to refine the Torah.

Rav Kook goes on to tell us that when the mitzvot and teachings of Torah are not combined with "the noblest of principles,"[97] and are enforced upon those who are not ready for them, the results can be destructive and nihilistic. In such cases "their influence on ill-prepared students have led so many to reject them and to mock them."[98] At this point then our approach to Torah, both as individuals and in our teaching of it, is itself part of the problem. It is "as a result of negligence, the light of the inner Torah whose pursuit needs a high state of holiness has not been properly established in the world."[99] The influence of the righteous and their participation in Israel's historical redemptive task might be key to the cosmic levels of repentance, but the manner in which religious Jews relate to the rest of the nation can also be a significant obstacle.

This is unsurprising given that Rav Kook believes that we are unaware of the inner mystical meanings of the higher Torah, but this lack of awareness becomes particularly problematic given that full

---

95. *"Yissurim Memarekim,"* in *Orot*, 126. Translated as "The Pangs of Cleansing," in Bokser, *Abraham Isaac Kook*, 264.

96. *OHT* 21: 58.

97. Ibid., 17; 53.

98. Ibid., 16: 52.

99. Ibid.

repentance requires a level of contemplation that addresses these very same "deeper levels of Torah and divine wisdom concerning the mystical dimension of the world."[100] Full repentance requires the study of this higher Torah, which requires the desire for a constant cleaving to God. At the same time, "one cannot succeed in the study of the mystical dimension of the Torah without repentance,"[101] leaving us apparently in a vicious circle where repentance requires awareness of this mystical Torah, but study of mystical Torah requires repentance. One might argue that it is only the *awareness* of this higher Torah that is required for repentance, and that it is through repenting that we actually come to *understand* this mystical level of which we had become aware.

Prayer is presented as having a role in unlocking the doors to repentance,[102] which may suggest that the awareness of the higher mystical Torah motivates prayer as a route to repentance and subsequently to mystical understanding. But however we are to understand this, the key idea seems to be that repentance, at least in the fullest sense, is not a straightforward return to the Torah as we currently understand it. It cannot simply be about saying sorry, or redressing the errors one has made regarding particular mitzvot. What is needed is for people to study Torah in the correct manner "to enlarge our spiritual perspective so as to recognize the proper connection between the particulars and the universal categories of the spiritual."[103] It will only be through the reestablishment of Torah in its true sense that we will be able to achieve the type of individual repentance that connects us to the nation of Israel which can then go on to redeem the world.

CONCLUSION

Rav Kook's *Orot HaTeshuva* is one of a number of twentieth-century works that co-opt ideas originally intended as a critique of religion in the service of religious ends.[104] But it is the combination of these

---

100. Ibid., 30; 73.
101. Ibid., 31; 77.
102. Ibid., 32; 78.
103. Ibid., 16; 52.
104. Many of Rav Soloveitchik's works are further examples. See Rynhold and Harris, "Modernity and Jewish Orthodoxy."

modernist sympathies with deeply mystical foundations that renders Rav Kook such a unique and fascinating character, and makes his work on repentance stand out. Certainly his version of the Torah revolution is yet to materialize. When he wrote that the "profound disturbance of the spirit" that manifests itself in repentance "must come to expression in literature," and that what we need most of all is a "poet of repentance, who will be a poet of life, a poet of rebirth,"[105] he probably wasn't envisaging a contemporary religious world dominated by utilitarian religious institutions that seem unlikely to produce such visionaries. Saying that, it is not as if "poets of life" are a type that can be produced to order by institutional design. As things stand then, Rav Kook's own work is probably the closest we will come to the type of literature he thought we needed, and while in a sense its continuing attraction is surprising, that we continue to read him may yet indicate that we still aspire to some of his ideals.[106]

FURTHER READING

The standard version of *Orot HaTeshuva* is the oft-reprinted version published by Mossad HaRav Kook, currently found in a volume together with a selection of his other works, including *Orot HaTorah* and *Musar Avikha* (Jerusalem, 1985). It has also been translated as "Lights of Penitence" in Ben Zion Bokser, ed., *Abraham Isaac Kook: The Lights of Penitence, Lights of Holiness, The Moral Principles, Essays, Letters and Poems* (Mahwah, 1978), 41–128. As mentioned, we now also have available the uncensored notebooks from which the passages assembled as *Orot HaTeshuva* were taken: *Shemona Kevatzim*, 2nd ed. (Jerusalem, 2004). As has hopefully emerged in this chapter, the structure of Rav Kook's thought is such that one could almost see everything he wrote as being

---

105. *OHT*, 58; 128.

106. I am very grateful to Dr. David Shatz, Dr. Jonathan Dauber, and Rabbi Shalom Carmy for their comments on and discussion of this chapter. Thanks are also due to Dr. Yoel Finkelman for his helpful comments on the final version. I am also grateful to Jay Orlinsky and Chaim Zakheim for our weekly study sessions on Rav Kook over recent years that helped me to place his views on repentance in a broader context.

related to repentance at one level or another. Thus most of his major works could be listed here as supplementary reading.

Regarding secondary literature, other than the various monographs, collections, and articles mentioned in the footnotes, Zvi Yaron, *The Philosophy of Rav Kook*, trans. Avner Tomaschoff (Jerusalem, 1991), is a good clear survey of Rav Kook's thought, and I recommend the following collections of essays: Lawrence J. Kaplan and David Shatz, eds., *Rabbi Abraham Isaac Kook and Jewish Spirituality* (New York, 1995); Benjamin Ish-Shalom and Shalom Rosenberg, eds., *The World of Rav Kook's Thought*, trans. Shalom Carmy (New York, 1991). This latter volume appears in the notes, but I mention it here to draw attention to Part II of the collection, which is dedicated to *teshuva*, and contains chapters on *Ḥasidei Ashkenaz* and the *Musar* movement, among others, rather than being exclusively focused on Rav Kook.

The Halakhist as Creator: Rabbi Joseph B. Soloveitchik's *Halakhic Man*

Rabbi Reuven Ziegler

Among the ranks of modern Jewish thinkers, Rabbi Joseph B. Soloveitchik (1903–1993) holds a special place. A talmudist of the first rank and a profound expositor of the Bible, Midrash, and other Jewish texts, he also brings to his writings an academic training in philosophy and broad erudition in Western culture. His highly distinctive and creative works explore the meaning and depth of Jewish religiosity, while at the same time speaking to the general human condition.

Born into an illustrious family of Lithuanian rabbinic scholars, Rabbi Soloveitchik was raised in small towns in Eastern Europe, where he received intensive talmudic training at the hands of his father. In his twenties, breaking with family tradition, he pursued a university education, earning a doctorate in philosophy from the University of Berlin. Upon immigrating to America in 1932, he was appointed rabbi of the Orthodox community of Boston. In 1941, he succeeded his father as a *rosh yeshiva* at the Rabbi Isaac Elchanan Theological Seminary of Yeshiva University in New York, continuing to shuttle weekly between Boston and New York for over four decades. Dedicating the bulk of his efforts to training advanced students in creative talmudic analysis, he also focused on matters of Jewish philosophy and public affairs, and was universally regarded as the intellectual and spiritual leader of Modern Orthodoxy (a term he himself did not use).

In his philosophy, perhaps his primary concern is the role that halakha (Jewish law) plays in the Jew's life – both as a system of thought and as a way of living. Halakha provides the Jew's central mode of relating to God, a medium for his or her religious experience, a guide to self-development and community building, and a means of understanding the world and engaging it. Yet, out of its commandments and insights there emerges a view of human nature and its potential that has universal application. The individual is majestic and humble, natural and spiritual, burdened by incompleteness, vulnerability, and distress but capable of creation, self-transcendence, and greatness.

Drawing on his understanding of Jewish tradition, Western thought, and human nature, Rabbi Soloveitchik also focuses his attention on another crucial issue: the confrontation of religion with modernity. He addresses not only the ideas and events of modernity, but also, perhaps most importantly, its temper, mindset, and attitudes. His works, which evince both an acute analytic mind and a deeply feeling soul, convey to moderns the conceptual and emotional depth, drama, and power of religious existence, and specifically of halakhic life.

I. THE DIALECTIC OF *HALAKHIC MAN*

In his first major publication, *Halakhic Man* (originally: "*Ish HaHalakha*"), Rav Soloveitchik – or the Rav, as he was called – sets himself an ambitious task: to portray the personality and goals of halakhic man, "the master of talmudic dialectics."[1] He proposes "to penetrate deep into the structure of halakhic man's consciousness and to determine the precise

---

1. "*Ish HaHalakha*" was published in 1944 in the journal *Talpiot*, vol. 1:3–4, 651–735, and reprinted in the volumes *BeSod HaYaḥid VeHaYaḥad*, ed. Pinchas Peli (Jerusalem, 1976), 39–188, and *Ish HaHalakha: Galui VeNistar* (Jerusalem, 1979), 9–113. It was translated into English by Lawrence Kaplan as *Halakhic Man* (Philadelphia, 1983); page

nature of this 'strange, singular' being."[2] Such a task had never before been undertaken, and as an unfortunate result, says the Rav, halakhic man "is of a type that is unfamiliar to students of religion."[3]

The difficulty of the task is compounded by the fact that halakhic man is a complex personality: "Halakhic man reflects two opposing selves; two disparate images are embodied within his soul and spirit."[4] Utilizing the typological method employed in many of his later works as well, Rav Soloveitchik begins his depiction of halakhic man by first presenting portraits of two other ideal human types, *ish hadaat* and *ish hadat* – that is, cognitive man and *homo religiosus* (religious man).[5]

Cognitive man is exemplified by the mathematical physicist, who concerns himself only with the world of physical reality and attempts to gain intellectual mastery over it. *Homo religiosus*, by contrast, is an otherworldly, mystical type, focusing on the mystery of nature and seeking to transcend the tangible world in favor of a pure, spiritual realm. Halakhic man is both like and unlike these two types – and therein lies his uniqueness:

> On the one hand he is as far removed from *homo religiosus* as east is from west and is identical, in many respects, to prosaic, cognitive man; on the other hand he is a man of God, possessor of an ontological approach that is devoted to God and of a worldview saturated with the radiance of the Divine Presence. For this reason it is difficult to analyze halakhic man's religious consciousness

---

references in this essay refer to the English version (henceforth, *HM*). A bibliography of Rabbi Soloveitchik's published works can be found online at: http://www.math. tau.ac.il/~turkel/engsol.html.

2. *HM*, 4.
3. Ibid., 3.
4. Ibid.
5. Much of Rav Soloveitchik's philosophy is formulated as the description of different ideal types of personalities. (They are "ideal" in the sense of being pure abstract types, not in the sense of being the best types.) Any specific real person can contain within him a conglomeration of various types. But the point of separating an individual into his component parts is to demonstrate the internal coherence of each personality's orientation, and thus to understand better the complex hybrid produced by their coexistence.

by applying the terms and traits that descriptive psychology and modern philosophy of religion have used to characterize the religious personality.... In some respects he is a *homo religiosus,* in other respects a cognitive man. But taken as a whole he is uniquely different from both of them.[6]

Halakhic Man is a sprawling, dense, and riveting work. To get a handle on it, we first need to analyze the personalities of cognitive man and *homo religiosus,* and to discern in what respects halakhic man is like each and in what respects he differs from them. That will be our objective in this section. Then, in the next three sections, we shall look at halakhic man's goals, try to identify on whom he is modeled, and attempt to discern the Rav's aims in writing this work.[7]

Before analyzing the "two opposing selves" of halakhic man, we should note that, contrary to the impression we gain from the programmatic statements above, *Halakhic Man* is not just a work of description and analysis, but also one of defense and advocacy. It both depicts *and* defends a certain type of religious personality, as well as a certain approach to religion and a certain understanding of halakha. To an outsider, the word "talmudist" conjures up images of a dry pedant squinting into the pages of a dusty tractate while remaining oblivious to both the world without and the spirit within. The force and originality of Rav Soloveitchik's vision sweeps away this false image, substituting for it one in which halakhic man – precisely through the rigorous study and practice of halakha – comes to embody what the Rav considers to be the best qualities of both cognitive and religious man.

Cognitive Man and *Homo Religiosus*

Cognitive man, the theoretical scientist, is characterized by majestic and creative intellectualism. *Homo religiosus,* the God-intoxicated mystic, is characterized by burning religious passion. Halakhic man, the talmudic scholar, would seem to be far removed from both. How,

---

6. *HM,* 3.
7. Many valuable studies of *Halakhic Man* have been written; for those most relevant to the topics covered in this essay, see Further Reading at the end.

then, can his personality be the product of a dialectic between them? We can gain insight into the dialectic that generates halakhic man by contrasting it with the dialectic between Adam I (majestic man) and Adam II (covenantal man) in Rav Soloveitchik's well-known work, *The Lonely Man of Faith* (1965).

Though not identical, Adam I and cognitive man share a close affinity. Both are active and innovative personalities; both have absolute faith in the power of the intellect; and both have limited interests, restricting their inquiry to the realm of the comprehensible and rational.

By contrast, Adam II and *homo religiosus* differ in crucial ways. Both Adam II and *homo religiosus* seek God; however, *homo religiosus* views the material world – in both its physical and social aspects – as an impediment to the spiritual, while Adam II displays no such dualism. Thus, Adam II seeks companionship; *homo religiosus* is solitary. Adam II desires a relationship with God; *homo religiosus* desires to lose himself within God. Adam II feels lonely in the world; *homo religiosus* feels trapped.

Adam II, covenantal man, tries to overcome his loneliness by forming relationships with God and with other people. *Homo religiosus*, a Romantic, attempts to escape the prison of physicality by exploring esoteric mysteries, leaping beyond objective reason into the realm of subjective intuitions. These bring *homo religiosus* to a dizzying vacillation between ecstasy and melancholy, often engendering asceticism, anxiety, and psychic torment.

Adam II is thus a much healthier sort than *homo religiosus*, and this fact impacts upon the nature of the dialectic in each book. For while *The Lonely Man of Faith* calls upon man to maintain the positions of both Adam I and Adam II in endless oscillation, the title character of *Halakhic Man* overcomes the duality of cognitive man and *homo religiosus* and thereafter does not return to the position of either. In philosophical terms, *The Lonely Man of Faith* presents a Kierkegaardian dialectic, wherein the thesis and antithesis remain in perpetual tension, while *Halakhic Man* presents a Hegelian dialectic, wherein the tension between two antithetical positions ultimately results in a third position, or synthesis. It would make little sense for Rav Soloveitchik to advocate a Kierkegaardian dialectic in *Halakhic Man* since he regards one side of the dialectic, *homo religiosus*, to be an exemplar of – or at least prone to be – what William James calls "the sick soul."

There is yet a deeper reason for the different types of dialectic employed in these two works. The fundamental dialectic in *The Lonely Man of Faith* is between conquest and sacrifice, while the fundamental dialectic in *Halakhic Man* is between this-worldliness and otherworldliness, or between materialism and dualism. The Rav values both conquest and sacrifice, which is why he maintains both of them in an unending dialectic in *The Lonely Man of Faith*. However, he *rejects* both materialism and dualism, which is why in *Halakhic Man* he must find a third position that overcomes the deficiencies of both.

This-Worldly Spirituality

Cognitive man, a materialist, acknowledges only the physical universe. *Homo religiosus*, a dualist, recognizes both the material and spiritual worlds but sees them as standing in opposition to each other; he wishes to flee the former to live in the latter. Halakhic man cannot accept either perspective:

> Halakhic man differs both from *homo religiosus*, who rebels against the rule of reality and seeks a refuge in a supernal world, and from cognitive man, who does not encounter any transcendence at all. Halakhic man apprehends transcendence. However, instead of rising up to it, he tries to bring it down to him. Rather than raising the lower realms to the higher world, halakhic man brings down the higher realms to the lower world.[8]

It is clear why, as a religious person, halakhic man cannot agree with cognitive man that the corporeal world is all that exists or all that should interest him. However, we confront the following question: If halakhic man agrees with *homo religiosus* that there is a transcendent realm and that it is desirable to encounter it, why doesn't he join *homo religiosus*'s quest to "ascend to the heavens"? Why must he remain firmly

---

8. *HM*, 41–42.

rooted in *olam hazeh*, this world, while pursuing his quest for transcendence? Why would a religious person wish to stay in a world that is *not* transcendent?

Rav Soloveitchik offers three reasons.[9] First, he considers *homo religiosus*'s position unethical:

> *Homo religiosus*, his glance fixed upon the higher realms, forgets all too frequently the lower realms and becomes ensnared in the sins of ethical inconsistency and hypocrisy. See what many religions have done to this world on account of their yearning to break through the bounds of concrete reality and escape to the sphere of eternity. They have been so intoxicated by their dreams of an exalted supernal existence that they have failed to hear...the sighs of orphans, the groans of the destitute.... There is nothing so physically and spiritually destructive as diverting one's attention from this world.[10]

Second, *homo religiosus*'s attempt to turn himself into pure spirit is unrealistic; man is unavoidably corporeal and must deal with this fact.[11] Third, the path of *homo religiosus* is undemocratic; it can be pursued

---

9. Ibid., 41–44.
10. Ibid., 41.
11. Similarly, in n. 4 of *Halakhic Man* Rav Soloveitchik offers both moral and "realistic" reasons as to why the religious experience should not be regarded as something simple and tranquil. The "realistic" reason is that such a portrayal is simply false; the religious experience "is exceptionally complex, rigorous and tortuous...antinomic and antithetic" (141). The moral reason is that the desire for simplicity and serenity stems from a rebellion against knowledge and objective thought (which raise questions and thereby disturb one's peace of mind), and this rejection of reason – by sanctifying instinct, intuition, and unrestrained emotion – ultimately leads to moral depravity. He concludes powerfully:

> And let the events of the present era [i.e., the Holocaust] be proof! The individual who frees himself from the rational principle and who casts off the yoke of objective thought will in the end turn destructive and lay waste the entire created order. Therefore, it is preferable that religion should ally itself with the forces of clear, logical cognition, as uniquely exemplified in the scientific method, even though at times the two might clash with one another, rather than pledge

only by a small elite, while halakha, in contrast, is meant to guide the entire community.

Rejecting cognitive man's materialism and *homo religiosus*'s dualism, halakhic man adopts a monistic stance that recognizes both the material and the transcendent and, rather than rejecting one in favor of the other, seeks to bring them together. In order to understand how he accomplishes this, we must now ask not how halakhic man differs from cognitive man and *homo religiosus*, but in what ways he is like them.

Like *homo religiosus*, "halakhic man reaches out to God" and "his soul...thirsts for the living God."[12] He, too, experiences the affirmation and negation of a finite being standing before the Infinite,[13] though, unlike *homo religiosus*, he overcomes this duality via the halakha – particularly through the realization that "the halakha set man at the very center of its world."[14] Yet in almost every other aspect, he resembles cognitive man: in his rigorous intellectualism, his balanced temperament, his rational and objective approach to the world, his quantifying methodology, and his fundamentally this-worldly orientation. Like cognitive man, he "holds fast, with all his being, to the concrete reality of our empirical world"[15] and "occupies himself with intellectual constructions – experiencing all the while the joy of discovery and the thrill of creation – and then coordinating his

---

its troth to beclouded, mysterious ideologies that grope in the dark corners of existence, unaided by the shining light of objective knowledge, and believe that they have penetrated to the secret core of the world. (ibid.)

See also *The Halakhic Mind* (New York, 1986), 52–55, where Rav Soloveitchik, clearly declaring that "The ethical implications of any philosophical theory... should many a time decide the worth of the doctrine" (52), again assails the Romantic rejection of reason, noting that "When reason surrenders its supremacy to dark equivocal emotions, no dam is able to stem the rising tide of the affective stream" (53).

It should be noted, however, that the use of reason and cold logic can also lead to moral travesties, as in the case of Communism. Therefore, employing the moral criterion may not always privilege rational approaches over non-rational ones.

12. *HM*, 40.
13. Ibid., 67–72.
14. Ibid., 70.
15. Ibid., 40.

ideal intelligibles [i.e., the creations of his thought] with the real world, as does the mathematician."[16]

How can a life devoted to the study and practice of halakha be compared to that of the mathematician? And how can such a life be said to bring transcendence into the world? To explain this, the Rav introduces two ideas: halakha as a cognitive system, and the doctrine of *tzimtzum*. These ideas define the nature of halakha and of the halakhist's activity, and highlight their uniqueness in the world of religion.

The Scientist and the Halakhist

The idea of "halakha as a cognitive system" must be understood by reference to the neo-Kantian view of science.[17] Generally, science is thought to be an empirical, a posteriori enterprise: this means that the scientist ponders reality with no apparent preconceptions, and when he finds some repeating patterns within it he begins to formulate laws to explain the observed phenomena. The neo-Kantian view, by contrast, is that the scientist constructs an ideal, a priori system of laws and then views nature through it. It is "a priori" in that its categories do not proceed from experience but rather from pure thought; it is "ideal" in that it does not have to conform to reality, but merely must be internally consistent. After performing this supremely creative act, the scientist then looks at the world through the categories he has conceived and correlates physical reality with his constructions.[18]

Rav Soloveitchik sees the halakhist's activity as parallel to the scientist's. Halakha, he maintains, is not just a normative system but

---

16. Ibid., 39–40.

17. More precisely, this is the view of the founder of the Marburg school of neo-Kantianism, Hermann Cohen (whose thought the Rav studied intensively, and about whom he wrote his doctoral thesis), as well as that of his students Paul Natorp and Ernst Cassirer.

18. Though this conception of the scientific enterprise may seem counterintuitive to the non-specialist, it was the view held by many of the leading scientists and philosophers of science at the time *Halakhic Man* was written. If we think in terms of mathematics instead of physics, this view becomes easier to comprehend. The mathematician creates abstract constructs and focuses his attention on them, without any reference to the concrete world of experience. Afterwards, he may investigate the world using these constructs and find physical phenomena that parallel his ideal constructions.

primarily a cognitive one as well. In other words, it is not just a system of laws that regulates the Jew's life, but also a system of concepts that mediates halakhic man's perception of the world, or a lens through which he views his surroundings. Halakhic man "orients himself to the world by means of fixed statutes and firm principles" of halakha.[19] To take a celebrated example:

> When halakhic man comes across a spring bubbling quietly, he already possesses a fixed, a priori relationship with this real phenomenon: the complex laws regarding the halakhic construct of a spring. The spring is fit for the immersion of a *zav* (a man with a discharge); it may serve as *mei ḥatat* (waters of expiation); it purifies with flowing water; it does not require a fixed quantity of forty se'ahs; etc. When halakhic man approaches a real spring, he gazes at it and carefully examines its nature. He possesses, a priori, ideal principles and precepts which establish the character of the spring as a halakhic construct, and he uses the statutes for the purpose of determining normative law: does the real spring correspond to the requirements of the ideal halakha or not?[20]

These halakhic statutes and principles, though revealed by God, are subject to human interpretation and conceptualization. Therefore, they are the main arena in which halakhic man exercises his creativity. "Halakhic man received the Torah from Sinai not as a simple recipient but as a creator of worlds, as a partner with the Almighty in the act of creation."[21] Because of this dual aspect of halakha, halakhic man both *discovers* the principles divinely revealed at Sinai, and *creates* his own conceptualization of them. After creating this ideal halakhic world, halakhic man then "orients himself to the world" through his system of halakhic postulates. Since "there is no phenomenon, entity, or object in this concrete world which the a priori halakha does not approach

---

19. *HM*, 19.
20. Ibid., 20.
21. Ibid., 81.

with its ideal standard,"[22] halakhic man must fix his attention upon all aspects of creation: nature, society, commerce, family, government, psychology, etc.

The Advantages of Halakhic Cognition

To summarize, the Rav presents halakhic cognition as having two stages: the creation of the ideal world, and its correlation with the real world. Each stage addresses a distinct problem.

First, given that halakhic man combines cognitive man's creative intellectualism with *homo religiosus*'s concern with transcendence, the question arises: how can one apply human intellect to the transcendent realm? As a thinker well trained in Kantian philosophy, Rav Soloveitchik tended to eschew metaphysics. Therefore, in *Halakhic Man* as elsewhere, he shifts the application of intellect from metaphysics to halakha. Although man cannot penetrate the nature or essence of God, man can study Torah, which is a projection or manifestation of God's will and wisdom. Human intellect thereby gains access to the transcendent realm and, furthermore, is supremely creative within that realm.

The second stage of halakhic cognition addresses a different problem: If halakhic man is so interested in the ideal constructs of his mind, how can he stay grounded in this-worldly existence (something the Rav considers necessary for the reasons cited earlier)? The answer is that he uses these constructs as categories through which to perceive the world. This stage of cognition keeps halakhic man's focus on this world; furthermore, it brings God into the world by applying to it the categories of transcendence. As Rav Soloveitchik puts it elsewhere, "He is not concerned with interpreting God in terms of the world but the world under the aspect of God."[23] The former enterprise ("interpreting God in terms of the world") was that of medieval metaphysics: applying the categories of the finite human intellect to understanding the Infinite. This, according to the Rav, is both an impossible and undesirable task. The latter enterprise ("interpreting…the world under the aspect of God") is that of halakhic man: applying the divine-human categories

---

22. Ibid., 19.
23. *The Halakhic Mind*, 45.

of halakha to cognize the world. This is both epistemologically possible and ethically-spiritually desirable.

The Kabbalist and the Halakhist

One way of bringing God into the world is by means of halakhic cognition, or *talmud Torah*; the other is by means of halakhic action, or *shemirat hamitzvot*. To elaborate on these ideas, we must introduce the Rav's presentation of a kabbalistic doctrine: *tzimtzum*, or divine contraction.

In Kabbala – and note that the kabbalist is a type of *homo religiosus* – *tzimtzum* is a tragedy. Before the creation of the universe, God filled all of existence, so to speak. Since nothing finite can exist within the Infinite, God had to "contract" His existence in order to make room for the world. "The mystic sees the existence of the world as a type of 'affront,' heaven forbid, to God's glory; the cosmos, as it were, impinges upon the infinity of the Creator."[24] The world thus serves as a barrier between man and God; if the world were to disappear, all would be united within God. Since the kabbalist's main desire is to unite with God, *tzimtzum* is a source of anguish to him.

Halakhic man understands *tzimtzum* differently. For him it is a source of joy and gives meaning to his existence. Harking back to a midrashic use of the term *tzimtzum* (Exodus Rabba 34:1), Rav Soloveitchik takes it to mean not the contraction of God *away from* the world, but rather His contraction *into* the world. Far from being an affront to God or a barrier between man and God, the world is the sole arena within which man can confront God. "God saw everything that He had created, and, behold, it was very good" (Gen. 1:31): God wants man to live in this world and to bring His presence into it. The means by which man concentrates God's infinite presence into the finite world is by realizing the halakha.[25]

---

24. *HM*, 49.

25. While Rav Soloveitchik's presentation of *tzimtzum into* the world, as opposed to the Lurianic view of *tzimtzum away* from the world, may be rooted in the writings of Chabad, Rav Soloveitchik strips *tzimtzum* of its metaphysics and cosmology and turns it into a halakhic concept in which transcendence enters the physical world through halakhic study and performance. I thank Dr. Yoel Finkelman for this point.

To complicate matters, the "realization" or "actualization" of halakha (*hitgashmut hahalakha*) seems to have two different meanings in *Halakhic Man*: the cognition of halakhic structures as they apply to the world, which we have already examined, and the performance of halakhic norms, which bring the real world into closer correlation with the ideal. This dual meaning, naturally, leads to the question of whether, for halakhic man, study or practice is paramount.

II. HALAKHIC MAN'S VALUES

Study and Practice

Halakhic man pursues two primary goals: the study of halakha and its practice. The study of Torah, as we have seen, means not just mastering texts, but grasping, via those texts, the a priori world of halakhic constructs: comprehending it, shaping it through one's own creative interpretation and conceptualization, and immersing oneself within it. By studying Torah in this fashion, halakhic man makes the Torah into his own possession, a part of himself. As Rashi (Kiddushin 32b, s.v. *uvetorato*) explains the verse, "But his delight is in the Lord's Torah; and in His [or, his] Torah does he meditate day and night" (Ps. 1:2): "At the beginning it is called 'the Lord's Torah,' and when he studies and masters it, it is called 'his [own] Torah.'"

Halakhic man's other goal, the practice of halakha, means implementing and actualizing these ideal constructs within the human world of action and experience. This has two ramifications. First, the performance of mitzvot concretizes, objectifies, and, one might say, externalizes halakhic man's subjective, inner religiosity. Second, by applying halakhic constructs within the physical world, halakhic man brings reality into closer conjunction with the ideal halakhic realm, thereby drawing divinity down into the world.

Which is more important for halakhic man – study or practice? At some points in *Halakhic Man* study seems paramount, while at others it seems that the implementation of halakha (following upon its study, of course) is more significant. While this tension remains unresolved, it seems to me that, overall, study gains the upper hand over practice. This is most striking when the Rav refers to the famous talmudic dispute on this very topic:

R. Tarfon and the elders were assembled in the upper story of
Nitza's house in Lod. This question was posed to them: Which is
greater, study (*talmud*) or practice (*maase*)? R. Tarfon answered
and said: Practice is greater. R. Akiva answered: Study is greater.
All [the elders] answered and said: Study is greater, for study
leads to practice. (Kiddushin 40b)

Of course, the conclusion that "Study is greater, for study leads
to practice" leaves open the question of which of these is more valuable
in itself. However, halakhic man's interpretation of this passage makes
the question almost moot. Noting that *maase* can refer either to "determining the...ideal norm" (a theoretical activity), or to "implementing
the ideal norm in the real world" (a practical activity), Rav Soloveitchik
writes, "Halakhic man stresses action (*maase*) in its first meaning." Thus,
both *talmud* and *maase* (understood this way) become aspects of study.

In a sense, halakhic man is almost *forced* to give primacy to
theoretical study, because even though every area of life is governed
by halakha, many areas of halakha are not practically operative today
(e.g., the laws of the Temple and of ritual purity). Consider the fact that
Maimonides, after enumerating the 248 positive biblical commandments in his *Sefer HaMitzvot*, lists only sixty (!) as *mitzvot hekhreḥiyot*,
commandments that are in effect in all eras for all people. Were halakhic man to lay his primary emphasis upon practice, he would be left
with far less motivation and justification for studying the vast areas
of halakha that remain in the realm of the ideal – and this would be
contrary to his very essence.

Although halakhic man of course keeps mitzvot scrupulously,
his deep desire to realize halakha in its fullness within the concrete
world is something of a messianic aspiration, and is not necessarily
his primary motivation on a day-to-day basis. Note what halakhic man
pursues actively and what he pursues passively in the Rav's summary
of halakhic man's activities:

He *creates* an ideal world, *renews* his own being and *transforms*
himself into a man of God, *dreams* about the complete realization
of the halakha in the very core of the world, and *looks forward*

to the kingdom of God 'contracting' itself and appearing in the midst of concrete and empirical reality.[26]

In this summation, halakhic man is active regarding *study* and *self-creation* ("creates," "renews," "transforms"), and passive regarding the full *realization* of halakha ("dreams about," "looks forward to").

Halakhic Man's Ethical Commitment
Earlier, we saw that halakhic man rejects the approach of *homo religiosus* because he finds it otherworldly and undemocratic. But if halakhic man indeed values study more than practice, can he himself really be considered this-worldly or democratic? In other words, if halakhic man lives within the realm of theoretical halakhic constructs that cannot all be actualized, in what sense is he this-worldly? And if he believes that halakha demands such a high level of abstract intellectual accomplishment, in what sense is he democratic?

Perhaps to combat the first charge, Rav Soloveitchik concludes Part One of *Halakhic Man* (which generally lays a heavier emphasis on study than on practice) in a manner reminiscent of the way Maimonides concludes his *Guide of the Perplexed.* Throughout the *Guide*, Maimonides presents a highly intellectualist version of human perfection. All human endeavors, it seems, should lead to the ultimate goal of intellectual perfection, or knowledge of God. Yet in the final chapter (III:54), Maimonides clarifies that this intellectual perfection is not purely contemplative, but rather entails concrete actions that proceed from knowledge. Similarly, after presenting throughout Part One halakhic man's pursuit of an intellectualist ideal, Rav Soloveitchik ends this section[27] by stressing halakhic man's ethical sensitivity and his commitment to ethical action. These are a major part of his commitment to the realization of the halakha as a whole:

> The standard notion of ritual prevalent among religious men – i.e., ritual as a nonrational religious act whose whole purpose is to lift man up from concrete reality to celestial realms – is totally foreign

---

26. *HM*, 137; emphasis added.
27. Ibid., 90–95.

to Judaism. According to the outlook of halakha, the service of God (with the exception of the study of the Torah) can be carried out only through the implementation, the actualization of its principles in the real world. The ideal of righteousness is the guiding light of this worldview. Halakhic man's most fervent desire is the perfection of the world under the dominion of righteousness and loving-kindness – the realization of the a priori, ideal creation, whose name is Torah (or halakha), in the realm of concrete life.[28]

Thus, for halakhic man, as for Maimonides, intellectual knowledge is both an end in itself and a spur to action. The Rav illustrates the seriousness of halakhic man's ethical commitment with a remarkable comment by his grandfather:

> My uncle, Rabbi Meir Berlin [Bar-Ilan], told me that once Rabbi Chaim of Brisk was asked what the function of a rabbi is. Rabbi Chaim replied: "To redress the grievances of those who are abandoned and alone, to protect the dignity of the poor, and to save the oppressed from the hands of his oppressor." Neither ritual decisions nor political leadership constitutes the main task of halakhic man. Far from it. The actualization of the ideals of justice and righteousness is the pillar of fire which halakhic man follows when he, as a rabbi and teacher in Israel, serves his community. More, through the implementation of the principles of righteousness, man fulfills the task of creation imposed upon him: the perfection of the world under the dominion of halakha and the renewal of the face of creation.[29]

Although highlighting halakhic man's ethical commitment may mitigate the charge that he is not truly this-worldly, halakhic man still remains open to the charge that, with his strong emphasis on rigorous and creative Torah study, he is not truly democratic. Rav Soloveitchik returns to consider this theme in *UVikkashtem MiSham* when he

---

28. Ibid., 94.
29. Ibid., 91.

explores the necessity of the exoteric and esoteric, or democratic and elitist, dimensions of halakha.[30]

The Structure of *Halakhic Man*

Let us pause to consider the overall structure of *Halakhic Man*.

(a)   Sections I–X of Part One (3–66) present the "ontological outlooks" (i.e., the perspectives upon the different domains of being) of cognitive man, *homo religiosus*, and halakhic man – specifically, how each figure relates to both concrete reality and the transcendent realm. While the first two figures view this as an either/or choice, halakhic man chooses to relate to both realms and to bring them together. Namely, halakhic man draws down the ideal constructs of halakha from transcendence into the real world by creatively cognizing them, viewing the world through them, and actualizing them in practice.

(b)   Sections XI–XV of Part One (66–95) explore how halakhic man's this-worldly spirituality, with its commitment to the ideal and attention to the real, shapes the contours of his personality, especially as contrasted with that of *homo religiosus* (who, indeed, serves as his major foil throughout the book).

(c)   Part Two focuses on halakhic man's creative capacity, as exercised in three domains: Torah, the world (sections I–II, 99–109), and especially the self (sections III–VI, 110–137).

We have explored (a) and the first part of (c). The topic of self-creation – the main focus of (c) – continues to figure prominently, and is developed at greater length, in Rav Soloveitchik's later writings on prayer, repentance, and suffering.[31] What *Halakhic Man* adds to his other treatments of self-creation is an analysis of providence and prophecy, not as articles of faith but as normative demands. Following

---

30. See *UVikkashtem MiSham* [*And From There You Shall Seek*], trans. Naomi Goldblum (Jersey City, 2008), 57–60, and my book, *Majesty and Humility: The Thought of Rabbi Joseph B. Soloveitchik* (Jerusalem, 2012), 115–118.

31. See the discussion in chapters 20, 22, and 23 of *Majesty and Humility*.

upon the Maimonidean doctrine that God grants individual providence (as opposed to providence over species) and prophecy only to people who have earned them, halakhic man takes these beliefs as commands: one must strive to make oneself worthy of both individual providence and prophecy. One accomplishes this task of self-perfection by developing one's individuality and exercising one's creativity. Indeed, it is quite striking that in Part Two, the Rav identifies *ḥidush*, creativity, as the central characteristic of halakhic man, a figure whom outsiders might consider outdated and fossilized. In fact, the Rav exalts creativity to the point that it becomes the highest form of imitation of God (just as God is a Creator, so should man be a creator[32]) as well as the source of all sanctity.[33]

What remains, then, is for us to consider (b), halakhic man's personality, which I would like to approach by asking: Who is a halakhic man?

III. WHO IS A HALAKHIC MAN?

In a sense, this question is unfair, for the Rav makes clear in the book's very first footnote that "the description of halakhic man given here refers to a pure ideal type.... Real halakhic men, who are not simple but rather hybrid types, approximate, to a lesser or greater degree, the ideal halakhic man."[34] Even so, however, we may ask which real figures correspond to the ideal halakhic man "to a greater degree." Let us start by considering one of Rav Soloveitchik's greatest heroes, Maimonides.

Many aspects of halakhic man's emotional profile correspond to traits Maimonides prized, and indeed seem to match what we know about Maimonides himself from his books and letters. Halakhic man is motivated by deep piety and a passionate love for truth.[35] His religious experience is powerful and penetrating; however, it is one that follows upon cognition, and it is modest, not flashy.[36] He avoids

---

32. *HM*, 99–105.
33. Ibid., 107–109.
34. Ibid., 139, n.1.
35. Ibid., 79.
36. Ibid., 84–85.

melancholy[37] as well as exaggerated joy,[38] possessing instead a festive dignity and solemnity,[39] almost a stoic tranquility and extreme self-control.[40] Halakhic man is confident,[41] individualistic and autonomous,[42] noble,[43] bold and assertive.[44] Supremely strong-minded,[45] he hates intellectual flabbiness,[46] does not seek anyone's approval,[47] and is scornful of piety not based on knowledge.[48]

Yet while emotionally similar, halakhic man and Maimonides diverge intellectually. Halakhic man approaches God solely through the medium of halakha, and is unconcerned with either metaphysical mysteries[49] or philosophical subtleties.[50] In this sense, he could not be more different from the philosopher Maimonides. (This also distinguishes halakhic man from another of the Rav's heroes, the kabbalist Nahmanides.) Halakhic man, indeed, regards the study of halakha in much the same way as Maimonides regards the study of philosophy: it is the best way to know God, the peak of human knowledge, and the goal of our messianic aspirations. While the study of halakha has an important place in Maimonides' system, the study of philosophy has no place in halakhic man's system.

There is another factor that distinguishes halakhic man not only from Maimonides, but from almost all *gedolei Yisrael*: he avoids serving in rabbinic posts and is reluctant to render practical halakhic decisions.[51] In light of this characteristic, the Vilna Gaon, who meets many of the

---

37. Ibid., 72.
38. Ibid., 76.
39. Ibid.
40. Ibid., 77–78.
41. Ibid., 72.
42. Ibid., 78.
43. Ibid.
44. Ibid., 79.
45. Ibid.
46. Ibid.
47. Ibid., 89.
48. Ibid.
49. Ibid., 49.
50. Ibid., 58.
51. Ibid., 24.

above criteria and never held a rabbinic post, would seem to be a likely model for halakhic man. Since a number of the anecdotes in *Halakhic Man* revolve around the Gaon, it seems that in the Rav's mind he indeed is a model for this type.

However, this identification of the Vilna Gaon with halakhic man is problematic.[52] The Gaon's worldview, which molded his entire *mitnagged* milieu, was not only suffused with Kabbala (a subject that does not hold halakhic man's interest), but was, like that of *homo religiosus*, otherworldly and dualistic. As opposed to the early *mitnagdim* who despaired of attaining religious perfection while still tethered to earthly existence, halakhic man "is completely suffused with an unqualified ontological optimism [that is, he is optimistic about the possibilities offered by life in this world] and is totally immersed in the cosmos."[53] Far from viewing death as liberation from the shackles of physicality, halakhic man abhors death, for "It is this world that constitutes the stage for the halakha.... It is here that it can pass from potentiality to actuality. It is here, in this world, that halakhic man acquires eternal life!"[54] Halakhic man, wholly focused on the mission and aspiration of studying and actualizing halakha, is entirely unconcerned with *Olam HaBa*:

> The World to Come is a tranquil, quiet world that is wholly good, wholly everlasting, and wholly eternal, wherein a man will receive the reward for the commandments which he performed in this world. However, receiving of a reward is not a religious act; therefore, halakhic man prefers the real world to a transcendent existence because here, in this world, man is given the opportunity to create, act, accomplish, while there, in the World to Come, he is powerless to change anything at all.[55]

Could it be that halakhic man's scientific mode of thought, bold individualism, optimism, and creativity indicate that the book is an

---

52. See Nadler's article cited in Further Reading below.
53. *HM*, 52.
54. Ibid., 30.
55. Ibid., 32.

autobiographical portrait? I think not, for the simple reason that halakhic man would have no interest in writing *Halakhic Man*, nor would he have the ability to write it. The writer of the book *Halakhic Man* displays intimate knowledge of Jewish philosophy and mysticism, Christian thought, general philosophy and literature; halakhic man himself, as described in this book, displays no curiosity about these subjects. Rather, halakhic man's entire mental world seems to be encompassed by the study of halakha. Furthermore, the person halakhic man and the book *Halakhic Man* employ entirely different methodologies in approaching their respective subjects of interest. The thought patterns that halakhic man (the person) uses to study halakha are akin to those employed in the natural sciences, which are suited to the analysis of abstract concepts and the formal interrelationships between them. However, the book *Halakhic Man*, as pointed out in its first footnote, depicts its protagonist by utilizing the phenomenological method of the human sciences, which describes states and structures of human consciousness. With his "*lomdish*," science-patterned approach, halakhic man can write commentaries and novellae on the Talmud, but not a book like the one that describes him.

Once we have excluded all the above, as well as others whom the Rav contrasts with halakhic man (such as kabbalists, the early figures of the *Musar* movement, and Hasidim), who, then, is halakhic man? All the stories brought to illustrate characteristics of halakhic man are drawn from the lives of Lithuanian *gedolim* of the eighteenth to twentieth centuries. The overwhelming majority of these anecdotes concern the Rav's grandfather, Rabbi Chaim of Brisk, and the Rav's father, Rabbi Moshe Soloveitchik. In fact, the Rav explicitly refers to each of them as a "halakhic man."[56] In light of this, we can understand the book's epigraph, which is drawn from a talmudic aggada concerning the Rav's namesake, the biblical Joseph: "At that moment, the image of his father came to him and appeared before him in the window" (Sota 36b). When drawing his portrait of halakhic man, it seems, the Rav had before his eyes primarily Brisker man.

---

56. Ibid., 36, 38.

Although the specific contours of halakhic man's personality follow those of Brisker man, some of his traits and ideas have much broader application to all intellectual religious types, or all those whose service of God is filtered mainly through the medium of Torah study. Halakhic/Brisker man is an extreme version of this type in that he seems to derive his *entire* spiritual sustenance from the world of *lomdus*. In *Halakhic Man*, then, Rav Soloveitchik portrays a type that he clearly considers beautiful and highly admirable. Yet, despite his great esteem for this type and even his identification with it, it describes only one facet of his own religious personality, which was open to a wider range of experience and feeling, and interested in broader areas and sources of knowledge, than those pursued by the pure exemplar of halakhic man he so powerfully describes.[57]

IV. THE GOALS OF *HALAKHIC MAN*

Description and Defense

Given the date of *Halakhic Man*'s publication (1944), many have speculated that the Rav wrote it as a philosophical eulogy for his father, who had died unexpectedly three years earlier, and perhaps for the entire Lithuanian yeshiva world that was being annihilated in the Holocaust. While there may indeed be an element of eulogy in this work, I suggest that we look closely at the Rav's explicit programmatic statements on its first and last pages, and at the carefully chosen terms he uses to characterize halakhic man throughout it. These will help us grasp – now that we have surveyed some of *Halakhic Man*'s major themes – what exactly the Rav is trying to accomplish in this work.

> It is difficult *to analyze halakhic man's religious consciousness* by applying the terms and traits that *descriptive psychology and modern philosophy of religion* have used to characterize the religious personality.... He is of a type that is *unfamiliar to students of*

---

57. For this reason, I believe, he felt compelled to write *UVikkashtem MiSham* as well; see Ziegler, *Majesty and Humility*, 385–389.

religion.... Our aim in this essay is to penetrate deep into the structure of halakhic man's consciousness.[58]

My sole intention was to *defend the honor of the halakha and halakhic men,* for both it and they have oftentimes been attacked by those who have not penetrated into the essence of halakha and have failed to understand the halakhic personality.[59]

In these passages, the Rav articulates two goals: analysis[60] and defense;[61] and he identifies two subjects that are to be analyzed and defended: halakhic man and the halakhic system. To be more precise, the Rav wishes to (a) analyze halakhic man's religious consciousness, (b) defend halakhic man, and (c) defend the halakha.

The Rav does not define against whom he wants to defend halakhic man and the halakha. However, it seems to me that it is the inability of "descriptive psychology and modern philosophy of religion" and "students of religion" to understand halakha and halakhic men that leads the practitioners of these disciplines (and, more importantly, the broader circles influenced by them) to denigrate and even attack both of them.

Psychology and Philosophy of Religion

The American psychologist and philosopher William James (1842–1910) is widely acknowledged as the founder of the field that the Rav calls "descriptive psychology of religion." In his survey of *The Varieties of Religious Experience* (1902), he describes numerous types of *homo religiosus*. Yet all of these types practice a religiosity based on emotion and tinged with mysticism. James cannot conceive of an intellect-centered religiosity like halakhic man's, in which experience only follows upon cognition, never preceding it. *Halakhic Man,* then, introduces an entirely new cognitive personality type to James' religious taxonomy.

---

58. *HM,* 3–4; emphasis added.
59. Ibid., 137; emphasis added.
60. Ibid., 3–4.
61. Ibid., 137.

The seminal figure in the "modern philosophy of religion" (as in many other areas in philosophy) is without a doubt the German philosopher Immanuel Kant (1724–1804). One of Kant's most basic distinctions is between noumena and phenomena, or things-in-themselves as opposed to things as observed through our senses. Human intellect can be applied to the realm of phenomena, but it has no access to the realm of noumena, which includes the entire area of transcendent metaphysics (that which lies "beyond" the physical world). Thus, the metaphysical propositions of religion – God's existence, immortality of the soul, and free will – are not subject to either proof or disproof. They are not matters of *knowledge* but of *faith*.

Human intellect can be applied fruitfully, however, to a number of different areas, including:

(a) *Science*: This area was developed more by neo-Kantians such as Hermann Cohen than by Kant himself (see "The Scientist and the Halakhist" above).

(b) *The study of human consciousness*: Even if we cannot determine whether many of the things we think about are real, we do know that our thoughts themselves are real, and they can be studied. In fact, Kant's main project in his study of knowledge was to identify the structures by which the mind cognizes. By drawing attention away from the analysis of *things*-in-themselves, Kant opened the way for philosophers and psychologists to study the thought processes and subjective awareness of the *think-ers*. This turn to the self had a lasting effect on philosophy and led to the rise of the phenomenological method that the Rav employs in *Halakhic Man* and *UVikkashtem MiSham*, which, as noted, studies perceptions and consciousness rather than what lies behind them.

(c) *Ethics*: Man can and must formulate the universal ethical norm purely by using his own intellect. This is termed autonomy, i.e., self-legislation: *auto* = self, *nomos* = law. If one acts properly because one has been given an external command, and not because of the dictates of one's own conscience, one is acting not morally but rather slavishly. Kant terms such behavior heteronomous, meaning that it follows a law dictated from the outside: *hetero* = other, *nomos* = law. (Following the dictates of desire instead of reason is also a form of heteronomy.) For him, only autonomous acts have moral worth.

Although, according to Kant's theory of knowledge, we cannot assess the truth of religious propositions, religion plays an important practical role in supporting Kant's ethical theory. For in order to posit the existence of a moral order, it is necessary to assume that man has free will, that the soul is immortal, and that God exists.[62] However, this is no longer religion as commonly understood. God, the heteronomous commander, has no place in this system. For Kant, having true religion means following the moral imperative of one's conscience for its own sake, and not because it has been commanded from without. Man cannot have a personal relationship with God, nor does God desire man's service or worship. Religious rituals and prayer, which constitute what he calls the "external cult," are meaningless. At best, religious worship has instrumental value in symbolizing and perhaps reinforcing man's commitment to the ethical ideal.

Kant and Halakha

Basing himself on Christian portrayals of Judaism stretching back to Christianity's very beginnings, as well as on the interpretation of Judaism offered by the apostate Jew and rationalist philosopher Baruch Spinoza (1632–1677), Kant views Judaism as nothing more than a collection of political laws and empty rituals designed to preserve group cohesion. For him, it lacks a moral core and any notion of autonomous duty; in fact, it makes no demands whatsoever on the inner self. Rather, Judaism demands the fulfillment of external observances, resulting in what he considered to be an ossified legalism. As the very epitome of heteronomy,

---

62. (a) If man lacked free will, he could not be a moral agent. (b) The moral agent seeks to perfect himself, and it is impossible to attain this goal within the span of a life; hence, we must posit the immortality of the soul. (c) A moral order entails that one's happiness should be proportionate to one's moral virtue. Yet only the existence of God can ensure that this will ultimately come about. For Kant, these are necessary postulates of his moral theory, and they are also factors that motivate moral behavior.

Judaism creates a servile personality and thereby damages the causes of human dignity and morality. By Kant's definition, Judaism cannot be considered a religion at all.[63]

Most subsequent attacks on halakhic Judaism derived from Kant's critique in one way or another. This is not because the attackers were all sophisticated philosophers, but rather because the constellation of values that Kant or his successors espoused – autonomy, individuality, freedom, intellectual rigor, boldness, and creativity – became regnant in modern Western civilization. Whether due to Kant's direct or indirect influence, or because the "spirit of the age" dictated an approach like his, his ideas (even if watered down) became almost taken for granted. And the values mentioned (autonomy, individuality, and so forth) were invoked as a major indictment against Judaism, which seemed so lacking in these qualities. How was a religion devoted to the seemingly calcified study of ancient texts and the fulfillment of heteronomous laws to respond?

We must distinguish between two distinct issues: whether Kant's approach to religion is correct and whether his views on the nature of Judaism are correct. Many Jews thought that Kant was correct on both counts. Therefore, they concluded, Judaism either should be reformed and brought into closer accord with Kant's religion of reason by eliminating halakha's "ritual" laws and keeping only the "moral" laws (this was the approach of Liberal Judaism), or Judaism should be abandoned altogether (the approach of assimilationists). Others Jews, as different as Rabbi Isaac Breuer and Hermann Cohen, felt that Kant's understanding of religion was essentially correct, but his understanding of Judaism was faulty – for Judaism in fact met Kant's criteria for true religion. A third group, though they would not have said so in as many words, felt that, on the contrary, Kant's understanding of Judaism was correct but his understanding of religion was wrong: Judaism is indeed heteronomous and proud of it. (This approach may be attributed to ultra-Orthodoxy.)

---

63. Kant formulates his theory of knowledge in his *Critique of Pure Reason* (1781; 2nd ed. 1787); his ethical theory in *Groundwork of the Metaphysics of Morals* (1785) and *Critique of Practical Reason* (1788); and his criticism of Judaism in *Religion Within the Limits of Reason Alone* (1793), Book Three, beginning of Division Two.

Finally, there were those who challenged both aspects of Kant's view: his approach to religion and his understanding of Judaism. Among this last group we can count Rav Soloveitchik.[64]

Critique and Response

On the one hand, Rav Soloveitchik accepts Kant's delimitation of the intellect to the realm of phenomena (things as they appear to us), and the consequent impossibility of pursuing metaphysics. Instead of studying the metaphysical claims of religion, Rav Soloveitchik, like others, turns to the self and studies the religious *personality*.[65] He of course does not assert that religion is a purely human creation, but he does study it from the human, not divine, point of view, analyzing its influence upon man, man's role within it, and man's task of shaping it in partnership with God.

Many Romantic thinkers took the "turn to the self" to an extreme, coming to regard religion as purely subjective and emotional. Rav Soloveitchik's focus on human consciousness and the inner self does not lead him in this direction. On the contrary, halakhic man, as we have seen, is far closer to cognitive man than to *homo religiosus*. Halakhic man's religiosity is based on the intellect, and his primary goal is to bring objectivity to religion. He does this both by objectifying halakhic concepts in his rigorous and precise Torah study and by actualizing them in his observance of mitzvot. Both of these commitments prevent him from being swept away by the tide of subjectivity and unrestrained emotion that characterizes many contemporary forms of religion.

Nevertheless, I believe that Rav Soloveitchik displays sensitivity to Kant's critiques even when he does not explicitly indicate that he is engaging in polemic or defense.[66] For example, Kant and others viewed

---

64. To be more precise, Rav Soloveitchik, as we shall see, challenged some aspects of Kant's approach to religion while he accepted others, but he completely rejected Kant's understanding of Judaism.

65. At various points in his career, Rav Soloveitchik studied the religious personality through phenomenological lenses, focusing on states and structures of consciousness, and through existential lenses, focusing on the concrete dilemmas of the individual, his ability to communicate and form communities, etc.

66. Whether the Rav confronted these critiques in the writings of figures from the Haskala (Jewish Enlightenment), Liberal Judaism, Protestant theology, general

the mitzvot as empty and soulless rituals. However, the Rav demonstrates in many of his writings – both halakhic and philosophical – that halakha addresses not just external observance but also the inner realm of emotion and experience. Furthermore, in *The Halakhic Mind* the Rav asserts that there are values embedded within halakhic norms, and these can be identified after rigorous conceptual study of those norms.[67]

As for Kant's indictment of Judaism as being heteronomous, Rav Soloveitchik responds in two ways. First, he shows that there is broad autonomy within Judaism (at least for the master of halakhic study). Halakha is the product of divine revelation; but once halakha was given at Sinai, human reason is its final arbiter both on the level of study (*lomdus*) and application (*pesak*). Second, he shows that heteronomy is also important and has its place. In fact, more than the Rav addresses the technical philosophical issue of autonomy, he fosters an *ethic* of autonomy, a positive evaluation of halakhic man's sense of freedom, individuality, and self-worth.[68] In *Halakhic Man* especially, Rav Soloveitchik is far more concerned with the consequences of heteronomy for the religious personality than he is with the question of the heteronomy of the halakhic system per se. While the heteronomous personality is passive, uncreative, and servile, halakhic man is active, creative, and majestic. Halakhic man achieves this sense of autonomy by the complete identification of his will with God's will (i.e., the halakha), attained through his creative partnership with God in determining and realizing the law.

The Rav's use of the term "autonomous" to describe halakhic man, even if not in the exact sense Kant used it,[69] leads us to a crucial

---

philosophy, the social sciences, or elsewhere, they all derive secondarily from Kant and from the Enlightenment *zeitgeist* that produced him. Therefore, I will not treat each critic separately, but instead will address Kant himself, the source of the critique.

67. Regarding halakha and inwardness, see Ziegler, *Majesty and Humility*, 79–87, 96–110; regarding the derivation of values from halakha, see ibid., 334–343.

68. See Sokol (cited in Further Reading below), esp. 299–302.

69. For Kant, autonomy does not mean doing whatever I want. Kant believes that norms are universal, and not based on individual desires. Autonomy is achieved when, and only when, human reason establishes that how I act is right – and it can tell me that only if my prescription for myself applies to everyone and is not predicated on my personal desires. In other words, my reason does not so much *innovate* the norm as

point regarding *Halakhic Man*. In describing halakha and halakhic man, the Rav consistently employs loaded Kantian and neo-Kantian terms: autonomous, a priori, creative, scientific, etc. By doing so, he is making two statements: first, he values many of the same characteristics as do the Kantian and other modernist critics of halakhic Judaism; moreover, these very traits and values can be attained precisely through the study and practice of halakha. As he states in a succinct and striking formulation, "The goal of [halakhic man's] self-creation is individuality, autonomy, uniqueness, and freedom."[70]

We can infer from here and elsewhere that the Rav is responding to critics of halakha who asserted that "a life devoted to Torah study

endorse or *appropriate* the universal norm. (See Kenneth Seeskin, "Ethics, Authority, and Autonomy," in *The Cambridge Companion to Modern Jewish Philosophy*, ed. Michael L. Morgan and Peter E. Gordon [Cambridge, 2007], 195–196.)

If we understand Kantian autonomy in this way, perhaps Rav Soloveitchik concedes too much when he writes, "The freedom of the pure will in Kant's teaching refers essentially to the creation of the ethical norm. The freedom of halakhic man refers not to the creation of the law itself, for it was given to him by the Almighty, but to the realization of the norm in the concrete world" (*Halakhic Man*, 153, n. 80). Even according to Kant, the individual is not really creating the law; he is assenting to it and identifying with it.

Of course, Kant also says that external revelation has no binding power, and the source of moral authority is the self. Rav Soloveitchik cannot agree with this. However, Rav Soloveitchik could respond that once revelation *has* occurred, the self can give authority to that which has been revealed, which is precisely what halakhic man accomplishes by uniting his will with God's. Rav Soloveitchik emphasizes the centrality of *brit*, covenant, which demonstrates that man is a free agent and assents of his own will. Man is not the source of the law, but he freely adopts it as his own. Furthermore, through his freedom of conceptualization, halakhic man participates in the unfolding and elaboration of the revealed law.

Thus, the gap between Kant and the Rav shrinks when we take into account two factors: (a) norms do not depend upon one's personal desires even according to Kant; (b) even a revealed norm can be endorsed autonomously by appropriating it after it is revealed. Note Hermann Cohen's observation: "God's law does not contradict the autonomy of the moral will. There is a difference only in the method of formulating the concept, which is the difference between ethics and religion" (*Religion of Reason out of the Sources of Judaism*, trans. Simon Kaplan [New York, 1972], 339). See also Rav Soloveitchik's *The Emergence of Ethical Man*, ed. Michael Berger (Jersey City, 2005), 154ff.

70. *HM*, 135.

stifles the mind and stunts the spirit; the halakhic way of life deprives an individual of his freedom and intellectual creativity, and robs him of individuality."[71] As one who had grown up among the giants of Brisk, the exemplars par excellence of halakhic man, Rav Soloveitchik saw these accusations as being patently absurd. It is reasonable to assume that he realized that if serious Torah study and halakhic commitment were to flourish in the modern world, it was necessary to elaborate the ideological underpinnings of conceptual *talmud Torah* and to portray the *talmid ḥakham* in a manner that would be both comprehensible and attractive to modern man. Halakha, he explains, is a cognitive discipline; it demands the scholar's creative input; and it fosters a majestic and fully realized personality while avoiding the excesses of *homo religiosus*. Thus, as David Shatz writes:

> The very values which modern critics felt could be realized only by leaving the *dalet amot shel halakha*, the four ells of halakha, could, in fact, be achieved by remaining squarely within them. *It is as if modernity is being turned against itself; its value system is revealed not to oppose tradition, but to support and vindicate it.* And we are not dealing here with … an argument that uses the premises of the modern critic only to convince the critic of the validity of Rabbi Soloveitchik's praise of halakhic man, without Rabbi Soloveitchik endorsing those premises. On the contrary, Rabbi Soloveitchik seems genuinely to accept the values of freedom, creativity, and individuality because they are affirmed in Jewish sources …[72]

V. CONCLUSION

In sum, *Halakhic Man* aims to accomplish several goals. First, it depicts a type of intellect-based religiosity and religious personality that is unfamiliar to modern psychology and philosophy of religion. Second, it defends halakha against charges that it is heteronomous, non-cognitive, non-moral, and slavish. Third, it defends the halakhic personality against

---

71. Shatz (cited in Further Reading below), 193.
72. Ibid., 196, emphasis added.

charges that he is otherworldly, passive, and uncreative. In the course of accomplishing these goals, *Halakhic Man* provides a justification for Torah study, explaining its meaning and significance in terms comprehensible to modern individuals; it argues for the superiority of halakhic man's religiosity which, through the use of reason and the maintenance of boundaries, overcomes *homo religiosus's* subjectivity and extremism; and it establishes the centrality of creativity in halakhic life: creativity in the realm of Torah study, creativity within the world (by realizing halakhic ideals), and creation of the self.

In *UVikkashtem MiSham*,[73] Rav Soloveitchik writes that people naturally seek to anchor their existence in something stable and transcendent. This is doubly true of modern man, who is perplexed and conflicted. Such a reader – and not only one already immersed in the world of conceptual *lomdus* – can find *Halakhic Man* quite compelling, despite the "strange, singular"[74] nature of its title character. The book begins by acknowledging that conflict is a creative force, a point with which many would agree but would be hard pressed to find in earlier Jewish sources. The book then proceeds to build a stable and objective, yet dynamic and creative, religiosity. This religiosity avoids the pitfalls that many associate with contemporary religion – be they passivity and otherworldliness, vapid ceremonialism and sentimentality, or technical ritualism and intellectual laziness. Halakhic man lives a life of high seriousness and heroism, of drama and engagement, as he immerses himself in the demanding and meaningful struggle to grasp and formulate halakhic concepts, to actualize divine ideals within the concrete world, and to craft an individualistic personality that is intellectual and ethical, creative and majestic.

It is hard to do justice in a single essay to the rich range of ideas overflowing from the pages of *Halakhic Man*. I can close only by paraphrasing the book's conclusion:

> These are but some of the traits of *Halakhic Man*. Much more than I have written here is imprinted in *Halakhic Man*. This essay is

---

73. 8ff.
74. *HM*, 4.

but an incomplete sketch of a few of *Halakhic Man*'s features. But it is revealed and known before Him who created the world that my sole intention was to explicate *Halakhic Man*'s basic themes and goals, for they have often been misunderstood. And if I have erred, may God, in His goodness, forgive me.[75]

FURTHER READING

Soloveitchik, Joseph B. "*Ish HaHalakha.*" *Talpiot*. Vol. 1:3–4 (1944), 651–735; reprinted in *BeSod HaYaḥid VeHaYaḥad*, edited by Pinchas Peli (Jerusalem, 1976), 39–188; and *Ish HaHalakha: Galui VeNistar* (Jerusalem, 1979), 9–113.

Soloveitchik, Joseph B. *Halakhic Man*. Translated by Lawrence Kaplan (Philadelphia, 1983).

Selected secondary literature:

Kaplan, Lawrence. "Rabbi Joseph B. Soloveitchik's Philosophy of Halakhah." *The Jewish Law Annual* 7 (1988): 139–197.

Nadler, Allan. "Soloveitchik's Halakhic Man: Not a *Mithnagged.*" *Modern Judaism* 13:2 (1993): 119–148.

Ravitzky, Aviezer. "Rabbi J. B. Soloveitchik on Human Knowledge: Between Maimonidean and Neo-Kantian Philosophy." *Modern Judaism* 6:2 (1986): 157–188.

Schwartz, Dov. *Religion or Halakha: The Philosophy of Rabbi Joseph B. Soloveitchik*. Vol. 1 (Leiden, 2007).

Shatz, David. "A Framework for Reading *Ish Ha-Halakhah.*" In *Turim: Studies in Jewish History and Literature Presented to Dr. Bernard Lander*. Vol. 2, 171–231. Edited by Michael A. Shmidman (New York, 2008).

Sokol, Moshe. "Master or Slave? Rabbi Joseph B. Soloveitchik on Human Autonomy in the Presence of God." In ibid., vol. 1, 275–330 (New York, 2007).

---

75. This essay is adapted from Reuven Ziegler, *Majesty and Humility: The Thought of Rabbi Joseph B. Soloveitchik* (Jerusalem, 2012), with permission of the Maimonides School.

Rav Isaac Hutner's *Paḥad Yitzḥak*: A Torah Map of the Human Mind and Psyche in Changing Times[*]

Dr. Yaakov Elman

Rav Isaac Hutner (1906–1980) was one of the most compelling personalities and creative thinkers produced by the yeshiva world in the twentieth century. His influence on the personal and communal level was deep and long lasting, and dozens of his students assumed important positions in Jewish communal life. Already as a teenager he was acclaimed as the "Warsaw genius," and was recruited for the prestigious Slobodka Yeshiva at age fifteen – an advent that raised some resentment. At twenty-six, he published a work of rabbinic scholarship that garnered praise from leading authorities – but, remarkably, never published any other technical legal work under his own name.

---

[*] My sincere thanks to Dr. David Berger and Dr. Yoel Finkelman, and to my son Zev David for their helpful, and sometimes challenging, comments. This chapter has benefited greatly from their comments; responsibility for its remaining defects remains, as usual, with me.

Instead, he concentrated on instilling in his students his views of the "laws of dispositions and duties of the heart" incumbent on a Jew, which were eventually incorporated in what became his magnum opus, the eight volumes of *Paḥad Yitzḥak* (1964–1982). These volumes were arranged by the festivals of the Jewish year, but contained within their pages discussions of basic issues of Jewish theology in general – the workings of divine providence, free will versus determinism, theodicy, the ebb and flow of Jewish history – undergirded by his own preternatural understanding of the workings of the human psyche.

And yet, the exposition is anything but straightforward. Rather it is in the form of a halakhic discourse with as much, or even more, emphasis on the process of dialectic than on the exposition of doctrine, though Rav Hutner is certainly concerned with setting his listeners (or readers) straight on matters of doctrine.

As Hillel Goldberg put it in perhaps the most perceptive sketch of Rav Hutner's life and work:

> A statement of Rabbi Hutner will, for example, take as its fulcrum a stock philosophical concept – such as the distinction between the unknowability of God's essence and the knowability of His activities – with no reference to any philosophic source. The reference will be to a seemingly tangential, legal source, which draws the distinction in a strictly legal context, without philosophic elaboration. One who brings no prior philosophic knowledge to the statement will not notice the mask, but, under the impression that he is studying law, will learn philosophy. One who does bring prior knowledge will, under the impress of Rabbi Hutner's analysis, observe the limits of law, philosophy, and Kabbala dilate, reaching into each other in hitherto unnoticed ways and to a hitherto unnoticed extent. All this is covert. Substantively the reader perceives the multifaceted topic without the mediation of any technical terms, but formally it is like reading in a hall of mirrors – you think you see one thing, but really see another – like reading (in the language of Rabbi Hutner himself) the secret Torah

(*nistar*) in the language of the revealed Torah (*nigleh*) – and one never knows whether one has comprehended all the allusions.[1]

Why is this? Certainly a large part of his decision to expound his views in this manner was due to the fact that his audience was not familiar with – or even aware of – all the areas of his concern, especially those that were beyond the usual borders of yeshiva learning: Hasidism, Kabbala, philosophy both Jewish and non-Jewish, and even beyond that, matters historical and textual, matters his own teachers had kept outside their purview. Part was also due to the fact that, as we shall see below, his views were not always in consonance with the *ḥaredi* world that was in formation. Thus, for example, we can understand why he removed the portrait of Rav Kook from the yeshiva sukka after years of having it displayed; and, again, why in 1948 he bent to Rav Aharon Kotler's will and abandoned his plan (with Rav Shraga Feivel Mendolowitz of Yeshiva Torah Vodaath), two years in the making, for a combination yeshiva and college in Brooklyn. The plan represented a tactical divergence from trends in right-wing Orthodoxy, which rejected (and still rejects) familiarity with cultural and scientific knowledge or training in order to ensure that one not be "infected" with modernism. In doing so, the opponents of secular education merely trade the dangers of associated with modernity for those of stagnation, insularity, and dependency. It should be noted that the success of Touro College and its branches has filled that gap, but even before that a number of members of prominent rabbinic families, including Rav Hutner's own, have earned advanced degrees, and most yeshiva students have gone to college in one way or another.

Nor were his hasidic interests free of controversy; I well remember the critical eye that was cast by outsiders on the question of whether he was a Lithuanian *rosh yeshiva* or hasidic *rebbe*. In truth, he was both, and his expansive intellect and personality could encompass both roles. But in his *maamarim* (discourses) he was first and foremost an educator, well aware of the limits of his audience.

---

1. Hillel Goldberg, "Rabbi Isaac Hutner: A Synoptic Interpretive Biography," *Tradition* 22 (1987): 18–46, see 35–36.

In sum, though, *Paḥad Yitzḥak* presents a view of Judaism – optimistic, expansive, world-embracing – quite different from the "circle the wagons" policy of much of the Orthodox world, in which humanity – Jews included – degenerates from generation to generation and we are bidden only to hold on to the past and resist the future. Rav Hutner's view presents the world as the siddur does, praising the Creator who renews and revivifies His Creation daily. He understood that by presenting such a negative view of humanity, we impugn God's creation and governance of that creation.

As to his hasidic side, again, as Hillel Goldberg put it in his perceptive essay:

> Although his paternal heritage derived from the Lithuanian sector in the predominantly hasidic, religious sector of Jewish Warsaw, he knew the larger hasidic community of his birth. His maternal heritage was hasidic. The attractive traits of the Elder [of Slobodka]'s *musar* he could locate in the iconoclastic, Polish hasidic eddy of Kotzk, with which an uncle was associated. He studied in the Gerer *shtiebl* in Warsaw. He absorbed Hasidism's dominant view that the ego, though not to be left untended, was not to be transformed, either. Whether the hasidic ethos shaped Isaac Hutner, or merely confirmed prior inclinations, we cannot know. We do know that he was able to reconcile a *musar* stress on criticizing the ego and a hasidic stress on nurturing it.[2]

Intellectually, Rav Hunter once commented that if his mind were to be compared to a building, the first floor would be the influence of the Elder of Slobodka, Rav Nathan Zvi Finkel (1849–1927), and the top floor would be that of Rav Abraham Isaac Kook (1865–1935), to whom he was related by marriage.[3] This statement points to two of the formative intellectual influences on him, as represented by two figures, each of whom represented a focus of Rav Hutner's thought: the ethical and psychological teachings of the *Musar* movement founded by Rav Israel

---

2. Goldberg, "Rabbi Isaac Hutner: A Synoptic Interpretive Biography," 27.
3. Rav Moshe Tzvi Neriyah, "*Shemesh UMaor*," *BiSdeh HaRe'iya* (Kefar Chabad, 5651), 419–438.

Salanter (1810–1883), and the spiritual-mystical teachings of the first Ashkenzic chief rabbi of British Mandatory Palestine, Rav Abraham Isaac Kook (1865–1935). Both the Elder and Rav Kook had a supremely optimistic view of humanity, its spiritual powers and potential – and a positive view of human individuality and autonomy.

Finally, there is the influence of the second Gerer Rebbe, Rav Yehuda Aryeh Leib Alter, the *Sefat Emet* (1847–1905), who died the year before Rav Hutner's birth and whose work represented a more conservative version of the Kotzker tradition, but who nevertheless emphasized the importance of creativity and change (see below). Thus, Rav Hutner was raised and educated in a tradition quite different in vital respects from the rural hasidic and ultra-conservative Lithuanian traditions that have dominated postwar Orthodoxy.

Nevertheless, that hasidic background also encouraged study of Maharal's writings, and Rav Hutner's theological positions generally reflect those elements of Maharal's system that entered hasidic tradition, stripped of much of its specifically sixteenth-century elements, as we shall see. This is especially true of that urban Polish hasidic tradition in which he was steeped from childhood: that of Rav Simcha Bunim of Przysucha (Pshischa/Parshischa) (1765–1827), Rav Menachem Mendel of Kotzk (1787–1859), Rav Mordekhai Joseph of Izbica (Izhbitz), known as the Izbicer (1801–1854), and Rav Tzadok HaKohen of Lublin (1823–1900), all of whom stressed the post-Renaissance values of individuality, authenticity, autonomy, awareness of the changing circumstances of the human condition and the consequently changing obligations of spiritual life (*hithadeshut*, renewal, and *shinui*, change). In Slobodka, too, he found a stress on individuality and creativity.

In this stress on individuality, autonomy, and creativity, that intellectual Polish school of hasidic thought represented by Przysucha and Kotzk were responding to a social and spiritual crisis, as were Rav Israel Salanter and the *Musar* movement. Alan Brill[4] and Glenn Dynner[5] have

---

4. Alan Brill, *Thinking God: The Mysticism of Rabbi Zadok of Lublin* (New York, 2002), 365.
5. Glenn Dynner, *Men of Silk: The Hasidic Conquest of Polish Jewish Society* (New York, 2006), 35–40.

suggested that these qualities reflected the crisis of an urbanizing Polish Jewish community, the community of which Rav Hutner was part.

The writings of Maharal and of Rav Tzadok would have been available to the young Rav Hutner in the Gerer beit midrash in Warsaw, where he studied. While Maharal's writings reflect sixteenth-century concerns, he has rightly been called the "unofficial spokesman of rabbinic theology," and the basic elements of his theological scheme undergird *Pahad Yitzhak*. As to the Gerer provenance of Rav Hutner's study, it is clear that *Pahad Yitzhak* shares a number of important themes with Rav Alter's *Sefat Emet*, though Rav Hutner develops them in a way different from the Gerer Rebbe's extreme spiritualization. For example, Rav Alter stresses the idea that the mission of Jews is to testify that the material nature of the universe is merely an illusion, and that in reality all is spiritual; Rav Hutner allows for both material and spiritual aspects to coexist, especially in the human psyche, and transforms the mission as one to extirpate evil from humanity.[6] Again, recognizing the illusory nature of the material world is the essence of truth and redemption for Gur;[7] in this context we may understand Rav Hutner's insistence that "truth and its opposite relate to a person's intellect. If the image of reality in the mind corresponds to reality, this then is a true opinion," and thus even God's promises must be fulfilled in the material world in order to be confirmed.[8]

Thus, *Pahad Yitzhak* may be seen as an attempt to come to terms with three hundred years of intellectual history, in particular with the post-Renaissance modern Western world, just as Maharal did with the sixteenth-century world. Maharal interpreted ancient rabbinic teachings in the spirit of sixteenth-century Platonism and neo-Pythagoreanism. The first of these accounts for both the philosophical and mystical currents in his thought, for example, his extremely dualistic view of the world. Thus, male Jews have great spiritual potential, while women and non-Jews are merely "material beings." *Pahad Yitzhak* moderates, or simply ignores, Maharal's frequent use of number symbolism (one is the number of unity, two of

---

6. *Pahad Yitzhak* Yom Kippur 12:8.
7. *Sefat Emet, Parashat Vayehi* 5636.
8. *Pahad Yitzhak* Shabbat/Sukkot, *Kuntres Birkat Avot* 15:2.

division, six is a perfect number, etc., all of which are to be found both in Maharal's writings and in those of the so-called neo-Pythagoreans). All of this is typical of sixteenth-century thought, from the hugely influential fifteenth-century Marsilio Ficino (1433–1499) through the rise of modern science, as represented by Johannes Kepler (1571–1630) and Tycho Brahe (1546–1601), whom Maharal met,[9] and René Descartes (1596–1650), and Galileo Galilei (1564–1642), whom he did not. In response to the challenge of emerging modern science, Maharal's underlying message was that the ancient rabbis had a profound understanding of the way the world works, similar to that of the Renaissance Platonists, neo-Pythagoreans, and geometrician astronomers. In doing so, he broke with geonic tradition which viewed some rabbinic statements as based on an outmoded scientific understanding; in contrast, Maharal defended every classical rabbinic statement by reinterpreting them by sixteenth-century standards; however, he did not take those statements literally, but allegorically. Thus, while not accepting Copernicus' heliocentric view, he did not reject it, either.[10, 11] Rav Hutner could thus take from Maharal the idea that contemporary challenges to religion must be met and not merely ignored, a view that mirrored that of Rav Kook, and the necessity of not understanding them literally, a lesson forgotten or ignored by some contemporary Orthodox writers.

Still, Maharal turned most of his attention to the obligations of humans to God and to each other; despite his mystical inclinations, there is hardly any mention of the kabbalistic upper worlds and the like. Maharal's view was that the ideal human being, like Adam before his sin, would and should be in constant communion with his Creator, without any notion of free will or autonomy. In contrast, as we shall

---

9. Note David Ruderman's comment on Maharal in his *Jewish Thought and Modern Discovery in Early Modern Europe* (Detroit, 1995), 70 and n. 55; see also Ofer Gal and Raz Chen-Morris, *Baroque Science* (Chicago, 2013), 60–78, 91–114, 161–181; and see 280–282.

10. Andre Neher, *Jewish Thought and the Scientific Revolution of the Sixteenth Century, David Gan (1541–1613) and His Times* (New York, 1986), 245–248.

11. On Maharal's ambivalent but basically positive attitude to natural science, see A. F. Kleinberger, *The Educational Theory of the Maharal of Prague* [Hebrew] (Jerusalem, 1962), 79–85, esp. 84–85; and see Maharal, *Be'er HaGola*, chs. 4, 6.

see, Rav Hutner stressed individuality and autonomy, and deferred the abolition of free will to messianic times.

Nevertheless, as David Sorotzkin has recently emphasized, in his works Maharal addressed seven issues that had become part of the European intellectual discourse of his time and place, and which continue to define the nature of Western thought: nature, order and lawfulness, the place of the collective, time, continuity and change.

> His system attempts to give an unprecedented, all-encompassing answer to questions such as the nature of historical time, the exile and scattering of the Jewish people, the status of Jewish legislation and the limits of the canon of aggadic Midrash. The most important and central theme of the Maharal's thought is the concept of "the separate" (*hanivdal*), which is developed in various contexts.

By this, Sorotzkin refers to the dualistic nature of Maharal's thought, as noted above.[12]

In sum, *Paḥad Yitzḥak* may be seen as Maharal's system, stripped of many of its specifically sixteenth-century aspects and as refracted through the prism of that strain of urban Polish Hasidism mentioned above, Slobodka and the approach of Rav Kook, leavened with a generous dollop of Rav Hutner's creativity and his engagement with twentieth-century problems.

INDIVIDUALITY, RENEWAL, AND DYNAMISM

In line with the hasidic antecedents of its system, *Paḥad Yitzḥak*'s appreciation for the uniqueness of each individual person also includes an appreciation for the uniqueness of each moment of time, both in an individual's life and in the era in which that life takes place, as well as in the history of both the Jews and of humanity as a whole. Indeed, an awareness of changing times and circumstances, and the consequent change in God's will, is

---

12. David Sorotzkin, *Orthodoxy and Modern Disciplination: The Production of the Jewish Tradition in Europe in Modern Times* [Hebrew] (Tel Aviv, 2011), 70.

one of the themes of the Izbicer's *Mei HaShilo'aḥ*.[13] As times change, the challenges posed to tradition also change, and must be met by rational analysis, on the one hand, together with imagination, intuition, creativity, and renewal/adaptation on the other; the result is the possibility and *obligation* of self-fashioning in accord with one's individuality. All this overlaid with the sheer joy of intellectual endeavor. But *Paḥad Yitzḥak* is also intensely personal in that it reveals the secrets of the human mind and psyche by looking within: we are privileged to understand ourselves because Rav Hutner reveals what he has observed in himself.

The system that emerged from the confluence of all of these influences viewed all the following values positively: individuality, authenticity ("to thine own self be true"), autonomy, renewal on the individual, national, and cosmic levels, and thus creativity (which includes the importance of doubt and dispute as spurs to further knowledge), and its attendant intellectual joy, as well as the importance of renewal and self-fashioning (as in repentance but in other instances as well).

Though rooted in the talmudic rabbis' appreciation of individuality that "Man was created as an individual" (Mishna Sanhedrin 4:5), Rav Hutner developed the idea in a way that emphasizes its existential quality and thus owes something to the *zeitgeist* of the modern era. This view is facilitated by a "Brisker" analytic approach, typical of the late nineteenth- and twentieth-century yeshiva world, but also by Maharal's dialectical approach. *Paḥad Yitzḥak* may thus be seen as an application of the Brisker system of analysis to questions of Jewish theology and human psychology, not only in a descriptive sense but also in a generative one. Its author expects to find – and often does – a binary dynamic within human and human-divine interaction, so this dynamic assumes a large role in his work.

It is thus not surprising that *Paḥad Yitzḥak* deals with modern philosophical problems, though employing its own terminology and modes of argument; *Paḥad Yitzḥak* is not a philosophical work, but a blend of hasidic and *musar* approaches, along with a plethora of the author's own psychological insights. In order to express the essence of these concerns in language that would be accessible to his non-hasidic

---

13. See vol. II, *Parashat Beḥukkotai* 54 in the Jerusalem 5768 edition.

yeshiva audience, Rav Hutner created a nomenclature uniquely his own, often based on references from the siddur or classic rabbinic texts, most often interpreted metaphorically. But once the existential referents are made clear, his work becomes a compelling narrative of the encounter of a twentieth-century "prince of Torah" with the modern world and its concerns, concerns which continue, and indeed, have only intensified, in the generation that has passed since their publication. Rav Hutner located the eternal verities of a God-created Torah in the workings of God's other creation, the human psyche. And thus within the pages of *Paḥad Yitzḥak* one will find disquisitions on the difference between the psychologies of generalists versus specialists, the tensions of the individual within human society, other problems of identity and personality, of change and renewal, the problem of mortality and other aspects of the human condition, and much more. It is this attention to the existential side of Jewish thought that makes for such compelling reading.

The world of *Paḥad Yitzḥak* is thus a joyful one: a dynamic world filled with creativity, renewal, and innovation, one that celebrates the products of the individual and of the individual human mind at its creative best, that is, in the study of God's Torah. It is also a world that does not denigrate the use of those intellectual tools when employed to enhance human life. Nor are those tools limited to rational discourse and logic; intuition and emotional engagement, and in particular the pleasures that accompany them, are essential parts of *talmud Torah*. In short, it is the world of Slobodka but with a Hutnerian flavor, a world that proclaims not only the greatness of God, but also the greatness of His Creation, and, in particular, the summit of that Creation, humankind. It is thus a world in which the individual can – and *must* – contribute something of his or her own unique selfhood.

It is also a world of poetic beauty and metaphor: Maharal does not teach us, he "implants" knowledge in us; the Vilna Gaon does not instruct, rather we "discover the pearl hidden beneath his words." These metaphors are not mere literary flourishes, but reflect Rav Hutner's inner world, a world that he wishes to share with us. It is a world mysterious but knowable; the controlling metaphors reveal the inner workings of the world and of the human mind and psyche, which are related analogically, for man is a microcosm of the macrocosm of which he is part. It is a world of parallels and analogies, analogies that connect the parallels. It is also a world of paradoxes, and those too must be reconciled, a world of strict judgment (*din*) but also a world of *ḥesed* (loving-kindness).

The metaphor of implanting reflects Maharal's own view of the world, which is a world of potential that must be actualized by human activity, as a plant grows from a seed under the farmer's care. The world is mysterious, but can be understood, and, once understood, will be seen for all its beauty, as is the pearl. That is one of the sources of the dynamism of Maharal's system, and that same dynamism characterizes the world of Rav Hutner.

In its valorization of individual creativity *Paḥad Yitzḥak* runs counter to two trends in pre-World War II Eastern Europe which have dominated the intellectual and cultural landscape of postwar Orthodoxy. I refer to a Manichaean view of the world in which absolute Good confronts absolute Evil, with no gray areas in between, in which the world has nothing of value to teach us; and a pessimistic view of human intellectual and moral potential such that the individual is not to be trusted and must be guided by those untainted by exposure to that world of Evil. As a result, all change is to be resisted.

Rav Hutner's view of evil and change is much more nuanced, as in *Paḥad Yitzḥak* Pesaḥ 76:14, where the constantly renewed power of evil cannot stem from evil itself, but rather from the *failure* of good to fulfill – and renew – itself:

> Certainly, Evil's power of renewal does not stem from the independent powers of evil, for since the general universal renewal [in messianic times] involves the destruction [of evil], the offshoot cannot have what the root lacks. Rather, the entire capability which we find on the part of Evil comes only from [the fact] that it is built on the destruction of its counterpart (Good). That is to say, as long as the side of Good does not utilize its power of renewal for its divine service, so too, in parallel, its power of renewal is added as a jewel to the building and palace of Evil. And the power of evil is strengthened by the addition of the powers of renewal [of the good, which have not been utilized for good]. When this one falls, the other one rises.

Moreover, though Rav Hutner does mention the "independent powers of evil," throughout *Paḥad Yitzḥak* he chooses to deal with the psychological processes involved in the struggle against that renewal, rather than discussing those powers per se, as one of his sources, Rav Tzadok, was wont to do. The focus of *Paḥad Yitzḥak* is overwhelmingly positive, even more positive than the focus of the outlook of the Slobodka yeshiva, Rav Hutner's *alma mater*, a school which, above all, emphasized the "greatness of humanity." For now, let us note that the Hutnerian material universe – though its figurative language is suffused with kabbalistic motifs – is nevertheless a Maimonidean one, which is to say, an Aristotelian one, at least outwardly: in it there is no kabbalistic "breaking of the vessels,"[14] no *sefirotic* realm, nor its antipodean one of evil. It is one in which demons exist *only* as projections of the human imagination. Nevertheless, the kabbalistic cast of Rav Hutner's thought is readily apparent.

It may be argued that these concessions to a modern, "scientific" worldview were only tactical, meant to provide an argument on humanistic grounds for devoting oneself to a life of Torah, designed for the intellectual climate in which mid-century American yeshiva students lived. Though the motives may have been tactical, at least in part, they do not diminish *Paḥad Yitzḥak*'s humanistic justification for a life of Torah study. Moreover, its system is in line with the "demystification" represented by the thought of Maharal and that Polish Hasidism on which it is based (except for Rav Tzadok, and, in his early writings, Rav Yehuda Aryeh Leib of Gur). That is, though the underpinnings of this trend may be found in mystical kabbalistic sources, on the whole it avoids both kabbalistic terminology and explicit kabbalistic concepts.

The same applies to the more universalistic elements of Hutnerian thought, which had its basis in Slobodka's optimistic view of the entire human race. Thus, in an excerpt from the *Kuntres Reshimot* of Shabbat 5:3, printed in the joint volume of Shabbat/Sukkot, Rav Hutner stresses the Torah's universalistic aspects, and in this case, the obligation of *imitatio Dei* on *all* humanity. In particular, he notes that this obligation implies that all humans are capable of following in God's ways of loving-kindness (*ḥesed*):

---

14. See Gershom Scholem, *Major Trends in Jewish Mysticism* (New York, 1995), 265–268.

Imitatio Dei is certainly without limits as to whom it applies. *Imitatio Dei* is not just an obligation – [it implies] that is how you should be, [for, after all,] one cannot say to someone: "Be what you cannot be." *Imitatio Dei* is thus prior [to the Giving of the Torah], for you *are* [already created] in the Image of God (lit., the Model of [the One] Above). And certainly a Noahide (a non-Jew) is also [created] in the Image of God.[15]

In championing this universalistic tendency, Rav Hutner opposed those increasingly powerful trends in the Orthodox world that demonized outsiders. Likewise, on the intellectual side, and in contrast to trends in the yeshiva world even in the heyday of the nineteenth-century revolution in methods of Torah study, his stress on creativity, which echoed similar calls from Slobodka, opposed the view laid down by Rav Elchanan Bunim Wasserman, quoting Rav Chaim Soloveitchik, that "it is not for us to innovate *ḥidushim* (intellectual innovations in Torah); only the *Rishonim* (the medieval commentators) had that in their power. Our task is merely to *understand* what has already been written."[16] Whether this statement does or does not involve innovation in talmudic interpretation is perhaps a fine point, but could easily be argued, even by Rav Chaim, who indeed devised a revolutionary method for understanding those *Rishonim*. This dogmatic formulation, however, remains highly influential, though the very human creative drive remains unabated in the world of the yeshivot to some extent.[17]

---

15. *Paḥad Yitzḥak, Shaar UVeYom HaShabbat*, p. 120.

16. Introduction to *Kovetz Shiurim*, published by his son, Rav Eleazer Simcha Wasserman, part I (Tel Aviv, 1964).

17. Although Rav Elchanan quoted Rav Chaim accurately, I doubt that Rav Chaim meant his words to be taken quite as literally as Rav Elchanan did. Rav Chaim could not have been unaware – his contemporaries were certainly aware – of the revolutionary nature of the methodology he introduced. But introducing revolutions within traditional societies requires all the more a sincere denial of change on the part of believers; for a general sociological orientation of the process, see Hans H. Gerth and C. Wright Mills, *From Max Weber: Essays in Sociology* (New York, 1958), 251–252, 294–299. My thanks to Dr. Haym Soloveitchik for directing me to this source, and discussing with me this particular view attributed to his great-grandfather and related issues.

There is another respect in which *Pahad Yitzhak* differs from the *haredi* world that was coming into existence during Rav Hutner's time in America: his attitude to change and progress. As we shall see below, *hithadeshut* ("self-fashioning" or, alternately, "renewal," or even "development," or "adaptation") was a prominent motif within the hasidic trends that were so formative in the making of *Pahad Yitzhak*. However, this emphasis of "newness" can be parsed both conservatively or more expansively. That is, it can refer to an individual's "renewal" of time-honored truths, as in repentance or simply in a new appreciation of timeless truths, or it can represent new developments in Jewish – or human – thought. Both elements are present in *Pahad Yitzhak*.

Nevertheless, the two are tightly connected, as the *Sefat Emet* emphasizes over and over, as for example in the commentary on *Parashat Hayei Sarah* 5734:

> The fact that God, may He be blessed, created this world to be renewed (*mithadesh*) every day and every year for better [was] in order that there should be a new enlightenment (*he'ara hadasha*) at all times (*bekhol zeman*). And on this we praise God (lit., "we bless"): He who renews the Work of Creation every day, for if Creation would proceed without any change (*shinui*), it would be distanced from the root of its life force (*hiyut*) as time went on (*beribui hazeman*). Therefore, God, may He be blessed, created [the world in such a way] that there is a plenitude of life anew, as noted above. Therefore, a man should see to it that there is at least one new insight every day. And in this way he will merit to feel a new thing every day, for every day proceeds from the epiphany (*hitpaalut*) of the day before, as it is written: "If it is heard of the old, it will be heard of the new" (Rashi on Deut. 11:13).

We gain a greater understanding of the scope of these insights and their consequences from Rav Tzadok, who attributes this insight to his rebbe, the Izbicer:

> All types of wisdom which the sages of the Nations innovate proceeds from the wisdom of Israel (*hokhmat Yisrael*). When one

of Israel gains a new insight in knowledge of Torah (*ḥokhmat haTorah*), which is the wisdom of God, this knowledge spreads throughout all the worlds, [including] the material world as well. In [it] some matter of worldly knowledge, corresponding [to the original insight] into God's Torah and into His service, may He be blessed, is innovated, and the sages of the Nations of that generation are able to absorb it and to produce an innovation, which the onlookers perceive as their own.[18]

This then is the hasidic response to the pessimistic view regnant in many sectors of Orthodoxy that humanity has been in constant decline and degeneration since Sinai, or even before; this optimistic view of human history can be traced back to Rav Simcha Bunim of Przysucha.

Indeed, the sense of innovation stemming from the "discovery" of the Zohar at the end of the thirteenth century, the rise of Lurianic Kabbala in the sixteenth, of Hasidism in its many branches in the eighteenth and nineteenth, and for the world of the Lithuanian yeshivot, the rise of the Brisker methodology and other systems of *lomdut* (e.g., that of Rav Shimon Shkop), not to mention the quickening pace of progress in the outside world, could not but have inspired some sensitive souls to consider the wider and deeper meaning of the praise we render to God daily, of "the One who renews in His goodness every day – continually – the work of Creation," as it did for Rav Tzadok HaKohen of Lublin.

Indeed, Rav Tzadok reports that the Izbicer reported in the name of Rav Simcha Bunim of Przysucha:

> Even though intellectual abilities (*hamoḥot*, brains) decline with each generation (lit., time), spiritual ability (*nekudat haḥayim shebalev*, the point of [divine] life in the heart) increases with each generation (lit., time) and has become purified through the tribulations of exile.

---

18. *Likutei Maamarim*, 139.

And he adds:

> Our Holy Master told [us] that this was something new to him
> when he had heard it in Parshischa, though he found this point
> explicitly explained in several places. He did not [at that time]
> elucidate his sources, but we have already traced the root of this
> principle [as is explained in a number of places].[19]

Thus, though intellectual abilities decrease, spiritual potential increases
with the concomitant advance of spiritual capabilities.

A statistic will illustrate the importance of this theme in that
strand of urban Polish Hasidism. The Bar-Ilan Responsa project lists
814 attestations of the noun *hithadeshut* (renewal). Of them, the lion's
share are distributed among those three writers of that trend of urban
intellectual Polish Hasidism stemming from Kotzk which serve as the
"basement" of the building of Rav Hutner's thought: Rav Tzadok, disciple of the Izbicer, himself a disciple of the Kotzker (173), Rav Yehuda
Aryeh Leib Alter of Gur, the *Sefat Emet*, grandson of the founder of the
Gur dynasty who, as noted above, was himself a faithful disciple of the
Kotzker to the end (292),[20] and Rav Shmuel Bornstein of Sochachow,
the *Shem MiShmuel*, a grandson of the Kotzker (107) – a full 70 percent.
Another 124 (15 percent) are distributed among various hasidic works,
from *Kedushat Levi* on. Among non-hasidic sources, the *hidushim* of
Rabbi Shimon Shkop, whose affinities to questions of the individual
and society I have pointed out elsewhere, also stand out – twenty-
eight attestations, the highest concentration outside of hasidic sources.

Moreover, in a search that included commentators on the Bible,
two moderns who dealt with problems of modernity are prominent:
Rabbi Yaakov Zvi Mecklenburg, author of *HaKetav VeHaKabbala* (6),
and Rabbi Meir Leibush Weiser, the "Malbim" (13).

---

19. *Peri Tzaddik*, end of *Parashat Va'ethanan*.
20. On the scope and importance of the theme of renewal (*hithadeshut*) in Gerer Ha-
    sidism from the *Sefat Emet* on, see Avraham Segal, "On 'Renewal' in the Writings
    of R. Yehuda Aryeh Leib of Gur and His Successors" [Hebrew], *Daat* 70 (5771):
    49–80.

Hithadeshut betokens a concern with process and change, both flashpoints in the encounter of tradition with modernity; it is no wonder that its use widens and broadens in modern times. In the works of Rav Tzadok, Rav Yehuda Aryeh Leib of Gur, and Rav Shmuel of Sochachow "renewal" refers both to natural/cosmic processes and human ones relating both to society and the individual, from daily, monthly, yearly, and seasonal cycles to the human resilience and renewal. All are included in the term "*hithadeshut.*"

In the case of *Pahad Yitzhak*, the result is a dynamic, progressive system which infuses new life into tradition. Thus, Rav Hutner cautions us not to be "small minded,"[21] he often "carries the line [of thought] forward" and does not "stop half-way."[22] Thus, in *Pahad Yitzhak* Pesah 76.10 (in a *maamar* devoted totally to *hithadeshut*) he observes that we have the capability of infusing a feeling of freshness to an action that has been repeated 101 times. This is *hithadeshut* on the personal level; but Rav Hutner is also sensitive to the radical changes in thought, perspective, and even instinct (as in the inclination to idolatry, abolished by the Men of the Great Assembly as related in Tractates Yoma 69b, Arakhin 32b) that have occurred in human history. Thus, he sees Purim as celebrating a watershed in human history, when the spirit of idolatry began to wane (and in parallel, following Rav Tzadok [*Resisei Laila, maamar* 56], the use of logical analysis in the interpretation of Torah replaced prophecy), and Hanukka celebrates another watershed, the rise of appreciation of individual gifts (see below).

The dynamism stems both from the dialectical nature of the thought of Maharal and of the Brisker revolution: by repeatedly emphasizing opposing elements in both the human psyche and the theological/philosophical problems we face, *Pahad Yitzhak* mirrors the complexity of human life, with implications on the individual, social, national, and cosmic levels. Indeed, some of this dynamism survived its conservative reworking in the thought of the author of the *Sefat Emet*, since he views the world (*olam*) as a place which, while hidden (*he'elem*), is also the locus of Israel's task of bringing to light its divine immanence, thus

---

21. See *Maamarei Pahad Yitzhak* Sukkot 65:7.
22. See, for example, *Pahad Yitzhak* Shabbat 2:3.

preserving the idea of progress. Nevertheless, the difference between them is palpable: for the Gerer rebbe, Israel's task in the world is to make clear the essential nullity of the world and to yield our free will to God's command; thus, *hithadeshut* relates not to temporal changes, but to the renewal brought about by *tzaddikim* who bring down divine blessings by means of their good deeds.[23]

In contrast, Rav Hutner defers the abolition of free will to the End of Days, emphasizes the survival of individuality,[24] and gives the individual intellect an essential role in that clarification.[25] For him, the mission of the Jewish people, and the purpose for which it was created, was to extirpate evil (as in the nullification of the drive for idolatry), and not, as the *Sefat Emet* has it, to testify to the nullity of the material world. Instead, he suggests that we testify to its secondary nature.[26] Moreover, while for Gur, truth and faith are one in that both reflect the nullity of the material world, *Paḥad Yitzḥak* sees one essential element of faith (as opposed to *kefira*, the rejection of faith) as the affirmation of the value of good deeds (*emuna be'erkan shel maasav hatovim*).[27] In sum, the material world is not an illusion, and it is not the task of faith to nullify it, but to believe in its improvement. Faith is more complex than that, of course, but in essence the Hutnerian view rejects this essential point of Gur and Chabad's view of the world.[28]

Thus, though superficially *Paḥad Yitzḥak* may be seen as "pre-modern" in its modes of interpretation of its sources (though hardly traditional), the values it champions are those to which the success of Western civilization may be linked, and which we have noted above: individuality, authenticity, autonomy, self-fashioning, creativity, the joy of intellectual discovery, and the consequent progress in the accretion of knowledge.

---

23. *Sefat Emet, Parashat Ḥayei Sarah* 5656.
24. *Paḥad Yitzḥak Iggerot UMikhtavim*, 70–71.
25. *Paḥad Yitzḥak* Shabbat 1.
26. See *Paḥad Yitzḥak* Shabbat 1:4.
27. *Paḥad Yitzḥak* Rosh HaShana 8:4; Yom Kippur 6:4.
28. See Yoram Jacobson, "Truth and Faith in Gur Hasidism" [Hebrew], in Joseph Dan and Joseph Hacker, eds., *Studies in Jewish Mysticism, Philosophy and Ethical Literature Presented to Isaiah Tishby on his Seventy-Fifth Birthday* (Jerusalem, 1986), 593–616, and Jacobson, "Exile and Redemption in Gur Hasidism" [Hebrew], *Daat* 2/3 (5738–5739): 175–215.

Paḥad Yitzḥak must be seen as a very personal expression of the immensely creative intellect of Rav Hutner, who plumbed the depths of his own psyche in order to help us understand ours, and to help himself understand his place both in the hasidic world into which he was born and the Lithuanian yeshiva world to which he aspired to belong.

Armed with tools that hasidic-kabbalistic epistemology provided, Rav Hutner could also expand the range of revelation. Two principles in particular, one derived from Kabbala and one from Hasidism, were of tremendous use. One was that Israel and the Torah are one, and the other was that God's revelation was embodied in two books, one the Torah, and the other the world, and that each may be utilized as a commentary on the other. Both appear in works of Rav Tzadok, and both could be employed to draw analogies from the world outside of our understanding of the Torah's teachings regarding the human condition. And, like Rav Tzadok, Rav Hutner used both to good advantage, as we shall see below, drawing analogies from one sphere of revelation to the other.

The stress on creativity mirrored Rav Hutner's own creativity, and in pointing this out, my intent is not to observe the conventional pieties of Orthodox discourse, but rather to point out salient features of his personality that will further our understanding of the system embodied in *Paḥad Yitzḥak*. The system of *Paḥad Yitzḥak* is an expression of Rav Hutner's yearnings as expressed in his journal (see below). The sciences of the mind which have progressed since his passing have mapped out features of human thought that serve to confirm and develop those features of *Paḥad Yitzḥak* that stand out all the more against the background of recent developments. Creativity requires openness to possibility, a comfort with doubt and possible error, an avoidance of dogmatism. And the human mind is open not only to reason, but to intuition and inspiration, and, indeed, it is the latter which enables creativity. All of these and more are features of the Hutnerian system.[29]

---

29. See, for example, *Paḥad Yitzḥak* Pesaḥ 70 on the role of the imagination in linking sensory perception and abstract thought.

Dr. Yaakov Elman

The following paragraph from *Paḥad Yitzḥak* Shavuot 17:8 combines the themes of individuality, renewal, creativity, and the life of the mind:

> Now, when we say that [a person's] unique quality inheres in the intellect of each person, we infer from this that the essence (lit., quality) of an intellect is that it is absolutely unique, for were it not that each and every intellect in this world were unique in its essence (lit., quality), it would not be possible for it to symbolize (lit., serve as) the crown of [human] uniqueness. For without the attribute of uniqueness, one intellect would be identical to another, while the potential for uniqueness [as inherent] in a person's intellect comes precisely from [the fact] that every intellect has something unique about it that is different from another's. We learn from this that the [unique] quality of each and every intellect inheres in the creative capacity that is found in it. And it is because of this that they said, "There is no beit midrash without any innovation" (Ḥagiga 3a). That is to say, the beit midrash is the place for the workings of the intellect, and the working of the intellect is in accordance with its essence (lit., quality). Therefore, the essential [product and proof of the] working of the intellect is the *ḥidush* (an innovation in Torah learning). [Producing a] *ḥidush* in the course of the workings of the intellect is inevitable, to the point that it is said that "there is no beit midrash without a *ḥidush*." The intellect finds its proper fulfillment in the full meaning of the word only at the time when it creates (lit., of creation). The essential quality of the intellect is the power to conceive. This alone is the intellect's mode of operation; during its [work of] analysis, the intellect's activity [may be perceived] as the urgent search for a new perception of the thing being analyzed: [that is,] before the analysis takes place, the object of the analysis was seen in a different light than it is after the analysis. This new aspect is the conception brought about by the power of the intellect. And this new aspect brought about by the intellect's occupation with the matter at hand is precisely the labor

of the intellect. And when you say "intellect without the power of [intellectual] labor," it is as though you said: "Fatherhood without the power of conception!"

Since the essence of a person is inherent in the intellect, the same is true of one's individuality, and both are fulfilled in creative activity, primarily that of Torah study. The seed of this view of humanity was planted long before: witness a letter from which Goldberg quotes in his biographical sketch, which itself quotes from a letter Rav Hutner wrote in 1933 and which quotes from an earlier journal entry.

> I am now becoming steeped in studies…. Study in its various guises absorbs me, and yet I know that the essence of my personality is the life of my soul and not the life of my mind…. For me to live a life of the soul means to live a life of soul-creativity. For myself, I cannot imagine any realm of life of the spirit to be without creativity. But this is the rub: I am not able to be creative in the life of the soul without first taking important strides – creative ones – in study and *madda*. And so, I am stuck between the insistent claims of the soul, which penetrate to my depths, and between the command of my personality to overcome these claims temporarily, [as I pursue my studies] to build for greater soul-creativity at a later time.[30]

As we shall see throughout this study, this championing of the individual and his creativity is a hallmark of *Paḥad Yitzḥak*, which it shares to a certain extent with the work of Rav Tzadok. This may also explain his emphasis on publishing volumes on Jewish thought rather than halakha. And, as we might expect, so was Slobodka with its emphasis on "the greatness of man." An examination of the discourses in the volumes of *Or HaTzafun*, which were not written by the Elder of Slobodka but reflect a consistent *musar* focus on the individual and his psyche, will enable us to see those threads strengthened. However, several strands are particularly prominent in *Paḥad Yitzḥak*, especially the emphasis

---

30. Goldberg, "Rabbi Isaac Hutner: A Synoptic Interpretive Biography," 27.

on the joy attendant on creative use of the mind and the importance
of that pleasure in fostering that intellectual side of humanity.

AUTONOMY, BUT ALSO RENEWAL,
SELF-FASHIONING, AND REPENTANCE

These bundled themes of individuality, authenticity, and autonomy were
an integral part of the stream of hasidic thought that Rav Hutner imbibed
from his Kotzker uncle. Let us begin with *Paḥad Yitzḥak*'s discourse on
authenticity, being "true to oneself." In Rosh HaShana 16:3, Rav Hutner
elaborates on an assertion by the medieval ethicist and rabbinic authority, Rabbenu Yona Gerondi (d. 1264):

> Indeed, we again return to Rabbenu Yona's statement, [whose
> importance] he implanted in us, that "truth is [one of] the foun-
> dations of the soul" [*Shaarei Teshuva, shaar* 3, no. 184]. These
> words were explained in [our] previous *maamar* [*Paḥad Yitzḥak*
> Rosh HaShana 15:6–8], that the foundation of the soul is the
> aspect of the image and likeness [of God] in it. And the essence of
> the quality of likeness and image is in [its] resemblance and fidel-
> ity to the Source/source. [Thus,] the meaning of truth inheres in
> the resemblance of the branch to the Root/root and the offspring
> to the Father/father. See there in the previous *maamar*. And since
> the knowledge of opposites is one [in the S/source, that is, all is
> unified in God's knowledge and there are no contradictions – YE],
> ineluctably the meaning of falsehood is in the contradiction
> between the offspring and the F/father and between the branch
> and the S/source. And from this wellspring we learn that these
> paired concepts of truth and falsehood do not exist at all in the
> Source itself. Truth and falsehood [exist] only [as] relations of
> offspring to its R/root and S/source. But the Source itself is cer-
> tainly faithful and conforming to Itself/Himself.

Humans are shaped in the Image of God; that is our Source, and that connection joins the truth of the soul with the truth of God's Creation, and
so the two must cohere without contradiction. To be true to oneself (in
the true sense) means to be true to one's self. But in order to search out,

discover, and express that soul's truth, we require autonomy. And so Rav Hutner repeatedly used this statement in his arguments in favor of human autonomy. This statement in *Paḥad Yitzḥak* echoes a notation by Rav Kook, written in London in summer of 1919 in anticipation of his return to Palestine:

> When we forget our souls, get distracted from looking into our own inner lives, all is confused and uncertain. The first repentance, which immediately lights up the darkness, is to return to oneself, the root of one's soul, and immediately one returns to God, the soul of all souls … and this is true of a lone individual, a whole people, all of humanity, or the *tikkun* of all of being, whose ruination always comes from forgetting oneself.[31]

Thus, Rav Hutner's play on the ambiguity of R/root and S/source, which point to both the soul and to its Creator, points to a true relation, one which merges individuality, autonomy, and authenticity, and echoes Rav Kook's notation. In this respect Rav Kook's position would have been familiar to Rav Hutner from the hasidic tradition of Przysucha and its successors, which were very much alive in Rav Hutner's Warsaw.[32] All stressed the need for autonomy. We find that Rav Simcha Bunim of Przysucha also stressed close and intense study of medieval philosophic works, perhaps as a counter to heterodox thoughts. As Michael Rosen observes in his book on Rav Simcha Bunim:

> He also taught that it was forbidden to extinguish the light of one's own inner world to conform to the charisma of a *tzaddik*. Just as intellectual acumen requires independent judgment and a sense of autonomy, so too – he argued – in matters of emotion and spirit one could only make contact if one were truly present, if one took responsibility for oneself, even at the moment of encounter with the *tzaddik*.[33]

---

31. Abraham Isaac Kook, *Shemona Kevatzim* 8, 213, as quoted in Yehudah Mirsky, *Rav Kook: Mystic in a Time of Revolution* (New Haven, 2014), 153–154.
32. Michael Rosen, *The Quest for Authenticity: The Thought of Reb Simhah Bunim* (Jerusalem, 2008), 25–26.
33. Ibid., 16.

But, as Rosen immediately adds, "these qualities of *autonomy* and *purity of motive* would bring Przysucha into direct conflict with the hasidic establishment." The emphasis is his, but reflects the sources. Thus, Rosen quotes Rav Shmuel of Siniawa (Shiniva) – one of our primary sources for Rav Simcha Bunim's thought – as follows:

> "And you shall seek from there...and find" (Deut. 4:29). That is to say: all wisdom and [the use of philosophical] analysis to comprehend God and His unity is called "there": that is to say, from somewhere else. But the real truth is literally in its place – that is to say, in one's heart. For when a person properly purifies his character traits, he will find the Divine in his heart. And that is the "finding," for you should know that you don't need to inquire about God, to seek and search from anywhere else, except in your heart and your soul.[34]

It should be noted that Rav Shmuel notes that the purity of character should be achieved according to Maimonides' prescriptions in *Laws of Personal Development*.

The question then remains as to how one ensures that one's autonomy – one's truth – coheres with the divine truth of the Torah. In other words, how does one reconcile the notion of truth in the soul with truth as inherent in its Source?

Rav Hutner touches on the problematic consequences of the drive for autonomy in his volume on Shavuot (36:3) and even in Rosh HaShana (16:3) with regard to which spiritual obligations take precedence to matters of personal choice. The following, from *Maamarei Paḥad Yitzḥak* Sukkot 27:3, also demonstrates Rav Hutner's acute self-awareness in his choice of modes of argument:

> Even though in general we apply examples from the life of the individual in order to explain processes in the life of society, here we find it proper to take the opposite step, and to apply a process taken from the life of the Nation in order to explain the parallel line of development in the life of the individual. For in truth, in

---

34. Ibid., 135.

every individual two intellectual powers are at work, each in its divergent way, in the path appropriate for it. For the intellectual [decision] which determines [the choice] in regard to questions which arise in connection with the fulfillment of mitzvot has set principles by which to be adjudicated. But the decision to be taken in matters of personal choice (*divrei reshut*), that is, which of two choices is to be selected, [is decided upon the principle] of which choice will result in a greater increase in the honor due Heaven[ly matters]. At times this increase is accomplished by means of [increased] effort, at time by means of *bitaḥon*, trust in Heaven [and thus a policy of passivity], at times by means of submission, at times by means of a struggle for victory, and so on. This decision has no set halakhot, but depends on factors related to the estimate of the situation at the time in question.

Much of life's decisions are complex, and not easily to be derived from settled halakha; decisions require educated – but autonomous – judgment. It is important to note that Rav Hutner opens this paragraph with the focus on the individual. This autonomy, despite its dangers to a halakha-observing community, is, combined with the proper purity of intention, a powerful basis for spiritual development, as Rav Hutner stresses in his explanation of repentance.

Rav Hutner expresses the dilemma somewhat differently in *Paḥad Yitzḥak* Rosh HaShana 11:20 and its parallel in *Paḥad Yitzḥak* Purim 29:2:

The person who deepens his recognition of the image of God within him, by means of this ineluctably deepens his acceptance of the divine yoke. And the unique characteristic of this exercise of free will is [a manifestation] of the image of God within the human being. And the acme of the power of this unique characteristic of human choice is in this view: when a person sees himself as a decisive actor in the continued existence of the universe. And thus (*mimela*) the upshot is that this concept of the human being as an essential determiner of the existence of the universe is the [manifestation] of the deepening and crowning of the glory of His kingdom, may He be blessed, on that man.

The glory of Heaven arises precisely from the person who chooses, [that is,] the one who possesses the freedom that comes from [being made] in God's image.

The central position of humanity within the (spiritual) ecology of the universe mirrors that of its Creator, and thus "a person sees himself as a decisive actor in the continued existence of the universe." This responsibility then tempers his drive for autonomy. However, the tension between the validation of autonomy and the demands of the Torah and human responsibility can perhaps not be reconciled; at one point one must yield to faith in the divine plan and surrender one's autonomy to the demands of faith.

The role of faith is nowhere more apparent than in regard to the issue of theodicy. In *Paḥad Yitzḥak* Shabbat 2:4, Rav Hutner *explicitly* admits that the divine mode of governance involving "the suffering of the righteous" is beyond our ken. Where reason fails, faith must perforce take up the slack, and this brings us to the issue of repentance. The awareness of our ultimate limitations, coupled with our capacity and need to change, enables us to repent, as we see in *Paḥad Yitzḥak* Yom Kippur 19:8 and 19:12:

> 8. The basic point of the work of repentance is not included within the essential separation from sin, but precisely in the awareness of change and in its work of cutting [oneself off from one's past – YE] .... The work of change and the awareness of renewal constitute the essential work of repentance. This is so much the case that the definition of repentance is not "to become better" but "to become *different*, in a better way."
>
> 12. We learn how much this motivating consciousness of change and consciousness of renewal constitute the separation from sin. [This is] so much so that when the consciousness of change and consciousness of renewal are not apparent, we require yet a new dimension of the power of repentance. The Rambam provided a special halakha – at great length – and wrote that a person should not say that repentance applies only to actions, etc. [but also to evil opinions and dispositions]. And all this consciousness of change and renewal is included in the "resolve for

the future" of the penitent. For only his "resolve for the future" incorporates within itself all these motivations.

Thus, the keystone of renewal (hithadeshut) *inheres in the process of repentance: in finding oneself within the process of repentance, one finds God; in finding God, one finds oneself.* The central concept of repentance is change and renewal – for the better, that is, in becoming closer to God. It is significant that the word Rav Hutner employs – *hithadeshut* – is central precisely in the school of hasidic thought that we have encountered over and over again. And that is precisely the point: it was from this hasidic school of thought that the centrality of this notion originated, as we noted above.

And this brings us to Rav Kook's thought and writings, with which Rav Hutner was intimately familiar. This does not necessarily imply that Rav Hutner learned any of the basic themes that characterize *Paḥad Yitzḥak* from Rav Kook; rather the relationship served to solidify the values that they both shared, among them the importance of individuality, authenticity, the power of the imagination, and renewal.[35] Still, a determination of the exact relationship of *Paḥad Yitzḥak* to Rav Kook's writings remains a desideratum.

Still, we may find in Rav Kook a way of reconciling the demands of autonomy and Halakha, as Benjamin Ish-Shalom puts it:

> The acceptance of the yoke of the kingdom of heaven is perceived not only as an expression of freedom's ability to contain itself; religious aspiration, or, as Rav Kook put it, "the striving toward closeness to God," is described as the "culmination of the great ideal of freedom, the object of yearning held dear by the best of men, for which the human soul and social life in its every shade so earnestly long."[36]

This not only helps us understand the context of Rav Hutner's view of autonomy, but will also help place in context Rav Hutner's view of

---

35. Benjamin Ish-Shalom, *Rav Avraham Itzhak HaCohen Kook: Between Rationalism and Mysticism* (Albany, 1993), 99–116.

36. Ibid., 114.

repentance.[37] And, needless to say, this comports quite well with the Slobodkan doctrine of the greatness of man.

In *Paḥad Yitzḥak*, Shabbat 1:4, Rav Hutner takes a divergent though related path. He begins by mining a halakhic source for the broader insights it might yield, quite in the style of Izbica and Sochachow:

> One who takes food less than the amount that would make him liable for violating the Sabbath [law against carrying from one domain to another] in a container is also not guilty for carrying the container, because the container is only an accessory to the food [and he had not carried enough food to make him liable], that is to say, even though the essential act of taking out the container is defined by all the rules [forbidding] transferring [from one domain to another] that make the carrier liable for violating the Sabbath, nevertheless, since at the time of the transfer the container was only an accessory to another act, [that is, the forbidden one of transfer of the food], this aspect of the action takes the act of transferring the container out of the category of "intentional labor" [which defines acts which violate the Sabbath]. And thus [that act] does not contradict the [commandment of] resting on the Sabbath. [With our understanding of this rule] we are prepared [to understand] the particular insight [to which] this *maamar* [is dedicated]: this matter of essence and accessory is not a particular rule governing only this situation among the many other rules governing Sabbath rest, but rather this rule of essence and accessory constitutes *the inner process governing the rules of resting on the Sabbath* [*instituted at*] *the Creation* [emphasis mine – YE]. In order to clarify these matters, we must return to those six days that preceded the Sabbath of the week of Creation. During those six days the Ten Statements [by which God created the universe] operated. By dint of these sayings the laws by which the essential *nature* of all the worlds were emanated, created, fashioned and made. However, [despite the operation of] the Ten

---

37. Shlomo Kasirer, "Repentance in the Thought of Rav Isaac Hutner in Light of its Sources in Hasidut, the Mussar Movement, and Twentieth-Century Thought" [Hebrew] (PhD diss., Bar Ilan University, 2009), 106–183.

Statements of the six days of Creation, the matter of sanctity was not yet mentioned at all. Only with the appearance of the Sabbath is the existence of sanctity mentioned for the first time. The general matter of sanctity here means that though until that point in the six days of Creation the substance of the worlds had become actual (*in actu*); only now, with the appearance of the Sabbath, did *the purpose and goal* of the existence of the universe issue from hiddenness to its revelation. "If I had not created day and night, I would not have put in place the laws of heaven and earth" (Jer. 33:25). The covenant is the purpose and goal of the laws of heaven and earth [playing on the likeness of *bariti*, I created, and *beriti*, my covenant].[38]

In short, humanity's place in God's creation requires the exercise of precise judgment, the ability to distinguish the essential from the secondary in all our activities. Needless to say, this is no simple matter, but the Torah provides guidance. Thus, in *Maamarei Paḥad Yitzḥak* Sukkot 27 (as noted above), Rav Hutner suggests that the operative principle for deciding on a course of action, especially when halakha is not determinative, is to choose that course which will increase "the honor of Heaven" to the greatest extent. By introducing this factor, the natural world is thus reduced to a *secondary*, or accessory, status, *tafel*:

> This is the essence of the existence of the Sabbath-rest of Creation, for because of the appearance of the light of the sanctity of the Sabbath the importance of the nature of the worlds and their substance was relegated to the level of [merely] a vessel and accessory – that is [what] the rest of the Sabbath of Creation [represents].

And, as he goes on to say in paragraph 5, the precipitating factor in all this is no less than the human intellect, *hadaat*:

> However, the determination of the weight of the values of essential and accessory cannot be accomplished without the power of the intellect. Only the intellect weighs and evaluates.

---

38. *Paḥad Yitzḥak* Shabbat 1:4.

As we have seen, for Rav Hutner, the human intellect is the crowning point of Creation, and at its apex stands human creativity, which is an expression of an individual's uniqueness.[39] That uniqueness and creativity is actualized in *talmud Torah*, which requires autonomy for its achievement, as we have seen.[40]

While rationality, precise judgment, and assessment are essentials in *talmud Torah*, Rav Hutner was also cognizant of the role of the irrational in the human psyche, as the founder of the *Musar* movement, Rav Israel Salanter, already stressed, though in a negative manner. As historians have noted, Rav Salanter's recognition of the role of the unconscious mirrors that of Sigmund Freud, and it is no wonder that it appears in *Pahad Yitzhak*. Thus, in *Maamarei Pahad Yitzhak* Sukkot 99:17, he compares the microcosm of the human mind to the macrocosm of the world; just as the world is divided between the habitable continents, and the oceans, which are not suitable for habitation, so too the human mind has an upper layer over an irrational subconscious; that is, as Psalms 24:2 has it, God created the continents *above* the watery depths, thus contrasting the rational, accessible part of the mind with its irrational subconscious, the place of "lack of free will," where subconscious thoughts are beyond our rational control.

Moreover, as *Pahad Yitzhak* Pesah 76:15 has it, the urges of our evil inclination – the unconscious forces – may also be the means of renewal (*hithadeshut*) when employed in the service of God. Renewal in this sense means in part to reinvigorate rituals that are in danger of becoming rote, as Rav Hutner suggests in 76:10:

> This vision [of renewal] is built on the basis of a wonderful secret of the soul's powers, for in a person's soul is located a special capacity whose name is: the power of renewal. When this power operates, a person whispers to himself something of the following: "Even though from the point of view of my limbs and senses the act that I am doing is merely a repetition [without change], nevertheless, emotionally I perform this act for the first time. So

---

39. *Pahad Yitzhak* Shavuot 17:8.
40. *Pahad Yitzhak* Shavuot 15:6, repeated from Hanukka 6:6.

much so, the spiritual ability of a person [enables the person] to impress the stamp of originality on matters that have been performed 101 times."

I would suggest that it is, at least in part, that this "power of renewal" is linked to the imagination and the subconscious, which provide new perspectives on habitual acts; Rav Hutner has thus found a positive use for those unconscious forces which Rav Salanter saw only in negative terms.

THE ROLE OF PLEASURE

It is worthwhile comparing the pleasures of Shabbat, which constitute a fulfillment of the mitzva of *oneg Shabbat* (the duty of spending Shabbat pleasantly), with the pleasure that accompanies *talmud Torah*, which is in the control of the person fulfilling that mitzva. And when we go a step further, and compare this aspect of *Paḥad Yitzḥak* with Rav Tzadok's thoughts on the matter, we will have gained a large measure of understanding of what makes the Hutnerian system distinctive. And so, let us look at *Paḥad Yitzḥak* Shavuot 15:6–7, and then *Tzidkat HaTzaddik* no. 262.

> 6. However, this matter will not be complete[ly explained] if we do not repeat a passage from *Paḥad Yitzḥak* Ḥanukka 6:11–12] – the innovative aspect that we find in regard to *talmud Torah* [in contrast to other mitzvot is this: In regard to *talmud Torah* we have the rule] that a person should study what his heart desires. It is clear that this decision relates to the study of Torah ... in which involvement in matters that his heart desires is the decisive point of the law itself. The explanation of this matter is that all of man's relation to reality outside of himself is by means of connection. All the senses work by means of connection. The sense of touch works by means of a connection to touch. The substance [of the thing touched] touches a man's body. The sense of sight works by means of its connection with light rays; hearing works by means of its connection to sound waves. And it is incumbent on us to know that the same is true in regard to intellectual apprehension. It is impossible for the intellect to come to comprehension [of any matter] except by means of connection with the thing

apprehended. This connection of the intellect with the matter to be comprehended is accomplished by means of the [working of the intellectual] pleasure which is embodied in the matter to be comprehended. The power of the intellect without the working of pleasure is like the power of the eye [to see] without the stimulation of light, or the power of the ear [to hear] without the stimulation of air. However, when the eye is pleased by a beautiful sight, or the ear by sweet sounds, the pleasure is something added to the essential action of the power of sight or hearing, while when the intellect is [merely] pleased by its apprehension [of something], that pleasure is *the very soul* [emphasis mine – YE] of the action of apprehension, which, without it, the intellect [may be compared] to a dumb stone. Therefore, the heart's desire [to understand] is a decision relevant only in matters of [the mitzva of] *talmud Torah*, for the mitzva of the study of Torah exists only by the power of apprehension and understanding. And [thus] any enhancement of the pleasure [of learning] at the moment of comprehension – is thus an enhancement of the apprehension [itself]. Not only that, but we see that it is only in relation to *talmud Torah* that a blessing [which includes] a request for the pleasure of the words [of Torah] was ordained, for we do not find an example of the blessing of *haarev na* (please make it pleasant) in regard to any mitzva aside from *talmud Torah*. And that is the point, for the pleasure at apprehending the words of Torah enters into the very substance of the mitzva, while in regard to other mitzvot it is [merely] a crown at its head – thus far the quotation from *Paḥad Yitzḥak* on Ḥanukka.

7. The upshot is that even though we give the intellect the crown of Torah to rule over the other powers of the soul, nevertheless, the essence of this sovereignty is predicated on the workings of the capacity for [intellectual] pleasure. And the reason for this is that the sovereignty of the intellect over the powers of the soul and its characteristics, its essential definition inheres in [the fact that] the powers of the intellect have the quality of dominion, [but] this dominion comes into being only after the intellect is energized – and it is this pleasure that brings the intellect into

play, [and without it] the powers of the soul that are located in the realm of the intellect's dominion never enter [into operation] at all.

This is a remarkable analysis on several grounds. First, Rav Hutner assigns pleasure a role in the (psychological) workings of the premier mitzva, and moreover, he compares the role of desire and pleasure in Torah learning to the workings of the senses, and thus understands that desire as a *natural* outgrowth of the pleasure to be attained in the course of Torah study. In this way, he also emphasizes the role of human autonomy within the domain of *talmud Torah*, as he assigns it a role within the process of repentance. But perhaps the most remarkable of all is the fact that pleasure here is viewed positively, and, indeed, *the joy of intellectual discovery is the very essence of* talmud Torah; *without it, one has not fulfilled the mitzva of* talmud Torah. Our mandate is to create, not merely stand fast and preserve.

In contrast, though Rav Tzadok views pleasure positively both in regard to *oneg Shabbat* and *talmud Torah*, and even calls pleasure "the food of the soul," he reserves true pleasure for the next world, which is, in his words, is "a world of [spiritual] pleasure." Moreover, voluntary pleasures taken in this world cause pain to the body after death.[41] It is enlightening to contrast Rav Tzadok's use of the theme in *Tzidkat HaTzaddik* 262 to that of Rav Hutner in *Paḥad Yitzḥak* Shavuot. Here is Rav Tzadok:

> As is known, pleasure is the soul's sustenance, for with the bodily benefits and pleasures that the body feels from something, [its] life force is increased. The next world is a world of [spiritual] pleasure in which [the souls] enjoy the light of the Divine Presence, as the rabbis say (Berakhot 17a), and so too in regard to the Sabbath, which is compared to the next world and in regard to which it is said (Ps. 37:14): "Delight yourself in God" (Shabbat 118b). But as to this world, as it is said: "There is no reward for mitzvot in this world" (Kiddushin 39b), for no one feels pleasure in his soul from a mitzva [that he performs] ....

---

41. *Kuntres Shevitat Shabbat* 4, 78b–79a.

In any case, deeds of loving-kindness and the other [mitz-vot] that are listed there [are similar in that] the benefits that [a person] grants to his fellow also arouse a feeling of pleasure in the person [who grants the benefit] in that he takes delight in the pleasure and benefit [which he bestows] on his fellow, and in what he benefits his fellow, or father or mother. This pleasure [that he bestows on others is accounted] a mitzva, and consti-tutes the fruit of this world of the essential future pleasure.... In any case, this pleasure too is [available] to an ignorant person, [and] there is in it food for [his] soul; this is part of the fruit of the true pleasure [of the next world].

Thus, pleasure's role is at best to give us an inkling of the real pleasure to be attained in the next world, a pleasure that is certainly not con-nected to the senses or the body. In his discussion of the spiritual role of physical pleasure on Shabbat, Rav Tzadok limits it to Torah scholars who devote their time all week to study, and even then seems inclined to interpreting this as referring to spiritual refreshment rather than to eating and drinking.[42] In *Kedushat Shabbat* 5, he defines this as appre-hending the hidden light which is beyond human comprehension; it is by this means that one brings pleasure (*oneg*) to Shabbat, and he notes that the mitzva is not for human physical pleasure, but to give pleasure to Shabbat in spiritual ways. Indeed, he goes so far as to assert that the fact that some sages are referred to as heavy-set individuals is due to their Torah study and not to physical eating and drinking.[43] And, it should be noted, of the ninety-seven times that the word *taanug* appears in his writings, it refers to this *oneg Shabbat*, and not at all to *talmud Torah*.

Thus, for Rav Tzadok there are physical pleasures and spiritual ones. The latter come in the wake of performing mitzvot, not only the mitzva of *talmud Torah*. In contrast, Rav Hutner stresses the pleasure attendant on intellectual pursuits, and in this regard, *talmud Torah* is not merely one of the 613 mitzvot, *but one that is particularly dependent on the joy of intellection*. Again, for Rav Tzadok, pleasure exists – either

---

42. *Kuntres Shevitat Shabbat* 7.
43. *Peri Tzaddik Shemini Atzeret* 42; *Pesaḥ* 42.

in this world or the next – as a reward, but does not serve any *instrumental* purpose, except perhaps to motivate good actions. Rav Tzadok bases himself on traditional rabbinic sources, but adds a bit of personal observation/intuition that is quite in line with current research on happiness: doing for others yields happiness for oneself.[44] It was the Elder of Slobodka who introduced the notion of pleasure's instrumental function in facilitating repentance, but hardly in the positive sense that Rav Hutner deploys it. Rav Hutner combined that Slobodkan view with Przysucha's valorization of individuality.[45]

Indeed, Rav Tzadok mentions the talmudic dictum that a person studies only "in a place that his heart desires" (Avoda Zara 19b), which is so important to Rav Hutner, only *once* and that only in passing,[46] and then not primarily in connection with Torah study. Rav Hutner's analysis of the role of pleasure in Torah study seems uniquely his own, though, as noted above, it owes much to Slobodka.

The central themes in *Paḥad Yitzḥak* assume particular resonance within the context of the ideological development of Orthodox Jewish thought in the twentieth century and beyond, in which the desire for autonomy is viewed as a danger to Judaism's continued existence. But, as Rav Hutner stresses, creativity requires a degree of autonomy, and creativity is the crown of the intellect.

In this short sketch, we have emphasized the humanistic elements of *Paḥad Yitzḥak*, but interested readers will find themselves in a rich,

---

44. See Dan Robotham et al., *Doing Good?: Altruism and Wellbeing in an Age of Austerity* (London, 2012), and for the role of pleasure in creativity, see Daniel Kahneman, *Thinking Fast and Slow* (New York, 2013), 50–70, regarding the role of "cognitive ease" in fostering associative reasoning. See also the discussion of the role of dopamine and other such chemicals in Antonio Damasio, *Self Comes to Mind: Constructing the Conscious Brain* (New York, 2010), 50, 204–205.

45. Kasirer: "The distinction between 'being' and 'becoming' stands at the foundation of Rav Hutner's teachings regarding repentance" (117); and see the section entitled "Epistemology and Talmudic Discourse: Recognition from Within," 294–298. "Becoming" for Rav Hutner is the result of the workings of the creative forces within a person. See *Resisei Laila*, sec. 25, beginning (32b) and *Tzidkat HaTzaddik*, 216, no. 92a (Bethel ed., 124a).

46. *Kometz HaMinḥa* 1:7.

multilayered theological universe which will provide them with fresh perspectives that will both enlighten and enliven their lives.

RENEWAL IN ITS WIDER CONTEXT

It is thus no surprise that the theme of *hithadeshut* runs like the proverbial red thread through *Pahad Yitzhak*, from the personal level onto the national level and beyond, not only in regard to Jewish history but also the history of the human race. According to Rav Hutner, history records a number of watershed events, two in particular that are celebrated by the holidays of Purim, Hanukka, and to an extent, Sukkot. We will begin with Hanukka, though it celebrates a later historical junction than Purim.

As we have seen, for Rav Hutner, the intellect is the essence of humanity, and creativity is its crown, and the joy of intellectual discovery ensures that creativity. With this, however, come doubt and dispute, which should however not be looked upon negatively, but as essentials for a creative, joyous intellectual life.

It is hardly surprising, then, that, against this backdrop, Hanukka represents for him a watershed in Jewish history, with the coming of an appreciation for the individual's contribution to Judaism's intellectual life, the study of Torah. Hanukka reflects the transition to an intellectual rabbinic Judaism, where study and intellectual creativity became the hallmark of Jewish life. Before the early rabbinic sages, the *Tanna'im*, we do not hear of individual contributions to Torah learning. And it is only with the advent of the tannaitic period that the study of the Oral Torah flourishes, with the value placed on that individual contribution, despite the limitations of finite human understanding, its doubts and disputes. Here is *Pahad Yitzhak* Hanukka 3:2–4:

> 2. Yose b. Yoezer and Yose b. Yohanan who lived in the time of the Greek war were the first [recorded sages] to disagree in regard to the laws of the Torah.... That is, because the Greek decrees forbidding Torah study caused the eyes of the sages to be darkened, this darkening/causing to forget was the cause of the first [recorded] dispute within the Sanhedrin that sat in the Chamber of Hewn Stones – so that the increase of viewpoints and the consequent differences of opinion in Torah discourse (lit., war

of Torah) to the present day proceeds directly from that darkening of the eyes of Israel by means of the enforced forgetting of the Torah by the Greek decrees....

3. But "at times the nullification of Torah is its [continued] existence" (Menaḥot 99b).... The breaking of the tablets [containing the Decalogue] constituted its preservation [when Moses shattered the first tablets which eventually led to a reconciliation with God]. Thus, the sages say that had the first tablets not been shattered, Israel would not have forgotten the Torah (Eiruvin 54a). We learn therefore that the breaking of the tablets led to the forced forgetting of the Torah, and from this we learn a wonderful insight: *the Torah can become enhanced by means of forgetting of the Torah* [emphasis mine – YE]. See what the sages have taught us: Three hundred laws were forgotten during the period of mourning for Moses, but Otniel ben Kenaz restored them by means of his analytic ability (Temura 16a). Thus, the words of Torah that were restored by analytic ability are identical to the laws that were multiplied only because of that forgetting of the Torah. Not only that, but the very increase of disputes in law occurred because of that forgetting, but despite this, the sages tell us that even though these declare an object ritually clean and others declare it ritually unfit, these declare it invalid and others declare it valid, these declare something permitted and others declare it forbidden, etc., both are words of the living God; the upshot is that the increase in views and approaches constitutes an enlargement of Torah and its glorification that proceed precisely from the forgetting of Torah.

4. An even greater insight than this proceeds from the foregoing: our perception of the power of Oral Torah as revealed through disagreements is greater than when there is agreement. For within the principle that "these and those are the words of the living God" is included the essential principle that even the principle that is rejected as legal practice is nevertheless a Torah view, when it is expressed according to the norms of the discourse of the Oral Torah. This is because

the Torah was given according to the sensibility of the sages of the Torah.... And if they then vote and decide according to the rejected view, the law then changes in a true sense.... The result is that in disagreement the power of the Oral Torah is revealed to a greater extent than by [the sages'] agreement. The "war of Torah" (Torah debate) is thus not merely one mode of Torah discourse among others, but rather "the war of Torah" is a positive creation of new Torah values, whose like is not to be found in ordinary words of Torah [where there is no disagreement].

The paradoxes pile up: the laws that issue from the divine mind and are transmitted by prophecy are forgotten, but restored by the analytic methods of the mere human mind; revelation becomes enlightenment. Rav Hutner once complained that he spoke poetry, but his students wanted prose. The paradoxes, in which he delighted, are the poetry; their explanation is prose. Paradox has become *process.* The paradoxes are produced by the conjoining of antitheses: light, darkness, doubt, certainty, good, evil; that conjoining produces the dynamism that characterizes the system of *Pahad Yitzhak.*

How is this done?

By Rav Hutner's adroit use of parallelism, *à la* the neo-Platonic system of Kabbala and its partial demystification in hasidic thought. Mystically speaking, God, His Torah, and Israel are one. The minds of the sages of Israel, when engaged in the study of Torah, mirror that Torah, which in turn mirrors the mind of the Holy One, blessed be He. Thus, doubt and dispute – the application of human methods of analysis to the task of dispelling ignorance and doubt – produces certain knowledge.

This positive view of doubt is that of one of Rav Hutner's hasidic sources, the work of Rav Tzadok, which I have described elsewhere. The result of this process is described in *Pahad Yitzhak* Yom Kippur 15:4:

And this is what we said [above], based on the principle of Maharal that the sanctity of the First Temple issued from the Giver, while the sanctity of the Second Temple came from the recipient [Israel], and this difference in the sanctity of the Temple was clearly recognizable in the building itself [since the

Second Temple lacked the Ark – YE], and so too this difference was revealed in the eras of the two Temples. For the governance of the Collectivity of Israel during the period of the First Temple was by the prophets, while its governance during the Second Temple period was by the Men of the Great Assembly and their disciples, as we have it in the Mishna (Avot 1:1), "the prophets handed it over to the Men of the Great Assembly." And the Men of the Great Assembly are the ones who said "erect fences to the Torah," and overwhelmingly the enactments, decrees, and "words of the Scribes" are from the period of the Second Temple, and we hold that all the enactments continue in force because of their spread among all of Israel. And all of this shows clearly (lit., shows with a finger) that even in regard to [the nature] of the period of the two Temples, that of the First Temple was closer to the Giver, while that of the Second Temple was closer to the recipient.

The Second Temple period signals a transition to the role of the individual, and is symbolized by the Ḥanukka lights, which represent that individual contribution to the intellectual Torah heritage which grows and deepens with each contribution. And, as *Paḥad Yitzḥak* emphasizes, acknowledging individual contributions, and the unique contribution of each individual, improves the community, in this case the "Collectivity of Israel." In the modern parlance: a "win-win" outcome.

Thus, Ḥanukka marks one watershed in human history: the rise of individualism, and the effect that had on the Jews and their understanding of the Torah, which became an increasingly human document – with God's approval. According to *Paḥad Yitzḥak*, however, that process began earlier, with the return of the exiled Judeans and the rebuilding of the Jerusalem Temple under Persian auspices and the direction of Ezra and Nehemiah – and another watershed event, which paved the way for the second one.

Rav Hutner points to a rabbinic source interpreting a puzzling verse in Nehemiah 8; the verse in question observes that the Jews celebrated Sukkot by building sukkot and living in them for the duration of the festival – something that had not been done since the times of Joshua bin Nun!

Dr. Yaakov Elman

How could that be, asks the Talmud (Arakhin 32b)? Could it really be the case that David, King of Israel and progenitor of the Messiah, that King Solomon, builder of the Temple, had not celebrated Sukkot as the Torah mandates?

The Talmud reports:

> He [Ezra] had prayed for mercy in regard to the passion for idolatry and he removed it, and his merit then shielded them even as the sukka [shields its inhabitants, from a root meaning "to shield"].

As Rav Hutner goes on to explain in *Paḥad Yitzḥak* Yom Kippur 7:2:

> These words are difficult to parse, for we have often found that the merit of mitzvot and good deeds protect and save [their doers] – without [the need for] comparisons and analogies! This [protection] is thus simple [to understand and requires no further explanation or analogy to the sukka].... But a deeper analysis will teach us that this act of Ezra in nullifying the inclination for idolatry [which had led to the destruction of the First Temple] was a unique event from the time of Creation onward to the End of Days and the salvation of humanity. For in all the unfolding of events of human history no analogue may be found to this nullification of an inclination so deeply rooted in the human psyche. And, indeed, this event relates to the End of Days, when, as the prophets foretell, our hearts of stone will be turned to flesh, the foreskin of our hearts will be circumcised, and so on – this change in human inclinations relates only to the End of Days.

Once again, Jewish history is shaped by a unique event – a *hithadeshut*, in the turn away from idolatry. In *Paḥad Yitzḥak* Yom Kippur 10:4, Rav Hutner connects this epochal event with another unusual event, the ceremony of the Rejoicing of the Water Drawing in the Temple on Sukkot, which, the sages inform us, represented the acme of joy. Rav Hutner explains this as a celebration of the end of idolatry. Moreover, this was a foretaste of another epochal event: the end of humanity's inclination to sin altogether, which will occur at that End of Days, when our bifurcated nature will be made whole in the service of God, as noted above in our quotation of *Paḥad Yitzḥak* Yom Kippur 15:4, which contrasts the role of the prophets in First Temple times with that of the sages toward the end of the Second Temple era. He then continues:

> And we continue to draw the line [of reasoning] further, from the difference between the two Temples in their building to the difference between the two Temples in their destruction, for Maharal taught us that the destruction of the two Temples stands within the secret of *zeh leumat zeh* (parallel development) in regard to their building. Since the sanctity of the First Temple was from the Giver, so too the breaches that caused its destruction were the sins and transgressions in relation to God, that is, the three most heinous transgressions [of idolatry, sexual crimes, and murder – YE]. However, in regard to the Second Temple, whose sanctity in its building was from the recipients, the breaches that caused its destruction were the failings in the actions of the recipients, that is, baseless hatred within the Collectivity of Israel itself.

As it happens, historians, following the German philosopher Karl Jaspers, have marked this period as an "Axial Age," when many cultures of the Eurasian continent underwent a decisive change – from Hebrew to Greek to Chinese – a change that turned them to a more inward but, at least for some, a more transcendental direction. One consequence was the end of idolatry, though the process was extended over hundreds of years. But for the Jews, Purim marks that change.

This in turn may be connected to another event that the sages connected with Purim. *Megillat Ester* states that the Jews of Susa fulfilled and accepted this new holiday; but, notes the Talmud (Shabbat 88a), should this not have been stated in the reverse? They fulfilled what they had accepted? Rather, this expression refers to their acceptance of the *responsibility* to apply human methods of analysis to the Torah's commandments, a responsibility that would find its apogee after the miracle of Ḥanukka. Ḥanukka and Purim share their status as festivals established after the Sinaitic revelation; they were initiated by human beings responding to what they perceived as miraculous events, thus passing a human judgment on a hidden divine act.

There is still more to this: the rabbis contrast this voluntary acceptance of the Torah with the scene at Mount Sinai, when, as the Talmud puts it: "The Holy One, blessed be He, overturned the mountain upon them like an [inverted] cask, and said to them, 'If you accept the Torah, well and good; if not, there shall be your burial.'" In other words, Purim, when the Jews accepted the Torah willingly, is the completion of a process which began on that first Yom Kippur, when Moses descended the mountain bearing the second set of tablets containing the Decalogue.

In sum, renewal, creativity, autonomy, and self-fashioning combine to construct a framework for the Slobodkan doctrine of *gadlut haadam*, the greatness of man.

FURTHER READING

Paḥad Yitzḥak

The eleven volumes of the extended corpus of *Paḥad Yitzḥak* are published by Gur Aryeh Institute for Advanced Torah Scholarship, and include *Paḥad Yitzḥak: Kuntres VeZot Ḥanukka* (1964), *Paḥad Yitzḥak: Kuntres Kiyemu VeKibelu* (Purim) (1966), *Paḥad Yitzḥak: Shaar Yarḥa Telita'ei* (Shavuot) (1971), *Paḥad Yitzḥak: Shaar Yeraḥ HaEitanim* (Rosh HaShana) (1974), (Yom Kippur) (1978), *Paḥad Yitzḥak: Shaar UVeYom HaShabbat/Kuntres Reshimot/Kuntres Birkat Avot/Kuntres Yeraḥ HaEitanim* (Sukkot) (1982), *Paḥad Yitzḥak: Shaar Ḥodesh HeAviv* (Pesaḥ) (1984), as well as posthumously published volumes: *Paḥad Yitzḥak: Iggerot UKhetavim* (1981), *Sefer HaZikkaron* (2nd ed., 1997), which includes, *inter alia*, a valuable biographical sketch, *Maamarei Paḥad Yitzḥak: Shaar Yeraḥ HaEitanim* (Sukkot) (2002), *Maamarei Paḥad Yitzḥak: Shaar Ḥodesh HeAviv* (Pesaḥ) (2012).

On Maharal and His Times:

Albertini, Tamara. "Marsilio Ficino (1433–1499): The Aesthetic of the One in the Soul," in Paul Richard Blum, ed., *Philosophers of the Renaissance* (Washington, DC, 1999), 82–91.

Cassirer, Ernst et al. *The Renaissance Philosophy of Man* (Chicago, 1948).
Iamblichus, *The Theology of Arithmetic: On the Mystical, Mathematical and Cosmological Symbolism of the First Ten Numbers*. Translated by Robin Waterfield (Grand Rapids, 1988).
Neher, Andre. *Jewish Thought and the Scientific Revolution of the Sixteenth Century, David Gans (1541–1613) and His Times* (New York, 1986).
Sherwin, Byron L. *Mystical Theology and Social Dissent: The Life and Works of Judah Loew of Prague* (Oxford, 2006).

On Hasidism:
Dynner, Glenn. *Men of Silk: The Hasidic Conquest of Polish Jewish Society* (New York, 2006).
Jacobson, Yoram. *Hasidic Thought* (Tel Aviv, 1998).

On Przysucha Ḥasidut and Its Successors:
Brill, Alan. *Thinking God: The Mysticism of Rabbi Zadok of Lublin* (New York, 2002).
Elman, Yaakov. "The History of Gentile Wisdom According to R. Zadok ha-Kohen of Lublin." *Journal of Jewish Thought and Philosophy* 3 (1993): 153–187.
———. "R. Zadok HaKohen of Lublin on the History of Halakha." *Tradition* 21/4 (Fall 1985): 1–26.
Faierstein, Morris M. *All Is in the Hands of Heaven: The Teachings of Rabbi Mordechai Joseph Leiner of Izbica* (Hoboken, 1989).
Rosen, Michael. *The Quest for Authenticity: The Thought of Reb Simhah Bunim* (Jerusalem, 2008).
Weiss, Joseph. *East European Jewish Mysticism & Hasidism*. Edited by David Goldstein (London, 1997).

On the Musar Movement:
Etkes, Immanuel. *Rabbi Israel Salanter and the Mussar Movement: Seeking the Torah of Truth* (Philadelphia, 1993).
Goldberg, Hillel. *Israel Salanter: Text, Structure, Idea: The Ethics and Theology of an Early Psychologist of the Unconscious* (New York, 1982).

On Rav Kook:

Ish-Shalom, Benjamin. *Rav Avraham Itzhak HaCohen Kook: Between Rationalism and Mysticism* (Albany, 1993).

Mirsky, Yehudah. *Rav Kook: Mystic in a Time of Revolution* (New Haven, 2014).

On Rav Hutner:

Elman, Yaakov. "Autonomy and Its Discontents: A Meditation on *Paḥad Yitzḥak*." *Tradition* 42 (2014): 7–40.

―――. "*Pahad Yitzhak*: A Joyful Song of Affirmation." *Hakirah* 20 (2015): 24–64.

Goldberg, Hillel. "Rabbi Isaac Hutner: A Synoptic Interpretive Biography." *Tradition* 22 (1987): 18–46.

Greenblatt, Matis. "Rabbi Yitzchak Hutner: The Vision Before His Eyes." *Jewish Action* (Summer 5761/2001).

Kaplan, Lawrence J. "A Righteous Judgment on a Righteous People: Rav Yitzhak Hutner's Implicit Theology of the Holocaust." *Hakirah* 10 (2010): 101–115.

Kasirer, Shlomo. "Repentance in the Thought of Rav Isaac Hutner in Light of its Sources in Hasidut, the Mussar Movement, and Twentieth-Century Thought" [Hebrew] (PhD diss., Bar Ilan University, 2009).

Schwarzschild, Steven S. "An Introduction to the Thought of R. Isaac Hutner." *Modern Judaism* 5 (1985): 235–277.

Shmalo, Gamliel. "*Radikaliyut Pilosofit BeOlam HaYeshivot*." *Hakirah* 19 (2015): 35–56 [Hebrew numbering].

Stolper, Pinchas. "Rav Yitzchak Hutner: A Biographical Sketch." In *Chanukah in a New Light: Grandeur, Heroism and Depth* as revealed through the writings of Rabbi Yitzchak Hutner, interpreted and adapted by Rabbi Pinchas Stolper (Lakewood, 2005), 227–237.

―――. *Chanukah in a New Light: Grandeur, Heroism and Depth* as revealed through the writings of Rabbi Yitzchak Hutner, interpreted and adapted by Rabbi Pinchas Stolper (Lakewood, 2005).

―――. *Purim in a New Light: Mystery, Grandeur and Depth* (Lakewood, 2003).

―――. *Shabbos in a New Light: Majesty, Mystery, Meaning* (Lakewood, 2009).

Contributors

Rabbi Yitzchak Blau is Rosh Yeshiva at Yeshivat Orayta and also teaches at Midreshet Lindenbaum. He is the author of *Fresh Fruit and Vintage Wine: The Ethics and Wisdom of the Aggada* (Jersey City, 2009) and associate editor of the journal *Tradition*.

Rabbi Shalom Carmy teaches Jewish Studies and Philosophy at Yeshiva University. He is editor of *Tradition*. He received his BA and MS from Yeshiva University, and his rabbinic ordination from its affiliated Rabbi Isaac Elchanan Theological Seminary (RIETS), studying under Rabbis Aharon Lichtenstein and Joseph B. Soloveitchik. He has edited some of Rabbi Soloveitchik's work for publication. He edited the Orthodox Forum volumes on *Modern Scholarship in the Study of Torah: Contributions and Limitations* (Lanham, 1996) and *Jewish Perspectives on the Experience of Suffering* (Lanham, 1999), as well as several other works. He writes a regular personal column in *Tradition* and contributes regularly on Jewish and general subjects to *First Things* and other journals.

Dr. Jeremy Dauber is the Atran Professor of Yiddish, Language, Literature and Culture and director of Columbia University's Institute of Israel and Jewish Studies. His research interests include Yiddish literature of the early modern period, Hebrew and Yiddish literature of the nineteenth century, the Yiddish theater, and American Jewish literature and popular culture. Professor Dauber's latest book is *The Worlds of Sholem Aleichem: The Remarkable Life and Afterlife of the Man Who Created Tevye* (New York, 2013); it received the Sophie Brody Honor Medal from the American Library Association and was a finalist for the National Jewish Book Award. He is currently working on a history of Jewish comedy, to be published by Norton.

Dr. Yaakov Elman is Herbert S. and Naomi Denenberg Professor of Talmudic Studies at Yeshiva University, the author or editor of eight volumes on Jewish intellectual history, as well as dozens of studies of rabbinic intellectual and cultural history. Among his books are *The Living Nach: The Later Prophets* (Brooklyn, 1996) and *Authority and Tradition: Toseftan Baraitot in Talmudic Babylonia* (Jersey City, 1994).

Dr. Warren Zev Harvey is Professor Emeritus in the Department of Jewish Thought at the Hebrew University of Jerusalem, where he has taught since 1977. He studied Philosophy at Columbia University (BA, 1965; PhD, 1973), and taught at McGill University before moving to Israel. He is the author of many studies on medieval and modern Jewish philosophy, including *Physics and Metaphysics in Hasdai Crescas* (Leiden, 1998). He is an EMET Prize laureate in the Humanities (2009).

Rabbi Dr. Ariel Evan Mayse is the Director of Jewish Studies and visiting Assistant Professor of Modern Jewish Thought at Hebrew College. He formerly served as a Research Fellow at the Frankel Institute for Judaic Studies at the University of Michigan, Ann Arbor. He holds a PhD in Jewish Studies from Harvard University and rabbinic ordination from Beit Midrash Har'el. In addition to several scholarly and popular articles on Jewish mysticism, he is a coeditor of the two-volume collection *Speaking Torah: Spiritual Teachings From Around the Maggid's Table* (Woodstock, 2013), and editor of *From the Depth of the Well: An Anthology of Jewish Mysticism* (Mahwah, 2014).

Rabbi Dr. Moshe Y. Miller teaches Jewish History and Judaic Studies at two New York campuses of Touro College. His Bernard Revel Graduate School of Jewish Studies doctoral dissertation concerned the views of nineteenth-century German Orthodox rabbis concerning non-Jews and Christianity.

Rabbi Dr. Gil Perl is the Head of School at the Kohelet Yeshiva High School in Merion Station, Pennsylvania, and the Chief Academic Officer of the Kohelet Foundation. He earned his BA from the University of Pennsylvania, his Masters and PhD from Harvard, and his *semikha* from Yeshiva University. As a Teaching Fellow at Harvard, Rabbi Dr. Perl was twice awarded Harvard's Certificate of Distinction in Teaching and as an Instructor of Jewish History at Yeshiva University he was awarded the Lilian F. and William L. Silber Professor of the Year. He is the author of *The Pillar of Volozhin: Rabbi Naftali Zvi Yehuda Berlin and the World of Nineteenth-Century Lithuanian Torah Scholarship* (Brighton, 2012), an intellectual biography of the Netziv, as well as numerous articles and a widely read blog. Rabbi Perl resides with his wife, Melissa, and their four wonderful children in Bala Cynwyd, Pennsylvania.

Dr. Daniel Rynhold is Director of the doctoral program and Associate Professor of Modern Jewish Philosophy at the Bernard Revel Graduate School of Jewish Studies. Educated at the Universities of Cambridge and London, Dr. Rynhold has previously held positions in the Department of Theology and Religious Studies of King's College London, and at the renowned Jews' College of London. He has published a number of articles on various topics in Jewish philosophy, including the problem of evil, Nietzsche and Jewish philosophy, and the thought of Moses Maimonides and Joseph B. Soloveitchik. He is the author of *Two Models of Jewish Philosophy: Justifying One's Practices* (Oxford, 2005) and *An Introduction to Medieval Jewish Philosophy* (London, 2009).

Rabbi Dr. Meir Y. Soloveichik is Director of the Zahava and Moshael Straus Center for Torah and Western Thought at Yeshiva University and rabbi at Congregation Shearith Israel in Manhattan. He graduated summa cum laude from Yeshiva College, received his *semikha* from RIETS, and was a member of its Beren Kollel Elyon. In 2010, he received his doctorate in Religion from Princeton University. Rabbi Soloveichik has lectured throughout the United States, in Europe, and in Israel to both Jewish and non-Jewish audiences on topics relating to Jewish theology, bioethics, wartime ethics, and Jewish-Christian relations. His essays on these subjects have appeared in *The Wall Street Journal, Commentary, First Things, Azure, Tradition,* and the *Torah U-Madda Journal.*

Dr. Shira Weiss teaches medieval and modern Jewish Philosophy at Stern College, Yeshiva University. She holds a PhD in Medieval Jewish Philosophy and wrote her dissertation on the concept of choice in the philosophic exegesis of Joseph Albo. She was awarded an NEH fellowship for college professors on Free Will and Human Perfection in Medieval Jewish Philosophy and has authored several articles. Additionally, she holds an EdD and is a member of the administration at The Frisch School, Paramus, NJ. She is currently writing a book on ethics in the Bible, funded by The Templeton Foundation and The Herzl Institute, which subjects challenging biblical narratives to contemporary moral philosophical analysis.

Rabbi Reuven Ziegler is chairman of the editorial board at Koren Publishers Jerusalem and Director of Research and Archives at the Toras HoRav Foundation. A founder of Yeshivat Har Etzion's renowned Israel Koschitzky Virtual Beit Midrash, he has served as its editor-in-chief for over two decades. He is the author of *Majesty and Humility: The Thought of Rabbi Joseph B. Soloveitchik* (Jerusalem, 2012) and numerous articles, and co-editor of Rabbi Soloveitchik's MeOtzar HoRav series. He is also the editor of many volumes in English and Hebrew, among them an adaptation of Rabbi Aharon Lichtenstein's oral discourses entitled *By His Light: Character and Values in the Service of God* (Jersey City, 2003, and Jerusalem, 2016) and a work on the teachings of Rabbi Yehuda Amital entitled *LeOvdekha BeEmet* (Jerusalem, 2011).

The fonts used in this book are from the Arno family

Maggid Books
The best of contemporary Jewish thought from
Koren Publishers Jerusalem Ltd.